*Handbook of Global and
Multicultural Negotiation*

Handbook of Global and Multicultural Negotiation

Christopher W. Moore
Peter J. Woodrow

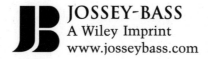

JOSSEY-BASS
A Wiley Imprint
www.josseybass.com

Published by Jossey-Bass
A Wiley Imprint
989 Market Street, San Francisco, CA 94103-1741—www.josseybass.com

Readers should be aware that Internet Web sites offered as citations and/or
sources for further information may have changed or disappeared between the
time this was written and when it is read.

Jossey-Bass books and products are available through most bookstores. To
contact Jossey-Bass directly call our Customer Care Department within the U.S.
at 800-956-7739, outside the U.S. at 317-572-3986, or fax 317-572-4002.

Jossey-Bass also publishes its books in a variety of electronic formats. Some
content that appears in print may not be available in electronic books.

Library of Congress Cataloging-in-Publication Data
Moore, Christopher W., date-
  Handbook of global and multicultural negotiation / Christopher W. Moore and
Peter J. Woodrow.—1st ed.
    p. cm.
  Includes bibliographical references and index.
  ISBN 978-0-470-44095-7 (cloth)
  1. Negotiation in business. 2. Cultural relations. I. Woodrow, Peter J. II. Title.
  HD58.6.M656 2010
  658.4′052—dc22

                                                              2009032175

Printed in the United States of America
FIRST EDITION

HB Printing   10 9 8 7 6 5 4 3 2 1

CONTENTS

FIGURES, TABLES, AND EXHIBIT

FIGURES

TABLES

EXHIBIT

PREFACE

Since the beginning of time, people from all cultures and nations have had to solve problems, negotiate agreements, and resolve conflicts among members of their own group or between members of their society and that of others. It is the rare culture indeed that has been so isolated that it has not had to figure out ways that its members could relate across cultures or internationally with people who were "different."

Historically, most cultures have had some contact with members of other ethnic or national groups, either within their own borders or at least with people from the near abroad (Fagan, 1984). People from Europe, the Middle East, Africa, Asia, and North and South America have long had diplomatic, commercial, religious, and in some cases colonial linkages and relations with each other (Brook, 1978; Wallerstein, 1976). Within regions or states, groups and nationalities have had to find ways to coexist in a peaceful manner and, when appropriate, seek relationships—diplomatic, commercial, technological, religious, cultural, or social—that result in mutual benefits. As internal migration, urbanization, and immigration from other countries have diversified membership or expanded regular contacts among groups, almost all societies have become multicultural.

In the first years of the twenty-first century, an increasing number of individuals, organizations, and nations are engaged in interactions, problem solving, and agreement making across cultures. Globalization is not only making the world smaller but is bringing people together who heretofore have never made direct contact (Friedman, 2007). This trend of increasing intercultural interaction occurs both within and between societies in numerous arenas: international peacebuilding and diplomacy; industry, business, and the workplace; humanitarian assistance and development; and political institutions, schools, and communities.

WHAT THIS HANDBOOK IS ABOUT

This handbook provides practical guidance for people working across cultures in a globalized world, specifically addressing issues such as these:

- How culture influences the definition of and approaches to problem solving and negotiation
- How people communicate, cooperate, compete, and engage in conflict with people from their own and other cultures
- How relationships are developed and valued across cultures, especially in the context of problem solving and negotiations and at a range of levels, from the interpersonal to business to international diplomacy
- How negotiators evaluate the potential outcomes of problem solving or negotiation with members of their own culture or another culture
- How proficiency in intercultural problem solving and negotiations can be increased so that individuals and groups from diverse backgrounds can work effectively together in multicultural situations

In our rapidly changing world, effective global negotiators not only must be familiar with a generic problem-solving or negotiation process that works in their own culture; they must also become familiar with cultural factors that affect the problem-solving approach of people from other cultures. They must learn how to adapt to cultural dynamics and patterns, respond in flexible and appropriate ways, and use a range of approaches for building positive working relationships and reaching agreements.

WHO WILL FIND THIS BOOK USEFUL?

This handbook was written for a wide audience of individuals and organizations engaged in problem solving, negotiation, or dispute resolution across cultures. It will be useful for people working in multicultural settings or a diverse workforce within a country, people who are working or visiting outside their country, and international negotiators working in a variety of settings and on a range of issues.

We have written the book to serve as a practical guide for negotiation practitioners who are conducting bargaining, problem solving, and conflict resolution. At the same time, we have drawn on considerable social science research to satisfy the concerns of academic colleagues who want to use the book in the classroom or to identify research topics in the critical area of intercultural interactions.

Two broad groups will find this book useful: negotiators of all types and those who assist negotiators (facilitators, mediators, and other intermediaries). Increasingly negotiators in many positions are called on to deal with people of different ethnic backgrounds within either their own country or other societies. The handbook provides conceptual frameworks that will aid them in understanding cultural factors that influence their own behavior, shape the actions and reactions of their negotiating counterparts, and have a deep effect on the institutions in which they work. The handbook also offers specific suggestions of strategies and tactics for handling intercultural negotiations and promoting successful talks and settlements.

While the handbook focuses on the negotiation process, the essential role of mediators and other kinds of intermediaries is to assist parties engaged in negotiations. Thus, mediators working cross-culturally or internationally will also find the work useful, as they must often structure effective problem-solving or negotiations processes. These insights apply equally well when assisting in the resolution of interpersonal, intergroup, intercommunal, or international conflicts. (See Chapters Fourteen and Fifteen for exploration of the roles of intermediaries.)

Specific kinds of negotiators will find the concepts, approaches, and procedures explored in this book useful

- *Global business negotiators.* The business world is increasingly globalized and diversified. Businesspeople from diverse ethnic groups and societies who are engaged in the development of mutually beneficial financial transactions will find the handbook helpful for understanding their own culture and how it influences their own negotiating assumptions and behavior, the impacts of culture on other bargainers, and the cultural context in which the bargaining is occurring.
- *Managers and workers in the multicultural or international workplace.* Many societies comprise multiple ethnic groups—and have for centuries. Others are newly diversified due to internal migration, immigration, and guest worker

programs. International companies also send managers to work in other countries, often with a diverse labor force, such as a Japanese manager working in a car manufacturing plant in the United States. Managers and labor representatives who are working with multicultural workforces in their own country or abroad will find the handbook helpful for understanding employees, managers, and groups that are different from them and for developing effective working relationships that can serve as the basis for handling day-to-day issues, negotiating more important problems, or developing a labor-management contract.

- *International diplomats.* Professional foreign service officers from specific countries and people working for international organizations, such as the United Nations, African Union, and the Organization of American States, will find the handbook helpful in promoting effective negotiations to address political, social, and economic development questions. Diplomats who move from country to country often need a broad framework that details "what to look for" in a specific culture's negotiating style. The handbook provides this general framework, as well as specific information about several national and regional styles.

- *International donor agencies and lenders and national government counterparts.* Every year billions of dollars (euros, yen, and so on) flow from lending institutions and wealthier nations to poorer countries in the form of bilateral aid or more specific relief and development programs. International institutions such as the World Bank, Asia Development Bank, and the European Bank for Reconstruction and Development are leaders in negotiating with national governments to determine the broad shape of international assistance, particular poverty-reduction plans. The International Finance Corporation and other multilateral and bilateral lenders provide capital to private companies engaged in projects that promote international development. We have also seen considerable effort devoted to the renegotiation of debts owed to international institutions. All of these require skills in intercultural negotiation—for which this handbook will prove useful.

- *International nongovernmental organization workers and local partners.* International nongovernmental organizations (INGOs), local nongovernmental organizations (NGOs), and community-based organizations (CBOs) are involved in humanitarian relief, development, human rights, and peacebuilding programs (usually supported by international donor agencies, private foundations, or individual donors). Such work involves constant negotiations: between INGOs and their local partners; between INGOs and host governments and donor agencies; and among INGOs, their local partner NGOs, and local communities. Relief agencies also find themselves negotiating with military forces and political groups that have their own agendas. Peacebuilding organizations organize dialogue processes among conflicting factions or serve as informal mediators or conflict resolvers. All of these groups, local and international, will find much useful information in this handbook.

• *Professors and other university educators.* Members of the academic research and teaching community at all levels will find the handbook useful as a text for preparing students to work in international or cross-cultural settings. This will be especially true in the fields of sociology, anthropology, political science, management, organizational development, planning, international relations, development studies, and the growing field of conflict transformation. University exchange programs or study abroad will also find helpful guidance. The handbook will sensitize students to some of the issues they will face when studying or working in another culture.

• *Educators, school administrators, social service administrators, and local government officials.* Migration and immigration have created multicultural schools, workplaces, and local communities. People who work in those settings need awareness and skills to handle a range of complex issues across cultural differences—many of which require some form of problem solving or negotiation. The handbook provides frameworks for understanding different approaches to conflict and bargaining that will be useful for people in these positions.

SOURCES FOR THIS HANDBOOK

This handbook presents what we have learned in our extensive practice of intercultural negotiations and dispute resolution, the experience of other practitioners, and the work of researchers in this field over many years. Each of us has almost forty years of experience working internationally in intergovernmental negotiations, humanitarian relief, development, and conflict resolution. This personal experience working and negotiating in many cultures—and helping others negotiate—provides the primary source for this handbook. We have also drawn on the rich literature in cross-cultural understanding, cultural anthropology, and international negotiation—as can be seen in the many sources cited in the text and the hefty References section.

We have also drawn on over thirty years of practical international and domestic negotiation and conflict resolution experience of our colleagues at CDR Associates (CDR), where we both serve as partners. Founded in 1978, CDR is an international collaborative decision-making and conflict resolution firm with offices in Boulder, Colorado. It provides professional decision making, organizational consulting, public participation, and conflict management assistance to the public, private, and nongovernmental sectors. CDR partners and staff members have worked in over sixty countries in Africa; Asia; the

Middle East; Central and South America; Western, Central, and Eastern Europe; and the Pacific region to promote effective collaborative negotiations among diverse parties.

Internationally our work has involved facilitation or mediation of multilateral international negotiations over Arctic nuclear cleanup among multiple nations in that region; transboundary river management issues between Botswana and Namibia; and economic cooperation and the resolution of commercial disputes among companies in Canada, Mexico, and the United States operating under the North American Free Trade Agreement (NAFTA). CDR has provided facilitation and conducted capacity-building initiatives to implement peace initiatives or accords in Afghanistan, Guatemala, the Middle East, Pakistan, and South Africa; promoted multicultural cooperation to resolve ethnic and religious disputes in Bulgaria, Canada, Indonesia, and South Africa; assisted in the resolution of environmental conflicts in Belize, Indonesia, the Middle East, Peru, South Africa, and Uganda; and helped to design, establish, and build capacities of dispute resolution systems or approaches that use negotiation and mediation to resolve civil, criminal, and land disputes in China, East Timor, Haiti, the Philippines, and Sri Lanka.

In the corporate and governmental sectors, domestic and international, CDR has assisted corporations in negotiating effective partnering and joint venture agreements between entities with highly diverse national and corporate cultures, resolving labor disputes, and settling grievances and charges of discrimination. CDR has also assisted corporations and governmental agencies in designing and implementing new dispute resolution systems, which generally involve negotiation and mediation, to resolve personnel conflicts.

In the domestic public arena, CDR has worked to solve problems involving Americans of diverse heritage (Asian, African, European, Hispanic, and Native Americans) over public policies, labor, and environmental issues. We have also worked in the nonprofit and community sectors to help with intercultural negotiations and problem solving.

THE APPROACH OF THIS HANDBOOK

We assume that most people will come into contact with people from cultural backgrounds different from their own. These cross-cultural contacts will lead to the need to create relationships, solve problems, and reach agreements. However, we are convinced that there is no "cookbook" approach for successful intercultural problem solving. Rather, this handbook provides broad concepts and frameworks that will help negotiators identify, understand, and interpret different cultural attitudes and behaviors and develop appropriate strategies that bridge differences. As a result, the handbook provides:

- A conceptual framework that presents a range of cultural factors that influence problem solving and negotiations, including attitudes toward relationships, communication, and competition, among others

- Clear delineation of the choices available for responding to intercultural differences

- A step-by-step exploration of the various stages and tasks of negotiation, with illustrations of how cultural factors operate at each stage

- Information about how specific illustrative cultures approach specific negotiation tasks and procedures

- A description of the range of intermediary assistance roles, as well as when and how to secure such assistance

In writing this book, we have been constantly aware of the dangers of addressing cultural differences. In presenting "central tendencies" found in the attitudes and behaviors of various cultures, we risk perpetrating stereotypes and even prejudice. However, people from the same culture do share some characteristics—which are then further shaped by personal experience, personality, and organizational routines (among other things). Therefore, we must acknowledge that negotiators from Japan or France or the United States, or any of the other cultures used as examples, *may* behave in the ways described—*or they may not*. Generalizations about cultures do contain important information, but that information must be held lightly and with a certain amount of skepticism. One of the most important points of this book is that negotiators must remain alert, expect the unexpected, observe and analyze constantly, and never assume that they understand someone from another culture fully.

Contents of the Handbook

The handbook is divided into three parts. A brief introduction at the beginning of each part provides more detailed information about the chapters that follow.

Part One provides a general overview of how culture affects conflict and negotiations, presents a framework for understanding cultural variables, explores general strategies for dealing with cultural differences, and describes several key cross-cutting issues that appear repeatedly throughout the rest of the book.

Part Two is a step-by-step guide to global and multicultural negotiations, working through preparation, early negotiations, issue identification, exploration of needs and interests, problem-solving and option generation, and reaching and implementing agreements. The chapters provide information on cultural variations, as well as suggested strategies for working across cultural differences.

Part Three addresses the possible use of "third-party" assistance to negotiation processes, including the roles of mediator and facilitator, but also outlines a wide range of intermediary roles used in different cultures.

ACKNOWLEDGMENTS

In writing this book, we are extremely indebted to our partners and other staff members at CDR Associates. We particularly appreciate the support of Susan Wildau, Mary Margaret Golten, Bernard Mayer, and Louise Smart, who worked with us on a variety of international and intercultural projects, helped clarify some of the concepts, and tested some of the procedures described in this book.

We also acknowledge and thank some of our domestic and international colleagues and clients with whom we have worked over the past thirty years. They have helped us immeasurably in developing our insights and procedures for intercultural negotiation and dispute resolution. These include Jack Lang y Marques of the Colorado Civil Rights Commission; Cindy Cruz, Zell Steever, Richard Ives, and Chris Kenney of the U.S. Bureau of Reclamation; Jerome Delli Priscoli, Lester Edelman, and Frank Carr of the U.S. Army Corps of Engineers; Ken Acton of the Saskatchewan Mediation Service; Jack Knight and Ellen Smeiser of the Continuing Legal Education Societies of British Columbia and Saskatchewan; Mary Ann DeSoet of the Rikswaterstaat in the Netherlands; Vasu Goundon and Karthi Govender of ACCORD; Sandra Fowkes, a private consultant; H. W. van der Merwe of the Centre for Intergroup Studies (currently the Centre for Dispute Resolution); Azikwelwa Zikhalala of the Negotiation Skills Project; Loet Dowes Dekker of the University of Witwatersrand; Athol Jennings and Vuyi Nxasana of the Vuleka Trust in South Africa; Gay Rosenblum-Kumar, John-Mary Kauzya, and Dekha Abdi Ibrahim of the United Nations Dispute Resolution Systems as Instruments of Governance Project in Africa; Norbert Ropers and Ulrike Hopp of the Berghof Foundation; Hannes Siebert of the One-Text Initiative in Sri Lanka; P. B. Heart, Kamalini de Silva, and Dhara Wijayatilake, Ministry of Justice and Law Reforms, Sri Lanka; L. Amarajeewa, M. Bandula, T. Y. Silva, P. Dematagoda, M.N.S. Gunawardena, M. T. Mubaris, S. Parathasarathy, A. De Seram, and M. Thirunavukarusu of the Center for Mediation and Mediation Training and former Ministry of Justice Mediation Trainers, Sri Lanka; Nilan Fernando, Dinesha de Silva, Ramani Jayasundere, Niro Nayagam, Eric Jensen, Nick Langton, and Kim Mckay, Asia Foundation, Sri Lanka; Sandra Dunsmore, Roberto Menendez, and Philip Thomas of the PROPAZ Program, Organization of American States in Guatemala; Zbjeck and Ela Czwartos, colleagues at the University of Warsaw, and Kinga Markert of

Markert Mediacje, Poland; Rumen Valchev and colleagues of the Bulgarian Center for Negotiations and Conflict Resolution; Mas Achmad Santosa, Wiwiek Awaiati, Mega Adam, and Takdir Ramadi of the Indonesian Center for Environmental Law and Indonesian Center for Conflict Transformation; Mehmet and Ipek Gurkanyak of the Hope Foundation in Turkey: John Marks and Bonnie Pearlman of Search for Common Ground; and Connie and Jeff Peck, Eleanor Wertheim, Tim Murithi, Tricia Reidy, Gao Pronove, and Lata Chandiramani, United Nations Institute for Training and Research and UNITAR-IPI Fellowship Programme in Peacemaking and Preventative Diplomacy; Gillian Martin, LEAD International; Winfried Hamacher, Stephan Paulus, and Carola Block, GTZ Germany; Meg Taylor, Amar Inamdar, Kate Kopishke, Rachel Kyte, and Henrik Linders, Office of the Compliance Advisor/Ombudsman at the International Finance Corporation; Steve Del Rosso, Pew Charitable Trusts; Pedro de Sousa and Edwin Urresta, Land and Property Directorate, Ministry of Justice, East Timor; Jonathan Stromseth and Ji Hongbo of the Asia Foundation, People's Republic of China; colleagues at the U.S. Agency for International Development and U.S. Information Service who supported projects in South Africa, Egypt, Jordan, Lebanon, and Morocco; Mary B. Anderson, Diana Chigas, Cheyanne Church, and Sue Williams of CDA Collaborative Learning Projects; and Frédéric Kama-Kama Tutu of Peace Tree Network, Kenya.

We are also indebted to several researchers whose intellectual work greatly influenced our thinking. First and foremost are Roger Fisher and William Ury for their pioneering work, *Getting to Yes: Reaching Agreement Without Giving In* (1981) and subsequent research and writing; and P. H. Gulliver, an anthropologist whose work *Disputes and Negotiations* (1979) set out the initial framework for negotiations in a cross-cultural setting that greatly facilitated Chris's thinking in the framework for his earlier book, *The Mediation Process: Practical Strategies for Resolving Conflicts* (1986, 1996, 2003). We also thank John Paul Lederach for his outstanding work in the field of cross-cultural dispute resolution in Central America, Africa, and Asia. He has not only influenced our view of international conflict and its resolution, but also has contributed to the way CDR trains in international settings.

Finally, we thank our editors, Seth Schwartz at Jossey-Bass, and Susan Geraghty, who assisted us immeasurably in making this book more readable.

∽

October 2009

Christopher Moore
Boulder, Colorado

Peter Woodrow
Cambridge, Massachusetts

For Susan and Linda,
patient partners in life and other adventures

And our many friends and colleagues around the globe
Who made this book possible

Handbook of Global and Multicultural Negotiation

PART ONE

THE ESSENTIALS OF GLOBAL AND MULTICULTURAL NEGOTIATION

P art One examines in detail cultural factors that influence intercultural negotiations and problem solving. Chapter One explores the concepts of culture and negotiation and the intersection of the two. Chapter Two presents an important conceptual framework: the Wheel of Culture. The Wheel of Culture explores broad factors that shape the context and parameters in which negotiations occur, as well as specific variables, including cultural views toward relationships, communications, cooperation, competition, and conflict.

Chapter Three explores a range of possible strategies for responding to cross-cultural situations, examining the merits of adhering to your own culture, accommodating another cultural way of doing things, adapting to another culture, or developing new approaches that incorporate elements of both or all cultures involved.

Chapter Four looks carefully at a number of cross-cutting issues that will be referenced repeatedly throughout the remainder of the book, including key cultural variables, three main approaches to negotiation, the composition of negotiation teams, and the uses of power and influence.

CHAPTER ONE

Introduction to Culture and Negotiation

The Context of Global and Multicultural Negotiations

Let's look in on Alex, who is struggling to cope in a cross-cultural negotiation setting. Here is Alex's message to people in his office. He might be a diplomat, a businessperson, or a development worker.

To: The Gang at the Office
From: Alex
Subject: Progress on negotiations for the new initiative

I thought I should give you all an update on how the talks about the initiative are proceeding. In my last message, I told you that our team had to meet the local leader prior to proceeding. Well, that meeting happened, and it was quite an event! Initially we were surprised to be met by a detachment of soldiers who we assumed were the leader's personal bodyguards. They were all decked out in elaborate uniforms and rifles. They formed a corridor through which we walked to meet the leader, who was standing at the end of the column outside an elaborate audience hall and palace. He shook hands with all of us, introduced us to his wife, and invited us in to sit with them at a low table surrounded by chairs. (Naturally he and his wife sat in the largest and highest chairs!) He motioned to his servants, who rapidly brought tea and some sweets, some of which were unrecognizable and very chewy. The leader initiated some small talk, asking about where we were from, what we had seen of the country, what we thought of the culture, and so on, and we reciprocated the small talk. Finally, one person on our team tried to talk directly about the proposed new initiative, but the leader dismissively waved his hand and said that we should discuss it later with some of his colleagues. We took the hint and returned to small talk.

Upon adjourning our meeting with the leader, our team was shown into another large audience hall adjacent to the palace and seated at the head table on a dais at the front of a large conference room with fixed tables in the shape of a U. About twenty or thirty men and three women filed in behind us and took their seats around the U. A number of people, who we assumed were their subordinates, also stood around the outside of the room and kept constantly coming in and going out while delivering messages to or taking notes from their bosses, who conferred and signed papers. (This went on throughout the meeting.) Occasionally a cell phone would ring, and the recipient of the call would take the call where he was sitting, often talking in a fairly loud voice, or would rush to the back or out of the room. It felt like controlled chaos!

Finally, we were asked to make our presentation. While most people seemed to be listening, there were also a number of side conversations going on. When we finished, the local participants began a long and elaborate discussion in their own language that didn't appear to have much focus either on us or on the program proposal. For long periods, they even seemed to be arguing among themselves. They occasionally asked us questions, but the discussion focused on several men who made fairly long, vociferous speeches, only portions of which were made in a language we understood or were interpreted for us. The group seemed to circle the question of whether to support our proposal, without ever explicitly supporting or rejecting it. I guess they wanted to get all of the views out on the table and assess the lay of the land without committing themselves. When it seemed appropriate, we added our comments and tried to answer their questions. Finally, one of the older men said he liked our ideas and suggested that talks continue at a later undefined time. I guess this will take longer than I figured! Please change my return air reservations to late next week. That's all for now.

⁂

Alex's message illustrates some of the difficulties of intercultural negotiations. Traveling businesspeople, diplomats, and development specialists writing to their home offices find that formal ceremonial events, a confusing decision-making process, and unclear power dynamics leave them stymied about how to proceed. Certainly local counterparts approach the negotiation process in ways that are strange—but are completely normal to them, of course.

This book is about the intersection between culture and negotiation. People who work across cultures, whether internationally or within nations, need general principles—a cultural map, if you will—to guide their negotiation strategies. Such a map will help them to:

- Identify the general topography of cultures—the beliefs, attitudes, behaviors, procedures, and social structures that shape human interactions
- Recognize potential hazards, obstacles, and pleasant surprises that intercultural travelers and negotiators might miss without a guide
- Select responses that will be more likely to achieve successful interactions and outcomes

Although many books have been written about the negotiation process and many more about culture, few analytical frameworks provide practical guidance about how individuals, groups, and organizations from different cultures solve problems, negotiate agreements, or resolve disputes. This book addresses this gap.

A DEFINITION OF CULTURE

Culture is the cumulative result of experience, beliefs, values, knowledge, social organizations, perceptions of time, spatial relations, material objects and possessions, and concepts of the universe acquired or created by groups of people over the course of generations. It is socially constructed through individual and group effort and interactions. Culture manifests itself in patterns of language, behavior, activities, procedures, roles, and social structures and provides models and norms for acceptable day-to-day communication, social interaction, and achievement of desired affective and objective goals in a wide range of activities and arenas. Culture enables people to live together in a society within a given geographical environment, at a given state of technical development, and at a particular moment in time (Samovar and Porter, 1988).

When we think of culture, we often think exclusively in terms of national cultures that are often reported in the media. However, we find cultural differences at many levels. For instance, women and men constitute the two largest cultural groups in the world (Gilligan, 1982). We also encounter subcultures in the beliefs, attitudes, and behaviors of ethnic groups, regional groups, social classes, tribes, clans, neighborhoods, and families (Kahane, 2003; Sunshine, 1990). Governments and their agencies, corporations and private firms, universities and schools, civil society and nongovernmental organizations have their own specific cultures and ways of doing things, often called organizational culture (Deal and Kennedy, 1982; Schein, 2004). Culture is also rooted in religious beliefs, ideological persuasions, professions, and professional training and in the levels and types of education (Smith, 1989; Sunshine, 1990). Finally, families have cultures that are a blend or combination of the cultures of their adult members or of their extended families (McGoldrick, Giordano, and Garcia-Preto, 1982, 2002).

Given all of these cultural variables and significant variations within cultures, how can we develop any conclusions about how a particular person or group from any one culture might behave in negotiations or conflicts? Despite the apparent insurmountable scope of the problem, specific cultures do contain clusters of people with fairly common attitudinal and behavioral patterns. These culture clusters occupy the middle portion of a bell-shaped curve (Trompenars, 1994), such as that illustrated in Figure 1.1.

However, every culture includes outliers—people who vary significantly from the norm and are outside the cultural cluster. Although they are still contained within the range for their culture, their views and behaviors differ significantly from those of their peers and may even look similar to those of people from other cultures. For instance, a businessperson or engineer from a developing country who was educated in the United Kingdom and has lived there for many years may have more in common with his or her peers in Europe than with people in his or her country of origin (Figure 1.2).

For this reason, we must be wary of making vague or sweeping generalizations about how people from a specific culture may think or act. Rigid notions about a group's cultural patterns can result in potentially inaccurate stereotypes, gross injustice to the group, and possibly disastrous assumptions or actions. Common elements and repetitive cultural patterns found in a group's central cultural cluster should be looked on as possible, or even probable, clues as to the ways that members of a cultural group may think or respond. However, the hypothesis should always be tested and modified after direct interaction with the individual or group in question. You never know when

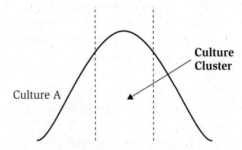

Figure 1.1. Distribution of Cultural Patterns in a Specific Group

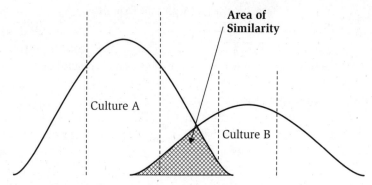

Figure 1.2. Overlaps and Differences Among Cultures
Source: Trompenars (1994).

you may encounter an outlier who acts out of cultural character, does not follow expectations according to stereotypes, and may think and behave more like you than you ever expected.

WHAT IS NEGOTIATION?

Before exploring the characteristics and cultural aspects of negotiation, we need a general definition of the term. Generally most Western negotiators and academics, when defining negotiation, emphasize the presence of incompatible positions or preferred solutions, a bargaining or problem-solving process based on an exchange of positions to address contested issues, or a process that results in specific tangible outcomes or substantive exchanges.

For example, Albin (2001, p. 1) states, "Negotiation is a joint decision-making process in which parties, with initially opposing positions and conflicting interests, arrive at a mutually beneficial and satisfactory agreement. It normally includes dialogue with problem-solving and discussion on merits, as well as bargaining and the exchange of concessions with the use of competitive tactics." Although this definition does identify some of the key characteristics or elements that may be present in negotiations, it fails to accommodate the full range of negotiation goals, approaches, procedures, and outcomes found across cultures. We explore some of these variables later in this chapter.

Within a broad definition of negotiation, we should also note that negotiations take place in a wide range of contexts, from simple market bargaining to complex processes to end wars within or between nations. Table 1.1 presents a schematic range of situations in which people from different cultures often engage in negotiation.

Table 1.1. Range of Negotiation Contexts

Less complex	⟶				*More complex*
Market bargaining	Contract negotiations	Negotiation of international norms	Negotiation of bilateral or multilateral assistance (development, humanitarian assistance, military aid)	Societal conflict:	International conflict:
Sales agreement (house, car, products, resources)	Trade agreements	Labor-management negotiations		Gang violence	Border dispute
		Environmental standards		Civil war	Dispute over a shared resource
				Secession	
				Rebellion	Invasion or takeover
				Ethnic conflict	Survival

Less conflict	⟶	*More conflict*

The examples in the table represent both simple and complex situations and ones that involve less or more conflict. Note, however, that situations of relatively little conflict can easily become contentious and move toward the right side of the table. For instance, trade negotiations are usually held in an atmosphere in which both sides are looking for mutual gain. However, if there has been recent perceived unfairness or disputes over certain kinds of goods, trade negotiations can become more contentious. And interactions that are generally straightforward in the context of a single culture can swiftly become conflictual due to intercultural misunderstanding. A European tourist might seek to purchase a carpet from a merchant in the market in Turkey. The interaction could begin amicably, with tea served and many carpets brought out for display. Although both buyer and seller expect a degree of over- and underbidding, either party might become angry based on perceived unfairness. A simple purchase can plunge into an irritated exchange.

Although the concepts in this book are applicable in all of the situations depicted in Table 1.1, they are most useful for more complex negotiations. The later chapters provide step-by-step practical guidance for all stages of negotiations. Such elaborate detail would be of little use for relatively simple transactions, but it becomes increasingly necessary as the stakes become higher and the level of actual or potential conflict rises.

CULTURAL VARIATIONS REGARDING THE ESSENTIAL PURPOSES OF NEGOTIATIONS

Members of different cultures see negotiations differently. For instance, some cultures place great emphasis on building positive relationships among negotiators—perhaps greater than their attention to any specific substantive decision or outcome. Many cultures also emphasize preexisting commonalties or areas of agreement or connections and procedures that develop consensus, as opposed to the exchange of positions or the use of threats. As we will see in later chapters, this difference in the basic conceptualization of negotiations can be considered a cultural frame.

Because of the range of cultural conceptions about what negotiations signify, the divergent goals that are influenced by culture, and the vast range of procedures and practices involved, we need a broad definition of the negotiation process and its potential outcomes. Our working definition of intercultural negotiation, used in the remainder of this book, is detailed in Box 1.1.

Although these elements occur in almost all negotiations, different cultures emphasize or value different parts. We now examine the elements of this definition in more detail and explore how the components of negotiation interact with culture.

Negotiation Is a Relationship-Establishing and Building Process

Negotiation occurs in the context of relationships: preexisting or newly created affiliations between individuals or groups. Relationships either bind parties together through common positive feelings of trust, respect, caring, obligation, or love, or drive them apart because of mistrust, pain, or hate. Constructive relationships, which on occasion are a precondition for productive negotiations, are generally established through the development of common positive feelings, perceptions, interactions, and reciprocal obligations or exchanges. Because the quality of relationships is often a key to the potential success or failure of negotiations, examining how positive negotiator relationships are established, maintained, or damaged across cultures is critical.

Box 1.1. Intercultural Negotiation: A Definition

Intercultural negotiation is a process initiated by individuals, groups, or organizations from different cultures that enables them to:

1. Jointly define the form of their relationship.
2. Clarify individually and together the goals and outcomes to be achieved.
3. Communicate about issues of individual or common concern.
4. Educate each other about shared and differing issues, interests, or needs.
5. Develop options that address their interests, needs, issues, problems, or conflicts.
6. Influence and persuade each other.
7. Reach mutually acceptable decisions and agreements.
8. Implement agreements reached.

Note: We are indebted to William F. Lincoln for his thinking on the components of the definition of negotiation.

Culture influences participants' views regarding what a relationship is: its goals, what goes into making a good one, norms and expectations for exchanges and reciprocity, appropriate interactions, activities and rituals involved, and things that damage or destroy them. It also defines what relationships are appropriate for negotiations. For example, in a small town in France, it is perfectly acceptable for a single or married woman customer to have a positive and friendly relationship with a man from whom she regularly buys vegetables at a local farmers' market. The negotiation relationship usually begins with a greeting: *"Bonjour Madame/Bonjour Monsieur!"* During their subsequent exchanges, it is within culturally acceptable limits for them to exchange pleasantries about each other's families or goings on in the village, as well as to dicker a bit over the price of the produce. The familiar exchanges preserve their relationship—and might also influence the price of the vegetables. The seller wants to preserve the relationship and may throw in some extra fruit to indicate that he values the connection, while also encouraging the customer to return. The buyer's exchange may be no more than a smile, a good story, or a promise to return to the stall next week, Nevertheless, the exchange is valued.

Contrast this negotiation relationship to the possibilities of a similar market interaction between a single or married woman and a male merchant in Middle Eastern cultures. In some countries and cultures in the region, an exchange like the one described in France would be totally acceptable, but in other settings, any interchange between a woman and a man would be forbidden. In still other places, a woman could buy from a male merchant if she were accompanied by a male relative. What is talked about, by whom, and for how long would probably be more highly circumscribed, but haggling over price might be more exaggerated, even if only as a ritual, than in the French example.

Relationships, mutual obligations, and trust are often valued as the cement that will ensure compliance with an agreement. In such settings, relationships are more important for compliance than abstract rules, laws, or court systems. For example, Jewish merchants in Europe, since the time of the Middle Ages, often acted as the bankers, lenders, and facilitators of commerce throughout the continent. Their network of coreligionists, who shared a common culture and similar values and were often connected through intermarriage, created bonds that allowed the lending and transfer of funds to be conducted in a fairly predictable and secure manner. It was the relationships and shared values and culture that facilitated these trusting exchanges, not the rule of law, although the latter often developed and was formalized from the model of these preexisting relationships (Putnam, 1993). Similar cultural relationship patterns have been found in networks of Chinese, Lebanese, and Indian merchants across the world (Sowell, 1996).

Negotiation Is a Goal- and Outcome-Oriented Process

Much of the literature on negotiation and statements from prominent negotiators in the West identify substantive agreements as the primary goal or outcome of negotiations. Substantive agreements involve coming to terms over money, property, performance, behaviors, and so forth. The focus is often on concrete and tangible outcomes, whether negotiations involve a reduction of the number of missiles possessed by nations, the adoption of a specific foreign policy, the intervention conditions for a peacekeeping force, development of a balance of trade, the definition of contractual relations in a commercial transaction between a multinational and a host country partner, terms for implementation of a development project, or even the price of a hotel room or taxi.

However, culture often defines what kinds of substantive outcomes are important or desirable. For example, in some more traditional societies, a person's wealth or status is measured in the number of cows and size of herd he possesses, not in the more abstract forms of wealth, such as money in coin or paper currency. An exchange of money, although of value, may not be the proper goal or outcome for negotiations.

Although substantive goals and outcomes are clearly important, they may not always be the primary outcome desired by all parties, especially those from different cultures. In some cultures, a relationship or psychological outcome may be just as important as any specific substantive agreement. In addition to substantive and relationship goals, some parties are concerned about the procedures used to achieve outcomes. The interactions among substantive, relationship, and procedural interests—and differing concepts regarding negotiation—is a constant theme in this book.

Negotiation Is a Communications Process

Communication is the lifeblood of negotiations, for to reach agreements, parties must communicate and exchange information with each other and be able to accurately interpret and understand data that have been presented. They need to be able to exchange information on their feelings, perceptions, concerns, interests, needs, goals, objectives, visions, and procedural preferences. Communication can be face-to-face, through intermediaries, written, over the telephone or Internet, or through symbolic gestures (such as gift giving), but it is a required element of effective negotiations.

Communication is deeply affected by culture. What, when, where, to whom, and how parties communicate is directly influenced by a negotiator's culture and background. Whether parties use respectful or pejorative language, speak directly or in a roundabout manner, quietly converse about a topic or debate it in a loud voice, or present specific or general proposals early or late in negotiations is governed by the cultural background of the participants. The cultural patterns of communication are explored in detail in later chapters.

Negotiation Is a Joint Education Process

At some time, the negotiators begin a mutual education process. This may be an explicit education process or indirect mutual learning through the presentation and exploration of positions. In most cases, in order to reach agreements, the parties must create informal or formal opportunities to educate each other about the connections they desire, the topics or issues for discussion, and their individual and collective needs and interests.

Cultures use contrasting approaches to educating one another. For example, a comparative study of business executives from the United States, France, and Germany concluded that many members of each of these cultures have very different styles and expectations for educational procedures in the context of negotiations. Hall and Hall (1990) noted that French executives often expect elaborate presentations that may include emotional content and literary or historical illusions: "The French like to provide masses of figures organized in complex patterns along with detailed background information. This is a result of their education, which stresses abstract thinking and the use of statistics and figures" (p. 103). In contrast, Germans in general provide more information on a subject than most other cultures either expect or require. Germans generally expect direct, clear, and highly precise presentations that provide a logical outline of facts, lots of data (including minutiae), and a summary at the end that repeats all major points. In still another contrast, American business executives generally expect direct and, on occasion, informal presentations (though not as direct as Germans) that are punchy, to the point, and often accompanied by some humor. Points are often made in headline or bulleted form, and a brief digest of key ideas may be submitted in written form. American executives appear to find general or background information less important than specifics that are needed to make immediate decisions. More will be said about cultural approaches to education in negotiations in later chapters.

Negotiation Is a Problem-Solving and Option-Generation or Proposal Process

Although negotiation serves many purposes and may achieve a wide range of goals, it is primarily a problem-solving process. Negotiators strive to identify a common issue, problem, or conflict and generate possible options to address their individual and collective concerns, interests, and needs.

In general, there are three broad procedural approaches to problem solving and negotiations, and related option generation: positional bargaining,

interest-based or integrative negotiations, and relationship or conciliatory procedures (Walton and McKersie, 1991). These approaches are practiced in
all cultures to some degree, although members of specific cultures typically
emphasize one approach over another. The approaches may also be conducted
separately or in combination. (See Chapter Four for a full exploration of these
three approaches.)

Negotiators from a given culture select the specific procedures they will
use depending on the specific situation; the particular issues or conflicts in
question; the parties involved and their rank, status, authority, or gender; the
perceived risks or stakes; their potential or actual means of influence; their
expectations or goals regarding current and future relationships; personal style;
and cultural norms regarding preferred negotiation approaches and a variety
of other factors, including the approach that the other party or parties adopt.
In general, outcomes of negotiation can be integrative or distributive in nature.

Integrative outcomes address to the greatest extent possible the individual
and joint aspirations, interests, and needs of the parties. Striving for integrative
solutions to issues, problems, and conflicts involves parties in identifying
individual and mutual interests and needs and then developing options, or
possibly an overall formula or package, that achieve the greatest benefit for all
involved. Distributive outcomes are negotiation consequences that result from
the division, sharing, or allocation of perceived or actual limited resources.
Money, property, time, performance, or activity can often be divided and
allocated among concerned parties.

The desirability of achieving integrative or distributive outcomes of negotiation is influenced by the mind-sets and cultural norms of the parties (Fisher,
1988). Decisions about the approach taken are determined by the issues,
who the parties are, perceived or actual scarcity, and preferred negotiation
procedures, among other things.

Relationship or conciliatory procedures are used to establish and build
positive personal, intragroup, and intergroup relations or repair or solve
problems in the context of relationships. In some cases, there are relatively
few substantive issues of concern, as negotiators focus on changes in attitudes,
expectations, or relationship-oriented behaviors.

Negotiation Is an Influence and Persuasion Process

In negotiations across cultures, the cultural acceptability of a persuasion tactic
may make the difference between a positive working relationship and deadlock.
Each party initiates activities to influence and promote change within the other
party. Generally these activities expand or narrow the range of potential options
for agreement.

Negotiators have many ways to influence each other, including cooperative tactics that provide positive benefits from collaboration, as well as more coercive means that may risks, and hurt or damage the other side if they do not comply. Some means of influence are exercising formal authority; providing testimony of experts or information; using connections or the influence of respected associates of another party; making suggestions on how to proceed with discussions; making threats or exercising coercion; being a nuisance; appealing to the status quo or traditional ways of addressing problems; exercising moral authority or appeals; or exerting personal persuasion (Mayer, 2000). Strategies and persuasion tactics have significant cultural elements that promote or discourage their utility or acceptability to members of other cultures.

Negotiation Is an Agreement, Decision-Making, and Exchange Process

Negotiations involve procedures by which parties reach agreements and exchange either tangible items (money, land, goods, or behavior) or intangible items (trust, respect, apologies, retraction of a statement or curse) to meet individual or jointly defined substantive, procedural, or psychological interests or needs. Members of diverse cultures often differ·sharply regarding what constitutes an agreement, how an agreement is reached, the degree of detail and closure involved, and expected procedures for implementation and compliance. The culture of the parties may also significantly influence what is exchanged, how exchanged items are valued, and what constitutes equity or fairness. More will be said about these aspects of intercultural negotiation in later chapters.

Negotiation Is an Action-Oriented Process That Requires Implementation

Negotiations are different from conversations or discussions in that they are outcome oriented. They generally result in changes of attitude, behavior, performance, or an exchange of something of value to one or more parties. This means that agreements have to be implemented. In general, negotiated agreements are either self-executing, in that parties make necessary exchanges in the negotiations themselves, or non-self-executing, which requires performance or exchanges over time. Each of these approaches may have culturally sanctioned or common norms regarding how they are confirmed. In some cultures, it may be a handshake, in others a meal, and yet in others the signing of a contract. Regardless of the type of agreement, usually some procedure is used to implement and a ritual performed to confirm the agreement.

PREPARATIONS FOR INTERCULTURAL NEGOTIATIONS AND DISPUTE RESOLUTION

An important first step in becoming an effective intercultural negotiator is to understand that culture can make a difference and pay attention to it. People just starting to work across cultures, and even those with extensive experience, often make several significant mistakes. First, they may start from a significantly ethnocentric viewpoint, assuming that all people are basically the same and denying differences because of ignorance or belief that their culture is the basic template from which all others are derived (Bennett, 1983). Such individuals or groups often believe that underneath our multipigmented skin, diverse languages, unusual clothing, and different behaviors, we all have identical wants and desires and similar approaches to negotiation and conflict resolution. Those who assert the basic similarity of cultures assume that if we can just communicate well with each other, all problems can be addressed or will evaporate.

Although this view is less common than it used to be, it is still frequently found in those with little experience with people from or working in diverse cultures. It is also prevalent among those of a second group who, when abroad, spend most of their time with colleagues and friends from their own culture or in international diplomatic, business, development worker enclaves, or tourist havens where either Western or international middle- or upper-class culture prevails or local culture is presented as a caricature of only the most acceptable, or in some cases romanticized cultural elements—a slice of the real thing.

Thus, when international travelers—whether tourists, businesspeople, or diplomats—visit countries such as Mexico, they are introduced to Mexican culture by mariachis (singing musical groups with guitars), sombreros, and margaritas. In Indonesia, they are likely to stay in an international hotel where accommodations are similar to those they might find in their home countries, they can choose Western or Japanese (or local) food if they care to, taxis or limousines whisk them (or get stalled in traffic) to meetings and meeting rooms that are similar to those found in developed countries, and so forth. If they take a break over the weekend, they are often likely to visit a Club Med type of resort in which only a slice of Indonesian culture is presented. In some cases, it may be limited to the gamelan orchestra—a percussion ensemble with xylophones, gongs, and other instruments—in the hotel lobby, masks and woodcarvings in the hotel shops, or the attire of the concierge, hotel staff, or servers in the restaurant. In these settings, it is perfectly possible to be abroad and never leave the comforts and culture of one's home culture and rest assured that "people in X foreign country live just like us."

A third group who are likely to think that all people within their cultures are basically the same—or should have the same values, cultural patterns, and behaviors that they do—are members of groups, organizations, or countries that are, or have been in the past, politically, economically, or socially more powerful and dominant than members of other cultures, or expatriates who have never had to accommodate or adapt to the cultures of others. For example, men in many cultures often miss or do not understand the culture of women and ask, "Why can't a woman be more like a man?"

In the United States, the majority of Anglos, or whites with historical origins in Northern Europe, frequently do not understand, dismiss, or are threatened by the culture and needs of long-term citizens in the Southwest of Hispanic origin (who have been there since the 1600s) or more recent Latino or Hispanic immigrants from other Latin American countries. They demand that non-Anglo groups integrate and become just like the rest of Americans, or "stay on the other side of the river" (Badillo, 2006).

Americans may not understand the culture or attitudes of Somalis and assume that they are striving for the same things that people from the United States want (Kaplan, 2003). Germans may not understand the cultures and sensitivities of members of central European or Turkish cultures and the joint history that they share with Germans (Kaplan, 2005). Russians may fail to accommodate to the cultural patterns and aspirations of Georgians, residents of the Crimea, Chechnyans, or former Soviet Republics (Nasmyth, Ku, and Pun, 2007; Sakwa, 2005). Chinese from the People's Republic of China may not understand the cultures or sensitivities of Tibetans, Taiwanese, Uyghurs, Inner Mongolians, Vietnamese, and so forth (Terrill, 2003).

In each of these examples of intercultural relations, power between cultures helps define and strongly influences relationships, interactions, procedures, and types of outcomes. "Culture needs to be taken seriously in debates over justice, in the sense that criteria for fairness are always rooted in particular cultural traditions, rather than in some transcultural definition of human reason, interests or rights. And particular cultures exist in relation to one another, in contexts always shaped by power—the sovereign power to coerce, enslave, or exterminate tying in with the ability to dictate the terms of political debate, while denying the cultural roots of these terms" (Kahane, 2003, p. 7).

As people become more familiar with other cultures, they begin to recognize differences but may still be defensive about the merits of their own in contrast to others. They take the view that while others exist, their culture is superior and the best. As they adjust further to differences, they may not judge other cultures as harshly, but they may still minimize differences, thinking that we are all basically the same despite some small differences (Wanis-St. John, 2005).

Another common mistake, currently in vogue, is to go to the other extreme: romanticizing culture and diversity and treating other cultures and their members as exotic, sacred, and deserving of protection from "cultural imperialism." Followers of this approach overemphasize differences among cultures, on occasion try to "go native," make extreme efforts to be culturally correct, and try hard to avoid unpardonable cultural errors.

Both views of culture hold some truth—there are many similarities among cultures, and cultures are unique. People get married in most cultures, but the kinds of relationships and relationship expectations that the couple have, the terms of the marriage contract, and rituals for uniting them may be extremely different. Children are educated in all societies, but what they are taught, how, by whom, and for how long are different across cultures. The education of students, in terms of subject matter, way of thinking, and the teaching-learning process in a Pakistani *madrasa* and one of the French *grandes écoles* are all quite different. People drive cars in many countries and cultures. However, the side of the road they drive on (left, right, in the middle or weaving between the two), where they drive (roads, sidewalks, or through fields), the way they drive (in an orderly and predictable or random fashion), and their observance of laws or informal driving practices (law abiding or adherence to situational ethics) may differ drastically. Leaders and managers in the private or public sector of various cultures and societies help define and oversee the work of subordinates. However, they do it very differently.

To move beyond the two extremes described and shift from a stance of ethnocentrism to ethnorelativism, a view in which there is greater acceptance of cultural differences and tolerance for them, individuals and groups move through three stages of development: acceptance, adaptation, and integration (Bennett, 1993).

Acceptance involves setting aside denial of differences and limiting or suspending judgments about merit, value, or appropriateness of different cultures, accepting that differences do exist and that it is all right for people to think and act in diverse ways. Adaptation means that "we become more skilled at seeing shared realities through different lenses and consequently can make adjustments to our understanding of an action, phenomenon, or idea different from our own" (Wanis-St. John, 2005, p. 124). Integration involves significant acceptance and understanding of cultural differences in thought and behavior, and comfort interacting within a cultural milieu that is different from one's own. Integration allows an individual or group to culturally adapt to a different culture and respond appropriately depending on the people, setting, issues, or tasks.

Just as individuals and groups may view their own cultures and those that are different from perspectives along a continuum of ethnocentrism to ethnorelativism, they may do the same when considering negotiation or the resolution of disputes. Some people believe that everyone practices these relationship-handling and problem-solving procedures in a universal manner and that culture makes relatively little difference in behaviors, strategies, interactions, or outcomes. At the other extreme are people who think that negotiation and conflict resolution practices are so particular and unique that they always have significant impacts on parties' interactions and outcomes and must at all times be taken seriously into consideration, with adaptations made when planning strategies, procedures, and behaviors.

The extreme views about culture and negotiation noted represent unhelpful outlooks. The truth lies somewhere in between. Cultural differences may be important factors in the success or failure of intercultural interactions and negotiations. Diversity can create barriers to agreement but also enable parties to find mutually acceptable solutions precisely because parties are different and have different interests, priorities, and goals. Seeing cultural differences in this way "has the potential to offer us 'foreign' strategies for reaching optimal, integrative agreements, or at least teaching us the relative merits of those approaches. It can also help us to understand that cultures need not incline us to conflict with each other" (Wanis-St. John, 2005).

In this respect, we need to move from acceptance of differences and toward adaptation and integration as successful strategies for intercultural problem solving, negotiations, and conflict resolution. While we must accept that culture plays an important part in interactions and negotiations between individuals and groups, we must not ascribe all problems encountered in problem solving or negotiations to cultural differences. Problems can also be caused by personal or group differences and styles of behavior, different approaches to negotiations, competing interests, or social structures.

The critical task is to determine what functions, roles, and impacts culture has on intercultural relations and negotiations and to develop appropriate strategies to accommodate these influences. To do this, we need a tool to help distinguish what may or may not be cultural factors and one that helps participants in intercultural problem solving or negotiations develop effective responses and strategies.

CONCLUSION

In an increasingly globalized world, we interact with people from other cultures in many contexts. Almost all countries are now host to large immigrant populations—political or economic refugees, people seeking new opportunities or fleeing oppression. Most modern societies are conglomerations of many cultures, requiring us to learn how to work across cultural divides in the business world, school, health care establishments, government, and other social institutions. As we work together, we depend on negotiation as an essential skill, and mastering negotiation across cultures has become essential.

Thousands of people enter other cultures on a daily basis—as business executives, diplomats, development and relief workers, or peacemakers. Like those struggling to operate in an increasingly multicultural domestic context, these international travelers must become conversant with the ways in which culture and negotiation intersect. Global and cross-cultural negotiation is no longer an optional competency. The next chapter presents a tool for identifying and understanding cultural differences that influence negotiations: the Wheel of Culture.

CHAPTER TWO

The Wheel of Culture

T abatha and Ming met in graduate school in Boston and fell in love. Ming proposed that they get married, and after some thought about the prospects of an interracial and intercultural marriage, Tabatha agreed. It was both exciting and problematic that Tabatha came from a traditional African American Southern Baptist family in Texas, and Ming grew up in a Confucian family in Taiwan. The planning process for the wedding could only lead to trouble!

Ming called his mother with the exciting news. After her initial shock that he was not marrying a "nice Chinese girl," she rushed to the local astrologer with the birth dates of her son and his fiancée to see if they were a good match. Immediately after getting the results, she called Ming. "You are a Tiger, and Tigers are bad luck—so you must stay away from the ceremony until the very last minute. And the wedding has to be on May 16, a very auspicious day. And I assume that you are coming to Taiwan for the wedding, right?" Ming already had a headache.

Meanwhile, Tabatha called her parents and broke the news. While they were relieved that their daughter was finally getting married—all of her high school friends had long since married and had children—they were a bit concerned about this stranger from Taiwan. In any case, they talked about wedding plans, when their church and minister would be available, and so forth. Of course, the couple would come to Texas for the wedding. Now Tabatha had a headache.

For months, Ming and Tabatha acted as both negotiators and intermediaries. They talked constantly with each other and their respective parents—mostly the mothers, as the fathers were wisely staying out of the way. If they survived this, the marriage would be strong for sure. At one point they proposed a single joint ceremony in Boston—which was equally unacceptable to the two sets of parents. For Ming's family, Tabatha would have to wear a red dress, the color of good luck for their culture—but the color of a harlot for Tabatha's folks. Of course, Tabatha's family insisted on a white dress for purity—but that was the color of death for Ming's family. And what would a joint Baptist-Confucian ceremony look like anyway?

After much negotiation back and forth, it was agreed to hold two ceremonies. One would be in Boston, where most of the couple's friends were. This would be a traditional Chinese ceremony on an auspicious date and time, with an embroidered red silk dress for Tabatha, and Ming, the dreaded Tiger, staying out of sight as much as possible. Tabatha's family would come to Boston for this event and do their best to adjust to what they considered to be the outlandish ways of their new son-in-law's family. Then the two families would travel to Texas for a traditional Baptist ceremony with a white dress and full church service, where Ming's family would have to bite their tongues and try to adapt to local ways.

In the end, it all came off with few hitches—but Ming and Tabatha were exhausted from the cross-cultural negotiations. They looked forward to their honeymoon in Greece, yet another culture!

∽

An important step in becoming an effective intercultural negotiator is to develop an awareness of how cultural differences influence problem solving and negotiation. Some of those differences are illustrated in the short story about Tabatha and Ming. Issues regarding values, relationships, communication, time and timing, and even venue are involved—and the beleaguered couple must act as both negotiators and intermediaries across cultures.

This chapter presents a framework for analyzing the impact of cultural factors on negotiations. We have used variations of this framework for about fifteen years. People who have applied it find that it is useful for understanding both their own cultures and other cultures in which they are working. The Wheel of Culture map (see Figure 2.1) identifies critical cultural variables that shape the ways that members of societies conduct problem solving and negotiate to achieve interests and resolve disputes.

We have found that understanding these variables helps people overcome communication hurdles and find mutually satisfactory solutions to both

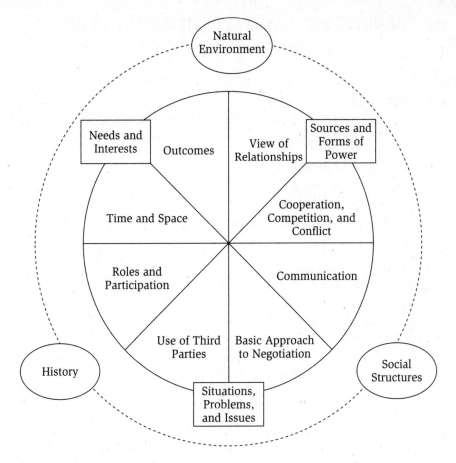

Figure 2.1. Wheel of Culture Map

simple market encounters and extremely complex negotiations regarding highly politicized and emotional issues. Of course, the importance of paying attention to these factors rises the more complicated the issues are, and the higher the stakes.

The inner and outer rims of the Wheel of Culture concern the broader environment in which negotiations take place, and a series of spokes represent key ways in which cultures differ in their attitudes and behaviors in negotiation settings. In the balance of this chapter, we provide fairly brief summary descriptions of these factors. However, these variables represent crucial lenses for examining the influences of culture on negotiation, and they are woven into the rest of the book. As you will see, the factors are not equally important. Some are addressed in great detail, while others merit only occasional mention.

THE OUTER RIM: NATURAL ENVIRONMENT, HISTORY, AND SOCIAL STRUCTURES

Negotiations are not isolated processes; they occur within a broad environmental and social context. The outer rim of the Wheel of Culture identifies the broad external factors that influence the development of a specific group's cultural approach to negotiations and conflict resolution:

- The natural environment
- History, events, trends, and adaptations that have occurred over time or are currently happening
- Social structures, both intellectual and physical, that people create to adapt to or survive in their environment

These three factors continuously interact and influence one another and the individuals and groups of any given culture. In order to understand why people think and act the way they do, it is helpful to understand how the natural environment and history have shaped their values, views, behaviors, and social structures.

Natural Environment

Are you dealing with a counterpart from an island nation or a country that is landlocked, large or small, desert or fertile? Tropical, temperate, or frigid? What natural gifts and vulnerabilities does the country have, including exposure to various natural disasters? Is the country remote or isolated?

Geography and the natural environment clearly affect the formation of the beliefs, attitudes, behaviors, and social organizations of a culture. They can also influence how conflict is addressed, not addressed, and resolved and the use of negotiations (Diamond, 2005; Reader, 1999).

Geography and environment have affected parties and negotiations since the earliest days of human interaction. In more recent times, geography and the proximity of parties, climate, weather, crops that are grown, and other natural resources have had significant effects on the culture of negotiations. One scholar notes:

> The high value placed on harmony in many African societies may have developed through social interaction with a particular physical setting. Africanist scholars have traced indigenous harmony models to a combination of specific environmental and technological conditions. Historically land had been relatively bountiful in West Africa, and local modes of production have relied on

intensive labor inputs. Wealth, status and prestige have been gained primarily through controlling people rather than land, leading to the development of harmony ideologies. . . .

In the Sahel region of Africa, the widespread aversion to conflict is in part a sociocultural response to a fluctuating environment characterized by regularly occurring extreme conditions and periods of scarcity [Davidheiser, 2006, p. 285].

Let us look at several other examples of how geography and environment influence culture and the approach to conflict and negotiations.

- *The Niger Delta.* For about sixteen hundred years, with its high point around 800 A.D., a vibrant civilization flourished in the inland Niger Delta in what today is Mali. The unique environment of the region created specialized roles and relationships that developed among the diverse ethnic groups in the area. Their ability to negotiate mutually beneficial arrangements played a role in the success of this civilization and the remarkable absence of major conflicts among its members. Due to the seasonal rise and fall of the waters of the Niger River, the area developed wetland crops including rice, dryland crops, animal pastoralism, and intensive fishing. Each of these activities was undertaken by a different specialist ethnic group during different periods during a yearly cycle and using the land—even the same lands—in different ways. In order to survive throughout the cycle of seasons, the groups depended on the production of others, which required the negotiation of a series of cooperative agreements about division of labor, uses of land and water, passage of animals and people, and exchange of products (Reader, 1997).
- *United States, Canada, and Australia.* Vast territories, sizable immigration flows, and patterns of widespread dispersal of immigrant groups shaped the more open and acquisitive cultures of the societies of the United States, Canada, and Australia and the ways that they have developed and applied negotiations (Althen, 1988; Potter, 1958; Stewart and Bennett, 1991; Hughes, 1988; Renwick, 1980). During the early development of their frontier societies, the ruggedness of the land, sparse population, and tensions with indigenous groups, especially in the United States and Canada, encouraged immigrants to engage in collaborative efforts for survival. Collaboration enabled people from diverse backgrounds to communicate, cooperate, protect themselves, and solve problems of common concern. At the same time, the availability of vast stretches of relatively unoccupied lands provided space for people to walk away from unsatisfactory relationships and move to other locales where relationships and the ability to accumulate wealth might be better. These environmental elements influence the negotiation patterns of parties from these cultures to this very day.

- *Japan.* The rugged mountains, small valleys, concentrated rice culture, and relative isolation of Japan during certain periods of its history influenced the development of a more homogeneous, closed, and collectivist culture in this society, as well as suspicion of foreigners. Due to years of isolation from outsiders, Japanese negotiators developed unique internal approaches to negotiations based on patterns of collaboration and mutual reciprocity. This reciprocity has been attributed to the collective action needed to grow rice (Doi, 1973; Embree, 1939; Nakane, 1970; Reischauer, 1989).

- *Egypt.* The natural environment has a strong influence on social structures that people construct for survival. For instance, historically, the dependence of the peoples of Egypt on the Nile River to provide life-giving water and the hostile desert climate surrounding them encouraged the development of a strong centralized and hierarchical authority to manage natural resources and construct water projects. Hierarchy and centralization, especially in government–civil society relations, remain cultural factors in Egypt (Bill and Springborg, 1990). This centralization of power generally has resulted in fewer negotiations and more command decisions in the governmental arena, in contrast with societies that are not as dependent on governments to mobilize resources for survival. Similar cultural patterns related to water and the construction of water projects can be found in the earlier civilizations of present-day Iraq and Sri Lanka. Interestingly, geography had an opposite impact on negotiations in the commercial arena. Egypt's location on the eastern Mediterranean made it, from ancient times, a central hub on the East-West trade route between China, the Ottoman Empire, and Europe. This made it a major trading nation at various periods of its history and contributed to the development of the *suk* culture of negotiations and its well-known process of haggling (Quandt, 1987).

KEY QUESTIONS ABOUT THE IMPACT OF THE NATURAL ENVIRONMENT

- Has the natural environment created scarcity or abundance of resources needed for a people's survival, and how might this affect their views of and behaviors in negotiations?

- Has the natural environment been a source of internal disputes among members of a culture, or conflicts with outsiders, because of scarcity of desirable or needed resources?

- Has the natural environment induced or required people to work together collectively to survive, or has its character allowed or required more autonomous action by individuals or small groups?

- Has the natural environment allowed or encouraged the mobility of peoples and exposure to different cultures, or has it isolated people and groups from each other?

History

History is made up of a series of individual and group experiences and events over time. It involves both interactions among individuals and groups within a culture and contacts with outsiders. Histories between entities (individuals, families, communities, nations) may be conflictual or collaborative. Many people and groups have mixed histories, both internally and with outsiders, including positive and negative experiences. Social histories encompass real and mythical events that have or are perceived to have shaped a society's self-concept as a distinct entity and its collective memory. Shared history influences how a society views its goals and interests and how members of a society interact with others and negotiate with people from other cultures.

History and culture are often so intertwined that it is hard to distinguish one from another. History influences culture, and culture influences history. However, by breaking the analysis of history and culture apart, it is often possible to gain a better understanding of why people and negotiators act the way they do and to develop appropriate strategies for overcoming obstacles and building on possible opportunities.

Members of a society inherit history from the past, and it exerts an influence on their worldview, attitudes, and behavior, even though they were not alive during the significant events that shaped the culture. Incidents that occurred decades or even centuries earlier persist powerfully in present-day consciousness. Such iconic events can become a core element of social identity. For Jews, the Holocaust represents such an experience. Defeat by the Turks in the fourteenth century shapes the Serbian worldview. At times, historical consciousness is held by a national society, but subgroups (for example, racial or ethnic groups, organizations, political parties, classes or castes) often maintain—and even nurture—memories of key events that form their identity and psychology.

Shared history also provides opportunities for competing or conflicting perspectives regarding the same events. For Palestinians and Arab nations, the Six-Day War represents a humiliating defeat; for Israel, it was a victory. Japanese nationalists still feel pride in the heights of the Japanese empire during World War II, whereas the many peoples occupied and oppressed by Japanese troops nurture distrust regarding the role of Japan in the region. Old-line traditional communists look back to the glory days of the Soviet Union, while for modern democrats in Russia the history of oppression and suppression dominates their view.

Not all of history presents negative experiences. Religious or racial groups may also have experienced times of tolerance and cooperation, such as the period in medieval Spain during which Muslims, Jews, and Christians lived in prosperity and harmony (Menocal, 2002). History provides examples of cooperation among ethnic and racial groups toward a common end, such as the coalitions among whites and multiple black ethnic groups in South Africa during the struggle against apartheid (Sampson, 2000).

Consider an example of Mexico and the United States and their long-standing, and often problematic, relationship: "The asymmetry of power determines how Mexico and the United States view each other. Differences of history, religion, race and language serve to complicate their relationship, to contrast their ways of doing things, to widen the gulf of understanding that separates them. But all these variables are overshadowed by the inescapable and unique fact that a vulnerable developing country shares a 2,000 mile border with the world's richest and strongest power" (Riding, 1986, p. 458).

In the late 1980s, two high-level diplomats from the United States and Mexico coauthored *Limits to Friendship: The United States and Mexico* (Pastor and Castañeda, 1989), a book that details the different perspectives of the two countries and their citizens on a wide range of issues and attempts to elucidate the roots of some of the tensions that have emerged between them. These tensions have often affected the abilities of negotiators from the government, economic, and social sectors to negotiate agreements. A few of the historical factors and perceptions of government officials, businesspeople, and citizens that influence relations and negotiations between the two countries are described in Box 2.1.

Box 2.1. Limits to Friendship: The United States and Mexico

Mexican Perspective

- Mexico has a strong sense of history; the United States lacks one. The United States has a short memory for historic events between the two nations.
- The United States has invaded Mexico or directly intervened in its politics a number of times in the past: the War of 1848 when U.S. armed forces took Mexico City; the occupation of Vera Cruz in 1913 during the Mexican Revolution; the intrusion of a military expeditionary force in Chihuahua led by General Pershing in retaliation for a raid on Columbus, New Mexico, by Pancho Villa; and conflicts over the nationalization of the oil industry in the 1930s.
- The United States took by force a significant portion of Mexican lands, first in the war over the succession of Texas and later in 1848, when Mexico was forced to yield the area that is now New Mexico, Arizona, and California.
- U.S. invasions have not been conducted for altruistic or what Mexicans often consider the "right" reasons. The United States has not helped Mexico and Mexicans as much as it might (and in some cases should).
- Mexico is poor and weak in many areas in comparison to the United States, which perceives itself and is perceived by Mexicans to be rich and strong.
- Mexico and Mexicans often feel ignored by the United States—unless the northern country wants something from them.

- Mexico has large oil reserves to which it perceives the United States wants access at prices less than advantageous to Mexico.
- In terms of the economy, culture, self-perceptions, and foreign policy, the U.S. presence is overwhelming.
- The United States has been, and is perceived by many Mexicans to be, actively meddling in Mexican domestic politics.
- Mexicans often feel that their maneuvering room to address basic structural features of their bilateral ties with the United States is very narrow.
- Mexicans on occasion follow the traditional aphorism of Benito Juarez for dealing with the United States: "Say yes, but never say when" (p. 24).

U.S. Perspective

- Occupation of western lands in North America was part of the manifest destiny for the spread of the United States, its culture, its political system, and democracy from coast to coast.
- "The United States is a nation that does not feel a need to remember its past, and the Mexican government feels it cannot afford to forget it" (p. 52).
- Most people from the United States know very little about Mexican history or politics: "History sits differently in the two countries. In Mexico, it is like a block of granite, inhibiting movement. In the United States, it is like a rolling stone. In Mexico, the 'past lives.' Mexicans are justly proud of their heritage, the great Mayan and Aztec civilizations, their colonial buildings, but are more pessimistic about the future. In contrast, Americans take pride in their newest building, the latest invention, the most recent success. The past motivates; it does not slow the future in the United States" (p. 47).
- Americans are not as interested in debating history as they are in discussing and reaching agreements on current policy.
- The United States is serving its interests when it helps Mexico—but Mexicans often believe that "one nation's development can only be purchased at the extent of another nation" (p. 8).
- People from the United States are problem solvers, but Mexicans frequently do not respond to or resist proposals made by parties from the United States.
- If Mexico would only release the state's control of the economy, Mexico would prosper.
- Mexicans seem overly sensitive to U.S. activities, and often feel slighted when this was not the intent.
- Mexicans are coming to the United States in significant numbers, and this influx is sometimes perceived by some as an invasion that poses a threat to U.S. culture, language, and economy.

The historical events and perceptions of Mexicans and Americans continue to affect negotiations between the two nations concerning a wide range of issues, including the North American Free Trade Agreement, Mexican economic development, oil sales, immigration, language, and drugs.

Source: Pastor and Castañeda (1989).

In assessing the potential effects of history on prospective negotiators and negotiations, it is helpful to know the relevant histories of the individuals and groups involved. Such knowledge can help you and other negotiators think about how positive historical events may help to promote agreements or, conversely, how strategies may have to be developed to overcome the effects of negative history that constrain positive relationships and settlements.

KEY QUESTIONS ABOUT THE INFLUENCE OF A CULTURE'S HISTORY

- What historical events within the society or culture have resulted in significant cooperation or conflict? Are there historical events that have shaped the consciousness of the individuals, groups, or the people as a whole that may affect negotiations?

- What has been the historical relationship of this country or culture to your own?

- If there was a colonial period or a time of occupation or slavery, were the members of the culture a colony or a colonizer, occupier or occupied, masters or slaves? If this country was colonized, what is the colonial legacy in terms of language, bureaucracy, governing structures, education, and so forth?

- Have there been any significant historical examples of collaboration, competition, or conflict between your culture, nation, organization, firm, or group and the counterpart with which you will be working? How might these historical events affect your future relationship and expectations concerning interactions, procedures, or expected outcomes?

- What has been the level of satisfaction in the other culture and in yours with historic transactions or the settlement of disputes? Are past satisfaction levels likely to influence current or future interactions?

Social Structures

Social structures are external factors or forces, institutional arrangements, or ideas and concepts, which are often beyond the direct influence or control of the people involved, that shape and influence the dynamics of negotiations. They may affect both physical arrangements, such as the way an institution is structured and internal relationships organized, as well as mental constructs and social norms such as laws, religious beliefs, and customary practices. Social structures play a significant role in determining how people of different ages, genders, classes, ethnic groups, and races interact. They also provide the basis for significant social systems, including the economic system, legal system, and political system, among others.

Social structures influence the dynamics of negotiations in many overt, but also somewhat subtle, ways. Some such structures directly influence the negotiation table, such as cultural preferences for how a negotiating team is organized or makes decisions internally. Social norms affect how a negotiation team fits into an organization and its relationship to other authorities. In some situations, existing laws will influence the permissible outcomes of negotiations.

Larger tangible social structures are external to the negotiations themselves, yet still exert a powerful influence. These include geopolitical relationships, ideology, religion, legal systems, government structures and bureaucracies, and corporate organizations. Negotiators bring these deeply embedded social constructs, parameters, and constraints with them into negotiations; they are not left at the door.

Cognitive structures, including thoughts, attitudes, and beliefs, are less tangible than organizational structures and are both the result of and influence the development of culture. However, they are every bit as influential on transactional negotiations or conflict resolution processes as more tangible social structural elements. For example, during the last half of the twentieth century, ideology, in the form of capitalism, communism, and fascism, had tremendous effects on international negotiation strategies.

Religious principles also influence tangible social structures, which in turn affect the course of negotiations. For example, banking practices based on Islamic law influence how negotiations over loans are conducted in Muslim states (see Box 2.2).

Box 2.2. Islamic Law and Banking

Concepts that formalized banking practices of Islamic financial institutions were developed forty years ago during meetings of the Organization of the Islamic Conference in Egypt. After many years of planning, the Islamic Development Bank, an intergovernmental bank, opened in 1975. Over the next twenty years, Islamic banks became active players in the world's financial sector. The first privately owned Islamic bank was opened in 1975 in Egypt. Since then, according to the General Council of Islamic Financial Institutions, 267 Islamic banks have opened worldwide.

The defining characteristic of Islamic banking is the prohibition of charging interest, since they are governed by strict rules derived from the Koran. Like Western banks, Islamic banks provide loans of funds. Earnings are derived from several special mechanisms that are based on profit-and-loss sharing and fixed markup (among others) instead of interest. Each Islamic bank employs at least one Muslim scholar, who determines what is acceptable under Islamic law. Investments in gambling and weaponry are prohibited. An Islamic bank can still be profitable, using concepts that are acceptable under its religious doctrine.

Source: "Islamic Banking Making Inroads" (2004).

KEY QUESTIONS REGARDING SOCIAL STRUCTURES

- *Family and community structures.* Are family systems patriarchal or matriarchal? Are families strong and intact, or fragmented and weak? Are traditional community structures operating, or have they been replaced by modern systems? Who exerts influence at the community level: Elders, men, women, elected leaders, religious or spiritual leaders? Are communities well organized to advocate for their interests or to initiate actions or are they fairly passive?

- *Legal and regulatory systems.* Is this a highly regulated society? What laws govern the topics under negotiation? What kind of legal systems are in force? Is the legal system working? Is a fair, timely, efficient, and inexpensive legal decision available or possible? If the legal system is not working, what alternatives do people commonly use to manage or resolve differences?

- *Political and bureaucratic structures.* Is the entity you will be working with a democracy, a dictatorship, a socialist state, a monarchy? Traditional or modern? Are government ministries, departments, and agencies bureaucratic or informal? Do they hire based on objective and merit criteria, or are family and friendship ties important? Does it take a long time and lots of red tape to get things done, or are systems fairly efficient? How do political systems exert influence on the issues under negotiation?

- *Economic structures.* Is this a free market, socialist, highly government regulated, or mixed economy? Is it an industrial or agricultural nation? What are the dominant industries, products, or services? What are the main economic resources and raw materials available? Is the economy mostly independent or dependent—and in what areas? Is this a rich industrial society or a developing country? Is income relatively evenly distributed or are the differences between rich and poor enormous?

- *Civil society and nongovernmental organizations.* Does this society have a strong tradition of civil society and nongovernmental organizations? If so, in what sectors—charity, environmental advocacy, human rights, development, business support (Chamber of Commerce, Rotary), women, youth? Or have such organizations been actively discouraged?

- *Belief structures, religion, and ideology.* What are the dominant philosophical systems in the society, if any? Is there one dominant religion or many? Is there a single ascendant political ideology, such as democracy, authoritarianism, socialism, or theocracy? How are religious or ideological beliefs or views played out in day-to-day interactions? Are specific discussion topics, behaviors, or settlement options considered to be taboo?

THE INNER RIM

The individuals or groups engaged in negotiations respond to and try to address different factors:

- Context, situations, issues, or problems that must be addressed
- Needs or interests they wish to have met in the outcome of problem solving
- Sources of power and influence

We examine each of these factors in turn.

Situations, Problems, and Issues

Culture influences how people define the social situations they face, the problems they encounter, and the issues or topics that are important to discuss (or avoid discussing). Members of all cultures deal with similar situations: raising or buying food, securing shelter, obtaining work to support themselves or their family, contracting marriages, purchasing needed goods, and interacting with peers, subordinates, and superiors. However, the meanings and importance that members of a culture place on these situations vary tremendously. This causes problems when people from different cultures must interact to get their needs met. An important element of preparation for any negotiation is to develop a clear understanding of how the other party defines the situation and the issues to be discussed and why. (For additional discussion of how people define situations, see the section of Chapter Four on framing.)

Transaction or Conflict Context: In general, the context of negotiation may be one of two types: a *transactional* interaction in which parties strive to build relationships and reach some form of agreement, deal, or contract regarding issues that are not necessarily conflicted; or a dispute or *conflict resolution* initiative in which the parties must attempt to resolve competing or conflicting views, tensions, interests, or actions.

Emotional Context: The context of negotiations has an impact on whether issues are framed as topics that will be discussed in a rational manner or with a high level of emotion. In a transactional process, relations and emotions are more likely to be neutral, positive, or only slightly strained. Agenda items and issues are generally addressed in a calm, rational, and problem-solving manner. In the case of an active disagreement or conflict, the agenda and individual issues are frequently emotionally loaded, and topics for discussion may be addressed in a strident, adversarial, and less rational manner (Kopelman and Olekalns, 1999).

On occasion, parties may not agree as to whether the context of negotiations and relevant issues to be addressed are primarily transactional or conflictual. Often the members of more dominant cultures or powerful parties frame issues in a transactional context. Conversely, members of less powerful cultures or parties, minority groups, or subgroups, who often feel one down or have suffered past harm, see negotiations and issues through a conflict lens. They frame negotiations as a forum to resolve a dispute, not to just make a deal (Kopelman and Olekalns, 1999).

KEY QUESTIONS ABOUT THE CONTEXT OR SITUATION IN WHICH NEGOTIATIONS WILL OCCUR

- Do the parties see the negotiations as a transactional interaction to reach a deal or contract, or as an initiative to resolve a conflict?

- Do the parties have a common view of the context for talks? If not, for whom is it different, and why?

- What might be appropriate actions or moves to clarify or coordinate views regarding the context of talks, if they are different? What might be the first steps that could be taken to move toward coordination? By whom?

- Does either party appear to carry intense emotions regarding the situation, problem, or issues?

- What does the intensity or lack of intensity of emotions about the issues in question indicate about their relevance, importance, or psychological significance?

- How is the intensity of emotions likely to affect future discussion of issues, and what might be done to address this dynamic?

Needs and Interests

Needs and interests are elements that individuals and groups require, expect, or desire. Needs fall along a continuum ranging from those critical for human survival on one end (such as food, shelter, health, and physical security) to identity needs (such as meaning, community, intimacy, and autonomy) at the other (Maslow, 1954; Burton, 1993). Interests generally refer to a party's preferred way of getting needs met. Thus, while we all need to eat, one person might prefer five small meals in a day, while another may want a big breakfast, a small lunch, and a full and rich dinner. In the process of negotiating, parties naturally advocate for their interests and needs.

A critical element of preparation for intercultural problem solving or negotiation is the development of a tentative understanding or preliminary theory about the needs and interests of the other party—and to become clear about your own.

While some conflicts are related to meeting survival and identity needs, a wider range of problems or negotiations in daily life focus on satisfying interests. We find that there are three kinds of interests: *substantive, procedural,* and *psychological/relational.*

Substantive interests are tangible outcomes or benefits a party wants to have satisfied, receive, or be exchanged as a result of negotiations. In transactional or conflict resolution contexts, exchanges may focus on the desire for and receipt of financial or political benefits, remuneration for past losses, exchanges of property, performance of services, or specific acts or behaviors. Examples of substantive interests include the terms of settlement for the division of property in a divorce settlement, favorable rates of salary and benefit increases (or decreases) in a labor-management negotiation, or the shape of a new broadly representative multiparty governance structure in accords to end a civil war.

Procedural interests refer to parties' preferences regarding the process by which problem solving, negotiations, or dispute resolution occurs and ways agreements are reached or implemented. They include the desire for an efficient and timely process, clearly understandable steps, and an opportunity for all parties to present their views. In a transactional context, procedural issues might include the timing of payments for the purchase of manufactured items or the schedule for delivery. In a conflict context, procedural issues may focus on who is included or excluded in the negotiation process itself or the process for verifying the disarmament and demobilization of combatants.

Psychological/relational interests concern how individuals or groups are treated, both in the negotiation process and outside of it. They also include how participants feel or want to feel about themselves and their counterpart, and how relationships are valued and shaped through negotiations. Psychological interests include an individual negotiator's desire to be trusted, respected, heard, and have feelings and experiences acknowledged. For instance, parties that have experienced deep injury in the past (such as Israelis, Palestinians, Native Americans, or First Nations) often need explicit recognition of that painful history in the context of negotiations.

In many negotiations, the nature of past, present, or future interactions among the parties may be an important topic on the negotiation agenda—or establishing or improving a relationship may serve as the basis for negotiations (Blake and Mouton, 1984). In some negotiations, parties want to find ways to terminate a relationship and have no further dealings with a counterpart, while in others, one or more participants want to maintain or create a positive future relationship.

Regardless of the types of needs or interests being addressed, how members of any cultural group define them and what they consider to be adequate satisfaction of them will be influenced by culture.

KEY QUESTIONS

- What do you understand to be the stated, or unstated, needs or interests of the other party? Your own? Consider substantive, procedural, and psychological or relationship interests.

- What appear to be the major issues or topics for discussion in negotiations? Are they substantive, procedural, or relationship and psychological in nature?

- Does there seem to be a lot that is unstated, understated, or vague or that hints about needs or interests, or is the counterpart specific or explicit regarding his or her wants or desires?

- Are needs or interests framed or described in a manner similar to how someone in your own culture might express similar needs or concerns? If they are stated differently, why do you think that this might be the case?

- Are they stressing the satisfaction of or ignoring substantive, procedural, or psychological interests more or less than you might expect from members of your culture?

Sources and Forms of Power

Power and influence can be defined as "the ability to act, to influence an outcome, to get something to happen (not to happen), or to overcome resistance" (Mayer, 2000, p. 50). Culture influences the preferred forms and sources of power and influence, and how and when they are used.

Culture also determines the options available when a party has more or less power than another or is in a superior or subordinate position. For example, a verbal slight to a man's wife by another person in some cultures might result in giving the commenter the cold shoulder or instead making a quick verbal retort. In another culture, the comment might be perceived as an attack on the family's honor, which could be righted only by a physical fight or, in extreme cases, the death of the offending person. In another case, a follower of Gandhi who believes that his or her rights have been violated may respond with *satyagraha,* or nonviolent resistance—a far different reaction from that of a guerrilla fighter who is a member of a violent separatist group. Good cultural analysis seeks to identify what forms of power and influence are most likely to be used, by whom, and in which situations.

As we will see in subsequent chapters, negotiating power derives from many sources for different people and parties. For some, power is based on the ability to make and carry out physical threats through personal arms, police, military, or other forms of force. Other people hold recognized moral authority that arises from their personal reputation or position. The pope and the Dalai

Lama exert influence based on their recognized moral authority. Still others claim power based on the rightness or fairness of their position or clear legal rights. For instance, a labor union might assert that a company is mistreating workers or violating labor laws, thereby gaining a certain amount of bargaining leverage at the negotiating table. People who are recognized experts or possess special knowledge may also exercise a form of technical power. Politicians or the leaders of a social movement might enjoy power derived from widespread public support.

While all of these forms of power clearly exist, cultures differ with regard to which forms of power are considered to be legitimate and under what circumstances. During the first decade of the twenty-first century, traditional religious leaders hold dominant power in Iran, whereas most religious voices hold little influence in Northern Europe. A Taiwanese negotiator might consult a reader of signs, portents, and the stars before making any major decision, while his American counterpart might consult his financial advisor.

Negotiations inherently involve efforts by negotiators to influence each other to achieve their goals and meet interests. However, the means used vary tremendously, and they may be significantly influenced by culture. Influence efforts during talks may be subtle and merely hinted by nuanced body language, a phrase, or an off-the-cuff suggestion in an informal setting. They may also be more direct and coercive, such as threats of withholding cooperation or payments, walkouts from talks, strikes, demonstrations, employer lockouts of workers, lawsuits, seeking United Nations sanctions, or gunboat diplomacy such as a blockade. Influence may also involve provision or withholding of information: substantive financial, technical, or scientific information that a negotiator believes will be important or compelling to a counterpart; psychological information such as personal impacts of harm or costs imposed on them or that they will impose on their counterpart; or direct or indirect procedural information conveyed by how a negotiator bargains or procedures this person will or will not use to get some interests met. Chinese negotiators, for example, may appeal to their desire to build friendly and fraternal long-term relations, reciprocity, or the propriety of stronger parties providing advantages to weaker ones. French negotiators may use logic and advocate the acceptance of principles that will guide decision making on all subsequent issues. Americans may try to persuade their counterpart that their ideas or proposals are the most efficient, cost-effective, and timely way to achieve their ends.

As in other intercultural aspects of negotiations, coordination of different cultural means of influence is often critical for parties to reach agreements. A number of years ago, one of us served as a mediator in an international dispute among several countries. The process of preparing for face-to-face negotiations had taken many months. Tentative agenda items and draft proposals had been circulated by two of the delegations with requests for all to comment on them. Representatives of two of the three nations—those who had initially sent out the drafts—provided extensive commentary. The third country remained silent.

When the delegations came together for their first face-to-face session, the delegates from the two countries that had submitted ideas were stunned by the negotiating posture and behavior of their counterpart from the third nation. The representative came into the talks with hard-line positions rejecting all of the proposals out of hand and identified twenty or more areas where he had major disagreements. He started out with both a strong critique and a refusal to accept any of the proposals on the table.

The representatives of the two other delegations were nonplussed by the response of the third. They had put together proposals in good faith, solicited input from all parties, and tried to be cooperative, accommodative, and open to making changes. They were astounded that their cooperative strategy was not working and was being met instead by stonewalling, strong language, and indications of distrust.

Later, with help from the mediation team, all of the parties analyzed the differences in their negotiation styles. At that point, they realized that they had different views about how they should influence each other, based partly on their historical experiences and cultures, especially their colonial heritage. Representatives of one country, which had an oppressive colonial history and had experienced years of civil war, believed that assertive exercise of coercive power was the only way to survive and get their way. Their educational system also was based on Continental deductive reasoning and argumentation. Thus, they used highly adversarial strategies, presented absolute "no's," made sweeping objections, asserted disagreements over principles, and engaged in point-counterpoint dialectical argumentation to get their way. The other two nations, with British-based colonial history and educational systems, and one of them with a long democratic history, used a more collaborative problem-solving approach, with appeals to logic and attempts to meet the identified interests of all concerned parties. In spite of these differences in assumptions about power and influence, the parties did reach agreement on the total document, but it took a long time and lots of blood, sweat, and tears.

KEY QUESTIONS

- What means of influence or persuasion have you heard or learned about that might be effective with the culture you will be working with?
- Are the means of persuasion and influence being used by the other party toward you significantly different from what you might expect from a member of your own culture in a similar situation?

- Do your means of influence or persuasion fail to persuade the other party, or do they signal that they are inappropriate?
- Does the other party react either more or less positively to either coercive or more positive persuasion tactics than might be expected from someone in your own culture when faced by similar tactics?

THE SPOKES OF THE WHEEL

While the inner and outer rims provide insights regarding the broader context of negotiations, the spokes of the wheel delineate areas where specific culturally based patterns of belief and behaviors influence interactions between individuals and groups. These factors are influenced by the natural environment, social structures, and history of a cultural group, as well as the specific situations or problems to be addressed.

Roles and Participation

Culture often determines who will participate in negotiation processes, based on deeply held views regarding gender, age, and status, among other important factors. Both cultural and tactical considerations determine the choice of negotiators or negotiating teams and when different people engage in the process. For instance, two parties may decide to conduct the bulk of negotiations using midranking teams of technical experts and engage authoritative decision makers only in the final stages. The negotiating team from an egalitarian culture might be made up of men and women, as well as older and younger staff, while counterparts from a more hierarchical culture might be composed entirely of older men.

Some cultures are quite explicit about who holds decision-making authority, while others may deliberately obscure the true power players. Chinese negotiators (representing the People's Republic), for instance, famously hide powerful party officials within larger delegations, while the apparent leaders and spokespersons may be lower-level officials.

Another variable that influences participation concerns how much emphasis a culture puts on the individual or on groups or collectivities. Some cultural analysts have described this as the individualism-collectivism continuum (Hofstede, 1984), with cultures falling along a spectrum of orientations. Cultures that are oriented toward individuals generally value individual autonomy, initiative, creativity, and authority in decision making. Those more oriented toward collectivism generally value and emphasize group cohesion, harmony, and decision making that involves either consultation with group members before deciding or consideration of the well-being of the group over that of the individual. It is helpful to know, before entering negotiations, whether a culture is oriented toward individualism or collectivism in comparison to your personal or organizational culture.

Cultures also vary with regard to the need for consultation away from the table. In some settings, negotiators would not finalize an agreement without consulting with people higher on the organizational ladder or wider constituencies. For instance, in labor-management negotiations, the labor negotiating team may seek a vote among the entire union membership before accepting a final negotiated contract. At the same time, the management team might consult with top managers and legal counsel.

KEY QUESTIONS

- What are the culture norms regarding rank, status, gender, and age? Is this a relatively egalitarian culture or one in which hierarchy and status are quite important?
- What is the makeup of negotiating teams? Are they mainly technical people addressing substantive issues or powerful leaders? What are their ranks, and do they have decision-making power?
- What is the division of labor among different people in the negotiation process at different stages?
- Do the parties in negotiation have the same or contrasting approaches to roles and participation? How will you coordinate differences?
- Who is not at the table? Are they deliberately excluded—and if so, why? Are there mechanisms for consultation with important parties not represented directly in negotiations?

View of Relationships

Some of the most striking differences among cultures are the variations in how they view relationships—how they start a relationship, build it, maintain it, and the boundaries they establish for it. Described next are some of the major variations in how cultures approach relationships. Although some of the variations described may appear to be polar opposites, most of these factors in fact lie along a continuum, with only a few cultures at the extremes. Most cultures are variations and combinations of these factors, which, when merged with individual differences, create a rich tapestry of possibilities—for conflict or for cooperation.

Task or Relationship Focus. People view negotiations as having either an instrumental/task or relational/relationship focus (Wilson and Putnam, 1990).

People in some cultures when engaging in negotiations focus primarily on the substantive tasks at hand: the business to be accomplished, the work to be done, or the contract to be agreed on. For example, "For most business executives and lawyers, particularly in North America, the goal of a business negotiation, first and foremost is achieving a signed contract between the parties. For them, the contract is the definitive set of rights and duties that strictly binds the two sides, controls their behavior in the future, and determines who does what, when, where and how. According to this view, the parties' deal is their contract" (Salacuse, 1998b, p. 5). Such individuals and groups often establish only enough of a personal relationship to get the job done, and no more. In fact, in many instances, it would seem that the sole purpose of developing a personal connection is to expedite the business; relationships are at the service of the task.

In other cultures, the people engaged in negotiations appear to take significant pleasure in meeting people, establishing close personal connections, and engaging in social activities—and view doing business as almost secondary or incidental. They would never consider making a business deal or negotiating an agreement with someone they do not know in some depth. They view establishing a personal connection as a necessary precursor to accomplishing tasks. This approach, often seen in Asia, considers "the purpose of negotiation as creating a business relationship. This view recognizes that, just as a map is not a country but only a very imperfect sketch thereof, a contract is not a business relationship. Although the contract that results from negotiations may describe the relationship, the essence of the deal between the parties is their relationship, not their contract" (Salacuse, 1998b, p. 5). Thus, the major focus of parties with this orientation is on creating, building, and negotiating the terms of the relationship. They often take extended time prior to and at the beginning of talks to establish and build interpersonal connections. They take a long-term view toward relationships, see negotiations as happening throughout participants' lives (rather than being a one-time event), and are open to using third parties to assist them in resolving any interpersonal or intergroup issues and substantive problems that arise (Salacuse, 1998).

Acceptance of Tensions in Relationships or Striving for Harmony. Cultures differ concerning the acceptability of or comfort with tensions between members or with outsiders. Some are at ease with disagreements or conflicts and place less importance on the development or maintenance of smooth interpersonal or intergroup relations. Others are very uncomfortable with direct expression of disagreement or engagement in disputes and strive for harmonious interactions, relationships, and positive affective feelings among people. All cultures have tensions and disagreements among members, but some accept them more than others. Cultures with strong harmony orientations strive to eliminate, suppress, or ignore tensions between members and take action to prevent conflicts from arising or being expressed. Traditional Chinese, Philippine, and many African societies are examples of harmony-oriented cultures (Murithi, 2006; Orendain, 1989; Chen, 2003; Goh, 2002). In Chinese society, cultural norms place a priority on appropriate and harmonious relationships between people of different rank and status—emperor and those ruled, husbands and wives, parents and children. Harmony is seen as benefiting both the people involved in relationships and society as a whole. This means that "in a society where harmony is the ideal and 'doing the right thing' is essential for good relations, one often does what one believes to be socially desirable even if one's attitudes are inconsistent with the action" (Triandis, 1989, p. 80).

In the Philippines, significant emphasis is placed on establishing, building, and maintaining smooth interpersonal relationships: "The value concepts that are predominant in the Filipino culture and relevant to the development of skills for conciliation, mediation and dispute settlement are *hiya* or an emotion-laden attitude involving honor, dignity and pride; *amor-propio* (self esteem) or the principle of reciprocity; *pakikisama* or the tendency to level with someone who is out of line and the curbing of antisocial attitudes by disallowing privacy; and paternalism which implies a deep respect for elders in consideration of age, stature or place in the community" (Orendian, 1989, p. 89).

Many societies in East, Central, and Southern Africa have the concept of *ubuntu*—the characteristics in their best sense of what it means to be human (Murithi, 2006). Tutu (1999) defines *ubuntu* in this way:

> *Ubuntu* is very difficult to render into a Western language. It speaks of the very essence of being human. When you want to give high praise to someone, we say, *"Yu, unobuntu"*; "Hey, so-and-so has *ubuntu*." This means that they are generous, hospitable, friendly, caring, and compassionate. Then you are generous, you are hospitable, you are friendly and caring and compassionate. You share what you have. It is to say "My humanity is caught up, is inextricably bound up, in yours." We belong in a bundle of life. We say, "A person is a person through other persons." It is not, "I think, therefore I am." It says rather, "I am human because I belong. I participate, I share." A person with *ubuntu* is open and available to others, affirming of others, does not feel threatened that others are able and good, for he or she has a proper self-assurance that comes with knowing that he or she belongs in a greater whole and is diminished when others are humiliated or diminished, when others are tortured or oppressed, or treated as if they are less than who they are [Tutu, 1999, p. 31].

A societal, group, or individual harmony orientation means that significant effort in negotiation or negotiation relationships is likely to be placed on maintaining smooth interpersonal relationships, keeping tensions under control, and, in the case of conflicts, striving for reconciliation.

Degree of Intimacy or Privacy. Cultures maintain different expectations regarding the degree of intimacy or distance in personal, family, social, and business relationships. More intimate relationships are characterized by trust, significant disclosure of information, informality, and multiple layers of interaction. At the other end of the spectrum, people proceed with more formality, caution, limited disclosures, and fairly circumscribed interactions.

Some cultures expect that business relationships will include some degree of social interaction, including eating or drinking together, attending local entertainment, and welcoming visiting business associates into private homes. Typically cultures with a stronger relationship (versus task) focus will also expect greater social interaction to provide the appropriate settings to build the relationship. However, a social setting and pleasurable activities should not be confused with expectations regarding the level of personal connection. How visitors are entertained may simply reflect a norm regarding politeness or the proper role of a host. The nature of the interactions during such activities—such as the kinds of personal questions explored—reveals whether greater intimacy is expected.

An example of different expectations regarding intimacy and disclosure is illustrated by contrasting behaviors of French, German, and U.S. business negotiators. Europeans are often very surprised by the level of both openness and disclosure exhibited by Americans and the degree to which they will invite foreigners into various parts of their lives. Americans are likely, especially in off-hours after a day of doing business, to invite foreigners into their homes to meet the family, "give them a real American experience," and disclose stories about divorces and problems with children, for example. Most Europeans are not as likely to invite people whom they do not know into their homes or reveal as much about their private or personal lives (Carroll, 1987). Germans frequently retain more formal relations, and often use formal titles—Mr., Mrs., or Doctor—even with people whom they have known for a long time. Because of different expectations regarding intimacy and disclosure, Europeans on occasion see Americans as forward, somewhat false, and shallow because they are willing to disclose aspects of their personal lives that Europeans would share only with very close friends.

Boundaries: Holistic Versus Compartmentalized. Some cultures divide life into neat compartments in which work focus or business life (diplomatic, commercial, manager-subordinate relations, and so forth) is separated from family or social networks. Such views might be reinforced by laws, regulations, or explicit ethical frameworks to prevent conflicts of interest, nepotism, and favoritism. People in many other cultures do not compartmentalize relationships, view all of life as connected, and observe only fuzzy boundaries at best between different kinds of relationships. For members of these cultures, business, friendships, family, and social networks intersect in endlessly fascinating and overlapping ways. For instance, in such cultures, it would be considered perfectly normal, even expected, for a businessperson to hire or give contracts to relatives or close friends—after all, they are known entities—while these actions in more compartmentalized cultures would be considered corrupt.

KEY QUESTIONS ABOUT ESTABLISHING, BUILDING, AND MAINTAINING RELATIONSHIPS

- Are the cultures involved more task oriented or relationship oriented? How will this affect the negotiation process?
- How are relationships established? How much time is devoted to relationship building prior to task-oriented activities?
- What degree of tension or conflict is permissible? Is maintenance of harmony a strong value?
- Are the cultures involved open and disclosing or relatively closed and distant?
- Do negotiators see life as a seamless whole or more compartmentalized?

Cooperation, Competition, and Conflict

Because culture has such a significant impact on the way that people interact with each other, it can and generally does affect their views and behaviors related to handling differences, tensions, disputes, and conflicts. By conflict, we mean situations in which there is significant perceived or actual divergence of interests of the involved parties, or a belief on their part that their current aspirations or goals cannot be achieved simultaneously (Rubin, Pruitt, and Kim, 1994).

Negotiators who are begining discussions, problem solving, or bargaining with someone from another culture will do well to try to identify the probable cultural orientations of their counterpart concerning how differences or conflicts are viewed and common norms for how they should be addressed. This includes understanding how a counterpart is likely to view and use various approaches to managing differences or disputes such as avoidance, accommodation, cooperation, competition, or engaging in overt conflict promotion, escalation, or resolution behavior.

Cultures differ dramatically regarding how they view the existence, importance, expression, and impact of differences among people and the desirability or undesirability of specific means for surfacing, managing, or resolving them. People in some cultures actively embrace differences and conflicts and willingly, if not always enthusiastically, make efforts to cooperate or compete to resolve them. In other cultures, people abhor discussion of differences or conflict. They engage in avoidance or suppression of tensions or find ways to cooperate and compromise so that differences are quickly resolved and perceived or real harmony can be restored.

Each culture generally exhibits a central tendency in their orientation toward the acceptability of differences and preferred means for managing conflict. However, in every culture, there are outliers who do not subscribe to cultural norms. In other words, although there may be a general cultural pattern of conflict behavior, many in the society will fall outside the norm—as any normal distribution curve does. Thus, we must be careful of accepting central tendencies and treating them as stereotypes; we must always be prepared for individuals and even groups to act outside the norm for their culture.

Three Attitudes Toward Conflict. In general, there are three broad cultural orientations toward conflict and its management and resolution:

1. *Conflicts are negative, unnatural, unnecessary, risky, bad, destructive, or dysfunctional for individuals, groups, and society.* In cultures that take this view, differences, disputes, and conflicts should, whenever possible, be ignored, avoided, suppressed, or dissolved (that is, made to disappear); or compromises should be made to manage them with minimal disruption to social relationships or group harmony.

2. *Conflicts are positive, normal, beneficial, and can catalyze greater understanding and learning and motivate individual, group, or societal change.* Members of cultures that take this view generally believe that disagreements, disputes, and conflicts should be encouraged and used to achieve positive change or favorable outcomes. They generally expect differences and different views to exist and are not uncomfortable in examining and addressing them.

3. *Conflicts are neutral but normal, inherently neither favorable nor unfavorable, good nor bad.* People who hold this view generally see that differences, diversity, or disputes are not bad in and of themselves and can result in either positive or negative impacts or outcomes. The key variable for members of cultures with this view is how differences are expressed and handled to achieve positive outcomes, not their existence.

Anthropological and sociological research has demonstrated a range of cultures that subscribe to one or more of these orientations toward the expression and management of differences, tensions, and conflicts.

Cultures that emphasize the first orientation, that overt expression of conflict is negative, generally see "conflict as dysfunctional and threatening to the social order, a phenomenon to be diffused. This notion of conflict presumes societal consensus about rights and values," which members are expected to adhere to and not challenge (Nader, 1990, p 47). Many Asian countries and cultures such as China (Chen, 2003), Indonesia (Mulder, 1996; Geertz, 1960), Japan (Nakane, 1970), and Thailand (Mulder, 1992); African societies (Channock, 1985); and traditional cultures such as Zapotec Indians in Mexico (Nader, 1990) or indigenous groups in Indonesia (Slaats and Portier, 1992; Von Benda-Beckmann, 1984) view tensions, assertiveness, aggression, or conflict in this relatively negative light.

Nader (1990) notes that cultures with negative orientations toward the overt expression of differences are often influenced by cultural "harmony ideology." The bias toward harmony is often based in religion or ideology, desires by members of a culture to find compromises that maintain the integrity of their community in the face of external threats, or as means for authorities to maintain power and control over other members of society.

Cultures whose members subscribe to the second view, that conflict is common, natural, and positive, are also quite common worldwide. For example, in some Melanesian societies, there is "a tolerance of and even enjoyment of quarreling" (Nader, 1990, p. 49). A number of anthropologists (Brigg, 2003) have also reported accounts of Australian Aboriginal people fighting because it is enjoyable or entertaining (Macdonald, 1990; Myers, 1991; Jarret, 2001).

This view is not limited to traditional societies. Cultures that have been influenced by Marxist ideology, in which class struggle is seen as the major engine for social change, frequently advocate surfacing, expressing, and dealing directly with differences and engaging in overt conflicts to achieve desired ends. For example, although Russia and many former Soviet Republics are no longer ruled by Marxist governments, their orientation toward the acceptability of vigorous engagement in overt disagreements and social conflict prevails.

The third orientation asserts that differences and conflicts are neutral, being neither good nor bad or destructive nor constructive. This view is common in Western European societies and those in the United States, Australia, and New Zealand, where individuals and groups emphasize conflict management and feel that conflicts need not be destructive and, in fact, may be productive for positive change. Of course, much depends on how conflicts are handled. Similarly, the personal growth or development movement of the 1970s highlighted the possibility that disputes can be viewed as opportunities for empowerment and personal transformation (Harrington and Merry, 1988). For subscribers to this view, social conflict could serve positive functions, such as binding individuals and groups together, providing a safety valve for the expression and diffusion of differences, establishing and maintaining balances of power, and facilitating the creation of associations and coalitions (Coser, 1956).

Strategies for Responding to Conflict. Closely related to orientations toward disagreements and conflict are the strategies various cultures prefer for respond- ing to them. In general, individuals and groups use five approaches to address common issues, problems, or conflicts:

1. *Avoidance strategies,* with maintenance of the status quo or stalemate outcomes

2. *Competition strategies,* in which one party generally strives to win signif- icantly more than another or attain totally win-lose outcomes

3. *Compromise strategies,* with shared gains and losses that are mutually acceptable to involved parties, often achieved through negotiation

4. *Accommodation strategies,* in which one party suppresses his or her own needs and agrees to meet the interests or needs of another, possibly at his or her own expense

5. *Cooperation strategies,* which involve the use of integrative interest-based problem solving or negotiation and result in solutions with joint gains and mutual benefits for all concerned.

These strategies are illustrated in Figure 2.2, which presents the approaches and strategies from the perspective of party A. The configuration of strategies would be reversed if B was placed on the *x*-axis. We will return to a discussion of these approaches in Chapter Three.

KEY QUESTIONS

- In the cultures represented in the negotiation, are cooperation, competi- tion, or conflict generally desirable or to be avoided?

- In what contexts or situations are members of cultures likely to cooperate, compete, or engage in conflict?

- Are disagreements or conflicts expressed and handled directly or indi- rectly?

Communication

Negotiators consider good communication to be central for productive negoti- ations. The negotiation process comes to a halt if participants fail to speak and listen to one another and gain a close approximation of each other's meaning and intent. Each of us has struggled to understand someone from our own cul- ture speaking our native language, especially at times of tension. This difficulty is magnified with people who come from different cultures and are not native speakers of the language. Luckily, people from different cultures expect some difficulty with communication and often put more energy into the process.

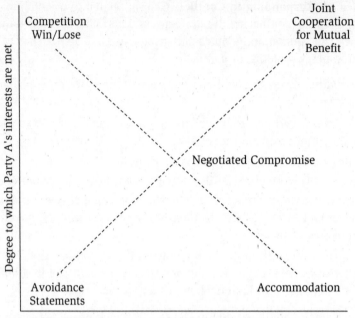

Figure 2.2. Basic Approaches to Conflict (from Party A's Point of View)

Many books have been written about communication and language within and between cultures. We address five major considerations for communication in the context of cross-cultural negotiations: direct versus indirect dealing, explicit versus implicit communication, the expression of emotions, nonverbal communication, and the meaning of yes and no. We also provide a note on the issue of language interpretation and translation.

Direct Versus Indirect Dealing. People in some cultures feel quite comfortable dealing directly with another party in negotiation or in conflict resolution. They prefer meeting face-to-face with the people most directly concerned in order to try to reach agreements. Such people usually discuss a wide variety of issues quite openly, freely express emotions, and engage in arguments over important points. Most people from majority cultures in northern Europe, the United States, Canada, Australia, and New Zealand, and from India and Pakistan exhibit direct-dealing behavior.

In contrast, people from indirect-dealing cultures, especially in situations where there is actual or potential friction in their relationships, frequently prefer to carry on communications through a formal or informal intermediary.

From their perspective, indirect communication allows face saving (honor or self-respect) for themselves or their counterpart, preserves smooth interpersonal or intergroup relationships, prevents direct confrontation, and can avoid uncomfortable interactions among people of different status or rank. Members of these cultures often find it embarrassing and needlessly disruptive to talk openly about conflicts, feelings, or competing interests, preferring to keep discussions general, noncontroversial, calm, and unemotional. People from many indigenous cultures around the world, and some cultures from southern Europe, the Middle East, South America, and much of Asia prefer indirect communications.

The choice of direct dealing or indirect dealing is somewhat determined by the issues under discussion and the degree of tension that exists around them, the comparative rank or power of the two parties, and the risks if direct communications occur. In some cultures, business or government matters may be handled quite directly, while personal, family, or disputes over issues of honor might be addressed only indirectly. Relatively equal parties may engage in direct negotiations, while people of different ranks may be required to deal through others or feel more comfortable taking that approach.

Explicit Versus Implicit Communication. Often closely related to the direct versus indirect factor, cultures display a preference for explicit or implicit communication. Anthropologists Edward and Mildred Hall (1990; Hall, 1987) developed a framework for understanding cultures along a continuum from high context to low context.

In high-context cultures, communication and much of the rest of human interaction is highly contextualized—in other words, the ways that people talk and deal with each other are culturally coded and dependent on prescribed patterns of relationships that in many cases are obscure to the outsider. Insiders follow unwritten rules—often quite elaborate ones—that they learn from childhood. The very meaning of words depends on the context: who says what to whom, the issues involved, and the degree of tension or controversy, for example. Communications among people in high-context settings are often imprecise, nuanced, and oriented toward saving face, preserving relationships, and allowing tactical flexibility.

High-context cultures are usually fairly homogeneous and maintain highly stratified social structures. Examples include many indigenous or tribal groups worldwide, and the cultures of Japan and parts of China and Indonesia. Many of the countries of the Mediterranean and the Middle East are also high context. In addition, every county has subcultures that are high context, including extended family systems, some organizational cultures, and religious and other closely knit communities.

People in low-context cultures are much more explicit in speech and action. Discussions are more overt, detailed, specific, and clear, leaving little room for misinterpretation. The rules and expectations of interaction are often written down or even posted publicly. In a negotiation, people from a low-context culture might present a set of written proposals or demands, leaving little room for interpretation and, incidentally, often locking the parties into positions. Low-context cultures are often found in countries that have diverse populations due to immigration, such as Canada, Australia, South Africa, and the United States, where people from diverse backgrounds have become more explicit in their communications in order to work and live with each other; amalgamated countries in which diverse groups have been unified into a common nation-state, such as Germany, Russia (and the former Soviet Union), India, and Pakistan; or countries that have been colonized by any of these nations. In addition, countries with relatively egalitarian traditions and or laws, such as the United Kingdom, the Netherlands, and the Scandinavian countries, also generally use very low-context communications.

In a study, Salacuse (1998a, p. 230) inquired of 310 business executives, lawyers, military personnel, diplomats, other professionals, and graduate students from North America, Latin America, and Europe about their communication styles, and whether they had either direct and explicit orientations or preferred more indirect and implicit patterns of talk during negotiations. His results show the percentage favoring indirect communications:

Country	Percent
Japan	27
France	20
China	18
United Kingdom	12
Brazil	11
India	11
Germany	9
United States	5
Argentina	4
Spain	0
Mexico	0
Nigeria	0

Japanese, French, and Chinese respondents indicated that they had a stronger orientation toward indirect and implicit communications. When Salacuse (1998a) controlled for gender, he found that 90 percent of the males and females responded to this question identically, with only 10 percent claiming an indirect style. It should be noted, however, that these were self-reports of a limited sample, not observed behaviors.

Expression of Emotions. Negotiations are not simply about substantive issues, such as the price and amount of a sale, the provisions of a labor-management contract, the division of land or water, how power will be shared, or the shape of government policy. Parties at the negotiation table bring feelings with them—about the other party, their roles inside and outside the negotiations, history, the substantive issues themselves, and a host of other potential matters. Without such feelings, negotiations might be a completely rational process. However, feelings of affection, frustration, respect, trust or distrust, satisfaction, impatience, betrayal, anger, and many others are integral to the negotiation process. Negotiators ignore them at their peril.

Cultures vary widely regarding the degree to which emotions can be shown or expressed. Some cultures strongly disapprove of the open demonstration or expression of feelings, especially negative ones. In accord with their preference for social harmony, people from many Asian cultures, such as Thailand, the Philippines, Japan, and Indonesia, value maintaining smooth interpersonal interactions and avoid direct emotional confrontation, except in extreme circumstances (Mulder, 1992, 1996; Orendain, 1989; Hall, 1987; Mulder, 1996). For many of these cultures, even overt expression of positive feelings may be subtle.

People from some other cultures expect a show of emotions in the process of negotiations and might even become suspicious if their counterparts show no feelings. For instance, in some settings, labor-management contract negotiations in the United States open with an almost ritualistic exchange of denunciations, insults, claims of bad faith, recitation of how one party or the other has acted badly, and wildly unrealistic demands. After a time, the negotiators usually buckle down to productive discussion of the issues on the table, but further eruptions of feelings may occur at any time. In these circumstances, both sides seem to feel that unless hard words are expressed, the negotiators are neglecting their job or failing to show how important the issues are. If the negotiations were conducted entirely in an atmosphere of polite respect and decorum, the constituencies outside the room might suspect that their representatives had not fought for the best deal possible.

Negotiators from some cultures appear to use feelings as a negotiating tactic. Officials from the former Soviet Union, Russia, and North Korea are known for expression of strong feelings of friendship, anger, or belligerence, sometimes accompanied by yelling, drama, and put-downs of their counterparts (Smith, 1989; Schecter, 1998; Snyder, 1999). People from the less expressive cultures might easily find such behaviors offensive or insulting. During the Cold War era, U.S. diplomats, while normally comfortable with some expression of feelings, were often confused by such tactics and unsure how to react, or they developed a strong aversion to them.

Comfort or discomfort with expression of feelings is not only culturally determined; individuals vary widely as well within cultures based on family upbringing, personality, and training. Negotiators must therefore be wary of assuming that someone from Japan will always act in a smooth and polite manner, or that someone from Italy will prove to be highly emotionally expressive or volatile.

Nonverbal Communication. Much has been written about nonverbal communication. Suffice it to say that each culture maintains norms and taboos about a number of areas—for example:

- Greetings (bows, handshakes, standing when someone enters)
- Meaning of head gestures (nodding, tilt of the head)
- Meaning of smiles and laughter
- Eye contact
- Placement and movement of arms and hands
- Use of right hand or left hand, or both hands
- Touching and closeness (by whom, where, when)
- Where to sit (chair, floor)
- Posture and position of legs and feet
- Dress, covering or exposing parts of the body
- Table manners, way of eating

Many books, even simple tourist guides, mention the most important of these norms in advising travelers to other countries. For instance, women travelers to Arab cultures are often advised to keep their head, arms, and legs covered in public—depending on how strictly the culture adheres to Muslim norms. It may take time and interaction with people from the other cultures to pick up the more subtle issues.

The Meaning and Frequency of Yes and No. When you are an outsider visiting another culture, you may run into difficulty with the concepts of yes and no, because your counterparts will not necessarily mean the same thing as you do by these terms. If you are from a direct-dealing and explicit culture you might expect that someone saying yes really means, *Yes, I hear, accept, or agree with what you have said.* For instance, when you ask for an appointment to see an important official and your guide (from an indirect-dealing and implicit culture) says, "yes," he or she may in fact mean, "I will make inquiries to see what can be done (but I doubt it will be possible)."

A classic of issues involving parties' interpretations of yes and no is that of Japanese or Indonesian Javanese negotiators who might respond to a request by saying, "That will be very difficult." An American might interpret this to mean that although the request might be hard to meet, everything will be done to accomplish it. However, the Japanese or Javanese person probably means simply no, but is unwilling to make such an explicit rejection.

Sometimes the difficulty comes from the actual language. Some languages do not have the exact equivalent of the English yes, but express agreement or disagreement in other ways. The Vietnamese language, for instance, does not have a single word that means yes; rather, agreement or disagreement is indicated in various ways depending on the context of the conversation. To make matters more confusing, Vietnamese constantly utter a particle that is a politeness meaning essentially, "I am hearing you." Unfortunately for Europeans and Americans, that participle sounds exactly like the German *ja* (pronounced as the English *ya*)—so it sounds like agreement to Western ears, but it is not.

If you are from an indirect and less explicit culture, you may have the opposite difficulty. You may be tempted to doubt a yes or no from a northern European or North American, while they will consider a firm yes as a verbal commitment.

Cultures also differ in the frequency that they say yes and, especially, no. One study of ten cultures (Graham, 1993) found that Brazilians are likely to say no more times in negotiations—41.9 times in a bargaining period of thirty minutes—than are members of nine other cultures. Members of other cultures who say no less often, but still fairly frequently, are the French and, to a much lesser extent, Germans, British, and Americans. The cultures that say no least frequently are Japanese and Chinese.

Issues of Language, Translation, and Interpretation. An obvious issue in communication among cultures is language. Even when people from two cultures appear to speak the same language, regional and national differences may cause confusion. Parisian French is not the same as Québécois in Canada. British, American, and Australian English have significant differences.

More important than these minor differences is the difficulty of communicating when you and your counterpart do not speak the same language. Even if one of you has learned the other's language, miscommunication can occur, since full fluency is relatively rare and the nuances are frequently important in negotiations. For this reason, unless you are experienced in negotiating in another language, it may be important to secure the services of an interpreter or translator for anything beyond informal communications. An interpreter usually provides immediate verbal translation of a conversation or other exchange, while a translator typically works with the written word (documents and agreements, for example).

A good interpreter will go beyond simple language issues to provide guidance to one or both parties regarding cultural differences and meanings. For instance, following an important meeting between a Chinese representative and an American businessman, an interpreter might meet with the American to go over what was said and help decipher what was meant, since the clues might have been subtle or even oblique.

Even with excellent assistance, language difficulties will persist. For this reason, if you have to work through interpreters, expect to slow down, clarify more than you think necessary, put agreements in writing (when culturally appropriate), and provide and receive a degree of forgiveness for minor misunderstandings.

KEY QUESTIONS ABOUT COMMUNICATIONS

- Are you or your counterpart direct or indirect in communication?
- Are you or your counterpart explicit or implicit as to content or meaning? Are you from high- or low-context cultures?
- How permissible is the expression of emotions, and in what context?
- To what extent is communication nonverbal or verbal?
- What do yes and no mean in this context?

Basic Approach to Negotiation

People from different cultures place a different emphasis or meaning on the negotiation process, including the follow eight perspectives:

1. Negotiation is a relationship-establishing and -building process.
2. Negotiation is a goal- and outcome-oriented process.
3. Negotiation is a communications process.
4. Negotiation is a joint education process.
5. Negotiation is a problem-solving and option generation and proposal process.
6. Negotiation is an influence and persuasion process.
7. Negotiation is an agreement, decision-making, and exchange process.
8. Negotiation is an action-oriented process that requires implementation.

Of course, these are not mutually exclusive propositions, but people from different cultures stress one or two of these over the others.

There are also three dominant approaches to negotiations that are influenced, although not determined by culture: positional bargaining, interest-based or integrative negotiations, and relationship or conciliatory procedures. The choice among these approaches is also affected by the cultural orientation toward competition and conflict. Many cultures that accept a degree of overt conflict and competition also tend to use a positional bargaining approach, and even aggressive or hard-nosed negotiation tactics. Cultures that are more interested in maintaining harmony frequently opt for interest-based strategies that engage parties in a mutual search for solutions using some form of consensus building. Cultures that place great value on creating and sustaining relationships might support an interest-based or integrative approach, although some cultures permit a fair amount of hard bargaining among people with strong relationship ties.

In a sense, this entire book is an exploration of the full range of culturally influenced approaches to the negotiation process. As we will see in subsequent chapters, in addition to the choice of a broad approach (positional or interest based, for example), parties to negotiations also make many microlevel procedural decisions that constitute elements of their approach to negotiations. The following questions address some of these factors, which will be explored in detail in later chapters:

- What are parties' concepts of negotiation, and are they the same or different?
- What is the role of relationships and trust building in the negotiation process?
- How do parties prepare for negotiations?
- Do parties commonly use positional or interest-based bargaining styles and in what contexts or types of issues?
- How do the parties accomplish various stages or sequences and tasks of negotiation?
- What means of persuasion or influence are commonly used?

Outcomes

Parties have markedly different views regarding acceptable and unacceptable outcomes to negotiations. As we have already seen, some seek to preserve or enhance relationships, including saving face and preserving respect. Others emphasize mostly substantive gains: division of material goods, access to resources, payment for goods or services, or payment of reparations in recognition of past abuses. Outcomes can also be distributive, in that they divide up scarce resources with gains and losses for the parties. Or they can be integrative, in which an attempt is made to address the combined interests of all parties (also called *joint gains* outcomes).

In some cases, the form of the result is important: Is an agreement written or oral; detailed or just broad principles; provided legal standing or not?

These dimensions (and more) are explored fully in Chapter Eleven. For the moment, the following questions provide a preliminary sense of the issues involved:

QUESTIONS ABOUT PREFERRED OUTCOMES

- What are the orientations of the parties toward "winning" or "losing"?
- Do the parties want or expect joint gains, or do they want to gain advantages over their counterpart?
- Do the parties value or not value consensus decisions?
- What role does or should power play in determining outcomes?
- Do parties have preferences concerning substantive, procedural, or psychological emphasis or components of outcomes?
- What is the preferred format for the outcome, and who must approve or ratify it?
- Are there culturally acceptable or sanctioned norms about outcomes?

Time and Space

Venue and Space. How the parties participating in problem solving or negotiations using physical space and venue is very much a cultural issue (Hall, 1990). Some cultures prefer to negotiate indoors, and others prefer to be outside. Many like more formal settings to transact business, while others would rather make agreements in more informal social settings. A number of cultures use religious venues or places of some spiritual significance to conduct negotiations, while others use only secular settings. Some negotiators prefer to sit and talk in close physical proximity with their counterparts, while others want to maintain greater personal distance or use electronic communications media—telephones, computers, or teleconferencing facilities. The management of space and venue can also have symbolic meaning for participants. How the parties are placed at the table (if there is a table!) can be a matter for much discussion in the preparatory phase.

Cultural differences in the use of venue and space can often either promote or hinder effective relationship building and agreement making. A better understanding of how venue and space are viewed and used in various cultures can help negotiators preparing to work in another culture.

KEY QUESTIONS REGARDING THE USE OF VENUE AND SPACE

- Do the parties prefer public or private space for negotiations?
- Will negotiations take place in a neutral place or in the space of one of the parties?
- Should the setting for negotiation sessions be formal or informal?
- What is the preferred physical setup? Where should people sit, and how is this related to rank or status?
- Should different stages of negotiation take place in different settings? Is there a need for a final ceremony?

Time and Timing. Edward Hall (1984) refers to time as "the dance of life" because temporal parameters frame the ways "people are tied together and yet isolated by invisible threads of rhythm and hidden walls of time" (p. 3). He sees time as a "primary organizer for all activities, a synthesizer and integrator, a way of handling priorities and categorizing experience, a feedback mechanism for how things are going, a measuring rod against which competence, effort, and achievement are judged, as well as a special message system revealing how people feel about each other and whether or not they can get along" (p. 3).

Time is one of the core systems for organizing cultural, spiritual, social, business, interpersonal, or personal relations. Our view of time influences everything we do, our perceptions of the world around us, and how we interact with other people. For most of us, our sense of time is deeply embedded in our culture, and no two cultures perceive time in exactly the same way. People from cultures that view life in terms of centuries may have difficulty negotiating with a group from a culture that values immediate progress and change and focuses only on the next fiscal quarter or even the next day. Individuals from fast or speedy cultures may find it difficult to work effectively with cultures that take things more slowly and prefer extended talks and deliberations before reaching agreements.

Time strongly influences negotiations across cultures, including when negotiations begin, allocations of time for social- and task-oriented activities, how long deliberations will take, what the pace of talks will be, what people do during various phases of the process, and how they end discussions and implement their agreements. As one scholar notes:

> Time itself can, indeed, be the implicit or unconscious source of conflict, and conflicts about time may themselves create the need for negotiation or cause negotiations to fail. Conflicts may arise expressly about time and timing when parties have incompatible expectations about the "best use" of time, or about the importance of punctuality, or about how to run meetings efficiently. But as important as these tangible differences about time may be,

the often unarticulated assumptions that often underlie them—about building relationships, the connections between social and task oriented activities, and the impact of history on current conflicts—may be even more significant [Mcduff, 2006, pp. 32–33].

Closely related to time is *timing:* strategic understandings and expectations regarding when specific actions or activities are appropriate and should or should not occur. Culture can affect the expectations of parties regarding when they think it is appropriate for parties to come together for talks, what is done or said at the beginning of discussions, when the emphasis should be on social relations versus when substantive discussions should take place, and when proposals are put on the table and agreements can be or are reached.

KEY QUESTIONS ABOUT TIME AND TIMING

- What are the parties' expectations concerning the duration of negotiations?
- When do parties believe that negotiations actually start?
- What are the views regarding the timing of various negotiation activities?
- What timing is to be allowed for agreement?
- What is the expected timing for implementation?

Third Parties

It is not unusual for parties to reach an impasse in negotiations. Or they may encounter any one of a wide range of problems related to miscommunication, misunderstanding, interpersonal clashes, interpretation of data, the use of power and influence, or different approaches to the negotiation process itself (among others). In these circumstances, negotiators often seek the help of a third party or intermediary, such as a mediator or facilitator. Some cultures, especially indirect-dealing ones, use intermediaries as a matter of course, and they are an expected element of any serious negotiation process. Other cultures seek such assistance only when they are truly stuck, although recent decades have seen an exponential growth in the field of alternative dispute resolution. Chapters Fourteen and Fifteen discuss the different causes of difficulty or impasse, present a range of intermediary roles, and discuss the roles of mediators and facilitators in detail.

KEY QUESTIONS ABOUT THE USE OF THIRD PARTIES

- When is it necessary to seek the assistance of a third party or intermediary?
- What is the relationship of an intermediary to the parties? Completely separate or a trusted person known to all?

- Is the intermediary expected to be impartial, or is an influential but biased person acceptable?
- What kinds of procedures does an intermediary use?
- Will the intermediary be involved in substantive issues or address only the negotiation process?

CONCLUSION

The Wheel of Culture is an analytical tool that can be used as a guide for identifying and understanding cultural factors that influence individual and group interactions during negotiations. It provides a conceptual framework and guidelines for negotiators to analyze possible cultural factors that may be influencing negotiations, begin to identify cultural norms held by their negotiating counterpart (a potential partner, buyer or seller, authority, opponent, or ally), develop responses that will be considered appropriate or acceptable in both or all involved cultures, and implement them to achieve coordination.

Ultimately the end goal of a successful negotiation is an outcome that meets all parties' needs and interests to the greatest extent possible. If their needs cannot be met through talks, a negotiated agreement may not be desirable, and the parties will have to determine if there are better ways for them individually or jointly to reach a satisfactory outcome.

To achieve a successful negotiated outcome to an issue, problem, or conflict, negotiators from any culture or country must find ways to coordinate their views, needs, interests, approaches, strategies, and tactics. This is never easy and requires significant effort on the part of all parties to accomplish. However, the task of coordination is vastly more complicated when talks involve parties from different backgrounds, cultures, or countries. The cultural factor is an additional component of complexity and often poses potentially problematic dynamics that may hinder or totally block parties from reaching agreements.

Because coordination is critically important for successful negotiations, especially when working across cultures, this book focuses on how intercultural coordination can best be achieved. In the process of exploring this kind of coordination, we examine a range of national and ethnic group orientations toward the concept, task, and process of negotiations; diverse approaches commonly used in collaborative talks; and various strategies and tactics that are frequently initiated as a means to reach agreements.

Moving beyond an understanding of how members of specific cultures approach negotiations, we explore how coordination can be achieved when negotiators come from two or more cultural backgrounds. We present a general framework that negotiators can use to analyze their own culture and that of their counterparts, interpret factors that may influence the focus and dynamics of their talks, and develop and implement more effective strategies to achieve coordination. We also provide concrete suggestions for responding to the specific cultural differences or dilemmas they pose.

CHAPTER THREE

Strategies for Global Intercultural Interactions

A number of years ago, one of us was working in Vietnam on a relief project. After several months living and working in a remote town, one of his Vietnamese colleagues, Anh Ry, invited him and several of the other foreign workers to dinner on the anniversary of the death of Ry's father—an important observance for Vietnamese. Ry promised it would be a special meal—a real Vietnamese treat! With a twinkle in his eye, he said that the meal would be "Dog Seven Ways." Peter and his friends assumed that this was just a humorous expression—like the Chinese dishes containing "dragon" meat.

On the designated evening, Peter and his friends arrived at Ry's home and sat down to a sumptuous Vietnamese meal. The first two courses included a strange meat: first a soup with some strange meatballs, and then kebabs with some odd flavors—interesting, but not familiar. When the third course was served—a spicy rice and meat dish—it again contained the same meat that he did not recognize. Peter continued to eat politely but began to wonder what this meal really was.

At the conclusion of the third course, his host stood up and made a short speech that in essence praised the family dog, which guards the house, remains a friend and member of the family, and finally gives its life to provide a special meal. This was a toast to the animal that had provided the meal! Anh Ry proudly described the courses that make up Dog Seven Ways, indicating that four more courses were to come. Peter nearly dropped his chopsticks. He

61

rapidly regained his composure, but then had to figure out how to respond to this uncomfortable intercultural situation, and what to do with the four additional courses of dog!

Peter had several strategic options. If he had realized ahead of time what was going to be served, he could have *avoided* going to dinner, perhaps saying, "I appreciate the invitation and would very much like to visit with you, but I have another commitment that evening." Or he could have become "sick" that evening. Another option was to stop eating the meal and *adhere* to his own cultural norms and values. He could do this indirectly by explaining that he was feeling uncomfortably full and could not eat anything else. Or if he thought it would be appropriate (which it might not be), he could be more direct: "We really appreciate all the trouble you have gone to, and we are honored by this special and excellent meal. However, in my culture, we normally do not eat dog. May we just stay and visit?" Yet another approach might be to *accommodate* or compromise by eating just a little of each course to be polite, and pushing the remaining dog meat under the lettuce leaf that was served on the plate with each course. Yet another possibility, in the event that he liked the meal or could stomach eating four more courses of dog, would be to *adopt* Vietnamese cultural norms, continue to eat the meal enthusiastically, and comment, "Best dog I ever ate!" A final approach, again if he had realized that he was truly going to be served dog, would be to *advance* an alternative to having dinner at the host's home. He could propose another option that both parties might accept and enjoy: "We would really like to share a meal with you. You have been such a valued colleague, that we would like to treat you and your family by taking you out to dinner. It will be great fun!"

Those were the options. However, in the situation, avoiding or advancing an alternative were not options, as he was already sitting down to dinner. What should Peter do: Adhere to his cultural norms and values, accommodate and eat a little bit of the meal, or go with local custom and proceed as if there were no problem at all?

∽

We all want to succeed in our intercultural interactions, and we each have a number of measures by which we determine our success: meeting essential needs, interests, or goals; establishing longer-term relationships; or achieving personal satisfaction with our performance in an unfamiliar setting. Reaching our goals and obtaining success requires embracing a strategy—whether consciously or unconsciously. For many of us, our strategies are unconscious; we simply follow well-worn paths that have served us well in the past. Or we may improvise as we go, offering resistance or keeping flexible as events and interactions move us.

This chapter, indeed this entire book, takes a strategic approach and provides some of the information needed for making conscious choices related to strategies for successful, substantive, and relationship-oriented negotiations across cultures. Making informed choices requires understanding the options and the potential consequences of pursuing a particular option.

Part of the challenge and fascination of cross-cultural negotiations is its dynamic and interactive nature. You may make certain strategic choices based on your best understanding of a culture, only to discover that your counterparts are also making choices that will influence your decisions and the negotiation process. You must carefully observe your counterpart and be prepared to change your strategies and decisions in order to respond appropriately to achieve your goals. Strategic choices are part of an ongoing and dynamic process.

As discussed in Chapter Two, people essentially bring three different interests to any negotiation process: substantive, procedural, and relationship or psychological. To review, substantive interests are tangible or observable: money or other profit, land, resources, certain actions or behaviors, recognition of rights. Procedural interests refer to the negotiation and decision-making processes: defining speaking protocol (such as who can talk when and guidelines for speaking without interruption), whether parties choose to use positional or interest-based procedures, acknowledging the role of spokespersons (whether the parties will speak themselves or whether there will be lawyers, for example), or creating some definitions for fairness so that trust can be established.

Relationship or psychological interests refer to personal expectations for treatment or the kind of relationship that is desirable during and after negotiations. Will everyone be treated with respect? Will all comments and contributions be equally acknowledged, or will some be ignored? Will the process be free of intimidation or threats? Are the parties emotionally prepared to negotiate?

A significant portion of this book focuses on procedural and psychological interests, related to cultural differences and the effect they have on the negotiating parties. It is important to distinguish substantive, procedural, and psychological interests in developing a negotiating strategy. If the primary concern is with substantive outcomes (the basis for a peace accord, rights to water from an international river, the amount of a contract, or the volume or terms of trade), you may want to be fairly flexible regarding the procedural approaches. For example, if your counterpart is highly sensitive regarding what she considers to be appropriate negotiation procedures, you may want to be more open or flexible and devote more energy to developing a compatible approach so as not to create procedural resistance to achieving your substantive goals. Consider your goals; then bargain wisely.

BASIC NEGOTIATION STRATEGIES

We have identified five basic strategies for conducting cross-cultural negotiations: adhering, avoiding-contending, adapting, adopting, and advancing. The choice is dependent on your ability or willingness to adapt to another culture and your counterpart's ability or willingness to adapt to yours. Figure 3.1 illustrates these strategies on a behavioral grid for both sides in the negotiation.

If you have a low willingness or ability to accept another's culture, there are two possible results depending on your counterpart's choice. If your counterpart is somewhat more flexible, you may be able to stick to or adhere to your preferred style; this is shown on the grid as the *adhering strategy*. If your counterpart also has a low willingness to change, the intersecting point on the grid is the *avoiding-contending strategy*— marked by avoidance of interactions and potential misunderstandings or by ongoing competition regarding whose style will prevail (*contending*).

When both parties are somewhat knowledgeable about each other's cultures and fairly willing to adapt to each other, you may coordinate your strategies and arrive somewhere near the midpoint of the grid—the *adapting strategy*. Each side compromises, probably adhering to his own style in some areas and adapting the counterpart's style in other areas, resulting in a mixed set of procedures.

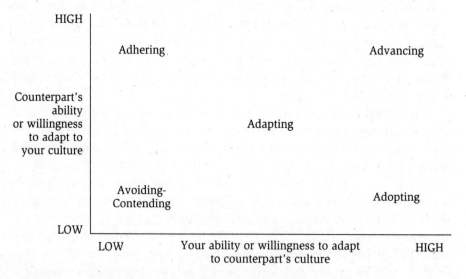

Figure 3.1. Strategic Choices for Intercultural Interactions

If you understand the other culture and are willing to change your style but your counterpart is unwilling to change, the intersecting point on the grid is the *adopting strategy;* you will end up adopting the cultural style of your counterpart.

An intriguing fifth option is also available: if both you and your counterpart understand each other's cultural norms and exhibit a real willingness to change, you can move into the advancing strategy and invent a new style that combines both cultures. The new style shares some attributes of the adopting strategy but goes beyond compromising to create new, shared norms for interaction that are completely comfortable for both parties.

Each strategic choice is described in more detail in the following sections.

Adhering

If you are unwilling or unable to deviate from your cultural style of conducting business and your counterpart is able to accommodate your style, you may choose to follow the adhering strategy.

People adopt an adhering strategy for many reasons. Some do not notice or acknowledge differences and therefore are not aware that other attitudes or behaviors may be appropriate. Others believe that people are the same everywhere and see no need to alter their responses in another cultural setting. Some think their cultural ways are "right," or believe they are not personally required to or capable of change. Finally, some adhere to their cultural norms as a negotiating ploy, believing that if they can force negotiations to operate according to their cultural terms, the other party will be at a disadvantage in discussions of substantive issues.

Chris, while working in a Central European country, was stopped by the police and charged with a traffic offense. He was asked to pull over to the side of the road and produce his license and passport to review. One of the officers took the documents to his car, while the other asked the author to pay a fine on the spot. Chris had been in the city for over a week, had watched traffic out of his hotel window take the same route that he had just taken, had taken taxis that followed the same route, and had also seen police officers observe the same traffic pattern and not take any action. When the officer demanded a payment, Chris assumed that he was collecting fines to augment his small income. (The issue was complicated by the fact that neither spoke the other's language, but the police could point to an amount that needed to be paid on a piece of paper.) Although Chris was sympathetic to the financial plight of the officers, he was not willing to pay a bribe to proceed. It was against his personal and cultural values to pay a fee that was not legal or fair. The police insisted, Chris stood his ground, and there was a standoff: no negotiations. After a half-hour of waiting, during which the police halted a number of other cars and collected "fines," a superior officer called Chris over to his car. The officer realized that the police power play was not going to work and gave Chris back his documents. However, the officer directed him to return to his car by a route that did not pass in front of the arresting officer, probably to save face. Once back in the car, Chris's colleague Susan asked how much the police were asking and what the fine was to be. Chris thought about it and said, "Less than a U.S. dollar, but it is the principle that matters!"

In order to pursue an adhering strategy for very long and still reach an agreement, your counterpart will have to be willing, or may be forced, to adapt to your cultural norms. Otherwise you will have to change your approach, or you will find yourself in the avoiding-contending mode.

There are times when an adhering strategy is appropriate or may occur naturally. At other times, adhering may be inappropriate or destructive.

When Adhering May Be Appropriate

- You do not know enough about the other culture to change your behavior to be credible within the other's cultural norms.

- Your counterpart is clearly willing to adopt your cultural norms. This often happens when this person is a visitor to your country.

- You both are operating in a third culture, such as an international diplomatic culture or the organizational culture of a large corporation with strong and pervasive norms.

- You want to adhere to certain attitudes or behaviors as a matter of principle, such as equal treatment of all races, genders, ethnic groups, or religions. (You may be able to adhere to certain behaviors while adapting or adopting others.)

- You find it extremely uncomfortable to change your behavior, and your behavior in the proceedings does not seem to hinder the relationship.

- You sense that attempting to adopt norms or actions from your counterpart's culture will appear artificial, demeaning, manipulative, or condescending.

- You find that your counterpart admires and respects your culture and is willing to adapt to your style, so you can act as you normally would, adhering to your norms.

When Adhering May Be Inappropriate

- Your counterpart clearly wants to conduct business on her or his cultural terms.

- You are thoroughly familiar and comfortable in the counterpart's culture and are more concerned about substantive outcomes than with how you reach agreement.

- You know that adhering to your way of doing things will cause a serious rupture in a relationship that is important to you.
- Your efforts to learn and adapt to another culture will be an important gesture of goodwill—even if you cannot behave in a perfectly congruent way.
- Your questions of status, ritual, and pace are unmistakably important to your counterpart.

Avoiding-Contending

When neither you nor your counterpart is willing or able to adapt to a different cultural style, two patterns may emerge—one personal and one political. In one scenario, you simply miss each other in the dark. You are uncomfortable with the cultural norms represented by your counterpart, so you personally seek only minimal contact. In a classic case, a business associate holes up in a Western-style hotel, attends the business meetings, and closes the deal in the hotel restaurant, developing only a minimal working relationship before taking a taxi back to the airport. This is an extreme case but not necessarily an uncommon example. In this case, the counterpart also avoids creating a relationship, keeping contact to a minimum to get the job done.

At times, avoidance of interaction is dictated by political circumstances. A political regime may deliberately limit contact or social relationships between its citizens and foreigners. During the Cold War, many Eastern European governments restricted citizen interactions with people from the West. Westerners who visited behind the Iron Curtain were also wary of making close connections with local people; avoidance seemed a prudent path. Some cultures may also engage in a private arena, such as a religious ceremony, secret society, or certain governmental deliberative meetings that are closed to outsiders.

The avoidance strategy is rooted in several sources. First, some people are comfortable only within their own culture and prefer to socialize or do business with others from their culture or with those who can operate according to their cultural norms. There are many examples of this "huddling" behavior within the diplomatic community, the expatriate staff of nongovernmental organization staff, and members of business circles abroad. Second, some people lack the energy and stamina needed to sustain intercultural interactions, which can be draining. In extreme cases, this may lead to culture shock, the psychological inability to deal with sharp cultural differences, characterized by withdrawal and even irrational fear. Third, some people dislike challenges to their way of thinking or acting represented by other cultures. Finally, some avoid other cultures due to various forms of ethnocentrism.

For example, a U.S. business firm was invited to do some work in Korea with a traditional organization. The Americans were told directly by the Korean organization's representative that it would not be wise to send a woman to do the job and that men were strongly preferred as counterparts. The U.S. firm placed a high value on gender equality and assigning the most qualified person to do the job, who in this case could have been either a woman or a man. It did not want to be forced to send a man, because this would have violated one of the company's basic values, but it also really wanted to do the Korean project. For a significant period of time, the U.S. firm avoided committing to do the work, because it did not want to violate its own values, but at the same time, it did not want to alienate the Korean firm or overtly reject the work. Ultimately, after indirect exploration of various options through an impartial person who was knowledgeable about both cultures—sending a woman with a male translator, sending a male-female team, sending a man for the first part of the job and shifting to a woman later—and receiving mixed responses from the Korean firm about these options, the U.S. company switched to an adherence strategy.

While on occasion you may prefer an avoidance strategy, sometimes it is not an option. You and your counterpart may have to work closely together in order to complete business deals, negotiate dispute settlements, or reach agreements regarding allocation of resources or other important matters. At the same time, neither of you may want to compromise your cultural norms of interaction. If there is a history (years, decades, or even centuries) of poor or hostile relationships, the mode of interaction itself may be a matter of fierce competition.

People contend for many reasons, including stubbornness, ignorance, arrogance, or desires to (re)establish dominance. Some people have never worked any other way, so it has never occurred to them that viable alternatives exist. In some cases, negotiating the negotiation procedure is as important as the negotiations themselves. Many remember the months of wrangling regarding the shape of the negotiating table as the Vietnamese, Russian, American, and other diplomats attempted to organize peace talks to end the Vietnam War. To outsiders, that discussion may have seemed pointless, but at its core was the crucial issue of who would be represented in the negotiations, as well as the symbolic status and ranking conferred by the physical positioning at the table.

When Avoiding May Occur or Prove Appropriate

- You are not entirely at ease or sure of yourself in your own culture, so attempting to deal effectively in another culture may be disorienting or confusing.

- You are exhausted and lack the psychological or physical stamina to respond appropriately to another culture.

- You wish to preserve or protect an important cultural value and fear that contact with another culture will taint its purity or integrity.

- Your culture is fragile or in recovery from trauma and needs protection from aggressive outside forces.
- Political forces dictate that cross-cultural mixing is not allowed.
- Making contact and developing relationships among counterparts in another culture may endanger them, and they are unwilling to take that risk.

When Avoiding May Be Inappropriate

- In order to accomplish your goals, you need to develop a good long-term relationship with your counterpart.
- Making an overt effort to accommodate your counterpart's cultural norms will be an important gesture or not making an effort will cause you to be rejected.
- Deliberately not cooperating with government or other constraints on contact may not gain you appreciation from other people with whom you want to work or develop a relationship.

When Contending May Prove Appropriate

- For whatever reason, you feel that the way that negotiations are conducted has important symbolic or practical consequences.
- You want more time to engage in a struggle over the form of negotiation and are not worried that it will prolong the negotiation process.
- You believe that adopting your counterpart's cultural norms for negotiation would be a perceived or actual sign of weakness by your counterpart or your superiors or constituents.

When Contending May Be Inappropriate

- You have time constraints, and struggling over the negotiation procedure will be a waste of time.
- You desire a long-term relationship based on trust and friendship.
- The debate over negotiation procedure has become unproductive and threatens to cause an impasse regarding important substantive issues.
- Getting a settlement agreement is more important to you than how you get there.

Adapting

In this strategy, both parties engage in give-and-take in adapting their responses to intercultural interactions and differences. This strategy requires that you both know at least a little about each other's cultures and that you remain fairly flexible to accommodate each other's cultural and procedural preferences. Each of you will probably compromise as a means to arrive at a way of proceeding that is comfortable to everyone—a mixed set of procedures.

A strategy of adapting may occur when your connections are fairly new but both parties want to establish a healthy long-term relationship. In these early stages, neither of you may know enough about the other to work from the advancing strategy, although that may come with time. (Sometimes parties who are capable of creating an advancing strategy may choose to simply adapt as a response to a single encounter with significant time constraints.)

When Adapting May Be Appropriate

- Neither you nor your counterpart has sufficient time to develop more elaborate means for interaction that are often required to develop an advancing strategy.

- You are operating in a neutral country, so neither party is guest or host.

- You are willing to change your behavior and learn something about your counterpart's culture, but not enough to adopt a totally new cultural style.

- You do not expect multiple opportunities for interaction, and therefore do not wish to invest in advancing totally new ways of doing things. Finding ways to adapt will suffice for the negotiation.

- Both you and your counterpart want to demonstrate a willingness to accommodate each other in order to benefit the negotiation process.

- You consider adapting in this circumstance as a prelude to later attempts to deepen the relationship and move into the advancing mode.

When Adapting May Be Inappropriate

- Even minor attempts to adopt your counterpart's culture will be seen as insulting or will be awkward.

- Your counterpart is actually more comfortable operating in your cultural mode than enduring your attempts to function according to his or her cultural norms.

- You and your counterpart already share an accepted and appropriate code of behavior in negotiations (which may require you to follow one of the other strategies), and trying to invent an adapting approach will be seen as deviation from the code.

Adopting

When you are thoroughly familiar with another culture and are comfortable with its approach to negotiations, you can adopt those ways. Adopting and adhering are continuums of one style; one party adopts the other's adhering style. You are more likely to adopt another culture's style if you are working within the culture, although there are occasions when the host is so familiar and comfortable with the culture of the guest that he or she will easily adopt the behavioral patterns of a visitor. An example of adapting might be when a member of a very fast time- and task-oriented culture decides to accept the cultural norms of his or her counterpart and takes days to get to know the interlocutor, build a positive working relationship, and share leisurely meals before getting down to the real business—that is, the substantive discussion.

An extreme form of adopting has been called (rather pejoratively) "going native." This term has a negative connotation because foreigners can appear strange, amusing, or even offensive when they adopt the customs of natives. Adopting another's cultural style can be a compliment to your counterpart's culture, but it is often difficult to achieve without sufficient familiarity, language proficiency, and good judgment about which behaviors to adopt and which to avoid.

For example, some civilian Americans working for nongovernmental organizations in Vietnam during the war in that country made an effort to learn the language and even wore the traditional black peasant pajamas and sandals made from tire treads. They did this because they thought that it would make relationships with Vietnamese easier and would facilitate working together and conducting business transactions. While the language abilities were often appreciated, the Vietnamese thought the middle-class Americans appeared quite strange wearing peasant clothes; Americans also ran the risk of making an unintended political statement of support for the groups fighting against the U.S. government.

In the United States, we often expect (consciously or not) foreign visitors to adapt to our ways by speaking English and wearing standard business dress. Most visitors know this and are prepared to comply with this unstated American bias.

When Adopting May Be Appropriate

- You know enough about a culture to function smoothly, without self-consciousness and without calling undo attention to yourself.

- You are a visitor, and your counterparts are clearly going to adhere to their own cultural approach, either because they are unable or unwilling to function outside that approach.

- Operating according to your counterpart's norms will be seen as a gesture in good faith.

When Adopting May Be Inappropriate

- You do not know enough about a culture (its language, habits, norms, or customs) to function comfortably.

- Your counterpart expects you to operate according to your usual ways and is comfortable working in your mode.

- The norms of the other culture require you to violate a core value or principle.

Advancing

Advancing is in many ways a more evolved version of adapting. You are still adapting, but not to each other's styles. Instead, you jointly invent or develop a third way that may or may not include elements from both cultures.

Advancing takes time and trust to develop. You need motivation to invent, a real willingness to adapt to a new way, and patience and flexibility to stick with a period of creative uncertainty. Usually this means that the participants are interested in a longer-term relationship and perhaps future encounters.

Advancing may be particularly relevant when there are more than two people or two cultures. When multiple cultures are present, the group can choose to operate according to a chosen culture—perhaps the host culture or another dominant culture—or develop a new set of group norms acceptable to that particular group. There are also examples of international cultures. In some ways, international diplomatic culture represents an evolving set of procedures that no longer truly belongs to any one culture, although it has clear roots in European modes of operation. At this point, however, diplomatic norms are usually accepted by all national representatives as the basis for interactions.

Many multinational corporations have also developed third cultures that are characteristic of the organization as a whole rather than any one of the national cultures where it operates. Levi-Strauss and Company, for example, has made a significant effort to develop a corporate culture that adheres to some core values of its home culture in the United States and broadened its range of acceptable actions and strategies to include components from its diverse cultural bases of operations.

When Advancing May Be Appropriate

- Everyone is interested in a long-term relationship and has the flexibility and knowledge to work together to invent new ways of interacting.

- You have been adapting and wish to move to a more sophisticated, stronger, and more durable approach.

- The cultural norms are antithetical to both parties, yet you have sufficient motivation to seek a third way rather than contend.

- Multiple cultures are involved, and no one culture dominates or has cultural norms that are acceptable or preferred by the others.

- The parties recognize that they have a history of poor interactions and want to find a new way of interacting that is more productive but does not involve adopting or adhering to any of the cultures involved.

When Advancing May Be Inappropriate

- The people involved do not have the necessary goodwill, flexibility, and knowledge to engage in the invention process.

- There is insufficient time or motivation to engage in the process of developing new norms of behavior.

- You and your counterpart (and others who are involved) are perfectly comfortable operating according to the norms of an existing culture or adapting.

MAKING NEGOTIATION CHOICES TO FACILITATE COORDINATION

Intercultural interactions by nature pose a degree of uncertainty. The strategies outlined represent a range of choices for interacting with intercultural counterparts. You can control your own behavior, but you cannot determine what your counterparts will do. The process is interactive and depends on all parties. The following suggestions will help you prepare and coordinate your interactions with your counterpart to the greatest extent possible or desirable:

- *Know yourself and your own cultural assumptions.* Develop an awareness of the values, norms, assumptions, prejudices, behaviors, and habits of your own culture and how your personal style is congruent or not congruent with it. It is difficult to choose to respond differently if you are not aware of your normal response. Similarly, you may encounter real shock if you are suddenly asked to do something in violation of your core values, especially if you did not even realize those values were so important to you.

- *Educate yourself.* Whether you intend to adapt to or adopt another culture's norms or adhere to your own, it is best to know as much about the involved cultural norms as possible (although time constraints may make it difficult to do a thorough job of research). As you educate yourself about normal cultural patterns, beware of stereotypes. Cultural information provides broad generalizations about societal behavior, but as we know from our own culture, there is enormous individual variation based on family background, class, race, language group, education, amount of intercultural interactions or international travel, and other factors. Most cultures have many subcultures. For example, among U.S. citizens operating abroad, you might expect significant differences (and also some areas of overlap) between an NGO staff member and a corporate sales manager. The key is to understand broad patterns of behavior but be prepared to deal appropriately with individual personalities.

• *Identify your priorities among substantive, procedural, and psychological issues.* It is important to recognize that you may have strong substantive interests in negotiations—the terms of a contract, financial payment for damages, specific actions, or establishment of rights, for example—that may be more important to you than how the negotiations are conducted. However, in some cases, showing flexibility around cultural norms and procedural issues may open up the potential for greater individual and mutual gains in substantive issues because the parties develop more trust, disclosure, and ability and willingness to search for mutually beneficial outcomes. In preparing for negotiations, you must weigh what is important to you and make choices about strategies—recognizing that your counterpart may make choices that will require you to change strategies and tactics as well.

• *Decide where you are flexible and where you are not.* Once you know your personal and cultural style, you are in a better position to decide where you can be flexible for change and where you need to remain true to your own way. Although this may also apply to the substantive issues you need to negotiate, here we are referring to flexibility regarding how you and your counterpart will conduct negotiations.

• *Prepare multiple approaches, and be nimble.* If your counterpart does not respond as you expected, you will need to alter your strategy and style accordingly. Perhaps you decided to adhere firmly to your cultural values or style because you believed your counterpart would accommodate you because of your common experiences in attaining educational degrees from the same university in your country. However, when you meet, that is not the case. They are responding to their national cultural norms and not their university background and experience. Your negotiations become stuck. At that point, you need to move gracefully toward your counterpart's preferred cultural style and strategy, either adapting or adopting.

• *Prepare for evolution.* In a negotiation process, you may start in one place and end up in another. You and your negotiating counterpart may begin adapting to each other's cultures, finding a comfortable set of compromises to guide your work. As you build trust and a track record of successful interaction, you may develop a unique form of interaction, characteristic of the advancing mode. (Or if you violate each other's trust, you might find yourself sliding into the contending mode.) An evolving approach is natural as you both learn more about each other's cultures.

CONCLUSION

We have choices when we interact with people from different cultures—whether in a domestic multicultural context or when working across international borders. Effective negotiators understand those choices and make conscious decisions about whether and how to take initiatives or respond to potentially difficult cross-cultural situations.

CHAPTER FOUR

Cross-Cutting Issues in Negotiation

I t was Jason Wright's first important international business negotiation, and he knew he had to make a good impression and bring home a deal. He had prepared well, studied the markets, worked with his legal team to develop viable proposals, and learned a few phrases in the local language. He thought he was ready for his first meeting with Mr. Moto, the representative for Shansu, the local company with which he was to make a deal.

Jason arrived at Shansu headquarters along with one of his legal advisors. He was ushered into a well-appointed room with comfortable easy chairs and offered something to drink. Soon Mr. Moto arrived, alone. Jason introduced himself and his colleague, and they all sat down.

Mr. Moto looked at Jason with an enigmatic smile and said, "I see."

"But I haven't said anything yet," said Jason.

"Ah, you have said many things."

"Really? Please explain."

"Yes, I see that you have not been 'hearing' me—at least not yet."

"Now I am truly confused."

Taking pity on the young man, Mr. Moto explained: "Your company has sent a young man under thirty years old to negotiate an important commercial contract, while I am old enough to be your father. I am here alone, yet you have brought your lawyer—and I see that he has a large document that looks like a proposal to me, although I could be wrong. I can see that you are eager to start talking about this deal we are to make. On the other hand, while I think I understand a bit about you, I don't know you—and you don't know me.''

''I see,'' said Jason, beginning to sweat, and to fear that he would never get a decent bargain with this start.

''In any case,'' said Mr. Moto, ''let us chat a bit, talk about your trip and what you have already learned about my country. Later you can have a rest, and then you and I can go to dinner together to visit some more. I will ask one of my legal team to accompany your colleague. We will have a pleasant time—and any talk of business will come at the right moment.''

∽

This chapter covers several key concepts in cross-cultural negotiations. Some were introduced briefly in Chapter Two, but these concepts will come up repeatedly throughout the rest of the book, so we are providing this summary here, where the descriptions can be found easily in one place. First, we review several important cultural factors that deeply influence negotiations: indirect dealing and direct dealing, high context and low context, relationship oriented and task oriented, and contractual and holistic cultures. Then we examine three basic approaches to negotiations: positional, interest-based, and relationship and conciliatory negotiations. The third topic addresses the concepts of framing and reframing, which concern how matters are viewed and expressed. Fourth, we address the issue of who is involved in negotiations, based on culturally determined factors such as age, gender, status or position, and expertise. Finally, we examine issues regarding the use of power and influence in negotiations.

KEY CULTURAL VARIABLES THAT INFLUENCE NEGOTIATIONS

In Chapter Two, we provided a general overview of numerous variables that determine how negotiators act in the process of conducting business transactions or settling disputes. In this section, we review several of the most important elements; they cut across all stages and types of negotiations and show up numerous times over the course of this book. Table 4.1 provides a brief summary of these concepts.

You might be tempted to think that all of the categories in the left column line up and reflect certain cultures and those in the right characterize others. In some cases this may be true; a number of cultures exhibit all of the left-hand or right-hand attributes, but many cultures demonstrate a mix. For instance, Indian negotiators are mostly from high-context cultures, but the majority of

Table 4.1. Key Cultural Variables

Members of *indirect-dealing cultures* are seldom explicit in exchanges and often prefer to communicate through intermediaries. They avoid strong expressions of feelings or any hint of disharmony. The meanings of yes and no are not obvious.

Members of *direct-dealing cultures* tell you what they think, directly and in person. They do not mind expressing feelings and will even shout and argue. For them, a yes is a yes and a no is a no. While harmony is a nice ideal, "you can't make an omelet without breaking a few eggs."

High-context cultures understand meaning in context—based on who you are, your relationship with others, and norms that are universally understood by any member of the culture. Much is implicit and unexpressed because it does not need to be pointed out; everyone (except outsiders) understands already.

Low-context cultures create meaning through explicit expressions: clear and direct speech, unambiguous messages, detailed documents, rules, regulations, written norms and expectations, and so forth. Relationships are constantly formed, reformed, and defined in the moment as needed and, depending on the context, through direct discussion. An outsider coming into a low-context setting might even be given a manual explaining exactly what is expected.

Relationship-oriented cultures depend on a series of affiliations to function in life. These may be based on long-term connections—family ties, friendships, ethnic group membership, school or university associations, business relationships, or other affective bonds. The primary task in any kind of negotiation is to establish or improve a relationship, which will serve as the basis for any future agreement or deal. In some cases, the relationship may be more important than any substantive element of a settlement, as it will endure over time and provide the context for resolving any misunderstandings or conflicts.

Task-oriented (or substantively oriented) cultures focus on the substantive matters at hand and the issues that have brought negotiators together, whether a business deal or a deep conflict. While members of these cultures may spend some time building a relationship, this is normally a means to the real end: the substantive deal. In the extreme, task-oriented negotiators will sacrifice a relationship for a more advantageous settlement.

Holistic cultures do not separate relationships, feelings, context, specific joint activities, and substantive issues; they see them as integrally connected. They would rarely compartmentalize different elements of life: business relationships, work, home, social life. In these cultures, unwritten or verbal agreements are strongly valued, and in some cases, they may be seen as more valuable than written commitments or contracts.

Contractually oriented cultures tend to compartmentalize people, relationships, issues, and diverse activities. They separate specific kinds of relationships (business, family, social) and are likely to make explicit agreements in each. An old joke illustrates the extreme: "He would sue his mother if he thought it would get him a better deal." Written contracts are the last word.

Indians are also very direct dealing. Some subcultures in Indonesia are known for being blunt in their communications, while most Indonesians are indirect dealing and relationship oriented.

Each person is a member of multiple cultures. While each of us is part of a broad national culture that shares many characteristics in common, we each also maintain memberships in our family, a community or communities, and usually some form of workplace (company, government agency, non-governmental organization, school, and so forth), and each of these represents a somewhat different culture or subculture. Most families are high-context cultures: all members understand what is said and what is expected based on their years of interactions. Of course, families in some cultures have adopted some low-context elements, such as written rules or family decision-making meetings.

Organizational or work cultures probably exhibit the greatest variability, even within a single country. Although there are general tendencies among most workplaces within a national culture, some organizations are highly bureaucratic and regulated, with explicit rules for almost every occasion (and therefore low context), while others are informal and flexible, depending to a large extent on unwritten rules and personal relationships to determine how to proceed (and are therefore high context). When we take a new job, we must adapt to the prevailing organizational culture, and within months the norms will seem totally normal to us, whereas at first they might seem somewhat alien.

Throughout the remaining chapters of this book, we come back to these factors again and again. They are the main drivers of cultural differences among negotiators.

BASIC APPROACHES TO NEGOTIATION

All cultures have procedures for making joint decisions on important issues, reconciling differences, and resolving conflicts. These cultural procedures provide general frameworks, both conceptual and procedural, for problem solving and negotiations, both within and between cultures. Many terms have been used to describe efforts to explore differing views on issues, build relationships, and reach agreements: *conversations, dialogues, talks, disentangling* or *untangling, talking story, haggling, dickering, horse-trading, cooperative or collaborative problem solving, joint decision making, bargaining,* or *negotiating*. Although there are many shades to the meanings of each term, all are oriented toward constructing positive relationships among people, encouraging dialogue about topics of mutual concern, and trying to decide how an issue or problem should be resolved. For the remainder of this book, we use *negotiation* (and sometimes *bargaining*) as the general term to describe these relationship-oriented and problem-solving procedures.

Four factors influence how individuals or teams of negotiators approach negotiations and related strategies, tactics, and behaviors (Quinney, 2002):

- *Specific personality and personality traits* of an individual negotiator or members of a negotiation team
- *The general context of negotiations and issues under discussion,* such as whether parties are involved in a transaction or resolving a dispute; are engaged in diplomatic, commercial, or other kinds of talks; or are resolving substantive, procedural, or relationship or psychological issues
- *Structural factors,* such as the broader political-economic position of the negotiator or entities he or she represents and those of the counterpart, the political or economic systems in which negotiations are occurring, organizational structures, leadership, and decision-making structures and procedures
- *The culture or cultures of the people involved,* including gender, age, race/ethnic group, profession, education, rank or status, region, or national origin

The first two factors vary significantly from negotiation to negotiation. A negotiator may change strategy depending on his personality or feelings of the moment, or the kind of relationship he has with a counterpart, such as a close family member, friend, business colleague, or adversary. Negotiators also change strategies due to the specific context in which negotiations are occurring: negotiating a business contract, resolving a dispute, international diplomatic negotiations, labor-management talks, developing a strategic partnership, or seeking agreement on a humanitarian aid or development program. Structure and culture are generally more persistent and have more enduring and ongoing impacts on the approach, strategies, and tactics of an individual negotiator, team, or broader organization.

In this section, we examine basic approaches to negotiations: positional bargaining, interest-based bargaining, and relationship or conciliatory negotiations. In real life, negotiators are likely to use a mix of these three approaches, with significant variations of their use, emphasis, and timing. Counterparts will sometimes utilize positional bargaining to resolve disputes over perceived or actual scarce resources. They may use interest-based bargaining if they want to develop innovative and customized solutions to issues in questions or an ongoing relationship is desirable. Finally, they may use relationship or conciliatory negotiations if it is important to establish a new or mend a damaged relationship.

For the sake of clarity, we will describe each approach separately. We will also detail attitudes, procedures, and behaviors of negotiators using each approach.

Positional Negotiation or Bargaining

Positional negotiation, which is also often called *hard bargaining* (Fisher and Ury, 1981) or *distributive bargaining* (Walton and McKersie, 1991), gets its name from both the procedure used to reach agreements and the kinds of outcomes that commonly result. This approach is often used when counterparts believe that a division of goods, resources, or benefits will be required to reach a settlement and that the end result will most likely be some form of compromise between their two views on a desirable allocation (distribution). A positional approach is common when the outcome of negotiations is seen by one or more parties as having a potential winner or loser.

Positional bargaining in various forms is used in most cultures to address a wide range of issues, from dickering over vegetables in a local market to reaching accords on international issues. Salacuse (1998a) conducted a study over a period of four years involving over 310 diplomats, business executives, lawyers, military officers, and graduate students from twelve nations. He found that negotiators from Nigeria, Brazil, and Spain responded that they more frequently view negotiations as win-lose endeavors in which gains and losses were likely to be disproportionately shared, as were a larger proportion of lawyers, military officers, and graduate students in the study. Each of these groups responded that they were much more likely to pursue positional strategies to achieve their goals, winning more than their counterpart.

Positional bargaining frequently begins with an assumption of limited resources such as money, time, material goods, respect, status, or honor. To reach an acceptable outcome, negotiators either have to strive to win as much as they can or reach an agreement on an acceptable division of the resource in question—hence the term *distributive* negotiations.

Participants in positional negotiations develop a number of possible positions—specific solutions that meet their individual needs or satisfy their interests—that they present to the other party. Positions are generally sequenced so that the first position represents its advocate's maximum aspiration for gain, which may be an inflated claim calculated to reserve something to trade or concede in future bargaining. Typically each subsequent position offered by a negotiator either gives up some gain or benefits, makes some concession to the other side's demands, and requires fewer benefits to be exchanged in return for an agreement; or is a random trial-and-error approach to making offers in the hope of discovering a mutually acceptable solution (Walton and McKersie, 1965).

Thus positional bargaining is generally characterized by an offer and counteroffer or a position and counterposition dynamic, in which one party makes an offer and the other party rejects the proposal and counters with another offer, which the first party may reject. The process of offer and counteroffer continues until those involved are close enough in their offers to effect a compromise settlement in which gains and losses are shared or happen upon a mutually acceptable solution. This process often commits parties to specific solutions early in negotiations, requires concerted effort to relax commitment from previously advocated solutions, generally involves the exploration of only two potential solutions at any given time, requires the wearing down of parties' demands and expectations, and generally results in compromise solutions in which gains and losses are shared.

In analyzing the convergence process, negotiation theorists postulate that negotiators begin bargaining with the understanding that their opening position, or target, reflects a maximum or even inflated expectation of what might be gained or what they are willing to give in negotiations (see Figure 4.1). These opening positions are often referred to as the initial high demand or the initial low offer. Positional negotiators also usually determine for themselves a bottom line—the minimum or maximum conditions for settlement that they can accept and still satisfy their interests. The negotiator generally keeps this position hidden from the other side to avoid making premature or unnecessary concessions.

Between the opening position and the bottom line is a range of positions—secondary, subsequent, fallback, and others—that the negotiators are prepared to make to prompt offers or concessions from the other side. When the range of preferred positions of the negotiators begins to overlap, so that offers being made by one side are in the acceptable range of the other, the parties have what is referred to as a positive bargaining range. In this situation, a series of possible settlement options becomes available, any one of which is probably preferable to a stalemate or no agreement. Although the parties may continue to negotiate once they have achieved a positive bargaining range, the bargaining at this point is generally oriented toward refining agreements regarding the final gains and losses rather than determining whether agreement is possible.

A simple example illustrates the dynamics of positional negotiations. In many countries, taxis and the price of fares are unregulated. Drivers and passengers expect to negotiate a mutually acceptable fare for trips each time a journey is taken. The fare is based on cultural and situational norms and variables, including the relationship of cost to distance, price of gasoline, time

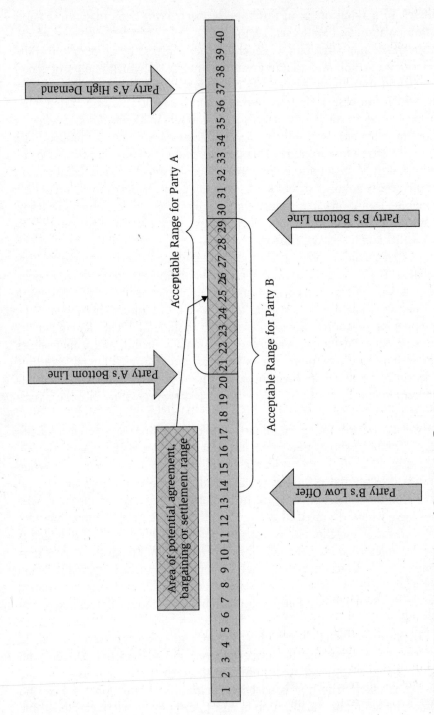

Figure 4.1. Positional Bargaining and Convergence Process

to make the trip, time of day, quality of cab, who the passenger is (local or foreigner), whether he or she has an ongoing or one-time relationship with the cabby, and so forth. Norms also include the process used to establish the price for the ride. People who live in the culture and use taxis frequently are familiar with how drivers normally calculate fares and know the price range for specific trips. However, many foreigners live in countries where taxis and fares are regulated or determined by a meter. Thus, when foreigners bargain over the fare, there is usually a jockeying between a high price demanded by the driver and a lower price requested by the prospective passenger. The back-and-forth discussion continues until the parties agree on a mutually acceptable price.

An example of this bargaining process occurred in Indonesia in a situation involving an Indonesian taxi driver and several non-Indonesian tourists from North America, Australia, and Europe, including one of us, Chris. He and the other tourists had all arrived on the island of Bali and headed for the small town of Ubud in the center of the island, where there was a pleasant rest house and lots of things to see and do. Chris met some of the other travelers, and the group agreed to hire a minibus and driver to take them to see some sights. They found a potential driver and asked him his price. He gave them what they thought was a very high offer. Based on their experiences hiring taxis in other parts of the island, they countered his offer with a much lower price. He said that he could not possibly take them for that amount. The situation was different in Ubud, he pointed out, where gas was more expensive, and drivers generally received more for a trip than we had offered. He countered by offering a fare that was a bit less than his original demand. One of the group at this point went over and talked to another driver to see if he could get a better price; when he returned, he whispered to us that the initial fare was the same as had been offered by the man with whom they were negotiating. The group talked with the driver a bit more, discussed the merits of the itinerary, and made another offer that was a bit more than their previous one. Finally, after some more offers and counteroffers, the group and the driver settled on a fee that was a compromise between their initial positions. They agreed to meet at 8:00 the following morning to go on the trip. As it happened, in the morning, another situation arose, which required a somewhat different approach to bargaining—and we will come back to this story later in this chapter.

Positional bargaining and the offer-counteroffer process can result in agreements without explicit identification or in-depth understanding of either party's interests by the other. A positional negotiator may propose a position, learn from what a counterpart says is wrong with it or a counterposition, and use that information to develop and offer sequential positions, each of which they hope will be increasingly more acceptable to the other party and meet his or her joint interests. In this trial-and-error approach, interests may never be overtly discussed. Positions are developed and agreements reached based primarily on the acceptability of proposed solutions (which are presumed to satisfy interests), not on explicit information about specific interests and efforts to craft customized options that address them.

Why Use Positional Bargaining. Why do negotiators use positional bargaining and strive for distributive outcomes to negotiations? It often has to do with the mind-sets and attitudes of individual parties and broader cultural norms or accepted practices regarding what negotiations are and how they should be conducted, plus the context and the issues at stake. Negotiators often choose to conduct positional negotiations in these situations:

- The stakes for winning are perceived to be high, and the negotiator cannot afford to lose—for example, the early arms negotiations between the United States and the former Soviet Union.

- The issue at stake is a matter of principle and requires a strong position to demonstrate the strength of the negotiator's commitment to it—for example, negotiations over whether discriminatory attitudes or behavior were exhibited in a company.

- Resources (time, money, psychological benefits, or something else) are perceived to be limited, and the only possible outcome will result in a distribution of gains and losses. Therefore, the negotiator must claim as much value or as many resources as possible, even at the expense of the relationship or the interests of the other side. Positional bargaining is selected for these reasons in some buyer-seller negotiations (Lax and Sebenius, 1986).

- The negotiator believes that the resource being negotiated is not divisible into multiple subissues or subinterests, which could facilitate trading items that are valued differently by the parties. For example, negotiations between a dealer and a collector regarding the disposition of unique and valuable archeological artifacts or a rare painting, which only one party could possess, would offer few opportunities for such trading.

- The interests related to the resource have been translated into symbolic solutions that are framed in terms of specific numbers (money, time, number of units produced, number of acts to perform a task) rather than proposals that meet the real interests or needs. Examples are negotiations over wages in labor management bargaining or the monetary figure to be paid in damages in a personal injury lawsuit. In both cases, the general interest is in fair compensation, for either work or bodily harm, but negotiators frame their demands in specific (and often inflated) financial terms.

If they were to address the true interests, they might explore other types of exchanges, such as apologies or other forms of compensation or benefits rather than financial remuneration.

- Both parties want exactly the same thing for the same purpose, and it appears that a win for one side automatically means a loss for the other. Examples include an intercultural child custody dispute, in which each parent wants legal custody of the child—and one country's customary or formal law awards custody to the father and the other country awards it to the mother, or a land dispute in which each party claims the same piece of property.

- The parties are not interdependent, will not pursue any future relationship or interaction, or do not consider any future relationship more important than immediate substantive gain. An example is a commercial transaction that is expected to occur only once, such as the purchase of a used car from the owner. Such one-time transactions are conducive to positional bargaining.

- The parties control adequate resources and coercive power to attempt a forced solution and damage the others if an impasse in negotiations occurs, and each believes that they can withstand or overcome the costs that will result from the exercise of the other side's coercive power. An example is the threat of ethnic insurgency or civil war.

- Posturing for a constituency and presentation of an initial, and often public, high demand is expected or required to maintain the credibility of the negotiator and the support of his or her followers. An example of this dynamic commonly occurs during Middle East peace talks when each of the parties makes extreme statements for the benefit of constituents.

- A negotiator believes that an initial high-demand or hard-line position is needed to educate the other party about the importance of the issue, the expected level of exchange, and the strong commitment of the initiator to a high settlement. Parties enmeshed in international trade negotiations often employ this tactic.

- The issue is not very important, it does not involve multiple interests to be traded, and the parties need a mechanistic procedure to split differences and arrive at a mutually acceptable solution. Or the ritual of positional bargaining is the norm and culturally expected. For example, in a vegetable market, haggling over the price within a well-understood range is expected.

Variations of the Positional Bargaining Process. There are some important variations of pure positional bargaining and the offer-counteroffer dynamic.

These blend positional bargaining with an interest-based approach (described below) and are informed by greater knowledge of the parties' concerns and interests. This process has two variations.

In the first variation, positional bargainer A presents an initial position early in negotiations. They may or may not explain the interests it satisfies. If the initial position is rejected by counterpart B, which it frequently is, positional bargainer A explains more about his or her proposal and may ask why, and what interests of counterpart B are not addressed or met by the position. If this information is provided, negotiator A uses it to modify the initial position to make it more acceptable or to develop a new position. This process may be repeated multiple times until a proposal is made that everyone can agree on. This process appears to be common to some Japanese negotiators, who present an initial position early in negotiations as a way to educate their counterpart about their interests. The initial presentation is followed by discussion in which more may be revealed about the interests of both parties, and the Japanese negotiator responds with a new position grounded in the new information (Adair, Weingart, and Brett, 2007).

The second variation begins much the same as the first. Positional bargainer A presents an initial position and explains the interests that the proposal satisfies. However, counterpart B, who is also a positional bargainer, rejects the initial position outright (often without providing much of an explanation as to why) and immediately proposes a counterposition that better satisfies his interests. In response, bargainer A may ask counterpart B why his alternative position is preferable to the first proposal. Bargainer A may also inquire about the merits of her proposal and problems inherent in the initial offer. Finally, A may ask explicitly about the interests satisfied by the counterposition from B. If this information is forthcoming, A can use it to formulate and present yet another counterposition that may better accommodate all parties' interests. Once again, this process may continue through multiple exchanges. After each proposal is presented, negotiator A and counterpart B continue to probe the merits and limits of each proposal and, if possible, explicitly identify interests to be met, until a mutually acceptable option is developed.

Interest-Based Negotiations

Interest-based negotiations represent alternative procedures for reaching agreements. In the positional approach, parties focus on advocating positions or specific solutions that meet their individual interests or needs and persuading opposing parties to accept their proposals. Interests may or may not be explicitly identified or articulated. In contrast, in an interest-based (or needs-based) process, negotiators focus first on identifying the concerns, needs, or interests of all parties, and only then do they individually or jointly develop integrative options to address them.

This process is also used in a wide range of cultures. In the Salacuse study (1998a) noted earlier, respondents from Japan, China, Argentina, France, India, and the United States reported that they were more likely to view negotiations as efforts to achieve win-win or integrative outcomes, as were the diplomats, public sector employees, managers of businesses, finance officers, teachers, and engineers. Negotiators from both the United States and Japan, especially when bargaining over commercial matters, are proficient in this approach for developing outcomes with joint gains (Brett and other, 1998).

In the field of dispute resolution, needs and interests are often distinguished from each other. Maslow (1943) identified a series of basic human needs, including absolute necessities (food, shelter, and safety), plus less concrete things (security, love, a sense of belonging, self-esteem, and self-actualization). Others have added recognition, distributive justice, meaning, and control over one's life or destiny as basic needs (Burton, 1990). Some conflict theorists argue that these needs are so fundamental that there can be little, if any, bargaining over them and that bargaining over basic needs in fact may border on the unethical.

Interests represent a specific way that a party wishes to have more basic needs met. Thus, interests are important preferences a party wants to have fulfilled. Interests may be broad, such as a desire for a general increase of economic benefits in a labor-management negotiation, or quite specific, such as the desire for a particular wage increase, cost-of-living allocation, or changes in specific working conditions. In many instances, interests can be satisfied in a number of ways. To review in more detail, there are three types of interests:

• *Substantive interests.* Substantive interests are tangible benefits a party wants to have satisfied or exchanged through negotiations. They include financial remuneration, the exchange of property, performance of specific acts or behaviors, and time commitments. For example, in a negotiation between a seller from the People's Republic of China and a buyer from Malaysia, the seller wants to sell goods at a reasonable price and receive monetary gain, while the buyer wants a specific product that meets desired specifications at an affordable price.

• *Procedural interests.* Procedural interests refer to preferences regarding the process by which problem solving, negotiations, or dispute resolution occurs and the way that agreements are reached or implemented. They include a desire for an efficient and timely process, clearly understandable steps, and an opportunity for all parties to present their views. Parties often have interests with regard to the agenda for negotiations—and whether their specific issues or topics are included and in what sequence. Parties may also want protection from emotional strain, personal attacks, or dramatic expression of feelings. For example, on the island of Java, people generally prefer to discuss business or diplomatic issues in an unemotional and nonadversarial manner, often through indirect dialogue rather than debate. Negotiations that involve direct confrontation or debate generally do not meet the procedural needs of Javanese negotiators. In a labor-management context, the union side often expresses the need for sufficient time to consult with and gain approval from their membership during contract negotiations.

- *Relationship or psychological interests.* These interests concern how individuals or groups are treated, both in the negotiation process and outside it, as well as how relationships are valued and shaped through negotiations. Psychological interests include an individual negotiator's desire to be trusted, respected, and heard and to have feelings and experiences acknowledged. For instance, parties that have experienced deep injury in the past (such as Israelis, Palestinians, Native Americans, or First Nations) often need explicit recognition of that painful history in the context of negotiations. In Japan, chief executive officers are frequently involved in the early formal and ritual stages of negotiations, and they expect their rank and status to be recognized in appropriate ways by their subordinates and negotiation counterparts. Psychological interests may lead to specific demands in the negotiation process, such as an apology, an acknowledgment of status, or even a title.

Relationship interests are closely associated with the psychological dimension of talks. In many negotiations, the nature of past, present, or future interactions among the parties may be an important topic on the negotiation agenda—or establishing or improving a relationship may serve as the basis for negotiations. In some negotiations, parties want to find ways to terminate a relationship and have no further dealings with a counterpart, while in others, one or more participants want to maintain or create a positive future relationship.

※

An interest-based agreement is reached because the parties have engaged either informally or formally in educating each other about their interests, jointly searched for options that address them, and found a balance among various interests that each party may value differently. The three interests or need components are illustrated in the triangle of satisfaction in Figure 4.2.

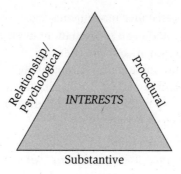

Figure 4.2. Triangle of Satisfaction

This diagram suggests that an agreement is possible when the three types of interests are satisfied, based on the importance that each party places on them.

Attitudes of Interest-Based Negotiators. Interest- or needs-based negotiations begin with general mind-sets, attitudes, and assumptions that are quite different from those common to positional bargaining. Interest-based negotiators assume that:

- *Zero-sum negotiations, in which one party will win and the other will lose, are not as common as most people believe.* Rather, the goal for bargaining is to strive for benefits to both or all parties. For example, in a long and bloody intrastate conflict between two ethnic groups, the parties may decide that a settlement that provides significant autonomy and recognition of cultural and language rights may be preferable to continuing the conflict and striving for one of the parties to achieve an all-out victory. Creative autonomy agreements may be able to address the cultural identity needs of a minority, while preserving the integrity of a state.

- *Resources being bargained over are not necessarily limited, and there may be a way to maximize gains for all concerned parties.* For example, rather than competing for tourists, several African countries that share the management of a river basin decided to cooperate in the development of a trinational campaign for ecotourism. The plan involves the joint development of tourist facilities and facilitation of visits by tourists to all three countries.

- *Resources may be expanded through concerted action; each party has the potential to gain more benefits from cooperation than from adversarial initiatives.* For example, in Sri Lanka after the devastation of the tsunami of 2004, both the government of Sri Lanka and the Liberation Tigers of Tamil

Eelam, the armed resistance movement seeking to create an independent Tamil homeland, could have secured more international financial assistance, increased goodwill, and confidence in each other by cooperating than they could gain unilaterally. (Unfortunately, despite the development of an agreement regarding the distribution of aid, each of the parties had other interests, so in the end, each received less assistance than they would have by working together.)

- *Any negotiation includes substantive, procedural, and psychological interests and needs that may be met in a variety of ways to reach joint gains.* For example, when Canada, Mexico, and the United States negotiated the North American Free Trade Agreement, they needed a mechanism to resolve disputes efficiently. The Mexicans, as the least wealthy partner and the most culturally different from what it perceived to be the Anglo North, needed to feel respected as an equal partner and to be consulted on the design of a dispute resolution process, rather than having procedures from Canada and the United States unilaterally imposed on them. They wanted substantive outcomes that they considered fair and involved equal treatment of all parties regardless of nationality.

- *Interests that have been expressed in numerical form (such as money, time, number of units produced, number of actions, and so forth) may be broken down into subtopics and associated interests that can be traded or addressed in a number of ways.* For example, the interest of a labor union for increased wages might be divided into the following interests: the actual amount of money desired, the timing of payments, the pace of future salary increases, or alternative forms of compensation or benefits (such as an improved health-care plan).

- *Parties may want different outcomes or benefits, value the items being discussed differently, or want benefits at different times or in different forms, providing the potential for trade-offs.* For example, in East Timor, several indigenous groups each claimed land that they had occupied at various times in the past. The current holders had the best claim and had occupied it the longest. However, each group placed different priorities on the crops that could be grown on the land and its use as rangeland for livestock. Negotiations explored the possibility for cooperative sharing of the land, allowing one group to harvest their preferred crop while allowing the other to use the land for grazing.

- *The ongoing relationship between the parties is valued both during and after negotiations, and a focus on meeting each party's interests will strengthen this relationship.* For example, in multiparty negotiations in the United States over the management of the Missouri River, twenty-seven

Native American tribes were potentially at loggerheads with the U.S. Army Corps of Engineers (USACE), the manager of the river, over issues related to the protection of their burial grounds on the banks or under the water of reservoirs. The tribes were opposed to any proposed flow changes that might expose the graves of their ancestors, which were very important to them. However, the tribes were also dependent on the USACE for helping them secure adequate drinking water for reservations and financing infrastructure projects. The USACE, while wanting to change the flow regime of the river to meet the needs of endangered species, also wanted to maintain good relations with the tribes, because tribal opposition to changes in flow could damage the agency's reputation and threaten legal challenges. In this case, both parties had strong interests in maintaining a healthy working relationship in order to meet their various interests.

The Interest-Based Negotiation Process. The process for interest-based negotiation differs from the positional approach. In brief, the interest-based negotiation process is as follows:

- *Define the issue or problem*. Each party identifies the issues or topics for discussion during negotiations.

- *Educate each other about interests and needs*. Each party educates the other about the specific interests and needs that they would like to be recognized and satisfied by a solution.

- *Clarify interests and needs, and identify criteria for acceptable agreements*. The parties individually or jointly clarify the interests and needs that have been presented. They may also identify criteria that could be used to guide option generation and evaluation.

- *Generate options*. The parties participate in developing multiple options that might satisfy the full array of their individual and joint interests. (See Chapter Nine.) Generally interest-based negotiators avoid the position dynamic used in the option development process of positional bargaining. Also, they generate options separately from the process of evaluating those options to encourage the creation of innovative and customized solutions.

- *Engage in bargaining and persuasion*. After the parties have generated a range of potential options, they may try to persuade each other about the desirability of one or more options. Ultimately they choose an option or combination of options that seems to meet as many of their stated interests as possible. Then they refine and adapt that option, based on all concerns, to work toward a final settlement agreement. This may mean modifying previous options, making trades, or developing new combinations of options. (See Chapter Ten.)

- *Evaluate options.* Once an adequate number of potential settlement options have been developed, parties either jointly or individually evaluate how well these potential solutions meet their individual or collective interests and needs. Parties frequently compare the options generated through negotiations with their best alternative to a negotiated agreement, or BATNA (Fisher and Ury, 1981), to determine which option has the best individual or joint value. In other words, do any of the proposed solutions match or exceed what they could achieve away from the negotiating table? They might also apply the criteria or standards that were generated earlier in the process to guide this phase. (See Chapters Eleven and Twelve.)

- *Implement and monitor the agreement.* The parties develop an implementation plan that details what is to be done, who will do it, when, where, and how. They may also develop procedures for monitoring the performance of the parties, evaluating how the settlement is working, and reopening issues, or handling future disputes or disagreements over implementation. (See Chapter Thirteen.)

We return to the simple negotiation example described earlier in this chapter to clarify some of the differences between interest-based and positional bargaining. As you will recall, Chris and some other tourists had negotiated a fee for a minibus tour around the island of Bali using a basic positional approach. However, when they met at the van on the day of the trip, some of the group members wanted to change the itinerary that had been previously agreed on. They said that they had already seen some of the sites planned for this trip and wanted to visit others. When they told the driver about the change in plans, his price for the day went up dramatically. He said that since we had changed the route, the trip would cost more. Some of the group members immediately thought that the driver had done a bait-and-switch on the price and was trying to take advantage of them, and they tried to return to positional bargaining. (The driver probably thought the same thing.) The back-and-forth of positional bargaining did not work; neither moved toward a compromise, and tempers were beginning to flare.

At this point, Chris decided to try an interest-based approach by exploring all of the interests and looking for a jointly acceptable solution. The tourists stepped outside the minibus to talk. First, Chris asked them what they really wanted to see on the tour. Their desires included temples, markets, a mountain lake, and a hike. Next, he explored what the options were for getting their needs met. They were (1) taking the original trip, (2) planning a new itinerary that was of similar cost and duration as the original one, (3) negotiating a new price with the driver for the new proposed itinerary, (4) taking their chances on negotiating an acceptable fare with another driver, or (5) not taking the trip at all. Chris asked which one of the options they preferred. They all said that if they could negotiate an acceptable fare for the new itinerary, that would be the best option; if not, they agreed to try their luck with another driver.

Having clarified the needs and choices about whether to negotiate and having assessed the options, the group returned to talk with the driver. Chris asked him if he really wanted to take a trip that day. He said he did: he had committed to go and was counting on our fee. The group affirmed that they too wanted to go on the trip with him if they could reach a mutually acceptable agreement. Next, Chris asked him to clarify why he wanted more money for the new itinerary. He explained that the original itinerary was shorter in duration, required less driving, and included more stops and more relaxed time waiting for his customers to swim and hike. He explained that the proposed new trip would be one to two hours longer, would mean going into the mountains, which would use more gas, and would include more kilometers to be driven than the other journey. He did not want to lose money or time by taking a longer trip for which he would not be adequately compensated.

With this information, Chris worked with the whole group, the driver included, to identify some general principles that could be used to establish a fee for a trip that covered the new itinerary. They all agreed that if the trip involved more distance, which it did, additional money needed to be paid for gas, and that if it involved more hours, an additional amount was due to cover the driver's added time. They then calculated the distance for the new trip, looked at the amount of gas that would be required and the cost per liter of gas, and added more money for each kilometer traveled. They added funds to cover an additional two hours for the driver's time, based on dividing up the hours that would have been covered in the original trip to determine his hourly rate. Finally, they agreed to cover all parking and entrance fees.

At this point, the driver was still not sure that it was a good deal for him, and some of the tourists feared that they had been cheated as well. Everyone took a moment and looked at their best alternatives to the current tentative negotiated agreement. The driver risked losing all his passengers for a day if he did not accept the principle-based fare. The tourists faced losing time away from a tour that they really wanted to go on and the prospect of new negotiation with another driver, the outcome of which was unknown, if a deal with this one could not be struck. After careful consideration, they all decided that the price negotiated for the new itinerary met most of their needs, although some still grumbled about the change in the fare and felt that they might have been taken advantage of. But they all finally agreed to proceed with the trip, shook hands, and took off on what turned out to be a wonderful day's journey to see the beautiful island.

Relationship or Conciliatory Negotiations

This type of negotiation does not focus on specific substantive or procedural issues, interests, or needs. Rather, it seeks to address the type and quality of the desired relationship between or among the parties. Conciliatory negotiations seek to improve the parties' relationship as a means to address substantive issues more effectively at a later time or as an end in itself. This typically involves actions and activities to develop trust and respect, enhance rapport, build confidence, encourage acceptance, and create understanding and, on occasion, empathy between the parties (Walton and McKersie, 1965; Burton, 1969, 1990; Rothman, 1992, 1997; Kellman, 1992; Fisher, 1997). Conciliatory bargaining may occur as a discrete activity prior to and independent of substantive negotiation initiatives, or may be an integral part of a substantive negotiation process. Because the process of building positive relationships differs significantly across cultures, the process of conciliatory negotiation must be tailored to meet specific cultural expectations and norms.

Peter worked as the facilitator of a major negotiation process regarding air quality in the Southwest United States. The negotiation groups included representatives of the business community (mainly energy companies, the biggest contributors to pollution), state governments, federal agencies, environmental advocates, and about ten Native American tribes. It was quite a diverse group—and the levels of distrust were high, based partly on previous experiences struggling, in court and out, over environmental regulations. The facilitation team and the organizing group worked hard to build relationships through informal gatherings, cocktail hours, and joint meals. And then a happy accident helped greatly. The full negotiation group met about every six weeks at different locations around the region, but it soon became apparent that the most convenient and least expensive location was Las Vegas—the gambling capital of the West. This turned out to be a lucky find; soon the business representatives, tribal members, and environmentalists could all be found making the rounds of gambling establishments in the evenings, all happily losing money together and then joking with each other across the table the next day during negotiation sessions.

Strategies for Coordinating Approaches to Negotiation

Coordinatation Among Positional Bargainers. If positional bargainers are able to find a solution within each other's bargaining range, they can proceed to an agreement. However, they may find themselves stuck after initial positions are stated or after several rounds of positions and counterpositions. In either case, the negotiators can:

- Continue advocating for the unacceptable position, with the hope that logic, the exercise of some means of influence or leverage, or a change of circumstances will encourage the other side to accept the proposal.
- Try to switch to an interest-based approach, encouraging each other to engage in joint problem solving to satisfy all interests and needs.
- Modify proposals or make a counterproposal that better meets the needs or demands of the other side, based on information gained about a counterpart's needs and interests.
- Identify a compromise position or solution in which gains and losses are shared.
- Break off negotiations.

Coordination Among Interest-Based Negotiators. If both parties begin negotiations using an interest-based approach, they may still have several coordination tasks. They may need to jointly define issues so that each party understands the problem or dispute to be addressed and associated subissues. In addition, they must clearly identify the interests (substantive, procedural, and relationship or psychological) that must be addressed and coordinate procedures for generating and evaluating options.

Coordination Between Interest-Based and Positional Negotiators. If one negotiator begins with a positional and the other an interest-based approach, there are several options for coordination:

- The positional bargainer may continue to try to educate her counterpart about the merits and logic of her position, and how it meets the interests and needs of her counterpart—and, if they are persuasive enough, move toward agreement.
- The positional bargainer may continue to advocate for his original position as stated, but at the same time will listen to what his counterpart has said, ask questions, and collect more information about the other party's interests. He may then use this information to show how his initial position meets the other's interests or develop another position that better meets all parties' interests.
- The positional bargainer may use her opening position as a place marker, but put it on hold while exploring the interests and needs of her

counterpart. A counterpart using an interest-based approach may be able to convince the positional bargainer to switch to a more collaborative process of problem solving.

- The interest-based bargainer may become positional and begin to advocate for specific positions or preferred solutions that meet his interests.

- The parties can divide up issues and apply different approaches to each, depending on whether they are more amenable to integrative or distributive solutions.

- The interest-based negotiator may convert the positional negotiator to the use of an interest-based approach.

Generally interest-based negotiators who want to persuade a positional bargainer to use a more integrative and cooperative approach must refrain from offering counterpositions or making explicit substantive proposals early in negotiations. Rather, they either directly or indirectly engage their counterpart in interest-based strategies and tactics.

Direct strategies require an explicit explanation and discussion of the interest-based approach with the counterpart and reaching a mutual agreement to try it. This requires a joint agreement to refrain from making positional statements or proposals, a commitment to spend time educating each other about individual and joint interests, an agreement to frame issues or problems to be addressed in a mutually acceptable way, and using collaborative processes for option generation. This approach can work well in cultures whose members are direct dealing, understand the value of process, and are willing to talk about how mutually acceptable procedures can be developed. Negotiators from the United States, the United Kingdom, and Germany are often amenable to discussions about process. However, not all direct-dealing cultures are open to such discussions. "The French have a very different outlook on the *process* of negotiations than do, for example, the Americans. There is no French equivalent of the word 'process' in the sense of its meaning in English of 'a particular method of doing something, generally involving a number of steps or operations' which may help explain why French diplomats have tended to regard the notion of negotiating process with disdain or at least little interest" (Cogan, 2003, p. 107).

Indirect strategies for transitions are used when a negotiator does not believe she can get a counterpart to agree openly to the use of an interest-based approach, or where it is not acceptable in the counterpart's culture to conduct explicit discussions about process. Common indirect strategies that can be used by an interest-based negotiator to encourage a counterpart to make the transition to a more collaborative approach include the following:

- Ignore any proposed positions. Neither accept nor reject them. Keep talking. Explain your interests, and state that you are open to exploring any proposals that might move toward meeting them.

- Ask whether the problem has to be solved in a win-lose manner. State that the joint goal of negotiators should be to find solutions that will be advantageous to all parties.

- Acknowledge the proposed position as one option, but note that there may be more than one way to meet your counterpart's interests and yours too. Ask your counterpart to explore other possible options that may better meet joint interests.

- Ask the counterpart to explain how she thinks her proposal meets your interests and what she thinks those interests really are. Use her response as an opportunity to clarify your interests and provide her with accurate information.

- Propose general principles, from those embedded in your counterpart's initial proposal or others that can be identified, that will provide structure and shape future option generation and, ultimately, agreements.

- Ask for clarification of the counterpart's position. Ask her why her position is important to her and (indirectly) what interests or needs it addresses. Probe to understand and clarify the substantive, procedural, and psychological interests embedded in her position.

- Where possible, acknowledge and legitimize a counterpart's interests, and state a willingness to look for solutions that will address them.

- State that for a mutual solution to be found and an agreement reached, all parties' interests and needs must be identified, jointly understood, and met to the greatest extent possible.

- Reframe the issue or problem to be addressed as a search for a way to satisfy interests rather than a means to persuade each other to agree to a specific position.

- Reframe the problem to emphasize commonality of interests or the possibility of joint gain.

- Ask other questions that refocus a counterpart on her interests.
- Negotiators can ask a variety of types of questions that can focus a counterpart on her interests and yours—for example:

  "Can you say a bit about why the solution you have proposed is important to you?"

  "What needs or interests are met by this proposal?" or "What benefits would agreement to this proposal give you?"

  "How do you think that this proposal addresses my needs [concerns, interests], because if I am to agree, some of my concerns will need to be met?"

  "I wonder if you could clarify what your long- or short-term goals are and how this proposed solution helps you to achieve them."

  "What concerns or doubts do you have about this issue, and how are they addressed by this proposal?"

  "What is most important to you about this issue [position, option, or proposal]?"

  "Can you be more specific about what it is you need [want, are concerned about, are afraid of]?"

Coordination Between Relational and Positional or Interest-Based Negotiation Approaches. Relational orientations toward negotiations are principally focused on creating positive emotional connections and commitments between parties that can ultimately be translated into reciprocal bonds of respect and obligation. Obligations may later be translated into mutually desired exchanges of intangible or tangible benefits, such as respect, honor, behavior, performance, money, goods, services, or land.

Coordination problems between relational, interest-based, or positional approaches, at least initially, generally arise over the tension between the time and energy required for establishing and building relationships versus a time-limited and immediate focus on procedural or substantive issues. Negotiators who subscribe to a relational approach usually want to spend more time getting to know a counterpart through socializing, identifying commonalities, and exploring and developing trust than do parties who adhere to the other approaches. Negotiators who want to move counterparts toward more of a relational approach can continue to spend social time with a counterpart, but offer specific information about when more focused substantive talks are likely to occur. Positional or interest-based negotiators can relax a bit if they know when substantive talks will take place.

For either positional or interest-based negotiators who want to move a counterpart with a more relational orientation in their direction:

- Accept that negotiations will probably take longer with these counterparts.

- Refrain from proposing or advocating hard positions early in negotiations.

- Take the initiative to demonstrate that you are a trustworthy and appropriate counterpart by reciprocating hospitality, identifying commonalities, affirming the relationship, and following through on promises or agreements, no matter how small.

- Spend more time doing informal sounding or making informal suggestions about the process and timing for discussion of substantive discussions.

FRAMING AND REFRAMING

Frames refer to the specific way that parties see or describe the situation in which they are involved. A frame includes how you see the problem or situation and your perspective on it. A party's description (frame) not only defines and assigns meaning to the broad underlying problem to be addressed and often the goals to be achieved, but also guides a negotiator's actions to achieve desired ends. Schön and Rein (1994) define a frame or a general frame as the story that a party tells himself or herself about a situation that for him or her is troublesome and needs to be addressed:

Each story conveys a very different view of reality and represents a special way of seeing. From a problematic situation that is very vague, ambiguous, and indeterminate (or rich and complex, depending on one's frame of mind), each story selects and names different features and relations that become the "things" of the story—what the story is about....

Each story constructs its view of social reality through a complementary process of naming and framing. Things are selected for attention and named in such a way as to fit the frame constructed for the situation. Together the two processes construct a problem out of the vague and indeterminate reality that John Dewey calls a "problematic situation." They carry out the essential problem-setting functions. They select for attention a few salient features and relations from what would otherwise be an overwhelmingly complex reality. They give these elements a coherent organization, and they describe what is wrong with the present situation in such a way as to set the direction for its future transformation [p. 26].

A negotiator's frames lie behind the presenting problem or purpose of negotiations. In that sense, each party's framing of the purpose, issues, problems, and interests remains relevant through the negotiation process. This concept is useful throughout the phases.

An example will illustrate how negotiators might frame a situation. In a divorce mediation, the wife might frame the process as, "How can I free myself from a destructive relationship?" while the husband might frame it as, "How can I make her suffer for leaving me?" And a mediator might frame the process as, "How can we restructure this family to bring closure to one set of relationships and establish workable new ones acceptable to the parties?"

In the Northern Ireland conflict, one side framed the extended negotiation process as addressing grievances related to basic justice and equality, while the other side framed it in terms of maintaining power and preserving a British identity. Both sides came from a minority frame, as the Catholics are a minority in Northern Ireland and the Protestants a minority in terms of the population of the whole island. For many years, it appeared that the two sides maintained incompatible frames. Only after considerable effort at reconciliation, a series of changed circumstances, and a gradual shift in public attitudes was it possible to construct a joint frame that allowed productive discussions to take place.

General frames for negotiations, or a negotiator's story, may be conscious and articulated, or unconscious, unspoken, or not even immediately recognized by the person or party holding them. Clearly it is easier to respond to conscious and articulated frames than those that are unconscious or unspoken. Note that several concepts are independent but all related: the context and general purpose of negotiations, the interests that negotiators hope to achieve, and negotiators' frames. In some situations, these may be virtually identical, and in others significantly different. As the concepts interact, how each is defined influences other definitions. Thus, the context of negotiations shapes the purpose. The purpose may shape the frame, and vice versa. Frames may shape and be used to attain specific interests (Schön and Rein, 1994). Although the definition of the purpose of negotiations and individual negotiators' general frames of the situation and goals are important in all talks, they can be especially so in intercultural transactions where culture can significantly influence the choice of frames.

Because of the importance of how parties describe the purpose of negotiations and frame the interests they hope to achieve, it is critical for them to be aware of possible conceptualizations and how they will influence negotiations. Negotiators need to be introspective throughout the process, trying to articulate, at least to themselves, how they define problems to be addressed and their underlying frames. They will then have to determine what should be expressed in negotiations, how their perspective (frame) can best be described to a counterpart, and what should be only privately acknowledged or remain unsaid.

In addition to understanding their own framing and implied goals for resolution of an issue, negotiators need to strive to understand the possible framings that counterparts may use in talks. In planning for negotiations, this often means extrapolating information about the other party from past encounters, written materials, or data from others who have had prior dealings with the counterpart. Once negotiations begin, negotiators have an opportunity to explore their counterpart's goals and framing for the negotiation process.

Coordinating Purposes and General Frames

In many negotiations, parties articulate and readily agree on the general purpose of discussions and have similar frames, or at least not mutually incompatible ones. Suppose that two parties agree that they want to complete a commercial transaction. One party advocates a relationship-building frame prior to moving to substantive discussions, and the other emphasizes a joint substantive gain frame (in which the parties try to understand each other's interests before reaching an agreement). They therefore have compatible, though different, frames, and productive discussions are likely to ensue, with agreements made.

In other negotiations, especially those initiated to resolve conflicts, parties often have frames that are at odds. In this situation, negotiators have to make efforts to coordinate their understandings of the purpose of negotiation and how they frame the process. In some cases, this requires redefining or reframing their views, so that they can conduct productive talks. (As we will see in Chapters Fourteen and Fifteen, an intermediary may also help parties to discover a joint frame or to reframe their views.)

SUGGESTED STRATEGIES FOR COORDINATION OF GENERAL FRAMES

- Avoid explicit presentation of your general frame until your counterpart presents his. If the other's description of purpose and frame is acceptable or marginally so, you can accept it as the premise for negotiations or modify it slightly to make it more agreeable.

- Advocate a purpose and underlying general frame and reject that of your counterpart, thus forcing him to accept your purpose and frame if he wants to reach an agreement.

- Advocate a general frame, and then, if necessary, adapt it to make it acceptable to all parties.

- Propose a general frame, listen to that of your counterpart, and, through mutual education, jointly shift to a totally new description of the purpose of negotiations and general frame.

As an example of this last point, imagine that one party in a negotiation initially describes the purpose of negotiations as a means to achieve revenge and punish the other party for a past harmful action: "We want you to grovel in the dirt and acknowledge the losses and pain that you have caused us. You will pay us one hundred times the damages that we have incurred, so that you will never do this again!" The other party had not realized the damage that he had inadvertently inflicted on the other group or the depth of feelings engendered, and had initially framed the problem as finding a solution where each party would benefit equally. These two definitions of the problem and related general framings were mutually contradictory. What to do?

Generally one of the parties will need to understand the underlying framing of the other and take the initiative to determine whether an alternative and mutually acceptable framing can be developed. For example, the "revenge" framing might be reframed as "restoring honor and respect"—or, in more complex terms, the process could be framed as searching for a solution that is acceptable to all parties, in which there are consequences for actions, and parties that were harmed are made as whole as possible. This reframing of revenge to a possible functional equivalent, if acceptable to the aggrieved party, may make negotiations possible.

Framing Issues or Problems for Negotiation

In addition to overall frames that define the purpose or goal of negotiations, parties frame issues in specific ways that can either promote productive talks or escalate tensions. In general there are four ways to frame an issue: as a (1) neutral topic statement, (2) statement of a position, (3) statement about a party's interests, or (4) joint problem to be addressed, which incorporates descriptions of two or more parties' interests or needs.

Framing Through a Neutral Topic Statement. A straightforward, neutral statement can define an issue and set parameters for its discussion—what may and may not be discussed—for example: "We want to talk about the price for purchasing two million widgets," or "We want to talk about the priorities for use of economic development funds." This kind of framing is common in direct-dealing cultures, in many international business negotiations, at problem-solving conferences, or in negotiations in which parties have a low level of conflict.

Framing by Stating a Position or Proposed Solution. Many statements of position include a proposed solution that then becomes an issue for discussion: "We demand to talk about a 20 percent wage increase," or "I want to talk about why you have discriminated against me on the job." This kind of framing is common in conflict situations, especially in direct-dealing cultures in which members are not afraid to verbally confront each other or overtly express differences. Subsequent problem solving usually involves discussion of the merits of the position, trying to discover underlying interests behind it, and developing either counterpositions or a number of jointly acceptable options. If the positional framing is particularly toxic, like the claim of discrimination, it may be necessary to reframe the topic before proceeding. For instance, the "discrimination" framing might be reframed as, "We need to discuss behaviors and actions by each party that have been problematic for the other."

Framing by Stating Interests. A statement framed in terms of interests identifies an individual or group's desires, wants, or concerns, but does not imply a specific solution to meet them. This approach depends on a negotiator's willingness to reveal information about specific interests—for example, "We want to discuss how authority can be delegated to people at lower levels in the organization, so that local people have a say in how the project proceeds." Or a union representative might say, "Over the past several years, certain categories of workers have received salary increases, while others have not. It's important to us to achieve greater parity."

Framing by Stating the Interests of Multiple Parties. This approach frames a joint problem statement in which more than one party's interests are identified along with a common or joint goal. The general format for this is, "We want to figure out a way that we can meet your interests pertaining to X and mine related to Y." For example, in a commercial negotiation, the parties might agree to this statement: "We need to discuss how to balance your need for timely delivery of the product with our need to ensure a quality product."

A classic case of reframing occurred in the 1975 negotiations between Israel and Egypt concerning the final status of contested territory and security issues in the Sinai Peninsula, which were the result of the Six-Day War. The Egyptians initially framed the issue for discussion as a position: "Israel must withdraw its troops from Egyptian territory." The Israelis responded with an equally positional statement: "We refuse to leave; only through control of the passes can we guarantee our security from future attacks." (These are paraphrased summary statements. The parties no doubt made longer and more complex arguments.) Eventually the issues were reframed as a joint problem representing both parties' interests, roughly: "How can Egypt regain sovereignty over its territory in the Sinai, and at the same time guarantee Israeli security so that they will not be vulnerable to attack from that region?" This framing allowed the Israelis and Egyptians to trade sovereignty and political control of the land for security and its demilitarization.

To summarize the four ways to frame issues, using the Egypt-Israeli talks as an example, we see:

Neutral topic statement: "We will discuss the issues of territory and security."

Positional statements: "We demand return of our land." And, "We refuse to leave, as occupation ensures our security."

Statement of interests: "We must regain control over our sovereign territory and want to be treated with respect." And, "Any agreement must include provisions that guarantee our security from attacks through the Sinai."

Joint problem statement: "How can we enable Egypt to regain control over its territory, while at the same time guaranteeing Israel's security from attack?"

Untangling Frames Through Reframing

How an issue is framed affects whether a party is even willing to talk about it, much less engage in productive problem solving. When a party frames an issue in a way that is unacceptable to the other party, one or the other will eventually have to figure out a way to reframe the topic in a manner that refrains from attacks, removes reference to a fixed solution, and invites joint problem solving. Reframing offers a number of possibilities:

- Translation from a win-lose or distributional approach to looking for joint gains or an integrative approach that tries to meet all parties' needs:

  Win-lose frame (cross-border water dispute): "The river rises in our mountains, and we have a right to use as much water as we need and want."

  Integrative reframe: "We need to develop a formula that works in wet and dry years and ensures a fair allocation of water to both nations that share the river."

- Redefining issues in either more general or more specific ways that allow problem solving:

  Overly general frame: "We need to discuss your treatment of people from our country."

  Reframe (more specific): "We need to discuss how border guards treat people from my country, including delays at crossings and the use of strip searches."

- Adjusting time frames if they are too short or constrained or too long and unlimited:

  Time-limited frame: "You promised delivery three weeks ago. The goods must be in our warehouse in three days or the contract is void."

Reframe: "We need to discuss the reasons for delay and consider appropriate actions, including possible compensation or price adjustments, based on late delivery."

- Translate one-sided frames to address the concerns or interests of multiple parties:

One-sided frame: "The mining company never gives the peasants who live closest to the mine anything for all the disruption that it has caused. We demand that the peasant communities receive 50 percent of all mining profits to compensate for their losses."

Reframe: "We need to determine appropriate compensation that the company will pay to all parties—the local peasants, their communities and municipalities—that have been adversely affected by mining operations."

- Remove toxic, adversarial, or judgmental language:

Toxic frame: "These foreign managers are slimy little dictators. They shut the door in our face, never listen to our concerns, and sexually harass the women workers. They have got to go!"

Reframe: "We need to discuss ways to ensure that worker concerns can be addressed on a regular basis and develop rules of conduct in the workplace that apply to everyone. We also need to deal with cultural differences that may be making matters worse."

WHO ENGAGES IN NEGOTIATIONS, AND HOW?

Another cross-cutting issue in global and intercultural negotiations concerns the people who are involved and the roles they play. This is also an area that displays considerable variation based on cultural norms, as well as the focus and circumstances of the specific negotiation process. Within the same culture, the size, composition, and roles of negotiation teams differ depending on whether the matter at hand is personal or familial, commercial, communal, governmental, or in the realm of international diplomacy.

Individual Negotiators or Teams

There are many possible configurations of negotiators or negotiation teams, including these:

- Individual negotiators, each representing himself or herself
- Individual negotiators, each representing larger entities, such as a community, organization, company, government agency, or national government

- Multiple individuals, each representing themselves
- Multiple individuals, each representing larger entities
- Teams of two or more people, each representing a larger entity
- Multiple teams, each representing a larger entity

Team Unity or Diversity

When teams are involved in negotiations, the situation becomes a bit more complex, and it is important to determine how the team is composed and the dynamics within it:

- The team may represent one group or organization and hold unified views regarding the issues, needs, interests, and outcomes that will be under discussion.
- The team may represent one group or organization, but individual members speak for different parts of the entity (even rival units) and may have individual interests different from other members of their team.
- The team may represent an informal or formal coalition of individuals or groups whose members have fairly similar views regarding the negotiations and the issues. Examples are representatives of an environmental coalition or a business association or trade group.
- The team may be composed of representatives of an informal or formal coalition of individuals or groups, but the members do not represent a unity of views or interests regarding the issues to be addressed in negotiations.

In most cases, the more unified a team is, with members coming from the same organization or holding common views, the easier negotiations will be, from an organizational perspective. Conversely, the more diverse a team is, with members representing only themselves, diverse parts of an organization, or coalitions of people or entities, the more in-team negotiations will be required both before and during negotiations, making talks somewhat more awkward.

Team Organization, Composition, Size, and Symmetry

The internal structures of a team have an effect on negotiation dynamics.

Team Organization and Decision Making. Teams representing national or organizational hierarchical cultures are usually organized in a similar manner, with a clear leader and other members in subservient positions. Similarly, teams from relatively egalitarian cultures have fairly flat organizational structures, usually including a coordinator or spokesperson who provides facilitative leadership for a group of relative equals.

Although it is easier to coordinate between teams that are organized in a similar manner, coordination when they are different is not impossible. Negotiations between teams that are hierarchically organized and teams that are coalitions are probably the most difficult. Members of coalition-based teams not only have to negotiate among themselves, as relatively equal team members, but usually do not have authority to make final agreements that will bind their organization, members, or constituents. Coalition team members may have to consult with those they represent or are responsible to at multiple stages of a negotiation process. Early on, the team may ask for ideas or options—and then engage in either consensus-building activities or voting on the options, before returning to the negotiating team members for further discussion, or prior to presenting a favored option to the other team or teams. In the later stages, the team may bring a final or near-final proposal back to constituents for approval. In contrast, the leader of a hierarchical team may have sufficient authority to approve a proposal, or the process of obtaining approvals further up a chain of command is relatively quick. Hierarchical teams can become impatient with the slower and more involved decision-making process in coalition teams.

Team Composition. The composition of a team is an important consideration in team formation. Issues involved in team composition include:

- The formal position and status of team members
- The personal or professional reputation and credibility of members
- The areas of expertise needed for the particular negotiations
- The personal style and perceived ability of individual members to promote agreements

Team composition involves both cultural and strategic considerations. At times, the most important drivers of team composition are strategic: How powerful and prestigious should the team be? How credible must the team be with respect to the substantive issues? Are we looking for a team of tough negotiators or a more conciliatory and cooperative team? At other times, these tactical issues are less important, and cultural norms are more important.

Who is on negotiation teams, and when they are involved, is often critically important in intercultural negotiations. For example, there is a great deal of variation across cultures regarding whether, how, and when key decision makers and midlevel managers become involved as members of negotiation teams or in less direct roles.

Some cultures almost immediately involve high-level leaders and decision makers in talks as spokespersons, decision makers, or regular, and even "hidden," team members. In those situations, leaders are engaged throughout the phases and tasks of negotiations, and they may be the final decision maker. The involvement of decision makers or high-level leaders is commonly seen as an indication to a counterpart or the broader public of the importance of the issues under discussion, the level of commitment demonstrated by having the powerful people at the table, the status of the individuals involved, and an approach that will enable parties to make agreements and get things done on the spot.

Involving leaders or decision makers directly in negotiations has strengths and weaknesses. Strengths include the opportunity for leaders, by their presence, to recognize the importance of negotiations and good-faith participation, determine if the counterpart is trustworthy and an appropriate interlocutor for further talks, and educate each other about the issues and interests in question. When leaders are involved, they can also directly help generate options and shape emerging agreements, which enables the teams to reach an accord without having to go through an elaborate consultation process. Perhaps the greatest advantage of this approach is the opportunity for key high-level negotiators to engage directly with each other, build relationships, generate agreements, and assess commitments to follow through on accords. The development of direct personal relationships among leaders can also provide the basis for the amicable resolution of differences if they do arise during implementation and for the relatively easy negotiation of future agreements. Historically, "walks in the woods" and informal discussions between national leaders have enabled them to explore and build more trusting relationships.

The weaknesses of the direct involvement approach include possible premature elevation of the importance of talks, the possibility of direct pressure on a decision maker to make an immediate decision, less flexibility to use time away from the table to reflect on a possible agreement with a decision maker who is away from the table, and an inability to bring a decision maker into negotiations at key points and as needed to provide encouragement to a team or break a deadlock.

Other cultures expect lower-level representatives of parties to begin talks. Higher-level leaders or decision makers are engaged only sporadically during deliberations to perform specific functions. Lower-level representatives are often used at the beginning and middle of talks for a variety of purposes:

- Engage in social activities with counterparts to get to know them personally and in a multidimensional way

- Explore whether a counterpart is personally and socially compatible and can be trusted
- Discover a negotiator's approach to and style of conducting negotiations
- Indirectly explore possible areas of agreement
- Informally discuss how formal negotiations might proceed
- Develop draft agreements for consideration by higher-level decision makers
- Establish conditions for the involvement of higher-level decision makers and determine the conditions and timing for their engagement

In this approach, higher-level leaders are typically brought in at various stages. For instance, they may provide formal recognition that enough trust and rapport has been established through informal talks that formal bargaining can begin. They may also establish general parameters, goals, or formal positions for talks. They may formally and publicly delegate responsibility for further discussions to teams, working groups, or subordinates. This is often the case in Indonesia and Japan. As progress is made in deliberations, leaders may take part in rituals or celebrations of progress or agreements. For example, various leaders may be brought in to banquets to celebrate the completion of various phases of negotiations.

If talks have become difficult, a decision maker may be asked to provide moral leadership and encouragement of negotiators to do their best and move forward in talks or to help break a deadlock.

Like the direct involvement approach, this method has strengths and weaknesses. Its major advantage is the opportunity to build negotiation relationships and procedures over time. As for disadvantages, it takes time, requires greater internal consultation by negotiators with their organizations or leaders, and creates gaps between the people directly involved in negotiations and final decision makers or implementers.

Additional Considerations Regarding Team Composition. Talks can be significantly affected by who is involved and when they engage in the process. Age, gender, rank, status, and qualifications or expertise all exert an influence on the progress of deliberations.

Gender Cultures differ regarding whether or how much men or women talk with each other, in what contexts, where, and what subjects are acceptable or taboo. Cultures also often prescribe what information men and women know about, should know about, and can share publicly or privately. Culture and associated social norms frequently determine how men and women are perceived in different contexts. The same statement presented by a woman as that of a man may be more or less acceptable, depending on the circumstances, the issues at hand, and the prevailing cultural norms and prejudices. For example, in negotiations over the development of local water projects in the Middle East, separate village negotiation forums had to be established for male and female villagers to solicit appropriate information and conduct problem solving for the project to move forward.

Cross-cultural tensions have increased on this dimension in recent years. Some cultures have become increasingly egalitarian along gender lines as a result of much social struggle, legal battles, legislative action, and personal change efforts. Other cultures have retained more traditional male dominance—and in some cases even increased restrictions on female participation in public life, usually for religious reasons. This situation causes potential dilemmas. Should an American or European company, operating under strong norms of gender equality, send a negotiating team headed by an unmarried woman to engage with a counterpart team from an Arab nation, where direct contact of a man with a woman is difficult—and even prohibited under certain circumstances? Using the terminology introduced in Chapter Three, should Americans or Europeans adhere to their own cultural norms or adapt to the norms of their hosts?

Age Members of some cultures believe that a credible negotiation team will include or be led by someone who has advanced somewhat in years (the exact number of years is variable). For these cultures, authoritative information and convincing ideas or proposals can come only from those with experience. Age is equated with experience, maturity, knowledge, and wisdom. Senior leaders are deferred to, listened to, and expected to engage in final deliberations and decision making. Other cultures are more open to exchanging information and negotiating with people of different ages, and wisdom and knowledge are seen as separate from age.

In the vignette at the beginning of this chapter, Mr. Moto notes that Jason Wright is half his age. He appears more amused than annoyed, but it clearly mattered to him. Another member of his culture might have taken offense and even refused to meet with such a young person.

Expertise Depending on the substantive issues on the table, it may be necessary to include, as members of the main team or in subteams or working groups, people with specific areas of expertise. Expertise comes in a variety of forms across cultures: financial, legal, or political matters; scientific or technical subjects; emotional or psychological dimensions; local cultural knowledge; or even spiritual factors. As with age, gender, and status, team composition is determined by a combination of tactical and cultural considerations.

Symmetry Between the Position and Status of Negotiators Members of some cultures wish to deal with individuals or groups of equivalent rank in terms of organizational position, social status, or political influence. Teams of people with significant differences in rank would be disturbing or even unacceptable to them. Other cultures are less conscious of status and more tolerant of differences between negotiating teams, but in general, parties expect to work with counterparts of more-or-less equivalent position, status, and authority.

For example, in 2006, representatives of the Government of Sri Lanka (GoSL) and the Liberation Tigers of Tamil Eelam (LTTE) agreed to meet in Geneva to restart stalled peace talks. The GoSL sent representatives that it felt were of appropriate status and position to address the issues on the proposed agenda and represent the government's views. The LTTE sent representatives to the talks from higher-level positions in its structure than those of their GoSL counterparts. They believed that high-level talks required representatives from the highest levels. When the parties reached Geneva, the LTTE accused the GoSL of not sending equivalent counterparts with authority to reach agreements and refused to engage in negotiations. This dynamic was one factor that caused the talks to collapse.

Size of Negotiation Teams The size of these teams is influenced by culture, as well as the context of talks and the complexity of issues under discussion. In general, cultures with more collectivist orientations favor having more members on negotiation teams than do more individualist cultures. China, a collectivist culture, is famous for the large size of its negotiating teams and the diversity of people on them.

Potential reasons for larger teams in talks include the need to recognize the status of key leaders by including a large number of advisors or retainers; the interest of various concerned parties to be recognized, included, and consulted; cultural or organizational norms for involving multiple parties as part of internal consensus building; and the desire to share collective responsibility for a decision rather than having liability rest on one person or a small group.

Individualist cultures favor smaller teams because of cost efficiency, norms regarding delegation of authority to representatives or spokespersons, and the willingness of members to take greater individual risk. Teams from the Scandinavian countries, Germany, Canada, Australia, New Zealand, and the United States are often much smaller than those of their counterparts from other parts of the world. The exception is in diplomatic negotiations, where larger and more politically powerful countries often send a large entourage of negotiators, legal advisors, and technical assistants to engage in or provide advice in negotiations.

Symmetry or asymmetry regarding team size can be important in coordinating intercultural negotiations. Naturally members of many cultures prefer that the size of their team and that of their counterpart be similar, although this is not always possible. Despite a preference for size parity, there is usually some tolerance in intercultural negotiations for variations in team size. Cross-cultural negotiators recognize that their counterparts often organize themselves differently.

Nevertheless, problems do arise when size differences among two or more negotiating teams are significant. Extraordinarily large teams are sometimes used by a party that perceives itself as either stronger or weaker than a counterpart, to awe or overwhelm them with numbers, impose their will, or compensate for weakness.

Very large teams, especially when sent abroad, may also be perceived by a counterpart as including many unproductive members or as indicating a lack of seriousness concerning the issues in question. For example, extended negotiations over a period of weeks to end the civil war in the Democratic Republic of Congo involved hundreds of negotiators traveling to and engaging in long talks in Addis Ababa in Ethiopia and later in Sun City in South Africa. Some observers and negotiators viewed these large numbers as wasteful and unnecessary, and saw that some of those attending peace talks were there to reap the benefits of travel abroad rather than to reach agreement to stop violence and bring peace to their country.

Conversely, in negotiations to end the civil war between Bougainville and Papua New Guinea, it was necessary to involve a large number of people from Bougainville in order to build a sustainable agreement between disparate population groups on the ground, and accommodate cultural norms that require building consensus on important issues before final decisions are made and implemented.

Smaller teams may be perfectly normal in some cultures but be perceived as a mark of disrespect, a failure to recognize the status of their country or group, or an indication that the substantive issues to be addressed are of low priority. Small teams and their leaders may be seen as arrogant and having an inflated view of their importance.

SUGGESTED STRATEGIES FOR COORDINATING TEAM COMPOSITION ISSUES

- Determine what the norms of your counterpart are likely to be regarding the presence, level of authority, and involvement of decision makers in negotiations. Ask your counterpart who may or will be attending upcoming meetings or negotiations and in what capacities. Decide if you want to mirror these norms, upgrade the negotiations by sending people of a higher level, or downgrade them by sending people who may be of lower status. Assess the potential impacts of involving people with different levels of authority in negotiations, and decide how any negative impacts that may result from this can be mitigated.

- Identify the cultural norms for your culture and that of your counterpart regarding the size and composition of negotiation teams. Decide if you want to adhere to your own cultural norms, adapt to or adopt those of your counterpart, or develop entirely new protocols.

- What are your cultural norms and those of your counterpart regarding the appropriateness, roles, and responsibilities of people of specific ages, genders, or status in negotiations?

- Do the cultures draw strong distinctions or prohibitions regarding the acceptability of younger or older people (women/men, high/low status) engaging in specific negotiation activities?

- Decide if you want to adhere to your own norms or accommodate the norms of your counterpart. What impact might your decision have on the negotiation process?

- What are your cultural norms and those of your counterpart regarding the kind and levels of expertise expected in negotiations? Think about the kind of expertise that will be convincing to your counterpart.

POWER AND INFLUENCE

Each party's power and influence operates as a key dynamic throughout the negotiation process, from first contacts through final agreement and implementation. Particularly in the early stages of negotiation, each party needs to assess its own sources of influence and speculate about where a counterpart might derive power. Power clearly determines the ability of a party to influence the outcome of negotiations, and it becomes an important factor in the final stages of negotiation, particularly if the parties approach deadlock or the negotiation process falls apart.

Power is the capacity to get what you want or get something done. Influence involves acts performed to change another's views or actions to achieve desired ends. In Chapter Ten, we examine the exercise of power and influence in more detail as part of the process of reaching agreements. Power comes in many forms—and each negotiator or negotiation team possesses multiple kinds of power. The appendix to this chapter presents a wide range of sources of power.

The existence of negotiator power does not, in and of itself, determine the outcome of negotiations. In order for power to work and achieve desired ends, negotiators must:

- Distinguish between actual power, which they already have and can exercise immediately, and potential power, which must be developed and cultivated before it can be used
- Develop the ability to mobilize their power and turn it into influence that can be used effectively
- Determine the costs and benefits of exercising different types of power and influence
- Ascertain how much power or influence they will have to use for specific ends
- Cultivate the will to use power when necessary
- Select from among different sources of power to use at appropriate times to exert the desired impact on a counterpart

In the context of negotiations, the least effective sources of power are position and coercion. Positional power works only if the holder also possesses a number of the other sources of power, such as perceived legitimate authority. Coercive power is effective only if a party actually possesses it, is willing to use it, can overcome resistance from a counterpart that the use of force provokes, and has accurately assessed the ability of the counterpart to withstand the exercise of this form of power (Fisher, 1976). If these conditions are not met, the use of coercive power will not only be ineffective, but may result in unanticipated negative consequences and make a situation worse.

Negotiators should use only the minimum amount of power needed to obtain a desired change (Boss, 2003). Overuse of any source of power may cause resistance on the part of a counterpart. For example, if more data than necessary are shared, a counterpart may be overwhelmed or feel that he is being talked down to, or if more coercion than necessary is applied, the counterpart may react by resisting and possibly damage all parties more than was necessary to resolve their differences.

Establishing and Managing Role, Authority, and Power Relationships

Parties' roles, rank, status, authority, and power relationships in relation to each other are often established even before talks begin. However, the first face-to-face meeting or meetings is often the place where power relationships and dynamics are exhibited and tested. Negotiation theorists have long postulated that some negotiators focus during the early stages of talks on establishing relations of dominance and appropriate relationships between superiors and subordinates (Stevens, 1963). This is especially the case when significant differences exist between parties about their roles, status, or influence or there is a conflict between them. Power factors and dynamics are commonly raised during early meetings, and they often continue to be a matter of ongoing struggle throughout the following phases of talks.

Negotiating parties establish the power elements of their relationship in the context of two competing goals. First is the need to create productive working relationships for successful negotiations. The other is to compete and posture to send the message that a negotiator or team represents a force to be respected, that its issues are important and must be addressed, and that failure to do so will have potential (usually negative) consequences.

Some parties are quite forceful, open, and explicit in projecting their power and exercising influence, while others prefer more subtle signals. Personalities, the issues in question, the resources and power that each party has at their disposal, and cultural norms for addressing and handling these factors all affect how the parties interact and the means they use to achieve desired ends.

In intercultural negotiations, these issues may be approached in ways that vary in their level of directness or indirectness. Parties try to clarify and establish their rank, status, and power relative to each other in these ways:

- *One-up or one-down behavior, gestures, or body language.* For instance, a negotiator who remains seated behind her desk and does not get up to greet a counterpart is sending an entirely different message than does a negotiator who comes from behind the desk to meet the interlocutor and moves to a more egalitarian setting of a sofa or two chairs. Similarly, the willingness to give culturally appropriate eye contact, shake hands or bow, or sit or stand near each other can send messages about whether positive or more adversarial relationships are expected.

- *Relationship-oriented statements that establish dominance versus more egalitarian or cooperative relationships.* If parties come from cultures that view the world in a hierarchically ordered manner in which individuals or groups are either one-up or one-down, and if they make overt statements that try to establish or emphasize their rank or status above another, they are likely to establish competitive relationships with their counterpart unless the latter acknowledges his subordinate position. Similarly, statements perceived by a counterpart that demonstrate genuine respect and openness, give honor, or save or give face are more likely to encourage cooperative and less competitive relations.

- *Emotional and positional statements versus more emotionally neutral statements.* Many negotiators come into talks knowing what they want and assuming that their counterpart wants exactly the opposite. Thus, they often present a forceful, emotional, and maximal position, which can be seen as a power move. Some negotiators, especially those from more competitive cultures, view this kind of tactic as less risky than disclosure of information about their interests and as a way to demonstrate resolve, exert influence, and educate a counterpart.

A number of researchers (Morley and Stephenson, 1977; Pruitt 1981; Putnam and Jones, 1982) agree that many "negotiations begin with spirited posturing that should be characterized more by influence than information exchange.... Because negotiators do not yet have an understanding of the other side's positions, needs, and interests, it would be difficult at this stage to make persuasive arguments that draw on rational argument about the issues. Thus at this early stage negotiators . . . focus on influence with respect to status and power. Affective persuasion is an influence appeal based on status, relationships and normative or other contextual factors" (Adair and Brett, 2005, p. 36). These dynamics are also seen in many international and cross-cultural negotiations. For example, Russian or (former) Soviet negotiators often fairly early in negotiations either adamantly reject a position proposed by a counterpart or present an equally maximalist one of their own (Smith, 1989; Schecter, 1998).

For negotiations to move forward to reflective information exchange, problem solving, and option generation, the parties have to move beyond efforts to establish dominance or superiority through posturing and positioning. If this behavior continues and they do not switch to alternative approaches, they will remain in an adversarial mode, become frustrated, and have difficulty moving forward—with the result that talks can ultimately stall and be broken off.

An alternative approach to handling status and power relationships is for one party to take the initiative to disclose information about his interests, preferences, and priorities—and invite his counterpart to do the same. This strategy indicates that a negotiator wants to cooperate, for in order to reach an agreement, parties must gain some understanding about what is important to each of them. Parties do not have to reveal all interests or needs, which can risk exploitation. However, they must reveal enough information to induce a counterpart to reciprocate with information. Researchers have noted that shifts from reciprocal posturing to beginning to explore parties' priorities and information sharing often occur for members of low-context cultures (Germany, United States, Israel, and Sweden) and when mixed low- and high-context negotiators are interacting. It is less common for high-context negotiators (Hong Kong, Chinese, Japanese, Russian, and Thai) to make this transition (Adair and Brett, 2005). High-context cultures tend to provide only general information on priorities and interests—and in less direct ways—than do members of low-context cultures. They often use positions, if and when they are provided, as means to send indirect messages about their interests and concerns.

SUGGESTED STRATEGIES FOR COORDINATION OF POWER AND AUTHORITY ISSUES

- Assess how important status, rank, authority, and power are to you and your counterpart, and the possible impact of establishing significant differences between you by using any of the means identified above.

- Consider potential impacts of the use of power on the process of negotiation and the likelihood of moving toward greater information exchange, option generation, or reaching an agreement.

- If you decide that you need to engage in positioning or posturing (to establish high goals, educate a counterpart regarding how important an issue is to you, or demonstrate your resolve, for example), consider ways of doing so that are less likely to cause resistance or damage potential positive working relationships. Avoid making threats or indicating possible negative consequences for nonagreement that you will have to back off from later or that you have neither the capacity nor will to execute.

- Think about how long you want to posture before beginning to share information with your counterpart about your interests and needs.

- Try revealing some information about your interests, and see if your counterpart reciprocates. If they do not, initiate questions about their positions that will help reveal more about their interests.

- If they persist in posturing, ask them whether the approach they are using is achieving desired results, and propose a shift to a more in-depth exploration of all parties' issues, needs, and interests.

- Determine what information you can share and at the same time minimize potential risks to what you want to achieve.

CONCLUSION

This chapter has presented information about several key cross-cutting dimensions of intercultural negotiations. These issues appear repeatedly throughout the rest of the book, especially in Part Two, which addresses each stage of negotiations and the cultural considerations important to accomplishment of the associated negotiation tasks.

APPENDIX: SOURCES OF POWER

Power and influence come in many forms. Before listing some of the more common sources, we note several important distinctions:

- Power can arise from personal attributes (qualities, skills, associations) or broader structures or systems (institutions, laws, position).
- There is a difference between perceived power and actual power—although perceptions are quite compelling, especially in an arena where psychological factors are important.
- Some persons or groups hold certain kinds of power and influence but are unwilling or unable to exercise that power—in which case, the strength is diminished. (Again, perceptions play an important role.)
- It is important to distinguish between sources of power and tactics for building or exercising power. This Appendix primarily lists sources of power—and there are myriad possible ways to increase power or use it. We have provided a few examples.
- Some sources of power exert a direct influence on the other party or parties, while other forms of power operate in relation to key constituencies, important persons not present, or larger societal forces—and therefore have an indirect effect on other negotiators.

A negotiator or a counterpart can draw on many sources of power to try to influence the outcome of negotiations (Boss, 2003; Moore, 2003; Mayer, 2000).

Individual Attributes as Sources of Power

Some sources of power derive from the individual characteristics of the negotiator. We see four subcategories of individual power: personal qualities, emotional power, expertise, and relational power.

Personal Qualities

- *Likability*. A positive and likable personality or character
- *Charisma*. Charm, magnetism, brilliance, and sexual attractiveness, for example
- *Respectability and reputation*. A good reputation, proven record of trustworthiness

- *Sense of humor.* Ability to see oneself and others in perspective
- *Compassion.* Showing sympathy through words or actions
- *Respect and deference.* Demonstrating respect, acknowledging status, position, or positive qualities
- *Intellect and logic.* Ability to think clearly and analyze information and to present it in a logical manner
- *Listening skills.* Ability to listen attentively and restate accurately what has been said
- *Articulateness.* Ability to articulate clearly one's own interests and perceptions and to present a compelling argument
- *Intuition.* Ability to sense the right way forward, strategically or tactically, based on what feels right

Emotional Power

- *Emotional maturity and management.* Self-perception and understanding, relative ability to manage emotions
- *Emotional expression.* The ability to express compelling emotions when appropriate
- *Empathy.* The ability to recognize and acknowledge others' emotions and to help them handle them
- *Apology or forgiveness.* The ability to meet someone's need or free one's own emotional resources through offering an apology or forgiveness in a timely and meaningful way
- Tactics for building or using emotional power:
  - ◇ *Recognize and emphasize shared feelings.* Acknowledging, articulating, and emphasizing common negative or positive feelings to create shared emotional bonds.
  - ◇ *Appeal for or promote harmony.* Stating your desire for smooth interpersonal relations that minimize or eliminate discord.
  - ◇ *Offer an apology.* To the extent you can sincerely—and with support from your own organization or constituency—take responsibility for a past action, it can reduce tensions and improve relationships.

Knowledge and Expertise

- *Expertise.* Possessing skills, education, experience, or training that is of value to others
- *Knowledge and information.* Having information or data that can have a positive influence on thinking or actions

Relational Power

- *Positive relationships.* The ability to create positive affective bonds that can provide emotional or substantive benefits to others (pleasure, goods, respect, cooperation)
- *Referent power or association.* Identifying with and creating connections and affiliations with people, groups, organizations, or other collectivities that give you or your group access to their sources of power and influence
- Tactics for increasing relational power and influence:
  ◇ *Food and drink.* Providing minimal or outstanding sustenance for a counterpart's benefit or pleasure or to provide a forum for relationship building
  ◇ *Creature comforts.* Caring for a counterpart's physical needs for shelter, comfort, and ease
  ◇ *Personal disclosure.* Disclosing through words or actions information that reveals some aspect of one's private self and may induce understanding, empathy, or reciprocal revelations from a counterpart
  ◇ *Face saving.* Acting or refraining from acting in a manner that risks or minimizes damage to a counterpart's positive internal self-view or avoids tarnishing the image this counterpart wishes to project to others or members of the public
  ◇ *Statements of good faith or honorable intentions.* Indicating explicitly through words or action your good-faith intention to seek or follow through on agreements or a request for similar commitment from a counterpart
  ◇ *Honor at risk.* Pledging or placing one's honor at stake, or obtaining similar promises from a counterpart, to demonstrate commitment
  ◇ *Reciprocity.* Developing expectations or creating requirements for reciprocal exchanges (information, tangible rewards or benefits, acting or refraining from acting in a specific manner) that each counterpart believes to be of value
  ◇ *Alliance building.* Creating visible bonds with other groups or individuals that increase your perceived or actual power

Structural or Systemic Sources of Power

In addition to the personal attributes listed above, power can be derived from existing structures and social systems:

The Power of the Status Quo or Tradition or a Vision of the Future

- *Status quo or tradition.* Existing systems and structures possess momentum (inertia), and changing them requires more energy than maintaining them. If you are on the side of protecting the current situation, you have inertia and tradition on your side.

- *Vision.* The capacity to develop and articulate a desirable, plausible, and compelling vision for the future.

Process Power

- *Process.* The ability to control the design and implementation of the negotiation process

- *Blocking.* The capacity to prevent progress in negotiations, or inhibit a counterpart from getting what he wants

- *Ritual.* Access to key symbolic actions, often associated with culturally meaningful rituals, but can also involve the breaking of a taboo or a dramatic gesture using cultural symbols

- *Control over time and timing.* The ability to control when things happen or to generate a sense of urgency

- *Imposition or relaxation of deadlines.* Actual or perceived control over deadlines and time frames

- Tactics for exercising process power related to time and timing:

  ◇ *Raise the "shadow of the future."* Raising awareness of potential or actual upcoming events, activities, or outcomes that may be positively or negatively influenced by current attitudes, behaviors, and activities. This means of influence is used to signal that current responses or outcomes are not independent of or divorced from the future.

  ◇ *Fading opportunities.* Indicating that time is limited to reach agreement or that possible benefits will diminish the longer it takes to reach an accord.

  ◇ *Time cycles.* Using natural or social cycles (seasons, planting and harvest, political elections) to establish or frame time lines in which certain activities can or cannot occur and to induce agreement making within time-determined windows of opportunity.

  ◇ *Time-out or cooling-off period.* Calling for a time-limited or nonlimited hiatus in negotiations to allow parties to reconsider how to proceed or handle strong emotions.

Position and Authority

- *Position or status.* Power derived from an individual or group's position or status within a group or community

- *Legitimate authority.* Power and authority conferred on an individual or group by widely accepted norms, agreements, or practices

- *Legal authority.* Power and authority of an individual or group based on laws, rules, or regulations
- *Religious authority.* Power vested in a person because of position within a formal or informal religious body or community
- *Traditional authority.* Power and authority derived by a person or group's position or role in a traditional society or institution; often vested in elders, traditional leaders, and shamans, for example
- Tactics for exercising or increasing religious or spiritual power:
  - ◇ *Moral appeals.* Appealing to widely accepted norms or standards of justice or fairness
  - ◇ *Prayer and request for assistance or intervention by a higher power.* Petitioning a higher power for strength, intervention, or help
  - ◇ *Gaining or providing opportunities for storing up merit.* Creating an opportunity for someone to gain from doing something that benefits the wider community (harmony, healing) or, in Buddhist terms, to attain merit

Options and Alternatives for Agreement

- *Reward power.* The ability to address and satisfy a counterpart's interests and at the same time meet your own
- *Creativity.* The capacity for generating creative options that address essential concerns of various parties
- *Having a viable alternative for meeting goals.* Possessing a good alternative to a negotiated agreement—which means that the negotiator can "walk away" if he or she needs to (best alternative to a negotiated agreement, or BATNA; see Fisher and Ury, 1981)
- Tactics for exercising or increasing options:
  - ◇ *Take a risk.* Taking a small risk when exploring a potential solution that puts you at a slight disadvantage in relation to your counterpart. Risk taking can demonstrate trust and promote reciprocal risk taking on the part of a counterpart.
  - ◇ *Make small concessions or create small wins.* Making a small or symbolic concession and requesting a reciprocal exchange in return. Gradually increase the number of offers while tying acceptance to reciprocal exchanges from a counterpart.
  - ◇ *Suggest a compromise.* Proposing a solution in which gains and losses are shared in a fair and equitable manner.

◇ *Demonstrate scarcity.* Demonstrating that resources available for settlement are scarce or time is limited to induce a shift of view or action in time to capture benefits.

Ability to Provide Benefits

- *Control over tangible resources.* Maintaining control over money, goods, services, or opportunities that can reward a counterpart

- *Control over intangible resources.* Holding control over desirable resources, such as status, recognition, legitimacy, honor, and respect

Negative or Coercive Inducements

- *Denial of benefits.* The ability to take away or withhold rewards or desired resources

- *Tangible sanctions.* The ability to impose consequences or punishments

- *Intangible sanctions.* The ability to impose emotional or symbolic punishment through criticism, shaming, damaging a reputation, or inducing guilt

- *Coercion.* The ability to force others to act or refrain from acting by making any alternative impossible or extremely costly

- *Physical harm.* Inflicting physical constraints, harm, or pain on a counterpart to induce cooperation, compliance, acquiescence, or surrender

PART TWO

A STEP-BY-STEP GUIDE TO INTERCULTURAL NEGOTIATIONS

P art Two examines, step by step, the stages of negotiation and the cultural factors that influence the behavior, strategies, and tactics at each phase. The chapters present negotiation in a fairly linear and logical sequence, but in reality, negotiations are much messier and iterative. Matters that seemed settled in the preparation stage may rise again in the final stages of coming to agreement. Problem-solving processes do not necessarily occur in one discrete period. Influence and persuasion strategies are employed by negotiators throughout the process.

Chapter Five addresses a series of important considerations in preparing for a negotiation process, including clarifying the purpose and conception of negotiations. Chapter Six follows parties into the first stage of negotiating, when they meet each other, engage in early relationship-building activities, and often make opening statements that lay out their initial understanding of the issues and needs.

Chapter Seven describes how parties from different cultures present issues—or fail to do so. Chapter Eight considers how the parties exchange important information about their needs, interests, and concerns and provides specific examples from nine cultures. Chapter Nine explores different approaches to solving problems and generating potential solutions, and Chapter Ten identifies how people from various cultures exercise influence; examples from eleven countries are offered.

Chapter Eleven examines how parties assess a possible settlement (a contract or treaty, for example); Chapter Twelve describes how the parties come to closure, including seeking necessary approvals or ratification; and Chapter Thirteen deals with issues concerning actual implementation of an agreement.

CHAPTER FIVE

The Preparation Stage

Marika and Sonuku are sisters who have very different approaches to doing their weekly family shopping. Marika carefully looks through all of her food supplies on hand and makes a list of the things she needs, thinking ahead about expected normal and unusual events in the coming week. She also calculates her food budget for the week and estimates what she will bargain to pay for each item, based on her knowledge of prices in the market. She sits at her kitchen table composing her list, marking the possible price, and totaling up her possible purchases. Then she sets out for the market, knowing exactly what she wants and what she will pay.

Sonuku simply grabs her shopping bag and a wad of cash from her food money jar and heads for the market. She is confident that she will be inspired to buy interesting things for her family and has a general sense of what she will need to get through the week. She cannot imagine why her sister spends all that time plotting and scheming!

Here we see two sisters from the same family (and therefore most likely the same class, education, culture, and upbringing) who show very different attitudes toward planning and preparation. There will always be different personal approaches to thinking ahead, making a clear plan, and calculating what might happen and what responses might be appropriate. As we will see, there are also cultural tendencies in this regard that influence how people prepare—or do not prepare—for negotiations. Let's consider another example.

The negotiation teams from Euroyl and the country of Saharaland are meeting to finalize an agreement that includes long-term leases for oil exploration, extraction, and transport. The Euroyl team is headed by the vice president for exploration, joined by technical and legal advisors. The team has been working on strategies for weeks, developing a series of scenarios, predicting the likely demands of the Saharaland government, calculating costs and revenues under multiple scenarios, and estimating their bottom line, their dream deal, and the most likely settlement. They are armed with tables and figures, multiple scenarios and associated budgets, as well as legal opinions from the company's legal experts, one of whom is on the team. They have also determined their likely strategy if the negotiations fail and the risks inherent in working in a country as unstable as Saharaland. The full team, including the vice president for exploration, participated in a strategy retreat in which they even conducted role-plays of negotiation scenarios, based on their research regarding the likely negotiation styles of the Saharaland team.

The Saharaland team is headed by the national vice president, who is joined by the minister for natural resources and several members of the oil resource unit within the ministry. The vice president has met with the president and received instructions to reach the best deal possible for the country; they have few other sources of revenue, other than foreign assistance and humanitarian aid, in the wake of twenty years of civil war. The president will review and approve any tentative agreement before completing the contract. The oil resource unit consists of two men with undergraduate engineering degrees who have done their best to estimate the kinds of revenues they might expect from the deal with Euroyl. They met briefly with their minister, who merely asked if they were ready, and they assured him that they were. They have not met with the vice president, although he is a distant cousin of one of the engineers. The vice president is also aware that the Euroyl vice president for exploration met with the president at a high-level summit on untapped oil reserves the previous year.

✍

Here we can see two organizational cultures and two national cultures at work as the two teams get ready to negotiate an important commercial deal. One team feels obliged to prepare thoroughly and in considerable detail, while the other focuses mainly on the decision-making authority of the negotiation team and relationship dynamics. While some of the variations in preparation can be attributed to the differences in available financial and human resources, much of it relates to the cultural orientations of the two teams.

A CULTURAL LENS IN PREPARING FOR INTERCULTURAL INTERACTIONS

In the context of negotiation, preparation involves forward-looking planning concerning approaches, strategies, and tactics that a negotiator believes will help him or her to satisfy key needs and interests to the greatest extent possible. Effective preparation can increase the probability that participants in negotiations will be able to engage more productively and meet their individual and joint goals as they engage in talks, deliberations, and decision making. The need for preparation increases as the stakes involved and the complexity of the matter increase. Unlike sister Marika above, most people engage in very little planning for simple transactions. Most of us are like Sonuku when the issues are straightforward. We have a general sense of our needs and assume that we can bargain effectively without a lot of preparation. However, if the stakes are higher and the issues and process more complex, we may need to plan, especially if the context is cross-cultural as well.

Preparation can help negotiators better understand the issues or conflicts they are engaged in. It can also enable parties to engage effectively with counterparts from other cultures who may exhibit perplexing behavior or use unfamiliar or uncomfortable tactics in trying to reach agreements. Some of these variations are personal, but some factors are also tied to culture. Preparation involves generic considerations that are applicable regardless of the issues, context, or culture, but it also has specific aspects to consider when working across cultures. This chapter discusses these cultural factors and provides a brief overview of generic preparation for negotiation. (*Note:* There are many useful texts regarding basic preparation for negotiations. Several of these are listed in the bibliography.)

FACTORS IN CULTURAL ANALYSIS

Preparation for negotiations and strategy formulation is very much a cultural process. Because planning and preparation are future-oriented processes, negotiators, teams, and organizations from different cultures often have very different approaches to preparing for the unknown based on their views of the importance of the future and degree of control they believe they have over it. Variations are often related to the orientations of members of a culture toward the past, present, and future; their acceptance or avoidance of risk; and the degree to which they believe that they can control what happens in the future.

Orientations Toward the Past, Present, and Future

Members of different cultures often have divergent views regarding the role and influence of the past, present, and future on their current lives. These variations can affect the amount of time and energy expended in preparation for negotiations.

Members of cultures that are past oriented often plan future strategies based on historic or past practices that help them return to a real or mythical golden age in their distant past or involve consideration of or consultation with ancestors or their spirits. For example, several years ago, one of CDR Associates' partners was working with a number of indigenous nongovernmental organizations (NGOs) in Guatemala developing reconciliation procedures to help heal the trauma that resulted from the thirty-six-year civil war. One of the goals was to reintegrate former combatants and their civilian supporters into their original home villages, which they had been forced to leave during the war.

Development of reintegration and ultimately reconciliation approaches required problem solving and negotiations between indigenous peoples, who make up the majority of the population, and Ladinos who are descended from Spanish conquistadors. When the CDR partner asked one of the indigenous leaders of an NGO what kinds of reconciliation procedures and structures would be appropriate and necessary to achieve long-term peace, he responded in a slightly embarrassed but nevertheless serious way that the ancestors would have to be considered and consulted regarding what would be appropriate. In addition, options would have to be negotiated that would meet the approval of both the living and the dead, that is, the ancestors of current former adversaries. He said that if the ancestors were not considered, true reintegration and reconciliation could never be achieved. This approach to the future was very much driven by the view of and importance of the past.

Present-oriented cultures focus their preparations for negotiations on meeting goals for the very immediate future rather than looking to the past or distant future. This orientation may be driven by a negotiator's need to meet immediate human needs, which requires people to live in the moment, an unwillingness to defer gratification until some unpredictable time in the future, or a belief that planning for the future is irrelevant or impossible because of unknown events or forces that may make planning irrelevant. Cultures that include elements of fatalism would also be present oriented.

An example of this orientation toward planning occurred during the 1990s when the United Nations and the Organization of American States placed a joint mission in Haiti to assist the government and citizens of that country to move toward democracy. The mission staff and international consultants repeatedly encountered a highly present-oriented focus and resistance to planning for the future on the part of many Haitians. When working with the joint mission, one of us was asked to consult on the development of a court-connected mediation process. As part of developing a culturally appropriate dispute resolution system and related procedures, he interviewed numerous Haitians and expatriates about cultural approaches to negotiation and conflict resolution. Many respondents noted that it was common for many Haitians, especially the very poor, to put little time into planning because the future was unknown and extremely unpredictable for them. Their response to planning seemed to be that if the future is so uncertain and can change regardless of what human beings do, why plan for it? Thus, planning for negotiations was conducted only for the most immediate future and to achieve tangible and immediate gains.

Future-oriented cultures, and related preparation and planning activities, seem to be of two types. One cultural approach emphasizes the development of long-term interpersonal relationships, which members see as critical for predictability, stability, and long-term gain for one or all parties. Japan is a prototype for this kind of future-oriented relationship-planning culture, with a strong emphasis on maintaining harmony. Cultures that hold this view, as do many in Asia and a large number of indigenous communities, believe that it is important to maintain harmony in the world and that people have the capacity to perform acts or rituals that can help achieve this goal. Negotiators from these cultures often place a high value on planning and developing future solutions that work to preserve harmony as opposed to significant gain for one party at the expense of another.

The second kind of future-oriented culture focuses on what will happen in the future and potential gains or changes that might result. Members of these cultures have a strongly linear view of time and progress (things are getting better all the time), believe that human beings can influence or control what will occur, and are willing to defer immediate gains for long-term benefits. Therefore, members of these cultures expend energy in planning for both the short and long terms. The United States and Western European countries exemplify this cultural orientation to preparation and planning for the future. However, even within cultures with many similarities, there may be differences in orientations toward planning. For example, in a comparison of 175 British, French, and German top managers, Horowitz (1985) found that French and Germans focus much more on short-term feedback and gains than do their British counterparts.

Orientations Toward Risk Taking and Planning

Risk taking or the avoidance of uncertainty also influences preparation. Cultures that value risk taking often emphasize preparation and planning so that they can take advantage of risks in exchange for significant gains. Similarly, members of cultures that are more risk averse may also emphasize extensive planning, as they hope to minimize risks and obtain more moderate and yet predictable gains. Hofstede's landmark study (1984) on the consequences of culture on work-related values and interactions explored the orientations toward risk and the avoidance of uncertainty among members of different cultures working in an international corporation. He found that a number of national cultures known to be extensive planners and preparers for negotiations can be found in both the high-risk-taking and high-uncertainty-avoidance categories.

For example, of the top thirteen national cultures that are willing to take significant risks in life and in negotiations, five are found in northern Europe (Denmark, Sweden, Ireland, Great Britain, and Norway). Three were settled predominantly by Western Europeans and currently have, or have had in the past, predominantly northern European cultures (United States, Canada, and New Zealand), and five were former British or U.S. colonies and were significantly influenced by their political and economic cultures (Singapore, Hong Kong, India, South Africa, and the Philippines, which was also a Spanish colony). Of those thirteen, eight have majority populations that are Protestant. The exceptions are Ireland and the Philippines, with Roman Catholic majorities, India with a predominantly Hindu population, and Singapore and Hong Kong with strong Confucian roots. With the possible exception of the Philippines and India, all of these national cultures are well known for their strong orientations toward planning and preparation, including for negotiations (Mole, 1990; Dunung, 1995).

Of the thirteen national cultures that are more risk and uncertainty avoidant, nine are Latin in origin or derived from Latin cultures (Portugal, Peru, France, Chili, Spain, Argentina, Mexico, and Colombia) or were strongly influenced by Latin culture at one point in their history (Belgium). All of these countries are predominantly Roman Catholic. Of the other four that rank high on uncertainty avoidance, one is Asian (Japan) and has been strongly influenced by Confucian values; two are on the border between Europe and the Middle East and have either Greek Orthodox or Muslim populations (Greece and Turkey); and the other is in the Middle East (Israel), with a Jewish population, many of whom came from Europe.

Which of these are known for their strong orientations for planning? The outstanding candidates are Japan, France, and Israel. Why are they in the uncertainty-avoidance category and plan extensively, while others in this category often do not? Historically, Japan has been strongly influenced by the cultural values of Confucianism and those of northern Europe, both of which emphasize planning. France and Israel have mixed values from both northern European and Mediterranean cultures. The French, while avoiding risk, engage in extensive planning, probably due to their philosophical and rationalist traditions and centralized state planning. Israelis prepare to ensure their preservation, because they have historically led a precarious existence in which risk reduction is considered paramount, and they have also adopted northern European traditions of planning (Klieman, 2005).

Emphasis and Activities in Preparation

Earlier in this chapter, we noted that cultures place different values and emphases on preparation for negotiations and vary significantly regarding the time and energy that they commit to it. Cultures also vary regarding what they emphasize and what they do when preparing for talks. Some of the variables are areas of focus and level of detail, protocol preparation, religious or spiritual preparation, psychological preparation, and communication preparation. Two additional factors, procedural and substantive preparations, are addressed in some detail later in this chapter. Before continuing with those issues, we will focus on preparation concerning the focus of planning, protocol development, spiritual grounding, psychological readiness, and how parties plan to communicate.

Focus of Planning. Closely related to cultural orientation toward control of the future and risk taking is the selection of the focus for planning and the level of detail. Some cultures focus almost exclusively on how to establish a positive interpersonal relationship with a counterpart and how opening rituals will be conducted. This pattern is especially common in cultures where personal relationships are seen as the glue required to bind parties and negotiated agreements together or, in more traditional societies, where the performance of correct rituals and adherence to historical protocol is seen to be important to getting talks off on the right foot. These cultures often leave detailed planning on substantive issues until the desirable relationship has been established.

Members of other cultures expend more energy on planning the process they will use in negotiations to elicit information about issues of importance from their counterpart, waiting until later to develop their own positions. Still other negotiators prepare by establishing general positions or principles to shape talks. For example, in French diplomatic negotiations, the Quai d'Orsay or the Secrétariat Général du Comité Interministériel (depending on whether the issue is to be dealt with unilaterally by France or by the European Union) will develop a general stance regarding what the government wants to achieve through talks. Agreement on such a position is often achieved by extensive consultations among concerned agencies or parties, with the goal of reaching consensus on a common opening position. This position generally consists of a broad set of general guidelines or instructions with specific points that negotiators are to achieve. However, the finer details are often not spelled out, and negotiators have significant leeway in how to attain identified goals (Cogan, 2003).

Members of yet other cultures expend considerable energy in developing an almost global or encyclopedic understanding of issues prior to negotiations. Germans, for example, probably plan more extensively for negotiations than almost any other national culture.

Protocol Development. Protocols are commonly acknowledged and practiced rituals and behaviors that members of a culture use to conduct negotiations. They may address the kinds of social activities that should precede substantive negotiations, where negotiations are traditionally held, room arrangements and physical setup, identification of appropriate refreshments that will be served, who enters the venue first, sequence of team members' entry based on rank and status, when people sit down, who talks first, what is talked about and for how long, when substantive issues are first raised, how the topics are discussed, and so forth. Cultures that value ritual often spend an extensive period of time planning for how it can be properly performed. This emphasis has led to a whole new profession in the West of protocol officers, who specialize in knowing about and informing parties about appropriate social etiquette and behavior (International Protocol Officers Association, 2002). Some cultures, such as a number of Native American and Asian ones, believe that proper performance of protocols and rituals is prerequisite to successful outcomes and that failure to perform them precisely may doom future activities (Mulder, 1992). For example, many Native American groups cyclically perform specific rituals year after year to make sure the world stays in balance and harmony. These beliefs about proper performance may also be applied to negotiations.

Spiritual Grounding. Religious and spiritual grounding refers to ways that individuals or groups who will be involved in negotiations gain the support of higher powers. This type of preparation may involve performing certain kinds of rituals, which create a bond between the supplicant and the gods and an obligation of the latter to grant the request. Mulder (1992) noted that this type of preparation for individuals who will be engaging in difficult tasks is common in Thailand.

In a second type of spiritual preparation, individuals or groups seek to become personally connected and grounded with a higher power or powers prior to beginning negotiations. Prayer, sitting meditation, walking meditation, or chanting may be used to help negotiators become more centered and spiritually engaged. For example, Gandhi stressed the importance of spiritual preparation for *satyagrahis*, nonviolent activists who practiced "truth force," prior to engagement in negotiations or direct action to end the internal oppression of Indians by other Indians and to gain independence from Great Britain.

Psychological Readiness. Individuals and groups strive to be personally effective in negotiations and in control of psychological factors that will promote success to minimize problems. Psychological preparation may include planning how to use or control the expression of emotions; planning how to remain centered, so that attacks by a counterpart can be ignored or deflected; working on staying calm; and using physical practices such as deep breathing to control physiological and psychological states (Dobson, 1994). The Japanese process of getting in touch with *hara,* or gut feeling, is one such practice (Matsumoto, 1988).

Communication Planning. Communication preparation focuses on the specific language (Thai, Zulu, Swahili, and so forth), syntax, phrases, expressions, stories, words, and logic that will be used in negotiations—in short, how important matters will be expressed. Communication preparation, either conscious or unconscious, is conducted by all negotiators in addition to a focus on content, which is the emphasis of substantive preparation.

Some cultures place high importance on the selection and preparation of the exact phrases or words that will be spoken, levels and timing for the expression of emotions, the degree of directness or indirectness to be used, and the amount of exaggeration or understatement that is appropriate or logic to be applied in discussions or negotiations. For example, during the seventeenth and eighteenth centuries in France (encompassing both the apex and nadir of the French monarchy), nobles at court verbally jousted with each other using stylish language, references to learned individuals or classical texts, cleverness, rhetorical flourishes, and multiple interruptions to express their ideas or debate the issues of the day. Some have said that French culture of that period measured a gentleman's character more by how he presented his ideas than what he actually knew. Some of these characteristics are still common today in French discourse and argumentation: "If we imagine conversation as being a spider's web, we can see the exchanging of words as playing the role of the spider, generating the threads that bind the participants. The ideal (French) conversation would resemble a perfect spider's web: delicate, fragile, elegant, brilliant, of harmonious proportions, a work of art" (Volk, 1988, p. 25).

Where intercultural communication conflicts often occur is when two or more cultures place different emphasis on the kind of communications and language to be used when talking to a counterpart from a different culture. For example, communication patterns during negotiations in the Middle East between Egyptians and Israelis are very different due to differences in Arabic and Hebrew, cultural differences in direct and indirectness, and differences in the rhetorical methods each culture uses (Cohen, 1997). Hebrew is a very explicit language with little nuance. It communicates ideas clearly and directly, with practically no verbal flourishes, detours, or room for ambiguity. Arabic is much less explicit, with a wide variety of words that provide opportunities for the communication of nuance and subtexts, looping to discuss more than one topic, and, on occasion, exaggeration for effect. When Israelis speak to Arabic speakers, their messages are frequently seen as lacking beauty or nuance and blunt. Conversely, Israelis often perceive Arabic speakers as being obtuse, lacking forthrightness regarding issues or commitments, failing to stay on point in discussions, or putting more emphasis on form than content (Cohen, 1997; Patai, 1983).

SUGGESTED STRATEGIES FOR COORDINATION OF PREPARATION

Negotiators working across cultures should identify the emphasis that they and their counterparts place on the nonsubstantive elements of preparation. If either party places a high value on preparation to follow correct protocols, engage spiritually with a higher power or force, prepare psychologically for talks, or consider how language should be used, the parties can make strategic accommodations to address these differences. In preparing to work with counterparts who may prepare differently:

- Make yourself aware of your own cultural and personal approach to preparation and planning.

- As much as possible, figure out the likely cultural approach to preparation of your counterparts.

- Identify whether you and your culture, or that of your counterpart, place a significant value on preparation or planning in any of the areas described.

- Consider how these different orientations to preparation may influence future negotiations, either positively or negatively.

- Determine what response will be best and most likely to promote cooperation from your counterpart. (See Chapter Three regarding the avoid, adhere, adapt, adopt, or advance strategies.) For example, accepting the other party's protocols can be a way of demonstrating respect or promoting feelings of comfort. Understanding that a culture places high value on the way things are said may create greater tolerance for different ways of communicating.

A BRIEF GUIDE TO PRENEGOTIATION PREPARATION AND PLANNING

This section outlines a number of general considerations concerning preparation for negotiations. Because this book concerns the cross-cultural aspects of negotiations, we will not discuss these in detail here, beyond providing the steps. We have also provided an exhibit (see Exhibit 5.1) on the next page that summarizes many of the preparation steps and questions and can be used as a tool for planning.

Exhibit 5.1. Situation Assessment, Conflict Analysis, and Negotiation Planning Framework

People and Parties Who Will Be Involved	Purpose of Negotiations and Parties' Framing of Goals and Outcomes	Preconditions: External Dynamics That Affect Talks	Parties' Issues	Parties' Interests and Needs	Importance and Emotional Charge of Interests and Needs	Parties' Willingness to Talk and Reach Agreements	Possible Options for Agreement	Parties' Alternative Means to Achieving Desired Goals	Parties' Means of Influence and Power	Possible Negotiation Procedures and Next Steps

139

Steps for Negotiation Preparation

Different cultures may do more or less of each of the preparation activities described below—or none of them at all. However, a well-prepared intercultural negotiator will find it valuable to implement some of these preparation strategies prior to meeting his or her counterpart because they can contribute significantly to the probability of successful talks and outcomes.

Step 1: Perform a Context Analysis. A context analysis permits a broad understanding of the situation in which negotiations will occur. Potential elements of a context analysis include the following:

1. Identify and understand the people and parties who will be involved in negotiations.
   - ◇ Who will participate in negotiation sessions—from your side and from the counterpart's side? What are the cultural implications and norms determining inclusion or exclusion of individuals from talks? (See Chapter Four for a discussion of this issue.) What is the structure of the two or more sides: a single individual, a team, or several subteams?
   - ◇ What kind of authority to negotiate do you and your counterpart have?
   - ◇ Who are the primary and secondary parties to the conflict or business transaction? What party or parties have been left out of the negotiation, and why?
   - ◇ What do you know about your counterpart as a group or organization and the individuals involved? What are their backgrounds and personal histories? Are they likely to adhere to traditional norms for their culture or work according to international business, diplomatic, or organizational norms?

2. Understand the situation in which negotiations will occur and the general purpose of the negotiations:
   - ◇ What are the general purposes and desired outcomes of the negotiation process? From your perspective? From the perspective of your counterparts? Are these in alignment?
   - ◇ Is the focus of talks on building a relationship, completing a transaction, or resolving a conflict? Is this a one-time process or part of a long-term relationship?
   - ◇ What is the history behind the negotiations? For specific individuals involved? For the groups, organizations, or nations? How might history influence the negotiation dynamics?

3. Identify positive preconditions for negotiations and develop strategies to mitigate negative ones. Typically, some (though rarely all) of the following preconditions for negotiations must be met for successful talks:

◇ Parties have been identified who are willing and ready to participate.

◇ The parties depend on each other to get their interests or needs met (interdependence).

◇ The parties agree on at least some issues and interests.

◇ The parties have the necessary resources, time, and energy to negotiate.

◇ The parties have effective means of leverage or influence.

◇ The outcome is unpredictable. (If the outcome were known or predictable, there would be no need to negotiate.)

◇ There is a sense of urgency and deadline (pressure to reach agreement).

◇ The parties have no major psychological barriers to participation or settlement.

◇ The issues are negotiable.

◇ The parties have the authority to decide.

◇ One or more parties lack a better alternative to reaching a negotiated agreement (see Fisher and Ury, 1981, regarding the concept—of the best alternative to a negotiated agreement, or BATNA).

◇ If necessary, the parties are willing to compromise.

◇ The parties believe that it is possible to reach an agreement and are willing to settle.

◇ External factors exert a positive influence or do not present barriers (for example, views of associates, political climate, economic conditions, security situations).

Step 2: Complete an Issue, Interest, and Power Analysis. In addition to analyzing the people, parties, situation, and preconditions, a negotiator needs to develop an understanding of the issues involved as the parties see them, the interests held by the various stakeholders, and the kinds of power they enjoy.

1. Explore the potential framing of issues (see the discussion of framing in Chapter Four):

◇ How do you frame the issues to be discussed?

◇ How does your counterpart frame them?

◇ Do you both see issues in approximately the same way, or are there stark differences?

2. Identify the potential interests of you and your counterpart:

◇ What are your interests in relation to the issues at hand? In the ideal, what do you hope to accomplish through the negotiation process? What would you settle for?

◇ What do you guess to be the interests of your counterparts—and their ideal and bottom line?

3. Assess the emotional charge of the negotiations, and develop potential strategies for handling it:

◇ Are the issues to be discussed fairly neutral for you and your counterpart, or is there a strong emotional connection for one or all? (Note that if the context is conflict resolution, there will almost always be an emotional component.)

◇ If there is an emotional charge for one or more parties, what are the potential strategies for handling those dynamics?

4. Evaluate the parties' willingness to talk and reach agreements and develop strategies for promoting effective talks or alternative means to get interests and needs met.

5. Assess the parties' means of influence and power (see Chapter Ten for a full exploration in relation to reaching agreements):

◇ What are your sources of power and influence? What are the sources for your counterpart?

◇ How might you mobilize your own sources of power—and what strategies will your counterpart likely use to mobilize his or her power and influence?

Step 3: Complete a Process Design. The list of procedural issues presented in Box 5.1 covers almost all of the issues that typically arise regarding the procedures for negotiation. In a simple negotiation process, many of these would be irrelevant or handled informally. In higher-stakes or more formal negotiations or those conducted under tension or conflict, these issues may become quite important. In fact, they may become the focus of a whole series of prenegotiations simply to bring the parties to agreement about how negotiations will take place. We have repeated experiences as mediators dealing with complex multiparty negotiations regarding volatile environmental issues in the United States. Often the parties include people from contrasting subcultures, including representatives of Native American tribes, state and

Box 5.1. Procedural Issues in Negotiations

A. Who Will Be Involved
1. Which parties (primary, secondary, and so on) will be involved—and how?
2. What will be the size and composition of negotiating teams? Any provision for substitutes or alternates?
3. Will the participation of observers be permitted?
4. Will legal counsel or other advisors participate and, if so, how?

B. Organization with and Among Teams
1. Role assignments within teams: spokesperson, topic or issue leaders, researcher, writer or editor, and so on
2. Designation of working groups, technical teams, or subcommittees by topic or issue

C. Basic Rules and Organization of Sessions
1. Will negotiation sessions be closed or open?
2. What is the agreed venue and physical setup of negotiation sessions?
3. What are the agreed behavioral guidelines among parties? Acceptable and unacceptable behavior (for example, respect for values, no personal attacks, no attribution of motivation, limits on emotional displays, and so on)?
4. What are the recognition and protection of legal rights and administrative mandates?
5. How will agendas be developed?
6. How will meetings be chaired or facilitated?
7. Is there need for a third-party neutral (mediator, facilitator . . .), and if used, what is the role or function of the third party?
8. What is the schedule of meetings, beginning and ending times?
9. How will basic rules be enforced?

D. External Relationships and Communication
1. How will the parties relate with their constituencies and decision-making authorities?
2. How will the parties interact with the media (press releases, briefings, and so on)—if at all?

E. Organization of Sessions
1. How will agendas be developed?
2. How will information be collected and shared among parties (especially if the negotiations call for gathering and analysis of new data through a negotiated process)?
3. Who will make initial opening statements, and in what order?

F. Reaching, Recording, and Implementing Agreements
1. How will parties know that they have reached an agreement?
2. How will the meetings be recorded and how will agreements be written?
3. What will be the process for final approval of agreements (including those directly involved in the negotiation sessions, and if needed, other people not directly involved)?

federal agencies, private corporations, as well as environmental organizations. Typically, two or three meetings are required just to work out procedural issues before the parties are ready to address matters of substance.

Revisiting Procedural Issues over Time. As we will see in subsequent chapters, these procedural issues often arise again even after negotiations have started—either because they were not addressed adequately at the beginning or because one or more of the parties realizes that they have procedural interests that are not being met. We have also noted that parties from different cultures will have different attitudes about whether agreements on these kinds of issues are even necessary. Parties from high-context cultures will assume that all of these issues are completely understood, so there is no need for discussion. Low-context cultures, however, will look for explicit agreements and written protocols in advance of negotiations. If negotiations will include parties from both low- and high-context cultures, it may be necessary to discuss whether and how procedural agreements are developed.

Cultural Impacts on Preparation

So what does preparation for intercultural negotiations look like in a specific culture, and how do its members address some of the prenegotiation planning tasks described thus far? We will present only two cases here, that of German and French cultures, because their members are known to be some of the most meticulous planners of all cultures and they apply somewhat similar approaches to multiple types of negotiations: diplomatic, economic, business development, and management in organizations. For the description of the German approach we have relied extensively on the work of Smyser (2003), Hall and Hall (1990), Ardagh (1987), and Craig (1983).

The roots of German orientation toward extensive planning are diverse. However, five are most important: (1) strongly held belief that with careful thought, the application of the correct logic, and extensive planning, people can control their environment; (2) a moderate degree of risk aversion and desire for predictability in ordering all aspects of life; (3) cultural norms of tenacity and persistence; (4) traditions of planning by the German military's General Staff, which expanded in the late 1800s to multiple elements of society; and (5) strong historical requirements and traditions prior to the rise to power of Prussian Chancellor Otto von Bismarck in the mid-1800s, during the interwar years of 1918 and 1933, and after World War II to negotiate carefully crafted, predictable, and acceptable compromise agreements between German states *(Länder)* and surrounding countries in Europe that did not place Germans in a position of weakness or disadvantage in regard to their neighbors (Smyser, 2003; Ardagh, 1987). Research and many interviews with counterparts of German negotiators have found that preparation for diplomatic, economic, business, and other forms of negotiation follows a similar approach. Three general characteristics of German preparations for negotiation are the breadth and depth of analysis and planning, consultation, and the length of time allocated to this task.

The first step is an in-depth effort to understand the broad context and environment in which the negotiations will occur. To accomplish this goal, Germans commonly collect a massive amount of primary and secondary data on the topics to be discussed and gather information about potential or actual views of future counterparts. They then analyze these data to determine what they mean, their importance to their counterpart, and potential impacts on the German state, *Länder,* corporation, business, or organization.

The results of the assessment and conclusions reached are often summarized in briefing books. Many counterparts of German negotiators, in both the diplomatic and business realms, have remarked that at the end of this analysis, the latter often understand the issues or business of their counterparts better than they do (Smyser, 2003).

Based on the extensive gathering and detailed analysis of information about future parties and their issues and interests, the government or business defines its goals for negotiations. This centers around the development of a general position to be pursued that will promote the satisfaction of their interests. The position is not established unilaterally and without seriously taking into consideration the interests and views of counterparts. Germans often even recognize the interests and needs of counterparts with whom they disagree. This approach is in direct contrast to how some other strong nations or businesses negotiate, which take a more unilateral style to position or option development.

This German approach to position development is in part due to German recognition that they as a nation or business often do not have the power to impose their will on counterparts, their willingness to work within the parameters of existing political and economic constraints, and a general desire to find potential solutions to problems that all parties can agree to and will generally support.

The next step is to prepare the details of the general position and logical arguments that will support it. To do so, Germans generally develop a *Gesamtkonzept,* a comprehensive or governing concept (Smyser, 2003). This framework provides a logical structure with intellectual coherence for the general position, articulates broad German goals and aims, elucidates general German interests, and often describes how the position will address the interests of counterparts. In general, Germans try to develop a framework and governing concept for negotiations that will encourage rather than close down discussion.

The preparation of the *Gesamtkonzept* and logical arguments to support it often involve consultations with a large number of internal German parties.

Depending on whether the negotiations are in the diplomatic or business realm, participants may include the chancellor, who sets broad government policy, ministers or their staff, representatives of *Länder,* and consultations with members of the Reichstag, or parliament. In the business sector, the role of bureaucracy may be less, but parties involved in preparations for negotiations may still include key corporate decision makers, leaders of leading divisions or departments, and technical experts who have an interest in the future outcome of negotiations. "Germans are very high on the monochronic scale, and their consensus decision-making process is often more involved and deliberate than the American, requiring many lateral clearances as well as considerable extensive background research. Because the Germans approach decision making slowly and laboriously, once a decision is made they stand firmly and unalterably behind it" (Hall and Hall, 1990, p. 35).

After elaborating the *Gesamtkonzept,* German negotiators identify specific issues that will have to be addressed to achieve it and the specific interests under each issue. This preparation is done in great detail, with nothing left to chance. Once issues are defined, a prospective order for their presentation and discussion in negotiations is determined.

In the process of preparation of the *Gesamtkonzept,* Germans conduct a concurrent and parallel analysis of their power and means of influence to achieve their goals. They also do a similar analysis of the resources of their counterparts in this area. In most negotiations, Germans prefer to use their initial *Gesamtkonzept,* or a modified governing concept that emerges from ongoing negotiations; logical arguments; provision of compelling data; pursuit of options that lower risks for all negotiators; and development of consensus-based solutions that appeal to or meet all parties' interests as means of reaching agreement.

This process takes time, often much more than that allocated by almost any counterpart cultures of German negotiators. Germans generally allocate more time for research and analysis, internal discussions and consensus building, the development of acceptable governing concepts, and elaboration of detailed strategies to address issues and common interests. They also prepare long and logical arguments to present their views. "When they explain something, they often find it necessary to lay a proper foundation, and as a result are apt to go back to Charlemagne. Such lengthy explanations make the average American impatient and drive the French crazy" (Hall and Hall, 1990, p. 35).

This description of German cultural patterns for prenegotiation preparation illustrates just one approach to this phase of deliberations and related tasks. It illustrates a model for in-depth analysis of parties, goals, frames for the purpose of negotiations, issues, and interests; development of a broad governing concept to guide future talks that takes into consideration and tries to address all parties' interests; and detailed planning for how specific issues and interests will be discussed and met. It also illustrates a process that commonly results in mutually satisfactory consensus decisions.

French preparation for negotiations, at least in the diplomatic realm, is also fairly detailed, involving multiple consultations among various hierarchically organized government agencies, with the president of the Republic being at the top (Cogan, 2003). The goal for the French is to enable their negotiating team to speak with a common voice and avoid having a counterpart see any variations in views or a fractured position. This requires considerable internal discussion, and on occasion debate, within the French government. Disagreements on views are referred up the chain of command.

In general, opening positions reached for presentation at the beginning of diplomatic negotiations are general instructions or points to be achieved, which provide some leeway on the part of negotiators regarding how they can be achieved. However, the general principle will be strongly advocated in the hope that the counterpart will accept it.

Because so much emphasis is put on an opening position, French negotiators often do not have elaborate plans if their counterpart will not accept their argument or if some circumstance beyond their control intervenes. Hall and Hall (1990), in their study of French business interactions and negotiations, noted that "long term planning is especially difficult for the French. They are all too aware of the many things that may prevent their keeping a commitment. Conditions may change, people may change. How can one predict the future?" (p. 89).

These examples illustrate some of the differences of focus, depth, and amount of planning that may occur in intercultural negotiations. However, individuals and teams preparing for negotiations should keep in mind the process commonly used in Germany: using your own preparation process and analyzing the parties, goals, issues, interests, and potential preparation process of your counterpart. Informed and prepared negotiators are better able to understand their counterpart, make proposals that meet joint interests and needs, and reach mutually beneficial and acceptable consensus decisions.

CONCLUSION

This chapter outlined a variety of cultural factors that influence preparations for negotiation. It also detailed a number of generic approaches for preparation and negotiation strategy design. With at least initial preparations completed, negotiators are now prepared to engage in face-to-face meetings.

CHAPTER SIX

Beginning Negotiations

A buyer and seller meet to discuss a sale in Lebanon.

SELLER: Welcome brother. I have not seen you for a long time.

BUYER: Why? I do come here from time-to-time.

SELLER: You ... from South Lebanon?

BUYER: Certainly, from the family of H.

SELLER: Oh ... I know some of the H's; they run for elections.

BUYER: Politics for politicians.

SELLER: My shop is yours—order and desire (*tlūb wi-t-mannā*).

BUYER: You are to order (*'int sāhib l'amir*). I want to buy some clothes for my children.

SELLER: What clothes?

BUYER: Ready made. Good quality and cheap.

SELLER: Shirts, underwear, pants?

BUYER: Socks and underwear for children of 7, 9, and 10.

SELLER: Best quality ... Italian made.

BUYER: But (they are) mixed with nylon?

SELLER: Slightly.

BUYER: Approximately how much?

SELLER: Pay as much as you want. We shall not disagree.

BUYER: Mr. K. M. told me that this shop is the most reliable one.

SELLER: I know him (Mr. K.) for a long time. He is a friend of yours? For your sake, pay لل 3 for each of these (underwear), and لل 1.75 for these (each pair of socks).

BUYER: Isn't that a little expensive for me?

SELLER: By God. It is only for you. The sum is لل 32. I give you لل 30.

BUYER: God is generous.

SELLER: This is as much as they cost. Please pay. God (will) send something better (*Allā bi-yifrijha*). Have pleasure in wearing them (*malbūus l-hana*) [Khuri, 1968, p. 705].

༺༻

Negotiations may be initiated directly by one or more of the parties or by a range of intermediaries, depending on whether one or more of the cultures is highly relationship oriented or prefers initial indirect dealing, or if talks are designed to resolve a highly emotional or difficult conflict.

This chapter focuses on the main tasks that negotiators must accomplish at the beginning of negotiations:

- Making initial contacts and connections
- Establishing, building, or maintaining working relationships
- Preparing and delivering opening statements
- Initiating discussions on substantive, procedural, or relationship issues (often accomplished through opening statements)

The dialogue between a Lebanese buyer and seller illustrates a number of these tasks. Although the buyer and seller were from the same country and the same Arab ethnic group, they may have been from different religious groups—Shia, Sunni, Druze, Maronite Christian, or Greek Orthodox—which might influence how they negotiate with one another. In the negotiation, the first four statements initiate the first contacts. The next ones establish common relationships and define roles and, to a lesser extent, authority and power relationship: the buyer is from the family of H.; the seller knows other family members who are politicians. The following sentences, which are about politicians, elaborate on the relationship and identify commonalities and focus on relationships and avoid discussion of differences; neither cares much for politicians.

Ultimately the seller shifts to a procedural opening statement in which he indicates an openness to discussion of more substantive issues and sets a positive tone: "My shop is yours." The buyer agrees, shifts the focus from relationship and connections to substantive issues, and begins to present a general frame for the purpose of negotiations: "I want to buy some clothes for my children." The buyer responds and makes a request for more information, "What clothes?" which he hopes will allow his counterpart to provide more data and establish the sequence for discussion or agenda. He then decides to make a request for more specific information in the form of a hypothetical question: "Shirts, underwear, pants?" He does this to draw out the buyer and allow him to educate him about his needs. The buyer counters with more information, "Ready made, good quality and cheap," provides information about their ages. The merchant then presents several options, again an educational process for his counterpart, which the parties discuss. The buyer asks, "Approximately how much?"—and problem solving over the price begins.

Although there are some similarities across cultures about activities and tasks that need to be accomplished at the beginning of negotiations, there are also considerable differences. For example, members of cultures often differ as to when they believe that negotiations actually begin. Cultures with a high task orientation and a need to reach concrete and tangible agreements rapidly often believe that negotiations begin only when parties start to discuss substantive issues. Everything before that is merely a preamble to the main task at hand, that is, conducting a content-focused discussion and achieving a deal.

Cultures that place greater emphasis on the development of affective relationships and building trust frequently see negotiations as involving a wider range of interpersonal or intergroup interactions, many of which must take place before substantive discussions can be held. Members of these cultures consider that negotiations begin as soon as the negotiators start communicating with each other, directly or indirectly, or meet face-to-face. For example, in Chinese commerce, "Negotiation sessions are preceded and punctuated by banquets and often karaoke sessions. These are used to strengthen relationships among the Chinese, to build trust, flatter associates and provide an ambience in which to talk about the negotiation in a relaxed way" (Blackman, 1998, p. 47).

This discrepancy of views regarding when negotiations begin can cause intercultural problems. One party keeps wondering why the other wants to take time for all this small talk or social interaction, and his counterpart wonders why the other is so brash as to keep pushing to talk about substantive issues when a positive relationship has not yet been firmly established. To begin to address these potential problems, we look at possible procedures for making first contacts and engaging in the first face-to-face meeting.

MAKING FIRST CONTACTS

Starting negotiations requires one or more negotiators to make contact with a prospective counterpart.

Contacts Prior to Face-to-Face Meetings or Negotiations

Contacts may be made directly or with the assistance of an intermediary. Direct contacts between individuals or groups who do not know each other are frequent in cultures where there are fewer differences in rank and status among members. In such cases, differences that do exist are played down, in keeping with a value of egalitarianism, and direct dealing and direct communications are the norm. In some such cultures, members of the society came historically from diverse ethnic backgrounds or subcultures and have had to deal directly with each other in order to get things done. For example, businesspeople from the majority cultures in the United States and Australia, both immigrant societies with citizens from diverse ethnic backgrounds, generally feel comfortable directly contacting unknown counterparts within their own culture or that of the other country to discuss business or political issues. Unless there is an extreme difference over topics that need to be discussed, intermediaries are considered to be unnecessary.

Unlike cultures where direct contacts are acceptable, other cultures typically expect intermediaries to set up first meetings. In these cultures, direct requests for meetings or negotiations by unknown persons in all likelihood will be ignored until a more appropriate means of contact is used.

China, Indonesia, and Japan are cultures where go-betweens or intermediaries are often used to open doors for initial discussions and possible subsequent negotiations. There are several reasons for cultural preferences regarding intermediary assistance in starting talks. For some cultures, negotiations and agreements are undertaken predominantly with people who are known quantities and share common networks of family, friends, or associates. To gain access to this network, outsiders need a person trusted by the member of the more closed culture to introduce them and possibly vouch for their integrity as a potential counterpart. In other cultures, intermediaries are used to bridge status gaps, where rank and status differences among members are often great and people of different ranks, especially those of lower status, do not readily initiate communications directly with superiors. Outsiders, whose rank and status are often unknown, need an intermediary to help manage status differences. This is especially the case in cultures where outsiders are seen as inferior to members of a self-perceived high-status culture.

Negotiating relationships with outsiders in these cultures are often initially established with the help of a mutually known, accepted, and trusted intermediary. An example of this role is the function of the *shokai-sha*, or introducer/go-between common in Japanese business negotiations. Contacts through the *shokai-sha* will help determine whether initial discussions can be set up to help parties determine if a positive future working relationship is feasible or desirable. At the *shokai-sha*'s suggestion, the Japanese firm will invite representatives from the other firm, generally midlevel managers, along with the *shokai-sha* for late afternoon tea at the Japanese company's offices. Tea is generally served in a fairly informal setting, with parties sitting in a room with chairs and one or more low coffee tables, or around a small table. The informal conversation is principally around nontask social and relationship-building issues designed to introduce the parties to each other and help them evaluate each other's character. About 6:00 P.M., the Japanese may suggest dinner and make reservations at a restaurant. Generally the hosting party pays for the meal. If Japanese hosts do not suggest dinner, it usually means that they do not want to proceed with negotiations, or at least not at this time (Hodgson, Graham, and Sano, 2000; Graham and Sano, 1979).

By making contact through a trusted intermediary, the parties can explore indirectly the potential for a future working relationship with a counterpart, minimize undue risks, prevent either party from losing face if a face-to-face meeting or long-term relationship does not emerge, and avoid either party's making premature commitments before the true intentions or character of counterparts are known. We discuss more about the potential roles and functions of intermediaries in Chapters Fourteen and Fifteen.

Given these two cultural extremes of cultures where hierarchical and power distance is high or low and members of the cultures are either indirect or direct-dealing, what strategies should be used to initiate initial contacts?

SUGGESTED STRATEGIES FOR COORDINATING INITIAL CONTACTS

- Determine if the culture of your counterpart is either hierarchical, with significant values and practices regarding behavior of or toward people or groups of different status, or fairly egalitarian.

- Assess whether the counterpart is more direct or indirect dealing when it comes to communication about important issues or those about which there may be significant differences or tension.

- If the counterpart's culture is fairly egalitarian and direct dealing, a direct contact may be acceptable. However, determine which means of initial contact are preferred in the counterpart's culture. In writing with a request for a meeting? By a formal or informal letter? Or will an e-mail do? Is a direct phone call acceptable? A letter followed up by a phone call?

- If a direct contact does not accomplish the desired result, consider using an intermediary who is trusted by your counterpart to make a connection or introductions for you.

- If the counterparts are unknown and their culture is fairly hierarchical and indirect dealing, consider using an intermediary to make a first contact for you. Generally the intermediary selected should be someone your counterparts trust but also has your confidence.

- Ask the intermediary to approach your counterpart, explain your organizational and personal background, what you want to accomplish through a meeting, and vouch for your integrity and capacity to follow through on any future agreements that might be reached. Note that what the intermediary relays about a party and his or her qualities depends on what the member of the counterpart's culture needs to hear in order to open discussions.

First Direct Contact Prior to Formal Meetings

Depending on the situation and culture, the first face-to-face contacts between a negotiator and her counterpart may take place before formal negotiations and at a different site. This might be a greeting at an airport or a social occasion. Because of different cultural expectations regarding when negotiations actually begin, it is important to develop a strategy for this first face-to-face encounter. Regardless of when members of cultures believe that negotiations begin, it is safe to assume that each party will be sizing the other up and making initial judgments about their counterpart before substantive discussions start. These initial meetings, no matter how brief, are often critical in shaping how counterparts view each other, and they can affect later negotiations (Gladwell, 2005).

Negotiators from task-oriented cultures, where socialization with counterparts prior to discussions is not common, often see this social time as unnecessary, merely going through formalities, or a waste of time. However, negotiators from relationship-oriented cultures view such social occasions as a valuable investment in a trusting relationship, which they consider to be critical for later substantive talks. Even at the level of simple trade, Sanger (2002) notes that shopkeepers in a number of cultures and countries go out of their way to welcome potential customers into their shops and build relationships before beginning substantive transactional talks:

> They often offer something to drink, typically tea. If it is a slow day, they will even sit down and drink tea with a customer themselves. I have encountered merchants who insisted on giving me a tour of their houses (which are often adjacent to their shops) before we began negotiations. One took me up on his roof to show me the view. One insisted we play a friendly game of backgammon before setting about negotiating over the price of the backgammon set. Others have introduced me to their children. Another even had me meet the animals the family owned including a cow, and several chickens [Sanger, 2002, p. 234].

In some cultures, carefully organized socializing may take hours or even days, and it may be initiated by one or more of the parties for a variety of reasons. They may be conducted so that counterparts can get to know each other personally and develop personal trust. They can also be designed to encourage participants to be more at ease with each other, and possibly let down their guard and disclose important information. Informal interactions may be used to conduct informal sounding about views on upcoming negotiation issues. Finally, they may allow the hosting party to demonstrate respect for the visitor. In some cases, this may establish expectations for future reciprocity due to the social exchanges that have been made or the care for creature comforts that have been provided. Many travelers have noted this dynamic among carpet sellers from Turkey to Afghanistan. Drinking tea, meeting the family, spending lots of time, and unrolling many carpets for the customer to peruse set up expectations that the visitor will buy, the merchant will make a sale, and each will gain "a new friend." Similar dynamics can occur in more complex negotiations as well.

The context, venue, and timing for socializing can be quite varied, depending on the cultural norms for prenegotiation activities and the kinds of talks that are to be conducted. Opportunities for socializing may include informal meetings over coffee, tea, or alcoholic drinks; having a meal together at a fine restaurant, a banquet hall, or the host's home; going on a historical or cultural tour or field trip, often to impress the visiting negotiator about the importance, longevity, and strength of the culture of the counterpart; attending a traditional cultural performance or engaging in a sporting event; or engaging in a prenegotiation cultural ritual common in the host's culture.

An example of a prenegotiation ritual can be seen in the culture of the Maori peoples of New Zealand. There negotiations traditionally begin either when Maoris are negotiating with each other or pakiha, non-Maoris, with the parties engaging in elaborate greeting rituals, especially when talks are to be held in a *marae,* the traditional Maori meeting house. The hosting party generally meets the visiting party outside the *marae* and verbally challenges the visitors to state their intentions. Once an explanation has been shared and demonstrated by respectfully picking up an object that has been thrown down on the ground by the hosting party as a test of sincerity, each party briefly begins to tell the story of their historic relationships with each other, often describing both positive and negative interconnections. If positive connections are recognized, parties may rub noses and "share breath," and then enter the *marae,* where stories and discussion of connections continue. After a period of time, one of the parties may raise a substantive issue of concern and the groups will begin to discuss it. Talks may be extensive, and a meal may be served and consumed in the course of deliberations (Tauroa and Tauroa, 1986).

SUGGESTED STRATEGIES FOR COORDINATING FIRST DIRECT CONTACTS

If You Are the Host

- Identify your norms and those of your counterpart regarding first face-to-face contacts and where and how such meetings might take place.

- As the host, examine your own cultural norms for first contacts, and try to determine how they will be received by your counterpart. If they are likely to be understood and well received, proceed to adhere to your common practices.

- Consider activities and times for socializing that will be comfortable and pleasurable for your counterpart, as well as provide opportunities for you to achieve other relationship-oriented goals.

- If you are the host and determine that adherence to your cultural norms may have an adverse impact on your counterparts or their views toward you, your organization, or your culture, consider how your practices for first contacts might need to be modified to achieve a more positive impact on the visiting negotiator.

If You Are the Visiting Negotiator

- Consider whether you will try to avoid complying with norms for first meetings that you are not comfortable with, adhere to your own cultural norms, adapt or adopt those of your counterpart, or introduce new behaviors or activities for the first contacts.

- If you are from a task-oriented culture and your host is from a relationship-oriented culture, be prepared to engage in extensive social activities prior to formal negotiations. Delay initiation of substantive discussions until your host indicates that it is time to shift to this focus. In relationship-oriented cultures, substantive discussions may begin to happen very informally and in the context of socializing. When substantive sounding does begin, take this as an indication that your counterpart is beginning to feel more comfortable about his relationship with you and has started to informally probe your views on the potential for and content of upcoming substantive talks.

- If you are from a relationship-oriented culture and your host is from a task-oriented culture, you may be asked to engage in substantive discussions before you feel ready, that is, before relationship-building activities have taken place. Consider whether you want to propose some form of interaction to meet your needs for getting to know one another, even if such interactions are very brief from your point of view.

First Negotiation Meetings: Physical Arrangements and Entry

Meetings of some sort are the normal forum for negotiations. They may be formal sessions with a high degree of protocol and held in formal settings; moderately formal talks, such as when midlevel counterparts of similar rank and status meet with each other in one of their offices or a conference room; or informal conversations, such as when counterparts meet for coffee, drinks, a meal in a bar or a restaurant or a nightclub, or just sitting and chatting under a tree or taking a walk together.

The venue for first-face-to-face contacts, and how people begin interacting in them, is usually influenced by the cultures of the negotiators. However, there are also occasions when negotiations take place in accordance with a set of norms that are from none of the cultures involved. For instance, many negotiations in the diplomatic realm follow international norms, which, while arising from Western diplomatic practice, are generally accepted by the entire diplomatic community. Before discussing the actual agenda and content of first meetings, we will address the location and physical setup of the negotiation venue and entry of negotiators into the venue.

Location and Physical Setup of the Negotiation Venue. The venue and the physical setup of the space for negotiations are determined by the kind of deliberations that are expected to occur. Many negotiations take place in quite informal and public environments. Examples are haggling in a public market with a street vender; making a sale or purchase in a shop with a public audience; deal making at a teahouse, coffee shop, or restaurant; serious discussions of conflict issues while sitting side by side on a log outside a local church (the experience of one of our colleagues working on conflicts among indigenous communities in Nicaragua); or negotiating with military or militias for safe passage at a checkpoint along a road during times of war. Kapuściśnski (2002) describes the touchiness of the venue and related encounters during the civil war in Angola.

On the more formal end, the venue for negotiations may be a large reception hall in a government building, meeting space at a corporate headquarters or conference center, or even in the officers' quarters at a military base where talks to formulate the Dayton Peace Accords to end the war in Bosnia were conducted. One of us participated in preliminaries to negotiations in the formal reception hall of the king of Yogyakarta in Indonesia and in another case facilitated negotiations regarding highly emotional species protection issues in Alaska, which were held on the floor of the Fairbanks Hockey Arena for 135 negotiators and 1,400 observers.

Some cultures use different venues at various times in negotiations, each designed to achieve a different purpose. Some may be oriented toward building positive social relationships, and others may be designed to promote more task-oriented goals. Hodgson, Graham, and Sano (2000) note that through a series of informal social interactions, often involving small groups and drinks at a restaurant, the Japanese are looking for integrity, sincerity, a cooperative attitude, and *wa*, a sense of harmony in a counterpart. These preconditions must be present before Japanese negotiators will proceed with the next round of relationship building and the initiation of more substantive negotiations in more formal settings.

If the right relations are established and the Japanese firm wants to pursue a relationship after the first meeting between midlevel managers, they set up an *aisatsu*, a formal greeting ceremony between the leaders of the companies. This meeting takes relationship building to the next step and symbolically moves the parties toward more substantive discussions (Hodgson, Graham, and Sano, 2000). The *aisatsu* is generally held in a medium-sized room with comfortable easy chairs spaced around the outside with low coffee tables in the middle of the room. The room setup may look informal, but it is the setting for a fairly formal Japanese meet-and-greet ritual between higher-status representatives of the two parties.

Some of the key considerations for selecting negotiation venues and their physical setup are (1) the level of informality or formality a party wants to convey to their counterparts or possible audiences by the setting; (2) the desired impacts of the venue on facilitation of social relationships or the accomplishment of substantive tasks; (3) the extent that privacy, intimacy, or openness to public scrutiny is important; (4) the need to emphasize or minimize the rank and status of different participants; and (5) the degree that proximity or distance between participants will either induce agreement making or possibly reflect the extent of differences between the parties.

An appropriate venue and physical setup can contribute toward getting negotiations off to a good start or impose physical and psychological barriers that push counterparts apart. When former President Jimmy Carter mediated negotiations in Africa between adversaries who had been warring for years, he and his mediation team seriously considered how the venue could best be arranged to promote productive talks. The team selected a neutral venue, a conference center in which all parties would feel comfortable, and they had the halls and meeting rooms painted in colors that were thought to convey tranquility and collaboration. His staff even put paintings on the wall that contributed to relaxation and cooperation.

A negotiator who is hosting talks should seriously consider what kind of venue will likely produce the desired result and impact on a counterpart. If the goal is to make the counterpart comfortable and cooperative and develop a positive relationship, one kind of venue may be selected. If the goal is to convey authority and power, another may be more appropriate.

The Entry of Negotiators into the Venue. Place and sequence of entry and other dynamics related to recognition of a negotiator's rank and status are important in all cultures. However, there are often differences in how they are expressed. The following vignette, which describes a formal meeting for a Japanese CEO, the vice president of an American firm, and their respective staff members, illustrates this point:

> The three representatives of the American firm and I arrived at the Japanese corporate offices at 2:00 P.M. We were greeted by a female employee in the uniform of the company who escorted us to a nearby formal meeting room. The room was furnished with sixteen expensive, but conservative, easy chairs arranged in a square with several coffee tables. We were not asked to sit, and shortly after our arrival three Japanese executives entered the room. The executives, whom I had met earlier in the week, were assigned specific management responsibilities related to the distribution of the American products. Introductions were made and business cards were exchanged, but in a relatively more formal manner than I had previously observed in other interactions with the same managers. The American vice-president was treated with obvious respect. The seven of us chatted in English about travel to Singapore and other non-task related matters.
>
> Behavioral scientists tell us that Americans are relatively uncomfortable with obvious status distinctions. As the conversation progressed it became apparent that all four Americans (including myself) were unconsciously imitating the respectful and formal behaviors of the three Japanese, thus equalizing the initial status distinctions. About the time this interpersonal equalization had been completed, three more Japanese executives entered the room. These three were members of the President's executive staff, much older than the first three (late fifties) and treated with utmost respect by the first three Japanese. Because the Americans had successfully established an ambiance of status equality with the first three Japanese, there now existed a large status gap between the Americans and the three Japanese executive staff members. This again was an uncomfortable situation for the Americans, who began to try and establish status equality with the three new Japanese executives. However, before this nonverbal status manipulation could be completed, the Japanese company president entered the room. The six Japanese already in the room acted most formally and respectfully, and thus, the status position of the Americans took another dip from which it never fully recovered.
>
> Once again business cards were exchanged and formal introductions made. One of the first three Japanese acted as an interpreter for the Japanese president, even though the president spoke and understood English. The president asked us to be seated. We seated ourselves *in exact order of rank*. The interpreter sat

on a stool between the two senior executives. The general attitude between the parties was friendly but polite. Tea and a Japanese orange drink were served [Hodgson, Graham, and Sano, 2000, pp. 4–5].

This description illustrates the cultural norms regarding the physical setup of the meeting room for the first formal face-to-face meeting, who is expected to enter the venue first (the host or the visitor), several possible sequences for entry of team members (leaders first, mixed in with other members of their team, or lower-ranking members first with individuals of higher rank entering later), and the importance of seating to indicate either the rank or equality of counterparts and their team members.

Because entry is often an important element of cultural protocol, an intercultural negotiator should consider how he wants or needs to respond to differing cultural expectations. This is especially important when negotiators and their counterparts come from cultures that differ significantly regarding norms related to hierarchy and egalitarianism.

SUGGESTED STRATEGIES FOR COORDINATING PHYSICAL SETUP AND ENTRY

- Consider the kind of venue and physical setup that your culture would expect to be used for the kind of negotiations that you are initiating. Focus on arrangements that are appropriate for the stage of negotiations that you will be conducting: early social-relationship-building activities, initial exploratory or sounding talks (in other words, talks about talking), or first formal meetings.

- Consider the possible venue norms and expectations of your counterpart for the first stages of negotiations. If they are the same as yours, proceed with what is commonly used in both cultures. If they are different, consider whether it may be desirable to change your usual preferences and attempt to meet those of your counterpart to achieve your desired goals: making the counterpart comfortable, recognizing rank and status differences, promoting privacy or openness, and so forth.

- Identify rank and status differences and the degree to which your counterpart will need these recognized. Then adjust the site and physical arrangements accordingly.

- Consider cultural norms regarding proximity and closeness, and ensure that the room setup places parties neither too close nor too far apart for intercultural comfort.

- Identify the norms regarding entry into negotiation venues for both your culture and that of your counterpart. If appropriate, consult with your counterpart or staff members regarding how they would like entry and the beginning of talks to proceed (negotiation of protocol).

- Assess the impacts on your counterpart of adhering to your own cultural norms regarding entry versus adapting to or adopting those of the other culture. Determine if adapting to or adopting the norms of your counterpart will put you at a psychological disadvantage or instead promote more productive talks. Determine if you want to adhere to your cultural norms and protocols regarding first meetings, adapt to or adopt those of your counterpart, or develop a third culture approach (such as international business or diplomatic norms).

- If you decide to adhere to your own cultural norms and your counterpart is likely to find them confusing, inappropriate, or disrespectful, consider what you can do to minimize any potential misunderstandings or negative consequences. Determine if there are ways that are culturally acceptable to you for interacting with counterparts from a hierarchical or egalitarian culture that will also convey respect for the other negotiator, his or her team, and their culture.

ACTIVITIES FOR FIRST MEETINGS

First meetings may encompass a wide range of activities depending on the people, issues, and cultures involved—for example:

- Welcoming comments, greetings, or speeches
- Introductions of individuals, team members, or other participants
- Rituals that affirm both the occurrence of the meeting and the connections being established between the parties
- Non-task-oriented talk to build or enhance relationships or to test the strengths of the parties' bonds
- Exchanges of gifts that symbolize the start of negotiation or the desire to build good working relationships among negotiators
- Expressions of willingness to engage in future substantive discussions
- Discussion of procedures for future negotiation
- General introduction of substantive issues that will be discussed in more detail in future meetings
- Formal opening statements that detail the parties' intent to engage in talks, propose processes for discussion, share general or specific views on issues, or present concrete proposals regarding issues of individual or joint concern
- Partaking of refreshments or a meal
- Watching or participating in entertainment provided by the host negotiation team

Brief descriptions of cultural approaches to some of these activities are provided next with suggestions for strategies to achieve coordination. Additional detail on openings focused on substantive issues is provided in the following chapter.

Welcoming Comments, Greetings, or Speeches

Most negotiations begin with a welcome by one or more negotiators. The welcome may occur either before parties sit down to begin discussions or at the beginning of formal talks. There is quite a range of practice regarding welcoming speeches. In some cases, a senior person may attend only this initial meeting to provide his or her blessing, wishing the parties success in their efforts. In some cases, only the host will offer a welcome. In others, a spokesperson or team leader of each team will make a welcoming statement. In some settings, it is expected that each person will make a brief welcoming comment. Welcoming comments may be brief and to the point, or quite long in duration, lasting up to an hour or more.

In welcoming statements, different cultures emphasize the psychological and relationship, procedural, or substantive issues to be addressed in future interactions.

- *Psychological and relationship welcomes.* These statements include recognition of existing connections between the parties; affirmation of positive feelings between them; recognition of the importance, rank, or status of a counterpart; emphasis on the importance of current or future talks; and expressions of goodwill or hope. The example of the first meetings between Maori delegations to negotiations or between Maoris and *pakiha* described earlier in this chapter illustrates this kind of psychological or relationship opening.

Negotiators from many West African nations often use elaborate psychological or relationship openings in interpersonal meetings, informal talks, and more formal negotiations, especially if a conflict is not at issue:

The course and temperature of the first greeting are of the utmost significance to the ultimate fate of the relationship, which is why people set much store by the way they salute each other. It is essential to exhibit from the very beginning, from the very first second, enormous, primal joy and geniality. So for starters, one extends one's hand. But not in a formal manner, reticently, limply; just the opposite—a large, vigorous gesture, as if one's intention were not so much to offer one's hand, as to tear the other's off. If, however, the other manages to keep his hand, whole and in its proper place, it is because, understanding the ritual roles of greeting, he has likewise executed the same broad, forceful gesture. Both of these extremities, bursting with tremendous energy, now meet halfway and, with a terrifying impact of collision, cancel out the two opposing forces. Simultaneously, as the hands are rushing toward each other, the two individuals share a prolonged cascade of loud laughter. It is meant to signify that each is happy to be meeting and warmly disposed to the other.

There ensues a long list of questions and answers, such as "How are you? Are you feeling well? How is your family? Are they all healthy? And your grandfather? And your grandmother? And your aunt? And your uncle?—and so forth and so on, for families here are large with many branches. Custom dictates that each positive answer be offered with yet another torrent of loud and vibrant laughter, which in turn should elicit a similar or perhaps even more Homeric cascade from the one posing the questions....

...If the laughter dies down, then either the act of greeting has come to an end and they will now move on to the substance of the conversation, or, simply, the newly met have fallen silent to allow their tired vocal chords a moment's respite [Kapuściński, 2002, pp. 29–30].

More formal meetings in these cultures often begin with the host or a specially designated person making a long and elaborate speech that recognizes the status of all parties involved. He or she may use multiple honorifics to describe the fine character of the participants, their past achievements, and the importance of their presence and involvement in current talks. In addition, the speaker may emphasize the value that he or she places on the meeting, the significance of the issues that will be discussed, and the importance to all concerned that the talks be successful. These greetings, while ostensibly focusing on the counterpart and future interactions with the counterpart, are also designed to bring honor to both those being welcomed and the speaker and his or her group.

A classic example of this greeting process occurred at the opening of the fiftieth anniversary conference of the African National Congress in South Africa. At this meeting, held to select the next executive committee, "a huge praise-singer in tribal costume pranced into the hall, chanting extravagant compliments with long vowels which slowly expired like a siren. In the silence that followed, Mandela appeared in his yellow shirt, walking slowly to the platform. A row of interdenominational priests blessed the conference, including the veterans of the struggle" (Sampson, 1999, p. 541).

Greetings in negotiations involving Chinese, especially those from the People's Republic of China, may also involve rituals that stress the importance of the relationship between the involved parties and the significance of the meeting. Chinese negotiators in their opening remarks often emphasize the importance of establishing bilateral friendships and enduring relationships characterized by trust and mutual respect. The opening is both a statement of the goal of future talks and a strong appeal for reciprocity from the counterpart—both to reciprocate with a similar verbal statement and to work toward achieving the Chinese definition of friendship.

Northern European and American negotiators generally make less elaborate welcoming statements that serve similar psychological and relationship purposes. They often stress similar points as those identified by Africans, but in a much abbreviated form and with fewer rhetorical flourishes.

• *Procedurally focused* welcomes or greetings. In contrast to the psychological and relationship openings, procedurally focused welcomes or greetings, while noting the importance of relationships and desired substantive outcomes, emphasize the need for discussion of procedures for the upcoming talks. This kind of welcome is characteristic of low-context cultures that are more explicit about negotiation processes or that place high value on transparency and procedural fairness. A negotiator using this approach for greeting a counterpart, after briefly welcoming the other team and introducing his or her own members, might proceed to say, "We truly welcome the opportunity to hold these upcoming talks and trust that they will be conducted in good faith by all involved. We expect that we will all engage in talks with open minds and that we will be forthcoming with data needed to make wise decisions. We trust that the process will show respect for all participants, enable us to explore each of our respective interests, and provide space for generating solutions that will meet all interests to the greatest extent possible. In our future discussions, we will describe the procedures that we would like to use for negotiations and outline a sequence of steps that we believe will lead to successful problem solving."

• *Substantive welcomes or greetings*. These openings spend time detailing the topics or issues that will be discussed in negotiations rather than focusing on relationship and psychological or procedural issues. In this approach, after a brief introduction and acknowledgment of the other participants, the speaker moves rapidly to an outline of substantive issues to be discussed or even concrete offers. This type of greeting might include the following topics:

◇ The history of the issues or problem to be discussed

◇ A listing of issues to be addressed

◇ The importance of the issues to one or all parties

◇ A description of the general or specific interests of one or more parties (either independent of or in association with specific issues)

◇ An outline of principles that might guide selection of solutions

◇ Possible options for consideration for settlement of issues or resolution of a conflict

◇ Specific offers, proposals, or positions to address concerns or satisfy interests

While we have discussed psychological and relationship, procedural, and substantive focuses for welcomes and greetings separately, many cultures blend the three, placing more or less emphasis on each depending on the culture or the type of negotiations to be conducted. The mix is dependent on the cultural orientations of the involved negotiators and what they expect to achieve at this stage of the negotiation.

Regardless of the form that welcoming statements take, they usually have the most positive impact on counterparts if they are sincere, genuinely stress the importance of discussions and the issues of concern to all parties, indicate a willingness of the speaker and his or her party to engage in good-faith discussions, express an openness to hearing the views of all parties, and indicate a commitment to find mutually acceptable and workable solutions. Welcoming statements that emphasize differences between parties, which rank them one above another or exhibit one-upmanship, generally do not promote mutually productive talks.

SUGGESTED STRATEGIES FOR COORDINATING WELCOMING STATEMENTS

- Identify the cultural norms of your counterpart regarding the content and process for making welcoming or greeting statements.

- Determine whether you will adhere to your own cultural norms regarding welcomes, or modify your response in a way that will be more culturally acceptable to your counterpart.

- If an elaborate welcome is required, spend adequate time developing one, and take care to mention all of the important persons who will be in attendance.

- Make the welcoming statement as positive as is realistically possible, given the importance of the issues that will be discussed.

- Consider who is the most appropriate person to make the welcoming statement and from whom it will best be received by your counterpart: the spokesperson or team leader, an authoritative decision maker, the most senior member of the team, a man or a woman, and so forth.

Introduction of Individuals, Team Members, or Other Participants

Either after or prior to welcoming comments or speeches, parties usually take time to introduce the participants in negotiations. Obviously introductions may be forgone if all of the parties know each other or have worked or negotiated with one another before.

What is included in introductions and how they are made is often culturally determined by the status and rank of the person making the introduction in their society or organization, what individual negotiators consider to be important to convey about themselves, and what they think a counterpart needs to know about them. A number of years ago, one of us was working with the staff of the Sri Lankan Ministry of Justice to set up a new nationwide mediation system. At the first meeting between the Sri Lankan and U.S. team members, individuals were asked by the Americans to introduce themselves. The Americans first made brief introductions, about three minutes each, describing where they came from, their organization, and a bit about their experience as mediators and setting up similar systems. The Sri Lankans introduced themselves by telling their family history, where they had attended university, what they had studied, the degrees they had received, a complete job history, and a description of the role they hoped to play in the new project. Each individual's introduction took more than twenty minutes! Similarly, one of us facilitated an interactive workshop with participants from all over the world. The Americans and Europeans generally introduced themselves in a minute or less, while the participants from South Asia and Africa were quite expansive, taking up to ten minutes each.

Depending on how they are seen by the person making them, what they want or do not want to convey to a counterpart, or what they are asked by a counterpart to communicate, introductions may serve a variety of purposes. They can:

- Provide a name to the face of a counterpart
- Give a title that describes what the individual does or responsibilities in the organization they represent
- Indicate the rank or status of the negotiator and how he or she fits into the team or organization participating in negotiations—as well as in relation to counterparts
- Define the formal role that the person will play during negotiations, such as spokesperson, facilitative spokesperson, technical expert, or recorder
- Indicate (possibly) the role the individual will play in team or organizational decision making
- Provide information on the educational background and expertise of the individual
- Present personal or family information about the individual (family background, parents, spouse, children and their ages, and so on)
- Give information about the groups to which the individual belongs or is affiliated with (family, kinship group, clan, tribe, honorific or secret societies, ethnic group, religious group, firm, organization, regional grouping, political party, country)

- Establish voice legitimacy in negotiations—that is, give each person a chance to speak, which can encourage later participation

In some cultures and situations, only senior people who will be directly engaged in negotiations and will be speakers are introduced. It is not unusual in these situations for a team spokesperson to avoid introducing his or her team members, saying rather, "The rest of the people you see here are members of my team. They are from relevant departments concerned about the agreement or will be involved in its implementation."

On occasion, the real decision maker may be neither the spokesperson for the team nor directly identified as the team's superior. However, this person will be in the room and able to observe negotiations. This pattern has been observed in some negotiations between Chinese from the People's Republic of China and negotiators from the West, or in high-conflict situations where the party that perceives itself to be in the weaker position is unwilling to take the risk of identifying its real leader to its counterpart. Depending on the situation, counterparts will need to decide if it is important for them to know the names and roles of all of the people present or if they will accept the structuring of participation in negotiations proposed by their counterpart.

Since introductions are one of the early places where negotiators can begin coordination with each other, care should be taken when considering how to make them and what kinds of introductions will help promote the best results.

SUGGESTED STRATEGIES FOR COORDINATING INTRODUCTIONS

- Conduct background research on how members of your counterpart's culture commonly make introductions—who makes them, in what order, what they think is important to say, what they want to hear, how long they usually take, and so forth.

- Decide how you and other members of your culture will make introductions and whether your norms are likely to be acceptable to your counterpart. Try to model similar levels of information and disclosure on that provided by your counterpart.

- Pay special attention to norms regarding rank and status when making introductions and whether senior people usually speak first or last.

- If the members of the culture that you are negotiating with are organized in a strong hierarchy, consider mirroring their sequence of introductions so that people on your team of corresponding rank and status are introduced in a similar way and sequence.

- Develop an opening statement that will be culturally acceptable to your counterpart and will provide this individual or the team with information that you think they would like to know.

- Avoid making introductions that your counterpart will dislike: bragging, exaggerating experiences, stating long lists of accomplishments, or putting significant emphasis on you as an individual over your group, unless these behaviors are culturally appropriate. In general, try to avoid one-upmanship when making introductions, because this behavior tends to create competition with other team members or with counterparts.

Building Working Relationships and Trust

In previous chapters, we explored a range of orientations toward creating and enhancing relationships between negotiators. At the beginning stage of negotiations, this process may only be getting started. Attitudes and behaviors exhibited by individual negotiators, team leaders, or members of teams at this stage of the process often have a disproportionate impact on future discussions. For this reason, great care must be taken to continue to build good working relationships. This may involve spending extensive time in social activities or engaging in relationship-building conversations. For example, in Islamic cultures, "one of the most important ways to build trust...is to conduct a leisurely conversation prior to discussing the issues themselves. Such conversation fulfills yet another objective of the early stages of negotiation, which is information gathering. If the trust-building conversation is successful, the particular information needed may be made available in a rather short time" (Alon and Brett, 2007, p. 61).

SUGGESTED STRATEGIES FOR COORDINATING RELATIONSHIP BUILDING

- Demonstrate nonverbally—by culturally appropriate eye contact, nodding appreciatively, leaning forward toward the person who is speaking, sitting still and not fidgeting, and not engaging in activities that indicate inattention—that you are listening attentively to what is being said.

- Avoid facial expressions such as staring at the counterpart without periodic breaks in eye contact; scowling; frowning; looking at the ceiling or floor; closing your eyes (although Japanese counterparts may do this), which can be perceived through the counterpart's cultural lens as indicating lack of interest; immediate disagreement; or hostility to what is being said or conveyed.

- Restate from time to time and in your own words what you have heard to show that the speaker has been heard and to give him or her an opportunity to confirm that you have understood accurately. However, avoid interrupting the speaker's presentation to do this.

- Ask occasional questions about what has been said, with the goal of increasing understanding and not challenging, demeaning, or objecting.

- Identify specific procedures that may be needed for future discussions, ask for procedural suggestions, or make proposals for alternative approaches that could be used.

- Avoid becoming positional about possible procedures that may be used or engaging in "process fights."

Initiating Discussions on Substantive, Procedural, or Relationship Issues

Parties enter negotiations with varying understanding of the topics to be addressed and how they are expressed (framing, discussed in Chapter Four). They also have different levels of information about their specific issues, interests, and preferred solutions and those of other negotiators. In some situations, issues and outcome possibilities may be clear, and negotiators will have to spend little time exploring details. In other cases, parties may lack information on a number of dimensions. Young (1972) notes that at the beginning of negotiations, a negotiator may be unclear about:

- The basic issue(s) at stake
- The range of alternative choices or strategies available
- The solutions that will best meet his or her interests or needs
- The number and identity of people who should be involved in the negotiations (or whom they will affect)
- The way that other negotiators will make decisions [p. 57].

The negotiating parties can gain a better grasp of these questions through early discussion of procedural or relationship-oriented issues.

Opening Statements

In formal negotiations, parties typically each make an opening statement. The emphases of such statements vary tremendously in terms of their focus on substance, procedure, or relationships. We will examine each of these strategies below.

Opening Statements Focused on Substance. The most common, but not always the most effective, way to open negotiations is to focus immediately on substantive issues to be discussed. In this approach, the negotiator elaborates on one or more topics. Moore (2003) and Lincoln (1981) list the common components used by negotiators who open with a focus on substance, and we examine each of these:

- Focus on presentation of history, need for a change, and position
- Focus on identification of issues and background facts

- Focus on issues and merit for change
- Focus on issues, priorities, preferences, and interests
- Focus on issue and presentation of an offer or position

Focus on Presentation of History, Need for a Change, and Position This combi-nation is quite common in many situations and cultures. The negotiator first reviews the background of the problem or dispute, describes the status quo (and in disputes why it has caused damage), identifies why changes are needed or desirable, and then, optionally, proceeds to detail an opening position that he or she feels would address or solve the presenting problem. This type of opening frequently forces the parties into positional bargaining.

Focus on Identification of Issues and Background Facts In some cases, a negotiator may dispense with a description of the history of the problem and proceed directly to identify the issues that he or she wants to discuss and pro-vide some of the relevant data related to them that will lay the groundwork for further talks. Issues and relevant background information may be presented in several ways:

- Defined only generally or vaguely and ultimately left for each negotiator to flesh out in later discussion
- Presented briefly in the form of a list of topics to be discussed with rela-tively little detail on each item
- Presented in an exhaustive manner that provides significant information on each

Vaguer or more general presentations of issues usually occur in cultures where it is not the norm to be direct or explicit, or in situations where a party wants to move more cautiously into substantive discussions. Many Asian, African, and indigenous cultures follow this pattern, as do cultures where there are significant power differences between parties or where honor or face saving is important.

Brief and explicit listing of topics is common in cultures that like to proceed to rapid and direct structured problem solving. U.S. negotiators often start with a listing of issues and provide lots of facts in a direct manner before beginning to explore positions, options, or possible solutions.

Focus on Issues and Merit for Change The negotiator introduces a topic for discussion and then focuses on educating her counterpart about why a change is necessary. Often the presenter avoids any detailed clarification of interests or presentation of a position or proposed solution until she feels that the counterpart has been convinced that the status quo needs to change. The assumption behind this strategy is that if a party can make a convincing case that the current situation is intolerable and that change is needed, reaching later agreement on a particular solution will be easier.

Focus on Issues, Priorities, Preferences, and Interests The negotiator identifies an issue or issues to be addressed and then details the substantive, procedural, or psychological or relationship interests that must be satisfied through negotiations. Focusing on interests instead of positions prepares the ground for possible interest-based negotiations and joint development of mutually acceptable solutions, although it does not guarantee this outcome. (See Chapter Four for a description of interest-based negotiations.)

Focus on Issue and Presentation of an Offer or Position The negotiator may dispense with any discussion of the history, the merits for change, or a description of interests. Rather, the negotiator briefly states an issue and immediately presents a preferred solution or position to settle it. Such a position may or may not be negotiable. At times, the negotiator presents an extreme position to educate the counterpart about how important the topic is to the presenter or about important interests. However, this style of opening can lead to a stalemate or even a walkout if the opening position is seen as too extreme. It also provides little information about why a solution is being proposed and makes it harder to explore other options that might satisfy the interests in another way.

Influences on Substantive Openings. Several factors influence the focus and content of substantive openings whether (1) a negotiator is from a low- or high-context culture (see Chapter Four); (2) the focus of negotiations is transactional (business) or the resolution of a dispute; (3) the parties are dealing with a single or multiple topics; (4) the issues at stake and potential outcomes are perceived to be either distributive or integrative in nature; and (5) one or both parties have sufficient power and influence to advocate for their preferred solution.

In general, when negotiations are focused on resolving a dispute, at least initially only a few central issues will be in question. When potential outcomes are more likely to be distributive than integrative or one party has significant influence, both parties are more likely to emphasize substantive openings and present positions or offers early in the process. Proposals are put forward to make demands, educate a counterpart, or serve as reference points from which negotiators may later make modifications or offer concessions. However, when negotiations are more transactional in nature, multiple issues are under discussion, there is potential for integrative outcomes, or parties want to downplay the exercise of power or coercive means of influence, negotiators pursue a varied range of approaches for presenting substantive issues.

In a comparative study of U.S. and Japanese transactional negotiations and strategies, Adair, Weingart, and Brett (2007) found that American bargainers (from a low-context culture) reach agreements with higher joint gains when they focus early in negotiations on information exchange about their specific priorities and preferences and those of their counterparts, and defer taking positions or making offers until later in talks, when the parties are better informed about each other's interests. U.S. negotiators, like those from the United Kingdom, tend to move fairly rapidly to identifying key issues and presenting detailed information about them.

In contrast, Japanese negotiators (from a high-context culture) ultimately reach settlements with greater joint gains when they present only tentative offers early in talks and then follow them up with a series of subsequent trial offers that are constantly modified based on information or comments provided by their counterpart. Japanese negotiators tend to use tentative proposal making as a way to share and gain information about their own priorities, preferences, and interests and those of their counterpart. They also use them to conduct informal testing regarding what options are acceptable. Interestingly, unlike many bargainers from low-context cultures, Japanese negotiators do not seem to become anchored inflexibly to their early offers or positions. They view presentation and discussion of offers as an important form of information exchange.

Let's examine the orientation of several other cultures toward substantive openings. Direct and rapid substantive openings in formal negotiations are common for French (Cogan, 2003), German (Smyser, 2003), and Russian negotiators (Schecter, 1998; Smith, 1989). Slower substantive openings are more common among Chinese (Solomon, 1999) and Japanese negotiators (Blaker, 1977a, 1977b; Hodgson, Graham, and Sano, 2000) and people from more traditional cultures.

French negotiators generally want to speak first and seize the initiative in talks. They believe that if they can frame the discussion and present concrete positions to address the issues, their approach will drive the agenda and give them additional leverage to achieve their goals (Cogan, 2003). The presentation itself is made in the form of a long speech that details their position on the issues. "The French mind-set is 'positional'; that is French negotiators come to the table with a clear idea of what is to be their final position" (Cogan, 2003, p. 120). They generally present their position, the solution that they are advocating to meet French interests, in a forceful, logical, and eloquent manner. They begin with an opening focused on principles, followed by a presentation of the facts, and a finally a summary in which they advocate what they see as the only logical conclusion: their position. Their logical approach is highly deductive, that is, they move from general principles to a final logical conclusion. They tend to save their most important point until the end of their speech. In the early stages of negotiations, French negotiators are often more interested in presenting their views than listening to and understanding the interests of their counterpart.

German negotiators generally consider their opening remarks to be the most important in the negotiation process. In a substantive opening, the first concept to be presented is the *Gesamtkonzept,* the governing principle that provides the logic for specific points advocated in their overall position, and it forms the framework for all subsequent discussions and negotiations. The *Gesamtkonzept* is presented in a manner that covers the most important issues to be discussed in negotiations, outlines the desirable outcomes, and demonstrates how it meets both the counterpart's interests and needs as well as German interests. The presentation of the *Gesamtkonzept* is almost always very detailed, because German negotiators want their counterpart to understand and accept the concept. Early mutual agreement on the governing concept is very important, because all following discussions about options flow from concurrence on this overarching principle:

> When they present their positions, German negotiators do not normally play shadow games. Nor do they waste time. They state their views openly and plainly. They have no mysteries and do not try to keep their proposals opaque. What you see is what you get. They know what they want. They do not try to present one position in order to advance another. They do not normally use devious tactics, such as presenting false issues as a tactical ploy while planning to drop those issues at the first opportunity. They simply outline, sometimes at staggering length and in painstaking detail, what they believe they can legitimately claim on the basis of the concept they have presented [Smyser, 2003, p. 74].

After the presentation and what Germans believe is a tentative agreement on the *Gesamtkonzept,* they may proceed with outlining subsequent issues and their initial positions. These too will be presented with similar thoroughness and detail as that used for the governing concept.

Russian negotiators commonly open negotiations with a focus on substance and an effort to seize the initiative, but their approach is different from the French. Russians often request that their counterpart provide an opening position and then proceed to counter it. In taking an opening stance, "Russian negotiators never open discussions with a position close to the final position. Russians rarely make an attempt to establish a mutual framework of agreement: rather they wait for the other side to reveal its position, and then, relying on carefully prepared instructions, open with a maximal demand. They make a concerted effort to intimidate their negotiating partner and establish a position of dominance and superiority" (Schecter, 1998, p. 68).

Chinese negotiators rarely open with a detailed focus on substance and, like Russians, often want their counterpart to make the first move or proposal. This cultural pattern is well illustrated by the beginning of negotiations between Chinese officials and Henry Kissinger in 1971. Zhou Enlai, the host, said to Kissinger, "According to our custom, we first invite our guest to speak. Besides you have already prepared a thick [briefing] book. Of course, later on we will give our opinions also" (Solomon, 1999, p. 76).

Openings Focused on Procedure. Another way of opening negotiations, which is not as common as direct substantive openings, is to focus on the negotiation procedures, which lay the groundwork for later substantive discussions. (See the list of procedural issues in Box 5.1.) Moore (2003) and Lincoln (1981) identified a number of advantages to opening negotiations by engaging both or all negotiation teams in a joint discussion about the procedures to be used in the negotiation process. (Clearly this is applicable only if the negotiation process will be either a single quite extended session or multiple sessions. Time and energy spent on procedural questions is rarely needed for short and simple interactions.) A procedural opening:

- Provides a jointly developed sequence for the negotiation to which all parties are committed
- Allows the parties to practice making decisions as a team
- Provides information about the behavior, attitudes, and trustworthiness of the other parties
- Allows parties to practice making agreements on problems that are neither substantively important nor as emotionally charged as the issues in dispute
- Provides an opportunity to build habits of agreement
- Demonstrates that agreement is possible and that the situation is not hopeless

Procedural openings that address specific stages and tasks to be achieved during talks are common in many diplomatic negotiations, where parties need to lay an adequate framework before commencing substantive discussions. They are also common in cultures that are highly aware of process, deem explicitness about procedures to be important, and emphasize transparency or involvement in determining how issues will be tackled. For example, American, British, and German negotiators (from low-context cultures) tend to place more emphasis on making process decisions explicit in negotiations than do their counterparts from high-context cultures, such as France, Japan, China, some Latin American countries, and indigenous communities. The low-context patterns of communication make the rules and assumptions about interactions more explicit. Members of the high-context cultures are also deeply concerned about process, but they have little or no need to engage in transparent discussion about it, as the rules and assumptions are "understood" in the context.

Openings Focused on the Psychological Conditions or Relationships of Disputants. This approach aims to improve the relationship of the disputants either before or as a major element in discussions of substantive issues or procedures. Openings focused on relationships usually involve statements affirming the past or current relationships of the parties, expression of positive expectations for the future, and emphasizing the value of building productive working relationships as a means of achieving mutual benefits. Psychological and relationship openings are usually followed by a shift to substantive discussions using one of the approaches already described.

Indigenous cultures and those that rely extensively on good relationships to establish trust and long-term compliance with agreements that are reached often spend considerable time at the beginning of negotiations discussing relationship-oriented issues: reviewing past connections among the parties, affirming friendships, stating visions for future relationships, sharing common experiences (meals, drinks, entertainment), or performing rituals that affirm connections. Maori greeting rituals and Chinese or African speeches that affirm friendly relations are examples of these kinds of openings.

Selecting the Focus of an Opening Statement. The choice of whether to make an opening statement with a primary focus on substance, procedures, or relationship depends on:

- The relationship of the parties and level of trust among them when entering this phase of discussions
- The type of issue, problem, or conflict to be addressed
- The level of emotional intensity parties feel about each other or issues that will be discussed
- The readiness or ability of the parties to focus on substantive issues at this stage in the negotiation

The choice about an opening is made based on several considerations:

- If parties have established a degree of openness, tolerance, rapport, positive relationships, or respect prior to or during the previous stage of negotiations, consider proceeding with a substantive opening.
- If there is significant apprehension, tension, or mistrust between parties, consider making a psychological or relationship opening statement prior to focusing on substantive issues or agree to discuss procedures prior to discussing content.

- If the issue is highly tension ridden or parties are contentious, consider focusing on procedures, such as how best to discuss issues about which there is significant disagreement.

- If it appears that parties are ready and willing to discuss substantive issues, determine which kind of substantive opening will be most effective and result in further productive discussions and best help you meet your needs. Think about the potential impacts, both positive and negative, on your counterpart of each form of substantive opening.

- Assess whether your counterpart needs to hear your views on the history of issues or merits for change, and whether she wants a listing of issues for future discussion or an in-depth presentation on how you see an issue or issues.

- Determine whether it is better to focus on a presentation of your issues, some of the interests or needs that you want to have addressed and abstain at this time from putting forth proposals or positions, or whether you want to put forward a position.

- If you determine to put forth a position in your opening statement, decide whether it should be an extreme one or a maximum high demand as a tool to educate your counterparts about the importance of the issue or solution to you and encourage them to readjust their sights regarding what they will have to provide in order to reach an agreement. Alternatively, put forth a more reasonable position as an illustration of what might work for you, but indicate that if your needs or interests (which will be detailed later in discussions) can be met in other ways, you are open to exploring other options.

SUGGESTED STRATEGIES FOR COORDINATING OPENING STATEMENTS

Opening statements cause problems when one party delivers one kind of opening and the other party delivers a different one. This is common between negotiators from cultures that are oriented toward tasks or substance and negotiators from other cultures that emphasize extended relationship building and indirect or gradual exploration of substantive issues. Ideas for coordinating these issues include these:

- Consider the kind of opening statement that your counterpart might use or expect, and deliver yours in a similar manner.

- Allow your counterpart to lead in making an opening statement and illustrate the kind of opening he prefers. Then decide if you want to adopt that approach, adapt yours to that approach, adhere to your own cultural norms, or explore the development of alternative ways to lay out issues for discussion.

- Adhere to your own norms for making an opening statement, but be prepared to modify or correct it after hearing the opening of your counterpart. For example, if you make a substantive opening with an emphasis on positions and your counterpart makes an opening statement focused on relationships followed by an explanation of some of her interests, consider following up her comments with some relationship-oriented statements of your own, or reciprocating disclosure of interests by sharing some of your own.

DEEPER EXPLORATION OF THE PURPOSES OF NEGOTIATIONS

Once formal or informal opening statements have been made, it is time for negotiators to deepen their common understanding of the purpose of negotiations, clarify the issues on the table, and establish agreement on how they will be discussed. This of course assumes that parties still agree to negotiate. Occasionally relationships have been seriously damaged by remarks in an opening statement—perhaps by harsh judgments about a counterpart, unacceptable behavior, or unreasonable or extreme proposals—and one or more parties decide to break off talks.

Some of the possible general purposes of negotiations that parties may decide on and possible framings were identified in Chapter Five on preparing for negotiations. In many cases, negotiators' opening comments or statements indicate their general goals or framings. In other cases, these will not be explicit and will have to be discovered through further discussion.

At this stage of negotiations, the hope is that parties have at least a minimal common understanding of why they are engaging in talks, even though each party's framing may be somewhat different. In the context of intercultural negotiations, some possible purposes include these:

- Establishing, solidifying, or concluding relationships
- Recognizing status and demonstrating respect for parties engaged in the process
- Granting recognition and legitimacy to specific issues or concerns
- Reaching general levels of agreement on issues, with details to be worked out later
- Reaching specific and implementable agreements on one or more tangible or intangible issues
- Developing implementation strategies for substantive or procedural agreements that have been developed in earlier informal or formal talks

An example of negotiations over clarification of the purpose of negotiations occurred several years ago in the context of diversity issues within a corporation. An African American manager, who was working in the American section of an international corporation, accused the company of discriminating against him. He claimed that the company and its leaders—all of whom were white—had not given him the financial recognition and rewards that he felt he deserved. The manager threatened that if the company did not negotiate with him and address his financial demands, he would file a claim with the Equal Employment Opportunity Commission, the federal agency charged to investigate and rule on workplace discrimination cases.

The company CEO and other senior managers were shocked at the threat and felt that no discrimination had ever occurred against the complainant. In fact, they believed that since his hiring, the company had made every effort to reward him for his work, accommodate his needs, and give him raises and bonuses when others had not received them.

But there were grievances on both sides. Over the years, other managers had found the complainant difficult to work with. He had repeatedly refused to follow corporate financial procedures, clashed with accounting staff, delayed or blocked promotion of other deserving staff, and consistently disrespected and maltreated clerical staff.

Fearing that other staff might eventually file a harassment or hostile workplace suit against the corporation concerning the behavior of the complainant and having lost all trust in him, the CEO and other managers decided that they should hold discussions with the complaining manager on conditions for termination only, not financial remuneration. In this case, both parties wanted to talk about financial issues but to achieve different ends. Only after several hours of negotiations did the parties reach agreement on the purpose of the negotiations: the termination of the employment relationship.

Parties do not have to have an identical understanding of the purpose of negotiations at the beginning of talks (or, for that matter, at the end). However, their purposes must not be incompatible or mutually exclusive. If the purposes are irreconcilable, parties may need to spend some time discussing the purpose and determining if there is enough overlap to proceed—or if talks should be broken off.

SUGGESTED STRATEGIES FOR COORDINATING PURPOSES

- Listen carefully to your counterpart's opening statement. Identify what is explicitly stated or implicitly implied as the purposes of negotiations.

- Identify whether your purposes and those of your counterpart are the same, overlapping, or compatible. Identify any differences of purpose, whether they are minor or major.

- If appropriate, explicitly affirm common views regarding the purpose of negotiations. If explicitness is not the norm or acceptable to your counterpart, indicate indirectly that you are in accord with the stated purpose of negotiations. This can be done nonverbally by affirming the relationship or interaction, or by more general statements of agreement, such as, "I believe we share the same views regarding what we need to talk about."

- If you have found both agreement and differences regarding your purposes, explicitly state that commonalities exist and that you want to build on them. Then state that although there are common aims, there are also some points of divergence that you are willing to discuss.

- If the purposes for negotiations are highly divergent, determine if they are parallel, congruent, and not mutually contradictory. Even if purposes are parallel or congruent but not the same, negotiations can probably still be conducted and reach a satisfactory conclusion.

- If purposes are highly contradictory, consider whether to revise your vision of the purpose of negotiations; try to persuade your counterpart to adopt your view; continue discussions, even though there is not a common purpose to see if one evolves or can be jointly developed; or break off negotiations. Consider the viability, benefits, and cost of each strategic choice, and then implement your strategy.

Once steps have been taken to coordinate the purposes of negotiations, parties are ready to address negotiation procedures.

Reconciling the Overall Approach: Positional or Interest-Based Negotiation

Opening statements, among other things, often reveal the approach that a negotiator prefers and will likely pursue throughout talks. As discussed in Chapter Four, parties generally show a preference for positional, interest-based, or relational negotiations. They often decide among these approaches unconsciously and merely do what they have always done. However, some negotiators make a conscious and strategic choice regarding their approach based on calculations about how they can influence the outcome of talks through the use of specific procedures and tactics.

The dominant negotiation approach is generally determined by one or more parties in taking the lead to initiate a specific approach, while their counterpart accepts and mirrors it; a direct or indirect struggle over approaches, without explicit disagreements over process; or overt discussion and mutual agreement regarding how to proceed. Reconciliation of approaches may occur gradually throughout the course of talks or through an explicit decision at a specific point in time.

Coordination of negotiation approaches is a bit like synchronization between two dance partners. At times dancers meet, start to dance, and everything goes very smoothly. At other times, they fumble over moves, step on each other's feet, or even trip and fall. If one partner knows only how to waltz, a formal dance in which couples hold each other and make fairly predictable moves, and their dance partner knows only how to rock and roll, a free-flowing individualist dance style with relatively spontaneous moves, they will probably have difficulty dancing together as partners. If you want to dance together, you have some strategic options: teach (or force) your partner to learn your dance, teach your respective dances to each other so you can alternate dances, or together learn an entirely new dance that may or may not incorporate moves from each of your familiar dance styles. The choices are similar in negotiations.

If both parties use the same basic approach—positional or interest-based bargaining—they will generally have fewer problems in coordinating the process. However, if one party is using positional bargaining and the other an interest-based or relational approach, the parties may have significant trouble dancing together.

How do negotiators know which strategic approach a counterpart is using? Usually the opening statement offers the first clue. If a negotiator lists issues and advocates preferred solutions in the opening statement, there is reason to believe that he is oriented toward positional bargaining. The French positional mind-set and process for beginning negotiations as described above is a good example of this approach for opening negotiations. French negotiators tend to open with maximalist positions and present the strongest case possible for adoption by their counterpart.

Some interest-based bargainers also open by stating positions. However, they do so not to attach themselves to a maximalist position, but to educate their counterpart about the importance of the issues, demonstrate their resolve, and indicate the underlying interests that must be addressed. Often after making a strong opening statement, they indicate that they are open to exploring other options that will satisfy their interests. They may then either shift to a detailed explanation of their interests, indicating flexibility regarding how they might be met, or offer (over time) modified positions that attempt to reconcile what they have learned from a counterpart's position or information gained about their interests. Japanese negotiators often follow this pattern, using positional negotiation as a way to share information about their interests rather than getting locked early into specific solutions (Adair, Weingart, and Brett, 2004).

An opening using a positional approach does not automatically mean that negotiators cannot or will not move to interest-based or relational approaches at some time later in negotiations. However, to make this transition, they may need help from their counterpart or, in some cases, a third party.

If a negotiator's opening statement lists only issues, issues and associated interests, or merits for a change, this person is likely to use an interest-based approach, at least at the beginning of negotiations. If appropriate, you can encourage this approach by responding in a similar manner rather than countering with a position.

Negotiators who begin with an interest-based approach may not adhere to it throughout talks or on every issue. They may switch to a positional approach in response to its use by a counterpart, because they have a nonnegotiable position on a specific issue or believe they have gone as far as possible using integrative procedures and devising integrative solutions and must use positional and distributive approaches to allocate perceived or actual limited resources. Even if the parties switch to a positional approach later in negotiations, the positions advocated are likely to be influenced by the greater knowledge about the interests of both parties gained through prior engagement in an interest-based process.

Determining Negotiation Protocols, Norms, and Behavioral Guidelines

In the box in Chapter Five, we presented a comprehensive list of procedural issues that often arise in negotiations. and these become the topics covered in a protocol that guides behavior and other issues in negotiation. The extent to which protocols or behavioral expectations are made explicit is influenced by culture. Negotiators from high-context cultures or more traditional societies, in which there is significant homogeneity among members, long traditions regarding appropriate actions in specific circumstances, and lots of shared assumptions, generally spend little time developing protocols. Everyone in these societies already knows and understands what proper decorum and behavior are and what is expected of them.

Those from low-context cultures have a stronger orientation toward explicit articulation of rules or laws. In cultures that are highly diverse or where members expect to relate to individuals and groups that are significantly different from themselves, negotiators generally become more explicit about expectations regarding norms and behavioral guidelines. These cultures are also more open to direct discussions about negotiation procedures, which are often drafted and approved.

An example of negotiations over a protocol occurred in the context of meetings of the Okavango River Basin Commission and the Okavango River Basin Steering Committee, its technical advisory committee—both composed of government representatives from Angola, Botswana, and Namibia. (The meetings were facilitated by one of us and another colleague.) The commissioners

and staff from Botswana and Namibia wanted to develop a written protocol to address how the commission and its members would conduct official
business at commission meetings, function effectively between meetings, and
consult among members to develop consensus decisions on both routine and
time-sensitive issues.

Such a protocol was very much in the tradition of Botswana, which has
a strong British-based governing process based on written rules of law, and
of Namibia, because of German and Afrikaner bureaucratic norms regarding
documentation. But the Angolan delegation was quite wary, and at times outright resistant, to codifying a written protocol for the commission's operation.
The Angolan delegation members argued that what mattered was how the
parties behaved in meetings, not what was written on paper. The basis of their
distrust of a written protocol, as articulated by a member of the delegation,
was that Angola and its people had a long tradition of making and abiding by
oral agreements, a destructive colonial history of one-sided and manipulative
written agreements that had placed them in a position of disadvantage, and
recent experience of broken peace accords. For these reasons, they distrusted
a written protocol.

With the help of the facilitators, a smaller working group developed an
acceptable protocol, which was then brought back to the full Commission for
approval. However, the Angolans would accept the written document only if
the other parties agreed that any country could propose to change the protocol
at any time. After considerable deliberation, all negotiators settled on an
acceptable amendment process. The party wishing to change the protocol was
required to submit a written proposal to the standing commission chairperson
prior to a commission meeting. The proposal would be distributed to all
members prior to the next session, with adequate time for each delegation to
review and consider it, before discussions would occur. At the next regular
meeting, a decision would be made to approve the change or not.

SUGGESTED STRATEGIES FOR COORDINATING PROTOCOL ISSUES

- Coordination between cultures that have implicit approaches to human
  interaction and those with explicit approaches is not easy. Cultures with
  implicit orientations generally cannot understand why expectations and
  protocol need to be clarified and written down. They often consider people who propose making the rules explicit to be rude or lacking proper
  upbringing. Conversely, cultures that favor explicit guidelines for interactions may consider counterparts from more implicitly oriented cultures to
  be secretive and manipulative.

- Negotiators seeking to coordinate between these two cultural orientations
  have several choices. They can adhere to their own cultural norms and

advocate for making expectations explicit or indirectly refuse to do so, engage in a process of accommodation to each other's approaches, or use a different approach, such as international diplomatic standards or specially developed guidelines for interactions within an international corporation that has employees from multiple cultures. Accommodation often entails making behavioral guidelines more explicit than the usual case in a high-context culture, but less detailed than the norm for a low-context culture.

CONCLUSION

At this point, the negotiators have made first contacts, laid out their views about the key issues at stake, and made initial presentations regarding their needs, interests, and concerns. The next chapter explores how they delve more deeply into the issues on the table in preparation for the processes of problem solving.

CHAPTER SEVEN

Identifying and Exploring Issues

Relationships have never been easy between the Tuscarora Nation (an Indian tribe), the State of New York, and the New York Power Authority (NYPA). This has especially been the case since 1960, when the U.S. Supreme Court allowed the NYPA to take 550 acres of tribal land to construct the Niagara Power Plant, the largest nonfederal hydropower facility in the country. Federal laws and regulations require that after a number of years of operation, a power plant's impacts must be reevaluated and facility owners must apply to be relicensed. The process requires an environmental impact study (EIS) of a facility's socioeconomic and environmental impacts on surrounding communities, identification of actions to be taken to mitigate impacts, opportunities for public participation in the process, and a final decision by the Federal Energy Regulatory Commission, the licensing agency. The time for the Niagara plant to be relicensed was at hand.

To gain public approval of the EIS, avoid future litigation over its adequacy, and have an uncontested application, NYPA initiated a collaborative stakeholder process to determine the focus, design, and methodologies to be used for the study and broader public ownership of the process and outcome. The Tuscarora Nation, arguing that the previous taking of tribal land had been unfair and resulted in serious social, economic, environmental, and psychological impacts on the tribe, refused to participate in in-depth talks without an agreement on preconditions and principles that included recognition by New York State and NYPA of the Six Nations treaties on land ownership to which the tribe and the U.S. government are parties. (In the United States, treaties are made between sovereign nations, tribes, and the federal government, not with states.) The governor and the state attorneys were concerned about the legal implications of formal recognition of the treaties by the state. After months of preliminary negotiations with the Tuscarora, the state agreed to language in a Memorandum of Agreement with the tribe that recognized "The Spirit" of the treaties. This framing was less than what the tribe wanted yet met its minimum requirement to participate in more comprehensive substantive talks. In addition, the two parties agreed on a two-track consultation process: formal government-to-government talks that recognized the tribe's sovereignty and a broader stakeholder dialogue involving concerned governmental and nongovernmental parties in which the tribe would participate.

∽

In previous chapters we have addressed preparation and planning for negotiations, as well as the initial meetings, including opening statements. One critical aspect of the opening meeting or meetings is the identification of issues to be discussed—the core of the negotiation process. In this chapter, we address how parties express issues, explore their importance, and begin the process of sharing information about them, all of which is influenced by cultural norms and habits.

Issue identification is necessary before moving on to clarification of each party's needs and interests with respect to the issues at hand, which itself is required before engaging in problem solving. At this stage, the parties need to complete the following tasks, which we address in this chapter:

1. Identify and agree on the issues to be discussed—including what is on and off the table.

2. Work to reconcile the parties' approaches to the processing of issues.

3. Determine an appropriate sequence for discussion of issues.

4. Start the process of exchanging information, including the parties' needs and interests.

Parties may address these tasks in the order listed, but depending on the cultures involved, the tasks could be taken up in any order.

IDENTIFYING AND AGREEING ON ISSUES TO BE DISCUSSED

At some point, generally early in talks, negotiators need to clarify what they want to talk about. Issues or topics for discussion may have been raised in informal planning or preparation sessions. Some parties will not even agree to meet with other parties unless the topics to be addressed (and those that will not be addressed) have been identified and approved. If the topics or issues have not been articulated prior to the start of formal negotiations, they may be presented through the negotiators' opening statements—although some cultures only hint at issues obliquely. In some cases, the issues have to be teased out throughout the negotiation process, based on the parties' informal or formal interactions and statements.

In terms of process, issue identification may occur indirectly or directly, and parties may provide significantly different amounts of detail about the topics. When negotiators are from the same or similar high-context cultures, they are likely to engage in indirect or implicit procedures for articulating issues. They may also share common cultural understandings about the issues in question and prefer to reveal or define the topics they want to talk about only gradually. This pattern is frequently found in traditional collectivist cultures, but is also common in national cultures such as Japan and Indonesia, especially in Java, where indirect dealing is the norm.

Such approaches may also be used when parties are from different cultures but have a common understanding of the topics to be addressed due to prior relationships or discussions and do not need explicit definition of issues in order to proceed with talks. Indirect procedures for issue identification are also common when one party is reluctant to make topics for discussion explicit for fear of rejection or losing face, as a tactical maneuver to obscure real issues or interests, or when a negotiator believes the situation or timing is not right for explicitness.

If parties are either reluctant or slow to reveal their real issues or concerns, people from more explicit cultures may be tempted to regard this as dishonest, purposely obscure, or nontransparent, or they may simply be at a loss as to how to proceed and what to talk about. Alternatively, a cultural explanation might be found in the reluctance of people from indirect-dealing cultures to state certain topics too openly, which would be considered rude or even offensive. At a more personal level, some people are not clear about their own needs and desires, so their true agenda may be revealed only through extensive discussion. While this may be frustrating for people who are usually clear about what they need to deal with and what they want, the negotiation process needs to make room for all cultural norms and all personal quirks.

Explicit procedures for issue identification are common in direct-dealing and low-context cultures where clear definition of issues is expected and seen as a precondition for productive talks. For instance, Israelis are especially known for their direct presentation of issues they want to discuss (Cohen, 1997; Klieman, 2005), as are Germans (Smyser, 2003). British and American negotiators are likely to present issues in a list, often with some elaboration of each item. French negotiators typically present a logical argument in their opening statements to support the topics or principles they want to discuss (Cogan, 2003).

At times, the inclusion or noninclusion of an item on a negotiation agenda is a delicate matter—and some negotiators may not be able to indicate open agreement to discuss certain issues. Thus, a negotiator may silently acquiesce or indirectly approve an issue's inclusion on an agenda. For example, in some circumstances, political constraints or the attitudes of a key constituency may require a negotiator to disapprove discussion of the issue—at least in public. However, the negotiator may indirectly approve the issue not by formally agreeing, but also by not overtly disagreeing to its inclusion on an agenda.

At this stage of negotiation, it is generally not necessary to generate complete specificity about the issues. Too much detail about them is often combined with the presentation of strong positions, which can prematurely lead to arguments over proposed solutions and prevent a deeper analysis of issues and interests prior to problem solving.

Sequencing the Discussion of Issues

Once negotiators have managed to identify the issues or topics for discussion, they need to create a sequence to address them: a negotiation agenda. Agendas are explicit or implicit agreements between negotiators about the sequence and, on occasion, the process that will be used to discuss specific topics. Overt decisions about agendas involve negotiators reaching agreements on the placement and sequencing of discussion topics. Agenda development involves questions and decisions about the focus of early, middle, and later discussions; which issues may be dependent on settling others; and when each issue should be addressed. Which issue should be taken up first? When negotiators can resolve this question, they demonstrate that a procedural agreement is possible, and the parties may be able to work together to resolve substantive issues.

Generally parties try to sequence issues in a manner that will result in progress and agreement making, especially for their own benefit. However, they may differ regarding which order will be the most productive. A negotiator may not want a difficult issue to be placed at the beginning of negotiations for fear that it might result in a deadlock. The placement of an issue at a specific time might force concessions that it would be better to hold in reserve to link to agreements on other topics or to include as part of a package agreement. For these reasons, negotiators need to think clearly about how to sequence issues, individually and jointly.

Following are some general criteria for determining the sequencing of issues:

∽

- *The emotional or psychological significance of the issue.* Issues around which there are strong feelings are often placed early in an agenda because parties will not be able to think or talk about anything else until those issues are raised and addressed. Early placement on an agenda may allow a counterpart to demonstrate that she has really heard the feelings of the other party, concretely demonstrate either cognitive or emotional empathy, and allow the other to vent, talk, and work through his emotions. It may also allow a negotiator to make a psychological concession by recognizing and legitimizing the perception or feeling of another party, and thus reduce emotional tension and polarization in negotiations.

• *Importance of the issue to one or more parties.* If a party thinks that an issue is very important, it will probably need to be addressed earlier rather than later, although it may not be the first agenda item. Proposing to discuss an issue of critical interest to a party later in talks can be interpreted by a counterpart as disavowing or dismissing its importance, a delaying tactic, or refusal to address critical interests.

• *Perceived difficulty or ease of reaching agreement on the issue.* The ease or difficulty of resolving an issue may influence its placement on an agenda. Often parties want to put the most difficult issue first. However, this approach frequently results in protracted arguments, an extended period of time before an agreement is reached, and significant frustration on the part of negotiators. An alternative approach is making the first issue on the agenda one that all parties are invested in but will not be difficult to resolve. This placement encourages early decision making, helps develop a pattern of agreement and saying yes, and promotes positive feelings and hope on the part of parties that that they can successfully work together.

• *Settlement of an issue as a prerequisite for agreement making on another.* Often in negotiations, one or more issues must be settled before others can be tackled. The reasons that some issues must be settled earlier are diverse. These may be key issues that unlock attitudes or opportunities in later issues; preconditions that, if met, allow discussion of other topics; foundation agreements that provide the structure for settlement of later issues; emotionally important issues that increase openness to discussion of substantive issues if addressed, and so forth.

• *Commonality with other issues.* Some issues are best grouped together because of common characteristics. For example, relationship issues might be grouped together and dealt with at one time, leaving related financial issues until later. Grouping of common issues, especially in cultures that prefer linear approaches to problem solving, prevents parties from hopping between issues that are very different in nature and hindering the progress of discussions.

• *Appropriateness of an issue being settled independently versus being linked with another or included as part of a settlement package.* Some issues can be settled independently from others. Others need to be considered together to allow links, trades, or the development of an overall settlement package that addresses the settlement of multiple issues at one time. While possible linkage of issues should always be considered when developing an agenda, possible connections may emerge only after some discussions have already occurred.

• *Impacts on power and influence relationships of negotiators if an issue is addressed earlier or later in an agenda.* Discussion and agreement on an issue can affect the power and influence a negotiator has to address issues later in an agenda. For example, if an issue is resolved and permanently closed early in a negotiation, that issue may not be available for trade-offs later in the talks. In negotiations involving coalitions, the settlement of one member's issue early on may reduce its commitment to other coalition members' issues that are to be addressed later, because it has already gotten what it needs. This strategy of divide and rule is often used in negotiations with coalitions.

Developing the Agenda

Sequencing agenda items can be accomplished by a number of methods, which we address in this section.

Ad Hoc Discussions. In this approach, a party proposes an agenda item for discussion. If the other party concurs, they discuss it until an agreement is reached. After the issue is successfully settled, parties select another issue for discussion. This one-at-a-time approach, with little regard for the total sequencing of issues, proceeds until all issues have been discussed. This process offers significant flexibility, and parties can often build trust as each issue is sequentially settled. However, manipulation is also possible if a party consciously selects an issue for the agenda at an opportune moment that may later influence another party's power or ability to make trades on future issues.

Group Conversation. In this approach, parties just begin talking about issues in general and ultimately begin to focus on one. A solution may or may not emerge as a result of general conversation, and without a structure, discussions may meander and become unfocused and time-consuming. Members of cultures who feel comfortable with many activities happening at once often favor this approach to issue sequencing. This style is also common in informal interpersonal negotiations, or in tribal or communal societies that have relatively unstructured decision-making processes and less-focused group dialogues. In each of these settings, the participants desire more holistic solutions that consider many variables and the input and interests of the whole group.

Alternating Choices of Items. In this approach, parties alternately select issues to place on the agenda for discussion. This process usually works initially, but often breaks down if one negotiator refuses to agree to the order or placement of an issue raised by another party. Like the ad hoc and simple agenda approaches, this approach may also create problems when issues of linkage and trading are required to reach agreements.

Creating a Simple Agenda. In this approach, one party proposes a complete agenda that contains all the issues to be discussed. The issues are then discussed and resolved one at a time, in the order the initiator proposed them. This process works well for meetings, conferences, or negotiations where there are no significant disagreements about the issues or no interrelated or linked issues or where significant individual advantage cannot be gained through sequencing. However, this approach to agenda formation may not be acceptable for complex topics, where issues must be linked in order to create solutions, or where conflict is high. Gulliver (1979) notes that the simple agenda approach often tends to subvert the ordering of items almost immediately in serious conflict situations. If parties feel locked into a simple agenda by premature procedural agreements, they may use manipulative stalling tactics to gain leverage on items later in the agenda.

Ranking According to Importance. Parties jointly select and place the most important issues at the top of the agenda. The process is often connected with a bargaining theory that assumes that if parties can initially agree on key issues, discussions about subissues will fall into place. However, parties often do not have the same assessments regarding the importance or priorities of issues. If this is the case, this approach to agenda formation may break down. Gulliver (1979) notes that this method generally works best when parties have no claims or counterclaims against each other, no previous offense has been alleged, or negotiators are trying to establish a new relationship.

Working from General Agreements to Details. In this approach, parties focus on identification and discussion of key principles or concepts that will serve to guide future discussion of individual issues. Such principles provide a framework that can both shape future solutions to specific issues and provide standards and criteria to which solutions should conform or comply.

Placing Less Difficult Items First. This approach has often been referred to as gradualism (Weiss, 2003): one or more parties sequence issues to be discussed from easier and less complex to harder and more complex, so as to facilitate a gradual sequence of agreements. Parties identify, individually or together, several important issues they believe will not take too much time to discuss, be too difficult to resolve, or be complex. Issues are often small, self-contained (not linked with others), less emotionally laden, and not symbolic of more conflicted issues. These issues are placed at the beginning of the agenda, and parties discuss them before tackling more complex issues.

"The logic behind the approach is that trust is low, and parties therefore need to take small steps to create initial trust and or foster a positive atmosphere, so that subsequent vital issues may be broached" (Weiss, 2003, p. 111, citing Etzioni, 1963). In addition, by discussing less-volatile issues first, parties experience decision-making success early on and create foundational agreements that they may risk losing if they do not continue the negotiations. This provides an incentive for approaching more difficult issues. For this process to work, the items placed at the beginning of the agenda have to be perceived as important and significant for formulating a settlement agreement.

Addressing the Boulder in the Road. Often in negotiations, one or more major issues are stumbling blocks for agreement on the remaining others. Unless progress is made on one of these barrier issues, the parties will become bogged down. The logic for this approach for agenda development and issue sequencing is that "it proposes to address the more complex issues first, thereby moving the 'boulder' or greatest obstacle; this enables easier resolution of the remaining issues" (Weiss, 2003, p. 112).

Grouping. Parties identify issues that have components in common and sequence topics according to similarity. Grouped items may be resolved individually or as part of packages that address a specific area of inquiry.

Trade-Offs or Packaging. Negotiators identify issues that are potentially related and link them together to facilitate the development of trades or package agreements. Linking is a common way to handle issues that cannot be settled independently or require concessions on one to reach agreement on another. The linkage, package, and trade-off processes for agenda formation are common when:

- Information and possible settlement options on all issues need to be identified and discussed before an agreement can be reached on any single one.

- One or more negotiators fear they will lose leverage for the favorable resolution of later issues if they reach an agreement on specific key issues early in negotiations.

- One or more parties believe that issues on which agreement has been reached and are considered to be closed may need to be reopened based on the settlement of later issues.

- A total package is the only way to reach an agreement because a package's total gains and losses on all issues are shared in such a way that they are mutually acceptable to all parties.

A common sequencing process for issues that must be included in a package agreement is for negotiators to reach a series of conditional agreements that can be modified and later combined into a total and comprehensive final settlement. Since the agreement for any one issue is conditional and each agreement may be modified before approval of a final package, the order in which they are discussed is less important.

Another sequencing process for packages is referred to by Zartman and Berman (1982) as the "leap-to-agreement" approach. In this variation, negotiators discuss all issues fully but reach very few, if any, agreements along the way. Toward the end of negotiations or as a deadline approaches, the parties individually or jointly assemble a total package that contains gains and losses for all sides and meets all or most of the parties' basic interests. Often a party proposes that a counterpart accept a proposed package as is or with minimal modifications, or the package will be withdrawn.

If a negotiator proposing a package understands the issues and interests of all parties and has taken significant steps to address and meet them in a "yes-able" proposal that the other party cannot refuse (Fisher and Ury, 1981), there is often a high probability that the proposal will be accepted in totality or with minor revisions by a counterpart. Package proposals are often positively received because they indicate a willingness of one party to recognize the interests of the other, demonstrate models for trade-offs, and do some of the hard work of putting together a proposal that the other party may not have the time or ability to do.

However, packages also are rejected because the recipients were expecting to make agreements throughout negotiations and resent the fact that a total package has been thrust on them, do not like the take-it-or-leave-it tone of the proposal, believe there are better ways to satisfy individual and joint interests, or prefer to be involved in the agreement and package development and have no procedural and psychological satisfaction.

Incremental or Alternating Discussion and Agreement. Parties initially discuss all of the issues, reaching agreements where they can and then moving on to other issues. Several more rounds of discussions are held, covering the same issues again in greater detail until agreements are reached on all issues. This method combines the grouping, group conversation, and package methods.

Assigning Smaller Issues to Subgroups. Often a large group will have difficulty adequately discussing all issues in the depth or detail necessary, especially if the topics are complex or the parties fraught with tensions. Frequently separating out specific issues (either simple or hard ones), fractionating topics into smaller parts, and assigning them to a subgroup of negotiators who work on them simultaneously are productive approaches to agenda development and discussion sequencing. Subgroups examine the issues, explore options, and develop recommendations or proposals that they bring back to the larger group for consideration and, everyone hopes, approval.

Dealing with "Unacceptable" Issues

Unacceptable issues are topics that, for whatever reason, one or more negotiators are not ready to or refuse to talk about, or will discuss only after other issues have been satisfactorily addressed or resolved. They are often couched or seen as extreme positions on a specific issue, nonnegotiable demands, or unacceptable preconditions for the continuation of negotiations.

Parties may propose issues that a counterpart may consider unacceptable for a variety of reasons. They may be issues that the proposing negotiator considers:

- Valid and legitimate preconditions for continuation of negotiations
- So important that they are at the core or the main purpose of negotiations
- Critical to have agreement on as necessary preconditions for discussion or agreement on other issues
- Symbolic, in that they are necessary to raise in order to preserve self-respect or honor
- Necessary to raise in order to gain and secure the support of superiors or constituents
- Throw-away issues that can be dropped in exchange for benefits received by agreement on other issues
- Throw-away issues to be traded for a counterpart's dropping of one of their issues that is also unacceptable

The reasons for a negotiator to raise an issue that is unacceptable to a counterpart may vary widely and range from matters of principle and honor to merely a negotiation tactic. Therefore, it is generally wise for negotiators not to respond too precipitously and immediately reject an issue that they do not want to discuss.

It is also important to distinguish between discussion of an issue and reaching an agreement. A negotiator can often agree to hear more about an unacceptable issue raised by a counterpart and hear the person out while not agreeing to reach a settlement on it. On occasion, all that a counterpart may want is to raise and explain an issue, with no expectation that an agreement can be reached on it. Raising the issue may be important to educate a counterpart about a concern, to defend honor, for symbolic or political reasons, or to demonstrate to a constituency that its issues and interests are being raised and aggressively advocated.

The strategic choice for negotiators after hearing a proposal for discussion of an unacceptable issue raised in an opening statement is whether to immediately reject it outright, finesse it by responding in a manner that neither accepts or rejects its discussion, or make a counterproposal to discuss it only after others have been handled and resolved.

In general, outright refusal to talk about a counterpart's issue should be considered only when a possible future agreement on the proposed topic, as opposed to discussion of it, will have one of these effects:

- Violate a nonnegotiable core value, principle, or belief
- Likely result in total defeat or loss to a party
- Raise such significant problems with a negotiator's superiors or constituents that he or she will be seen as a traitor and lose all ability to represent them in negotiations
- Lead to a total loss of dignity, honor, or self-respect for a negotiator, his or her team, the organization, or constituents

If any of these conditions is likely to result from discussion of an issue, a negotiator will have to decide how and when to reject its discussion. The process for how an issue is rejected may be as critical for future coordination of parties in negotiation as the rejection itself.

SUGGESTED STRATEGIES FOR COORDINATING UNACCEPTABLE ISSUES

As a negotiator, you have several options when considering whether and how to refuse to discuss an issue you find unacceptable:

- You can immediately and directly refuse to discuss the issue and provide:
  - ◇ No explanation for unwillingness to talk about it
  - ◇ An explanation or logic and a rationale for unwillingness to talk about the topic, which the negotiator hopes the counterpart will understand and accept

- Rather than overtly refusing to discuss the issue, you can
  - ◇ Ignore it unless it is raised again
  - ◇ Shift the counterpart's focus to other issues of joint concern or try to address another issue that is of interest to a specific individual or small group that the negotiator is willing to talk about
  - ◇ Indirectly communicate the unacceptability of discussing the issue by sending an indirect message, such as, "It might be difficult to talk about that topic at this time"
- You can avoid immediate refusal, and instead ask a clarifying question that raises doubts about talking about it. For example, you might ask a counterpart:
  - ◇ "Why do you see the issue as important to discuss?" and if an unacceptable logic and rationale is presented, refuse to talk about it at that time.
  - ◇ "How do you believe that we can discuss this issue without sacrificing a core value, principle, or belief or without one or the other of us losing our honor or self-respect?"
  - ◇ "Would you be willing to discuss this issue if you were in my position?"
  - ◇ "How do you think we can talk about this issue without my losing the support of my team, superiors, or constituents, which in itself would make any subsequent agreement that is reached unacceptable or unimplementable?"
- You can propose to defer discussion of the issue until a later unspecified time.
- You can propose to defer discussion of the issue until such time as other issues have been addressed and agreements have been reached.
- You can suggest deferral of discussion until the end of negotiations, at which time a decision will be made whether to discuss it, but without making a promise that any agreements will be reached.

Because outright refusal to talk about an issue of importance to a counterpart may raise the risk that talks will immediately fall apart, you should be careful and slow to use these strategies. Often it is better to agree to at least talk about the issue, and at the same time be explicit about not making promises that agreement is either desirable or possible. Discussion of even an unacceptable issue can allow you to gain greater insight into the logic and rationale of a counterpart and elements of an unacceptable issue. You may also find a way to reframe it so that it can be addressed productively.

Approaches for Discussing and Processing Issues

In order to talk effectively about issues, parties have to develop a common process for structuring their continuing conversations and analysis of topics of concern. In earlier chapters, we presented information about positional, interest-based, and relational approaches to negotiations. These approaches influence how the parties explore the issues that have been raised. (See Chapter Four for a full explanation of interest-based and positional bargaining, and strategies for coordinating across those approaches.)

The positional approach to information exchange and discussion usually occurs in the context of making proposals and counterproposals. New information is gained and exchanged from an examination of the sequential positions advocated by each party, rebuttals or critiques that each of them makes, probing questions, and extrapolation or logical deduction. Frequently there is little direct focus on or questioning about parties' specific needs, interests, or concerns.

The interest-based approach seeks to identify each party's needs, interests, and concerns before developing possible solutions. Parties alternate sharing information, asking probing questions, exploring how additional information for wise and informed decision making can be secured, and then framing the problem to be addressed in terms of meeting mutual needs and interests.

Both of these approaches for structuring information exchange and discussion also rely on several general strategies to organize talks and share data. At least nine approaches may be used to discuss issues:

- Ratification of the status quo
- Relationship approaches
- Personal storytelling
- Group conversation
- Circling
- General framework approaches
- Linkage approach
- Sequential building-block approaches
- Position and counterposition approaches

Different cultures have stronger or lesser orientations toward these approaches and may combine them or use different ones at various phases of the negotiation process. We believe that it is valuable to break each of them out as separate processes so that negotiators can more easily recognize them and determine appropriate responses. We begin our discussion of approaches with several that may be less familiar to some negotiators, especially those from Western European-based cultures.

Ratification of the Status Quo. This approach begins negotiations by identifying any positive elements of the status quo or current relationship that the parties want to keep or maintain in a subsequent agreement, and affirming that they will be continued. The process often is an extension of an opening statement that emphasizes commonalities or links among the parties. Once the positive ongoing elements of the current relationship are identified, approved, and included in an agreement, the parties may use one or more of the following discussion and issue-processing procedures to address other topics of concern.

Relationship Approaches. The fundamental assumption of this approach to discussion of issues and, later, agenda development is that all negotiations happen in the context of relationships. Whether they be good, fair, neutral, strained, or highly antagonistic, relationships are the water that negotiators swim in. For this reason, cultures that subscribe to this approach for discussing issues place a major emphasis on cultivating a relationship conducive to agreement making.

This approach generally seamlessly blends substantive, procedural, and psychological issue identification; agenda development; and issue sequencing, deliberations, and agreement making into the context of overall social interactions and relationships. At times, it may appear that resolution of substantive issues is merely an afterthought or side benefit of the broader social relationship that exists among parties, but this is not the case. Agreements are one of several major components in ongoing relationships among parties.

Negotiators who hold this view of both relationships and negotiations generally spend a significant amount of time—hours, days, months, or even years—cultivating and interacting with a counterpart to clarify both the kind and quality of relationship that exists and to feel out how they view issues and solutions that might address them. This is generally done in more of a conversational mode than in adversarial back-and-forth negotiations, though the approach may also be used in more formal talks. This approach to issue identification and agenda development is often characteristic of traditional or tribal societies where there are not high status differences between counterparts; cultures where a high priority is placed on building relationships, personal trust, and processing issues gradually; in negotiations between cultures where the goals of counterparts are not known and a direct approach would be seen as impolite, potentially risky, and possibly damaging to any future relationship; or where face saving is seen as important.

In cultures or situations with these characteristics, parties may meet explicitly, informally, or may even deliberately arrange "accidental" encounters to explore issues. During these meetings, a wide variety of social topics, as opposed to task-focused topics, are often discussed, such as health, common friends or colleagues, similar interests, the food or drink that is being consumed, family, current social individual or group activities, future plans for nontask-related activities, and so forth. At least initially, little mention of substantive issues of concern may be made. However, in the context of ongoing social discussions, an occasional, and often an oblique, reference may be made to a substantive issue of individual, group, or mutual concern. A counterpart may respond to an issue that has been raised in several ways. He or she may:

- Ignore the issue totally and continue the social conversation, which may indicate that the counterpart does not want to talk about it, the issue is too uncomfortable to discuss, or he or she may want to do more relationship building before tackling it

- Initially ignore the issue that has been raised and continue the social conversation, but later indirectly or directly comment on it

- Acknowledge the issue and perhaps indicate that there would be merit in conducting further conversations about it, but indicate either indirectly or directly that discussion of it should be postponed

- Comment indirectly or generally about the issue but not get into any detail

- Directly respond to the issue at the time that it has been raised

These behavioral clues can give the negotiator raising the issue ideas about how to proceed. Often it is only after a relatively long period of talk or time, protracted conversation, multiple informal soundings, and even several meetings that counterparts may move to a more focused discussion of one or more issues in question. Even then, deliberations may be conducted in a fairly slow approach-avoidance manner, with only a gradual exploration of each party's issues, needs, interests, and concerns.

Ultimately after the development of enough individual and mutual understanding, one party may make a tentative, indirect, or general proposal to a counterpart for how to proceed with further substantive discussions or perhaps a proposal on how to address the issue of concern. If a proposal is made, often it is framed in such a way that it can be easily ignored, disavowed, rejected, or modified in a way so that the party making the proposal or the counterpart receiving it will not lose face or have to break off conversation. Proposals may be made in an indirect manner, in the form of a metaphor or story involving people other than those involved in the actual negotiations, to illustrate how a problem might be solved in a satisfactory manner. The story in Box 7.1, told by a Navajo Indian peacemaker to one of the authors, illustrates this approach.

Box 7.1. Rattlesnake, Rabbit, and Coyote

Two Navajos were involved in a dispute and were sitting in a room with friends to discuss how it might be resolved. One of them told this story to illustrate how the conflict might be viewed and satisfactorily be addressed.

Two tribal members were in a conflict over disruptive and disrespectful behavior by one of them that offended the other. They agreed to meet with some other tribal members to discuss their differences. After describing what had happened, one of the men in the meeting said that their dispute reminded him of a story, which he proceeded to tell.

> Rattlesnake was sleeping peacefully under a rock. He was enjoying his nap when suddenly he was startled and frightened by a great thumping on the stone above him and lots of noise. He woke up, regained his wits, and slithered out of his burrow, where he saw that Rabbit was jumping up and down on the rock as happy as could be.
>
> Rattlesnake was irritated by the disruption and proceeded to wrap himself around Rabbit, said that he would never let him go, and he might even bite him as punishment for being so rude. Rabbit was panicked and squealed, "Help me, help me!"
>
> Well, at this time, Coyote happened to be walking by, heard the ruckus, and decided to investigate. Upon meeting Rattlesnake and Rabbit, he asked them what was going on. Rattlesnake explained that he was taking his regular afternoon nap and that it had been rudely interrupted by Rabbit jumping up and down on the rock above him. He explained that for this unruly behavior, he would never let Rabbit go.
>
> Rabbit explained that he was just taking his normal afternoon walk and that it was so beautiful that he was jumping for joy. He didn't even know that Rattlesnake was taking a nap under the rock. Now he really wanted to be free.
>
> Well at this point, Coyote thought a bit, and then told Rattlesnake and Rabbit that he wanted to try something. He asked Rattlesnake to release Rabbit and then asked Rattlesnake to return under his rock. He then asked Rabbit to go back a few paces behind the rock, hop forward until he was near the rock but not on it, and then hop up and down again just like he did before when he was so happy. Rabbit did what he was requested. Coyote then asked Rattlesnake if the noise bothered him. "Not at all," said the snake. "I hardly heard anything." "Well, Rabbit," said Coyote, "if you knew Rattlesnake was under that rock napping, would you have chosen to do your hopping on the top of his house?" Rabbit replied, "Of course not. If I had known he was there I would have given him a wide berth, and not disturbed him ... for a variety of reasons." Coyote then said to Rattlesnake, "Well, now that you have heard Rabbit's view, would that have worked for you?" Rattlesnake replied, "Yes, that was the way that it was supposed to be!" Coyote then turned and asked Rabbit, "Will you be more careful in the future?" "Yes, of course," responded Rabbit.

Upon completion of the story, the teller paused for a few moments of silence. Finally, one of the parties spoke up and acknowledged that the tale sounded like his situation, and that if the other party would only acknowledge the inconvenience and rudeness that he had caused, the dispute could be settled. Another moment of silence followed. Finally, the other party said, "Yes, that is the way it should be." He apologized, all men present nodded, as did his counterpart, and the dispute was settled.

While the relationship-building approach for the general shaping of discussions in negotiations, issue identification, agenda formation, and topic sequencing may appear to be highly ad hoc, undirected, and even chaotic to members of cultures with orientations that are more explicit and structured, it has an internal logic for members of cultures that subscribe to the approach. For them, it is logically reasonable, helps reduce risks, and is emotionally comfortable. It allows all parties to build a satisfactory comfort level before tackling difficult issues; enables participants to do informal sounding about a counterpart's character, views, intentions, and desires; allows face saving; and enables counterparts to back away from potentially unacceptable agreements without harming relationships or closing the door on future discussions.

Personal Storytelling Approaches. The personal storytelling approach to structuring discussions, issue identification, and agenda formation involves one or more parties narrating the history, or story, of their relationship with the other, including identification of various points where tensions, disagreements, or conflicts began; identification of issues that may require further discussion; and ultimately clarifying the current status of interactions and what one or more parties wants to be done. This style of issue identification and agenda formation is common in more traditional or communal societies; in cultures that value storytelling, recounting historical events and relations between parties; situations where storytelling is a normal part of ritual posturing and listing historical grievances; or where parties believe that a psychological tension is released and greater understanding achieved by recounting past events—and this a prerequisite for focusing on the issues.

This approach for discussion of issues may be initiated either unilaterally by one party, or all parties may subscribe to it and present and complete their stories before more in-depth discussion on any specific issues occurs. Stories may include appeals for recognition and affirmation of past positive connections, identification of individual or common values regarding what is widely considered to be fair or just, or detailed descriptions of how one or more parties has been wronged.

An example of the personal storytelling approach occurred a number of years ago during negotiations involving 135 parties concerning the development of a wolf management policy and plan to lower predation on declining moose and caribou populations in several regions of Alaska (Mayer, Moore, and Todd, n.d.). During the meetings, negotiators representing diverse interest groups worked to develop a consensus on policies that would be broadly supported by all concerned parties.

In one of the sessions, we had a public comment period where members of the public could propose approaches to handling the conflict over predation and wolf control. One of the speakers, an Alaska Native, came to the microphone and made a statement. He started out:

> I do not know how I can say what is in my heart in the limited time that I am allowed to speak, but I will say that I feel it is important enough to drive twelve hours from my trap lines to speak my mind. My ancestors have been on this land since time immemorial and have hunted and fished to stay alive. We depend on the game, the moose and the caribou, because without them, there is nothing to eat. Their survival is important to us, for our survival depends on them. For this reason, we cannot have wolves kill all the game [Alaska Native participant in the Governor's Wolf Summit, Fairbanks, Alaska, Jan. 17, 1993].

He provided an extended explanation about how his people lived and hunted, survived on game, had ceremonies around the animals that inhabited their region, and explained the impacts on his people's culture and survival if the game were gone. He ended with an appeal for people to listen to him and his people, feel the importance of his concerns, and include his people in the ecology that was being protected in Alaska.

Sequencing discussion of issues in the storytelling approach for topic clarification or problem-solving purposes may happen in several ways. Parties may try to reach agreement on issues during a party's narrative, and in the order that they are presented. Or they may implicitly or explicitly note places where they disagree and come back to them at a later time to discuss them in more detail, once the whole narrative has been completed or all other parties have had an opportunity to speak and describe their views of the situation and issues at hand.

In negotiations where issues are processed immediately after they are raised rather than waiting until a total narrative has been completed, discussions often degenerate into a series of arguments regarding what did or did not happen or who was wronged, and agreements to disagree stalemate on individual issues or a series of small agreements that may later be assembled into a total package. Situations where parties defer issue processing and problem solving until each party has been able to complete telling their story are more likely to result in more considered and deliberate discussion and problem solving. Allowing all parties to present their views first and having a more holistic view of issues to be addressed and needs and interests to be met is often helpful in enabling parties to address multiple issues together. They then may develop links and trades or comprehensive settlement packages that address substantive, procedural, or psychological or relationship issues.

Cultures where we have directly observed or have reviewed research on the use of the personal storytelling approach include Maori clans in New Zealand, Eskimo cultures in North America, Dutch culture in the Netherlands, and in dialogues among Palestinians, Jews, and Israelis in the United States. Some Maoris, especially those who are more traditional, begin meetings with each other, other clans, or *pakiha* (non-Maoris) with elaborate greeting, connection, and challenge rituals that involve recitations about historic links or disconnects between themselves and a counterpart and aggressive verbal challenges to the latter to state both their historic connections or affiliations with the other and intentions regarding whether the meeting is to be cooperative or contentious.

Some Eskimo cultures, especially those that have historically used song duels to resolve disputes, engage adversaries in preparing stories in the form of poems and songs that detail the content and sequence of tensions and conflicts. These are sung before the community as a means of elucidating the views of the adversaries, educating the community about the issues, and eliciting support for one or the other party's views or positions. In these cultures, great stock is put on the abilities of the singers in crafting their story and using word play to make their arguments both compelling and entertaining (Hoebel, 1967).

One of us observed a common storytelling process in The Netherlands while working with groups of social workers, social activists, and engineers. When asked how they wanted to process issues, they suggested that each make a general opening statement and then each would tell his or her own history of the events that occurred that led them to this meeting. When questioned about the process, one of the participants said that it was necessary to "go into the depths" in order for everyone to understand the history of the problem, the issues, and the importance that each participant placed on them. The process for sequencing issues on a subsequent agenda was as described above. Issues were either addressed as they were raised, or all parties deferred issue processing until everyone had had an opportunity to detail the shared history of the events that brought them together.

Group Conversation Approach. This approach to discussion and processing issues may not appear to be a formal process at all. It involves a discussion of all issues at the same time until a final agreement, which links all topics and acceptable solutions, is articulated by one or more of the negotiators. The group conversation approach may be relatively unstructured or may be an open conversation within the context of a larger ritual. In traditional societies, such as the Maori in New Zealand, the decision-making context, that of the *marae*, is highly structured. The format for speeches is culturally defined, and who speaks and in what order is also prescribed. What is not as highly defined is the direction of the conversation. Thus, the conversation could be linear or quite circular.

Ho'oponopono, a Hawaiian approach to issue identification, exploration, and problem solving that uses storytelling, has been used in cross-cultural dialogues and negotiations to address difficult issues between Hawaiians and non-Hawaiians (Shook, 1992). In these dialogues, about twenty people from different cultural groups engage in a facilitated discussion of issues of concern over a period of three days and nights. The process usually begins with a *pule*, or prayer, in which God, or the *'aumakua*, is asked to assist the group and bless the problem-solving process. Later conversations are also interspersed with prayers and shared meals.

After the prayer, a leader usually spends some time identifying the general problem that will be the focus of discussions, makes an effort to gain the commitment of all to engage in the process, and reviews the procedures for the talks. Once the proper environment has been established and the problem identified, the parties are encouraged to "talk story": "The process almost always begins with a Hawaiian telling a story. This first story then serves as a model for the rest of the group members. These stories...describe how the group members are connected to their families and community, and in particular how they feel about the issue on the table, including their hopes, fears, and the deep hurt of history. The core of the 'talk story' is its 'guts-on-the-table' approach" (D'Amico and Rubenstein, 1999, p. 391). As the discussion unfolds and various participants narrate their views, parties generally avoid confronting each other and avoid emotional outbursts. Understanding of issues is gradually deepened until one party, often an offender who has disturbed the harmony of a family or community, owns his or her role in the problem and begins to explore ways to make amends.

This process is not confined to traditional societies and is used by some religious groups, organizations, and subcultures in Western countries that have institutionalized a consensus decision-making process. A case in point is the religious Society of Friends or Quakers. In decision-making meetings, the group develops an agenda and discusses issues one at a time. However, they use a fairly free-ranging and open-ended discussion and dialogue process, which they would define not as negotiations but as a procedure to discern the will of God and make consensus decisions. An agreement is reached when the meeting, or group, finds what they call *unity*. Generally one member of the group, often the clerk, who is the group process leader or a respected member or elder of the meeting, will state what he or she sees as the "sense of the meeting" or consensus. If the group members agree, they say, "I approve." The clerk will then ask if anyone is uncomfortable with proceeding or moving forward. If no one dissents, the clerk will note that the decision is approved. If there is dissent, the group returns to reflection and discussion.

Circling Approaches. Circling approaches to the discussion of issues have some elements of both the relationship and the personal storytelling methods:

they often involve parties in discussion of wide-ranging social concerns interspersed with identification of the issues, problems, or conflicts they want to discuss. However, they are generally more substantively focused than in those two approaches.

There are at least two versions of the circling approach: spiraling and what we refer to as "sheep eating cabbage." The spiraling approach engages parties in gradual discussion of one or more issues with ever-increasing levels of specificity and detail. Parties begin by discussing an issue generally. They circle around each other by means of conversation, while gradually probing more deeply into the topic at hand. Each round in the spiral provides greater amounts of information and deeper understanding of the issues, motivations, needs, and interests of the negotiators, and moves parties toward identifying options or solutions. As more precise information is shared, either a consensus on what should be done gradually emerges in the course of the conversation, or parties may make general, tentative, or specific proposals to be confirmed, modified, or rejected. If proposals are rejected, circling continues until either a consensus emerges or a new acceptable proposal is presented and mutually confirmed.

The "sheep eating the cabbage" approach to discussing issues gets its name from the way that sheep who have gotten loose in a cabbage field consume the vegetables. Sheep eating cabbages do not consume a whole head of cabbage all at once. Rather, they nibble on one head, get tired of it, and shift to eat a bit of another. After trying a number of heads of cabbage, they return to the first one again and eat a bit more of that one. This eating one head, shifting to another, and returning to the first continues until the sheep have consumed all the cabbages in the field.

In the context of negotiations, parties identify a number of issues for discussion, in opening statements or social conversations. Through gradual discussion and processing of the topics—by "nibbling" a bit or conversing on one, shifting to discuss another, getting partial closure it, switching to yet a third or fourth issue, and finally returning to the first—they reach a number of agreements on the individual issues. Conclusions are reached by gradual "consumption" of each of the issues individually, by links and trades, or by simultaneous processing of all issues at the same time. Al-Omari (2003) observed this pattern in many negotiations among members of Arab cultures:

> The circular agenda means that issues are raised on an *ad hoc* basis rather than linearly, and more importantly, these issues are returned to several times from different angles.... the circular agenda has three uses. Firstly, issues are dropped when things get hot or confrontation becomes immanent. This gives each side [time] to rethink or reconsider declared positions. Secondly, the circular agenda enhances understanding, which is important in any

cross-cultural dialogue. Thirdly, it is a holistic style of negotiations where no decisions are made until all the issues have been discussed, or every stone has been turned, so to speak. The circular approach can also be described as being iterative and holistic rather than [the] linear, eliminative and reductionist style most common in the West [pp. 180–181].

While a number of cultures practice either spiraling or "sheep eating the cabbage," this form of issue identification and agenda formation is probably most common in some North and Southeast Asian cultures, especially those where consensus decision making is common. The spiral approach seems to be quite effective in helping groups develop integrative and consensus decisions. It enables participants to generally identify and explore all issues; gradually increase individual and group understanding of what needs, interests, and concerns are to be addressed; and incrementally reach a series of agreements on individual issues or packages of issues.

General Framework for Agreement Approaches. These approaches involve negotiators in the identification of either broad general frameworks for discussion or general agreements that shape subsequent approaches to deliberations and bargaining. There are at least six types of frameworks or approaches for structuring deliberations:

1. Agreeing on a general procedural framework for discussion
2. Reaching a general agreement or agreements and then moving to work out specifics
3. Agreeing on or tacitly accepting the use of ideological or religious principles to guide negotiations
4. Identifying common principles, objective procedural or substantive standards, and criteria that will be applied in future discussions
5. Developing a formula that contains components or elements of an agreement
6. Developing agreements in principle, tentative or conditional agreements, or a working hypothesis, the acceptability of which depend on working out mutually acceptable terms for details

General Procedural Framework Approach This approach involves parties in an explicit discussion about procedures they will use to discuss issues and develop solutions. Such a process agreement structures all subsequent discussions. Some common approaches are conducting a detailed overview and discussion of all issues first and allowing adequate time for detailed questions and answers without asking for or immediately committing to an agreement, looking for objective standards and criteria that can be used to shape future procedures or options for agreement, and allowing the initiating party to select the first issue to address, alternating choices, or other mutually acceptable procedures.

General Agreement to Specifics Approach This approach involves identifying one or more general agreements that all parties can support and using them as frameworks for discussion of subsequent ones. As negotiations progress, parties engage in developing ever more specific levels of agreement, with each previous level guiding the subsequent one. Moving from one level of detail to the next often involves using deductive logic, where a conclusion on one issue is deduced from a previous one at a higher level of abstraction.

For example, parties negotiating the terms of a new constitution after a civil war may agree that the new governing structure should include executive, legislative, and judicial branches. They might deduce that with three branches of government, there will inevitably be power struggles among them and that checks and balances of power will be needed to ensure that no one branch becomes too powerful or dominates another. Subsequently they might decide that since the judiciary will have oversight of the actions of both the executive and legislative branches, it should have a significant degree of independence. But how can this be achieved without the judiciary becoming dominant? One solution is for the executive to nominate judges and the legislative branch to approve them. As this example shows, each general level of agreement reached subsequently shapes later issues and details of agreements.

The rationale for negotiators using the general agreement and then specifics approach may be philosophical or pragmatic. For example, many cultures that prefer this approach uphold overarching philosophical traditions that explain how information is organized, knowledge is produced, and conclusions reached. They also maintain sophisticated educational systems that replicate this way of thinking. For example, many French schools teach a process of thinking that emphasizes identifying broad general principles and then deriving conclusions by deductive reasoning framed by these principles (Cogan, 2003). This way of thinking is applied in the realm of negotiation by negotiators who seek broad principles of agreement and then use these to deduce solutions to other lower-level issues. This mode of negotiation has been attributed to European continental philosophy and an educational system that values abstract thinking, deductive logic, and mathematics.

Similarly, Germans often develop and present their *Gesamtkonzept*. This is the governing principle that provides the logic for specific points advocated in their general position and forms the framework for all subsequent discussion and negotiation.

Other users of this approach do so for pragmatic rather than philosophical reasons. For example, Fisher and Ury (1981), U.S. negotiation theorists, advocate looking for agreements on broad principles as a way of positively shaping the later search for solutions on specific issues.

Ideological or Religious Principles Closely related to the approach of agreement in principle and then specifics is the use of an ideology or religious system to provide frameworks for negotiations, drawing conclusions, or reaching agreements. Marxism-Leninism in the past has provided such a framework for thinking and negotiations.

Many studies of Soviet-era negotiators, and Chinese negotiators to the present day, identify the use of the general agreement to specifics approach in which the general agreement has its premise in an ideological assumption—for example:

> Soviet representatives constantly demand settlement of general principles first, and will only then consider the specific instances, the technical and adminis- trative details, and the practical issues. There is only one "right" way to solve problems, especially political ones, and that is to agree on the principle first, and having [done that to proceed] to the particulars. This absolutist and deductive Soviet approach constantly clashes with the pragmatic and legalistic approach favored by the West [Wedge and Muromcew, 1965, p. 31].

Although the Marxist-Leninist ideological paradigm no longer guides many governments and has diminished influence, its logic will probably influence thought processes for many years to come. Schecter (1998) observed that this is the case for negotiators in post-Soviet Russia.

A similar dynamic regarding the use of overarching principles can also be seen in some negotiations with individuals or groups with strong religious beliefs that influence their interactions in all areas of life. Be they funda- mentalist Christians, Jews, Muslims, Hindus, Buddhists, or adherents of other religions, strong religious values can and often do influence principles that parties advocate as the basis for negotiations and subsequent agreements. For example, during the Iranian hostage crisis of 1979–1980, the Iranian students, Revolutionary Guards, and government representatives demanded that the United States accept broad principles regarding its past activities and acknowledge and apologize for perceived wrongdoing before any discussion of specific issues could begin. Some of the basis for the Iranian assumptions and demands (also reflected in the negotiation behavior of members of non-Persian Arab cultures) harkens back to Muslim views of Christians as a result of the Crusades (Maalouf, 1985).

Similar philosophical principles have guided some negotiators from Islamist movements. A historical example occurred in 1977, when a radical group of Hanafi Muslims took 124 people hostage in three downtown office buildings in Washington, D.C., and threatened to kill them unless their demands were met. To secure their release, three ambassadors from the Egyptian and Iranian embassies intervened. As a framework for reaching agreement on the release of the hostages, the ambassadors read and proposed sections of the Koran that stressed compassion and mercy. Agreement on these religious principles by the hostage takers and the ambassadors provided a framework for the release of the hostages unharmed ("Hostages Held at B'nai B'rith," 1997) .

Identifying Common Objective Standards and Criteria This approach to shaping discussions in negotiations is often referred to as principled negotiation because agreements are reached based on mutually agreed-on principles, standards, or criteria. The major proponents and elaborators of this approach are Roger Fisher and William Ury, who articulated it in *Getting to Yes: Reaching Agreement Without Giving In* (1981).

In this approach, early in talks negotiators identify and mutually agree on objective standards and criteria or principles, which will be used throughout the talks as guidelines, mileposts, or criteria to measure the viability or acceptability of options generated to address the issues. For example, a number of years ago, U.S. and Japanese negotiators were trying to decide how to address commercial disputes on specific projects that involved both governments. The Americans wanted to use arbitration, a process in which contending parties present their opposing views to an independent and mutually acceptable third party, who then makes a binding decision, as the first and only dispute resolution process to be used by the parties. The Japanese participants in the talks were reluctant to agree to the U.S proposal. They contended that arbitration and arbitrated decisions created an adversarial dynamic between parties, did not help preserve relationships, and would result in a loss of face for all concerned. They suggested that a guiding principle should be that the earliest dispute resolution procedures should promote cooperation and harmony, preserve relationships, and seek to find solutions with mutual gains before turning to more adversarial procedures. The Americans ultimately accepted this principle and worked with their counterparts to develop early dispute resolution procedures that involved informal talks, joint information exchange meetings, joint discussion, and identification of interests that needed to be satisfied, and, if necessary, shuttle diplomacy by a mediator as first steps in a dispute resolution process.

Formula Approach This strategy has been most clearly articulated by William Zartman and Maureen Berman in *The Practical Negotiator* (1982). The formula approach involves negotiators in the search for an acceptable formula:

> If [a substantive framework for agreement and a set of criteria for resolving details] does not cover the whole problem area, it presumably covers enough

of it to make an agreement worthwhile.... During this period the tactics of the parties are focused mainly on finding a favorable and agreeable framework and making it stick on one hand, and, secondly, on discarding other frameworks (of one's own or of other's invention) that are not favorable enough to merit agreement [p. 143].

This was the approach used by Henry Kissinger as a mediator to help Israelis and Egyptians reach an agreement on disengagement in the Sinai (Zartman and Berman, 1982). The process for developing the formula began with U.N. Security Council Resolution 242, which proposed "security for territory." It advocated Israeli withdrawal from occupied territory in the Sinai, respect for sovereignty, territorial integrity, and the right of every state in the region to live in peace with secure and recognized borders free from threats or acts of war. Using this framework, the negotiators and Kissinger worked out detailed agreements on how territory would be exchanged for security. The ultimate settlement included withdrawal of Israeli troops in stages, the development of a clear boundary, implanting a U.N. buffer zone at the top of passes, and creation of an elaborate monitoring and early warning system.

The Agreement-in-Principle Approach This framework for shaping discussions in negotiations, issue identification, and agenda formation involves parties in the identification and development of a series of conditional or tentative agreements or working hypotheses on issues, which enable them to explore possible settlement options without having to make final commitments to them. For example, a negotiator might say, "In principle, we can agree to X, if mutually acceptable solutions can be found to address our concerns about Y and Z. If no acceptable solutions can be found for Y and Z, we will withdraw our commitment to X." In this approach, final settlement of an issue is contingent on working out mutually acceptable concrete terms and conditions.

Salacuse (1998a, 2002) examined the approaches of 310 business executives, lawyers, military personnel, diplomats, and other professionals from ten countries regarding their orientations toward building agreements from the top down (the establishment of general principles and then working out the details) or bottom up (using a building-block approach to reach agreements on specific issues and then assembling a final settlement).

Respondents from India, Argentina, and, to a lesser extent, the United Kingdom indicated that they were likely to use a process to establish general principles first, from which other agreements could later be derived. The United Kingdom, China, Germany, United States, Nigeria, and Spain were likely to use either or both inductive or deductive procedures. Japan, Brazil, and Mexico were more likely to work on agreements on specifics first. (It should be noted that Japanese often use either a positional bargaining approach with proposals of tentative or trial positions or a circling approach to accomplish their goals.)

Respondents from different professional groups showed significant variation in their preferences for approaches. For instance, of the diplomats and civil servants, 71.4 percent preferred a bottom-up process, while only 38 percent of accounting and financial respondents took a similar view.

The Linkage Approach. This approach involves identifying issues that cannot be solved independently from the resolution of others. Linkage may occur because gains or losses on one issue must be traded for gains and losses on another for an agreement to be acceptable, because the settlement of one issue has to be part of a larger package, or because settlement of one issue in isolation might lead to the loss of a party's leverage on another that will be addressed later in negotiations. Linkage can be initiated for strategic or tactical reasons.

A key strategic decision in the early phases of processing issues is to determine which issues are, or have to be, linked versus which issues can be handled independently. Linkage is often related to the development of balanced exchanges in which each party believes that a fair distribution of gains and benefits has been achieved. For example, in negotiations among Canada, Mexico, and the United States over the terms of the North American Free Trade Agreement in the 1990s, the method to achieve a balance was a key issue. Agreements had to be reached in multiple sectors: energy, dispute settlement procedures, automotive, agriculture, glass, and others. Although links and trades on some issues in each sector were possible, each country was concerned about the overall balance of the agreement. An overall balance could be achieved only by making links and trades between sectors so that the total package would be acceptable. "In the words of a Canadian participant, the balance sought was, 'not an arithmetic but a political balance.' Mexico had to make enough concessions to provide the U.S. private sector an incentive to support the agreement in the U.S. Congress. The United States had to avoid trying to impose unacceptable conditions on Mexico" (von Bertrab, 1997, p. 47). For example, in the petroleum sector, Mexico wanted to prevent any discussions for constitutional reasons on PEMEX, the national oil company. However, in order to get an overall agreement on petroleum issues, it had to be willing to open and discuss purchasing agreements of the oil company and other parastatal groups. Opening up procurement to Canadian and U.S. suppliers in this sector was problematic, as the former countries had had no equivalent parastatal sector within which to trade potential contracts. This raised the potential of an unbalanced agreement for Mexico in this sector. Ultimately an agreement was reached that allowed Mexico to set aside a significant number of contracts from international bidding that it could use to help finance development of its capital goods industry (von Bertrab, 1997).

Aside from links and trades within one sector, each country had to estimate the values, viability, and desirability of linking issues and making trades across sectors. This can be a difficult balancing act for all concerned.

Sequential Building-Block Approach. The building-block approach to discussions in negotiations involves breaking issues, problems, or conflicts down into smaller parts or subissues, developing acceptable solutions to them, and then assembling these smaller agreements into a total and comprehensive settlement package. Cultures that prefer the building-block approach often have members who are pragmatic and compartmentalized thinkers and who value and appreciate logical step-by step approaches to problem solving. For members of these cultures, workable solutions, rather than those based on a specific principle or ideology, are often the goal. Members of mainstream cultures in the United States, Canada, Great Britain, Germany, and Scandinavian countries are often subscribers to this approach.

The Position-Counterposition Approach. This method of discussing issues is part of the broader positional bargaining approach to negotiations. In the position-counterposition approach, negotiators alternate taking, proposing, and relinquishing positions that meet their interests. A proposal is generally made by one party and is countered with a proposal from another. The first party may then respond with another counterproposal. The process continues until a positive bargaining position has been reached in which any settlement within a range is preferable to nonsettlement, differences between the parties are small enough that they can reach an acceptable compromise that shares gains or losses or splits their differences, or the negotiators happen on a solution that is mutually acceptable.

GENERAL STRATEGIES FOR COORDINATING THE STRUCTURE OF TALKS

There are three major sources of tension in structuring talks: (1) those between negotiators who use relationship-building, personal storytelling, group conversation, and circling approaches, and those who using more structured procedures, such as development of frameworks or principles and the building-block approach; (2) negotiators who want to link issues and develop packages versus those who want to solve issues individually; and (3) parties who want to use general frameworks or organizing principles for discussion of issues and those who prefer the building-block strategy.

Historically differences in approaches and strategies for discussing issues have on occasion often caused significant negotiation problems among individuals, businesspeople, and diplomats from traditional and developed societies and between nationals from Britain and the United States with France or Russia, whose citizens commonly adhere to and practice one or more of the methods. However, tensions also developed over approaches between countries during the process of reaching agreements on the North American Free Trade Agreement: "The United States was guided by an insistence on general principles that would then be applied to actual problems.... The Mexican approach was to seek trade-offs and accommodation in a 'sectoral balance of economic interests.' Mexico preferred a case by case approach to problem solving and therefore clashed on occasion with its counterparts" (von Bertrab, 1997, p. 42).

SUGGESTED STRATEGIES FOR COORDINATING AMONG APPROACHES

- Determine if it is comfortable or culturally appropriate to discuss the various approaches that can be used, agree to either accept or tolerate the use of multiple approaches, or agree on one or two that all parties will use.

- Discuss whether identification of broad mutually acceptable principles, standards, or criteria is possible, and then apply them to all topics for discussion on an issue-by-issue basis.

- Explore the feasibility of developing agreements on broad principles that can provide a general framework for addressing issues; then work to make more specific subagreements that conform to the general principles. Continue the process until additional agreement making using the approach of general to specific agreement making no longer works or parties are unable to reach general agreements. Then shift to detailed agreement making and the building-block approach.

- Identify general levels of agreements, principles, or formulas simultaneously with making specific agreements on similar issues. Work from general-to-specific and from specific-to-general at the same time.

- Work on issues separately and use the building-block approach until a combination of a number of individual agreements indicates a general principle that could be applied to other issues. Use these principles, and switch to one of the general-to-specific approaches.

- *Coordinating with negotiators using relationship, storytelling, or circular strategies.* The relationship, storytelling, and circling strategies are all relatively compatible with each other. Coordination problems generally occur between negotiators using any of these approaches rather than one of the general framework strategies, a building-block strategy, or a very direct linkage strategy.

- Negotiators who are using one of the general framework, linear building-block, or linkage strategies need to know that their preferred process will probably not be appreciated by a counterpart with a relationship, story-telling, or circling orientation. Negotiators using general frameworks, building block, or linkage approaches can:
  - ◇ Recognize that making cultural differences more explicit may neither be understood nor accepted by parties using relationship, storytelling, or circle approaches. Generally these are indirect-dealing cultures and do not like to make process issues explicit.
  - ◇ Allow more time than usual for counterparts to use approaches more familiar to them.
  - ◇ Purposely spend more time developing relationships.
  - ◇ Be tolerant of storytelling and recognize the cultural importance of this way of processing issues. Grasp the essence of a story, but it is not necessary to explicitly restate it. Consider appropriate responses to address the message that has been conveyed in the story, and then pursue more linear issue-processing procedures.
  - ◇ Explore ways of linking general framework approaches with circular approaches. It is possible, as parties are circling around issues, to identify a general principle and then move toward more focused and detailed discussions.
- *Coordinating relationship, storytelling, or circular negotiators with others using a general framework or principle, building-block, or linkage strategies.* Negotiators who use relationship, storytelling, or circling strategies often have difficulties coordinating with counterparts using the general framework, building-block, or linkage approaches. To them, their counterparts often seem excessively substantively focused, time driven, lacking in subtlety and finesse, and pushy. Negotiators using the first three strategies should:
  - ◇ Think about how time for discussing issues can be sped up, if culturally possible.
  - ◇ Accept that if counterparts do not understand messages about the value of relationships or personal stories, they are not necessarily doing it because of bad intentions or lack of subtlety. They are probably just adhering to their own cultural norms of being more explicit.

◊ If you are using one of the circling approaches, be open to looking for general agreements, frameworks, or linkages that can shape later negotiations. Use these frameworks to discuss issues in more detail. They can be especially useful in implementing the sheep-eating-the-cabbage approach.

- *Coordinating between negotiators using general framework/principles and building-block approaches.* This is a classic problem, common between negotiators from the continent of Europe and the British, and between Americans with Russians or Chinese. (French, Russians, and Chinese are more likely to use the general framework/principle approach than are British and U.S. negotiators. However, this is not always the case, as was illustrated by the United States in the North American Free Trade Agreement negotiations.) Possible strategies for coordination include:

  ◊ Recognize that these cultural patterns of processing issues are ingrained and may be hard to change.

  ◊ Determine if you are comfortable adopting the process proposed by your counterpart, and if so, do so.

  ◊ Make explicit the process you propose to use and describe how it might be helpful in addressing the issue in question.

  ◊ When appropriate, consider a blend of the two approaches. Work on general principles, and then apply them to concrete issues and resolve them one at a time.

Generic Information Needed for Discussions

As negotiators begin discussion of an issue, they provide each other with additional information, and ask and answer questions related to it. This process takes many forms, especially when it occurs across cultures. Negotiators typically present or request certain kinds of information:

- A more detailed history of the issue, problem, or conflict from the perspective of the party raising the issue

- Why the issue, problem, or conflict is of concern and important, especially for the party raising the issue

- A description of what motivated a party to raise the issue, problem, or conflict

- The logic and rationale for why the issue should be of importance to the counterpart

- Merits, if discussing the issue, for both the counterpart and the party raising it

- Downside or risks of not discussing the issue for the counterpart or the party raising the issue (this is optional)
- General benefits that could accrue to the party raising the issue and other parties if it is adequately addressed and resolved
- The basic needs of the issue, problem, or conflict that affect both the party raising the issue and, if appropriate, the counterpart
- The interests—substantive, procedural, and relationship or psychological—that must be addressed and satisfied for the party raising the issue and for a counterpart
- Why interests are important for the party raising the issue and a counterpart
- Identification of information that will be needed for the parties to make wise and informed decisions and will help address and satisfy their interests
- Identification of missing, incomplete, or inaccurate information that must be obtained or clarified before further discussion or option generation can occur
- Identification of and possible proposals for procedures to obtain and assess necessary information
- Discussion of how individual and team assessment of information and decision making will occur
- Identification of general or specific components that should be in a negotiated agreement
- Identification of possible principles, objective standards, or criteria that the parties might agree on to shape a future agreement or be used to measure the adequacy of options generated to address and meet needs or satisfy interests
- Possible options to meet needs and satisfy interests (optional)
- Proposals to meet needs and satisfy interests (optional)

Provision of this information can take place in a number of ways, most of them influenced by the culture of the involved parties. Information can be exchanged by formal or informal presentations, telling stories, reviewing history or historical events, dance or song, exchange of written documents, or examination and discussion of charts, graphs, or slides.

The information-gathering and exchange process can happen as a discrete task or can be accomplished as part of the generating-options process that will be described in the next chapter.

SUGGESTED STRATEGIES FOR COORDINATING INFORMATION EXCHANGE

As parties exchange information, they need to address these questions:

- What are your goals and those of your counterpart for information exchange and discussion? Consider substantive, procedural, and psychological goals.
- How do you think that your preferences for how information should be exchanged and discussed, and those of your counterpart, might be influenced by your respective cultures?
- Of the questions listed, which are most important for you to know about your counterpart or his or her team?
- Of the questions listed, which are most important for your counterpart to know about you and your team?

Information and the Specific Context of Negotiations

Clearly the context and specific substantive focus of negotiations and issues in question determine what information may be needed to make a wise and informed decision. For example, negotiators in an international business negotiation need to know comparative prices from other suppliers, a production plant's capacity, or information about past performance. In diplomatic negotiations over the inspection of a nation's weapons facilities, specific terms of access will be important. In development, lending, or grant negotiations, the lending agency or institution will want to know how the recipient country or agency will staff the project and keep accountable records. Cultural factors may also influence the kind and importance of information that may be relevant to negotiators. These cultural factors may be substantive, procedural, or psychological in nature.

The meaning and value of information is very much in the eye (or mind) of the beholder. Everyone interprets and evaluates information based on criteria that are often related to cultural values or norms.

A classic example of cultural values regarding information and what kind of data are valuable and to be conveyed is exhibited in cross-cultural automobile advertising in popular magazines. Compare, for example, advertisements for German cars—Mercedes and BMW—with Japanese cars—Infinity or Lexus. German car ads frequently list detailed car specifications at the bottom of the ad. The small print provides a complete list of information a buyer might want to know about the car. Japanese ads often provide only an image to encapsulate or emphasize a feeling. Sometimes the picture is not even of the car. It may be a landscape or a seascape. The image is intended to leave the reader with a certain impression that can be linked to driving the car: smooth, calm, and in harmony with nature, for example.

While Germans do value feelings, they generally prefer to have printed details about predictability and quality. These cultural preferences for data and information are often carried over into negotiations, where Germans provide significant amounts of technical information and expect to receive comprehensive information in return.

Japanese often want a high degree of technical information too, but they also want information based on feelings to assist them in decision making. The Japanese emphasis on feeling as an important factor in negotiation has been described in this way:

> What makes the Japanese tick? Evidence shows that the Japanese do not seem to possess principles, if the word principle is to be defined from the logic-oriented Western perspective. Logic is considered to be "cold" or "unemotional" in Japan and certainly not identical to the truth. By contrast *kimochi* (emotions) or *omoiyari* (caring), being "warm," are more likely to be used to avoid situations of conflict. If neither is used, a case can be made that the Japanese are not motivated by the mind or the heart alone, but by the *hara*: a primordial center both in man and nature [Matsumoto, 1988, p. 8].

A Japanese negotiator who is using *hara* in obtaining or giving information is yielding to intuition (nonlinear) rather than to intellectualization (linear) that is "enacted through effortless stylization rather than through the effort to appear natural." *Hara* is "utilized by men in the later seasons of life (autumn or winter) with practical experience, rather than by principled ideologists, uncompromising religionists or committed moral leaders." *Hara* occurs in "a confrontational setting where the interpersonal communication is based upon 'breath length,' and to be tacitly (not necessarily non-verbally) performed with appropriate *ma* (pregnant pause), rather than verbally with precise language" (p. 26).

Because of a focus on *hara* and the value of intuition, Japanese businessmen and diplomats often speak more slowly and more deliberately during presentations, with pauses and silence when appropriate. Japanese often like other negotiators to adopt their speaking style; they distrust highly verbal and articulate arguments.

Addressing Potential Resource Issues

Almost all negotiations are over some kind of resources, but they may be different in kind, amount, or degree of tangibility. For example, resources can include such diverse items as status, recognition, legitimacy, respect, time, proper behavior, performance of specific acts or ceremonies, listening, giving consideration to another's needs or interests, intellectual property, money, gems, agricultural crops, livestock, manufactured goods, provision of expertise or skills, and technical procedures or other tangible things.

When considering negotiations over resources, negotiators should ask several questions:

- What resources are the parties concerned about or will be negotiating over? Usually there are multiple resources that could be discussed or exchanged.

- Are negotiators concerned about or wanting the same resource, or do they want different things, that is, other kinds of resources? If parties want the same thing, negotiations may be harder. If they want different things, trades are generally more feasible and possible.

- Is the resource limited or unlimited? For example, giving respect or listening to another's concerns may be an unlimited resource. A specific piece of property may not be.

- Are there any ways resources could be expanded, used differently, or exchanged in mutually beneficial ways before negotiators attempt to allocate them? For example, negotiators may want to exchange money for a purchase and differ over the amount to be paid. But a monetary payment may be handled in a number of ways with many variations. It can be paid immediately or over time. Payments made at once may result in one price, and those made over time result in another. Payments can gradually escalate or decline over time. Part of a payment could be in cash and another part paid in the form of a financial or performance bond.

- Do negotiators value the resources in question in the same or different ways? Is the resource valued more or less by one or more negotiators? In this case, the difference in valuations may provide opportunities for trading.

- Would a trade or exchange of two or more kinds of resources be possible, so that each negotiator could get more of what he or she wants but would be "paid in a different currency"—for example, by exchanging an apology for a monetary payment.

- Might it be possible to create a package agreement in which different kinds of resources could be combined and exchanged in such a manner that gains make up for potential losses for each negotiator, and which all parties can accept?

Taking time to think about the kind, amount, and tradability of resources that will be negotiated can give negotiators added levels of influence in future discussions. It can also avoid getting enmeshed in negotiations over resources that seem to be limited, but may in fact not be, and help create trades and packages acceptable to everyone.

CONCLUSION

This chapter has described a range of cultural patterns in information exchange that are usually based in fundamental social and mental constructs. As the parties move toward problem solving regarding the issues that have been identified, they typically engage in a process of deeper exploration of the issues. Again, the approaches to issue exploration vary according to culture. This is the primary focus of the next chapter.

CHAPTER EIGHT

Cultural Patterns in Information Exchange

International mining, oil, and gas companies need the cooperation of members of local communities to extract resources efficiently, lower risks, and contain costs. This local cooperation is known as the *social license to operate*. Several years ago, it appeared that a mining company was losing its support from a small local community where it operated a mine in the Andean mountains of Peru. Multiple small villages of *campesinos*, small rural farmers who lived near the mine, were furious and fearful that their water would be poisoned and dry up due to the mining operation. They were worried that the water was not fit for them to drink, would make their animals sick, and was killing trout, which their forebears had depended on for food, as well as frogs. The *campesinos* had demonstrated against the mining operation and demanded that the company clean up their water.

The company was mystified. It had conducted numerous water studies in the past and had presented the results to the community. None of the studies indicated any serious problems with water quality, despite some minor issues. But the people did not believe the company or its numbers. They also felt the company was not examining the right issues and was not addressing questions that were important to them.

The company management was willing to take measures to address community concerns, but how could they talk to members of the community if there was no agreement on the data and the facts? The managers also wondered how *campesinos*, with little, if any, formal education, would understand the complicated scientific information that should form the basis for any future agreement.

Ultimately the company sought the assistance of a mediator and a hydrologist. The consultants helped the company identify what was really important to the *campesinos* and identify their interests. They also helped them jointly gather "knowledge from here" (that is, questions, concerns, and information from local community members) and integrate it with "knowledge from away" (scientific and technical methodologies and studies). Company representatives and *campesinos* walked the land together and examined the ponds and brooks where community members said that frogs and fish used to live and that they said were drying up. They discussed how the water could be sampled and developed joint community-company teams of *veadores* (observers) to observe the collection of samples and their delivery to a highly respected laboratory for testing and analysis (Atkins and Wildau, 2008).

When testing was completed, a company representative, several widely respected community representatives, the hydrologist, and the mediator assembled the results and data in a way that people from diverse social and educational backgrounds would understand. The result was knowledge and information that all could trust which provided the basis for negotiations and problem solving to address community and company concerns (from conversations by the authors with Susan Wildau, mediator, and David Atkins, hydrologist).

❧

In previous chapters we have explored the preparation for negotiations, initial contacts, first meetings, and opening statements. In Chapter Seven, we discussed how issues are identified and a basic structure for negotiations created. This chapter addresses how negotiators probe issues more deeply as an important further next step in the negotiation process. We look at how different cultures treat the question of information exchange, including the meaning of information itself. We also explore cultural norms regarding divulging or holding information close and cultural conventions regarding how to obtain information—through questioning or by other means. The patterns regarding information exchange of nine different cultures are presented.

DISCUSSING ISSUES AND INTERESTS AND EXCHANGING INFORMATION

After the agenda has been established, a sequence of issues established, and agreement reached regarding how issues will be explored, negotiators need to begin to examine issues in more detail. To do so, they must exchange information relevant to developing settlement options and ultimately coming to agreement. This part of the negotiation process usually encompasses three activities:

1. Each party provides information that they believe is relevant.
2. Parties ask questions or use other means to clarify their understanding of the information presented.
3. Parties refine their views concerning the needs and interests that must be addressed in agreements.

Each of these activities is influenced by the cultures of negotiators. The gathering and sharing of information can take place as a discrete task or may be integrated into the generation of options, described in the next chapter. As parties proceed to exchange information, they generally want to know the answers to these questions:

- What information is important to convey or obtain that will be needed to develop options, proposals, or solutions?
- How might the culture of the negotiators affect the information that each believes to be important and that can be disclosed appropriately?
- What are the cultural norms of negotiators regarding the method of information exchange?
- What are the cultural norms of the negotiators for asking and answering questions or using other means to gain or clarify information?
- What are the cultural norms for response when a party does not understand what another party is saying or wants to save face?

Generic Information Needed for Discussions

As they begin to discuss an issue, negotiators provide each other with additional information about the topic of concern and then ask and answer questions. This process takes many forms across cultures; however, negotiators typically offer and request certain types of information. We find that information needs fall into the following three categories and that a series of questions can be asked in each category:

Basic Information about Issues, Needs, and Interests

- How does each party view the history of the issue, problem, or conflict?
- Why is the issue important, especially for the party raising the issue, and why should the other party also view it as important? What are the risks of not addressing it?
- What benefits could accrue to either or both parties if the issue is resolved?

- What are the basic needs involved in the issue, problem, or conflict for all parties?
- What are the substantive, procedural, and relationship or psychological interests that must be satisfied for all parties?

Social, Political, Economic, and Technical Information

- What information is needed for the parties to make informed decisions and satisfy their interests? This might include technical information, financial data, scientific information, or other social, economic, or political assessments, depending on the type of dispute and the issues.
- Is information that must be obtained or clarified before further discussion or option generation can occur missing, incomplete, or inaccurate?
- What procedures for obtaining and analyzing information would be effective and acceptable to all parties?

Preliminary Options and Proposals

- What components or provisions should be included in an agreement or settlement?
- What principles, objective standards, or criteria might be useful and acceptable that could shape the discussion of specific issues or be used to measure the adequacy of options generated? This topic could be deferred to the option-generation stage.
- In a preliminary manner, what options might meet needs and satisfy interests? This is optional at this stage because it is part of the problem-solving and option-generation process. Nevertheless, parties may still offer proposals early in the negotiation process.

Context Specific Information

As noted in the last chapter, the focus and issue in negotiations may require context-specific information. For example, in international business negotiations concerning hiring of nationals to fill corporate management positions, a negotiator will need to know the number of positions to be filled, qualifications for the positions, the number of qualified candidates, and what additional training might needed and available to prepare candidates to do the work. In diplomatic negotiations over foreign aid, specific information about targeted population and communities will be required. In negotiations regarding an endangered fish species in river systems that cross international boundaries, negotiators need scientific information about the spawning habits of the species, seasonal water flows, water quality data over time, point sources of pollution, rate of fish take by all fishing enterprises, and so forth.

CULTURAL PATTERNS OF INFORMATION SHARING

Cultural factors also influence the kind and importance of information that is relevant to negotiators. These cultural factors may be substantive, procedural, or psychological in nature.

For many cultures, the medium and process for presenting information about issues, problems, or conflicts may be as important as the actual message or content. For example, Brett and others (1998) noted that Japanese and U.S. negotiators who placed a high value on information sharing in negotiations generally achieved agreements with higher joint gains than did counterparts from Brazil, France, Russia, or Chinese from Hong Kong. However, the ways that information is provided and shared can differ significantly. Experienced negotiators and researchers have noted that most cultures prefer certain styles of information exchange, which may be directly related to cultural patterns of thinking and processing information. Negotiators who follow culturally preferred methods for presenting information generally have a better chance of successfully communicating information in a way that increases the receptivity of a counterpart.

We will note a series of general cultural factors for sharing and obtaining information and conducting substantive discussions before discussing specific approaches.

Generally negotiators from any given culture expect and want information provided by counterparts in the same manner as they would present information themselves. We have already seen some of these variables in the context of establishing a structure or framework for conducting negotiations in the previous chapter. With specific reference to differences in the style of information exchange, we find the following important variables:

- Degree of decorum and calm versus allowance for free expression and argumentation
- Preference for oral versus written communication
- Degree of detail: general statements versus detailed exposition
- Focus on broad principles versus specific issues
- Lengthy versus brief presentations
- Timing for comments, questions, or rebuttals (during or after presentations)
- Range of questioning styles: not allowed at all, entirely oblique or indirect, gently probing, direct, assertive, or challenging

We describe how these general variables play out in negotiations by briefly examining nine cultures whose approaches to information exchange and presentations are different. We look specifically at negotiators from France, Japan, North America (the United States and Canada), China, Russia, Egypt, North Korea, Indonesia, and Mexico.

In each case, the cultural patterns described are based on general observations about these cultures. Thus, there is a danger that the descriptions might be taken as indulging in stereotyping. However, we are discussing a central tendency for the cultures addressed. In other words, many individuals from these cultures behave in approximately the ways described—but there are also many individuals who deviate from the cultural norm. Readers are therefore warned not to take the described cultural patterns at face value. It will always be necessary to observe carefully and make no assumptions about what other negotiators will or will not do in any specific context.

Cultural Patterns of French Negotiators

The French process of negotiation, presentations, and expectations for an information exchange have been significantly influenced by their educational system and the ways that members of the culture have been taught to think (Cogan, 2003). French schools are generally academically rigorous, and teaching is "deductive, rhetorical and very concerned with style. Students are required to analyze and synthesize their material and are trained to be articulate" (Hall and Hall, 1990, p. 99).

The French put a premium on logic and analysis, so they expect presentations to be organized, linear, and logical. Logic is intended to identify important principles to guide discussions. The focus on principles means that the French often prefer a focus on concepts as opposed to facts and often strive for discussions and agreements on principles and are less concerned about focusing on interests. Fisher (1981) noted that French negotiators tend to present universal or philosophical principles and then apply them to particular situations. The conclusions reached tend to reaffirm the original philosophical principle. For example, mathematics and broad statistical patterns are used to create philosophical principles or point to a logical direction in negotiations. These principles are then applied to specific situations, which verify the initial principles, in a circular pattern.

A focus on logic and principles has both disadvantages and strengths. French negotiators are often able to identify general patterns and specific problems within a complex situation. With this information, they can project consequences of different options and articulate general principles that can guide a settlement. Negotiators can universalize problems and identify the connections between issues and develop solutions that have creativity and objectivity:

> In business presentations, the French often like to provide masses of figures organized in complex patterns along with detailed background information. This is a result of their education, which stresses abstract thinking and the use of statistics and figures. Some foreign business executives have commented on the French habit of inundating them with financial data and all kinds of statistics, which to Americans is more overwhelming than enlightening. The French are not fact-oriented in the same way Germans are; rather they look for the *pattern* as expressed by the figures. Like all high context people, they are seldom satisfied with the prepared summaries preferred by Americans. They want to make their own contexted synthesis [Hall and Hall, 1990, p. 104].

There are also questions of style. Many French negotiators pride themselves on being well read and articulate. As a result of their classical education, their presentations may have references to literary, philosophical, or historical subjects, events, or principles. The French are also known to be moved by emotion and to have significant skills in presenting topics that stir up strong feelings. French presentations are commonly elaborate, may contain emotional appeal, often lack precise definitions, and may appeal to general principles related to honor and what they consider to be right.

The French dialogue process is at times polychronic—many activities or conversations take place simultaneously. This style works well with other polychronic cultures but may cause problems when a culture expects conversation, turn-taking of remarks, or listening to each individual who wants to speak. One North American observer described what happens when French and American cultures try to communicate:

> The French have a maddening habit of breaking into dialogues. One person is already talking to you and a second person begins to talk to you too. Personally I feel obliged to listen to the first person, but now this other person is talking to me...the French aren't bothered by this. Six persons will break into three conversations going at the same time. They seem to have developed a fantastic ability to hear two conversations at once, talking to this person here and following what is going on over there, and pretty soon they are back together! And then they will break up again. This is an ability that I've never learned [Wyle, 1991, p. 89].

Cultural Patterns of Japanese Negotiators

Japanese use different patterns of information sharing depending on the context and their perceived power relationship with their counterpart. In situations where Japanese believe that they are more powerful or have equal power in relationship to their counterpart, they are more likely to spend a shorter period of time gathering and sharing information before presenting an initial proposal or position. However, their initial positions are seen as a way to convey information about their interests and views rather than a fixed anchor from which they will not deviate. In fact, Japanese often utilize the presentation of multiple sequenced proposals with "trial" positions to indirectly communicate information over time about their interests. They engage in "offer exchange supported by argumentation and information exchange" (Adair, Weingart, and Brett, 2007, p.1060).

In situations when Japanese negotiators are not sure of the power relationship with a counterpart, or feel at a disadvantage, they often prefer significant information sharing before making a formal proposal or engaging in problem solving. They may use fairly indirect procedures, such as trial proposals presented in informal settings that allow a counterpart to infer their interests, needs, and priorities from indirect messages, signals, and clues (Hodgson, Sano, and Graham, 2000; Brett and others, 1998; Adair, Weingart, and Brett, 2007). Proposal making and receiving is followed by more extensive questioning than found in most other cultures (Graham, 1993).

Japanese negotiators, especially when negotiating between buyers and sellers within their own culture, but also on occasion when conducting talks with outsiders, use unique rituals for sharing information. They have clear expectations regarding the form and content of their presentations and expect the same from their counterpart. Their methods of presenting data can be highly ritualized. March (1990), in his analysis of business negotiations between sellers and buyers, notes that the Japanese ritual is like a fifteenth-century chant, a *naniwabushi*. The negotiation and the chant consist of three phases: "The opening, which is called *kikkake*, gives the general background of the story and tells what the people involved are thinking and feeling. Following this the *seme* provides an account of critical events. Finally, the *urei* expresses pathos and sorrow at what has happened or what is being requested" (p. 23).

Similar patterns in other negotiations were observed by Graham and Sano (1979). Japanese presentations open with a long and detailed general, and fairly indirect, explanation of the problem to be addressed. Next is a request for assistance, consideration, or reciprocal information to be provided. Finally, when negotiating with counterparts in their own culture, and often with foreigners, Japanese make a ritual apology for their request and express regret at putting their counterpart in any discomfort. A similar apology is generally not expected or required of foreigners negotiating with Japanese (Graham and Sano, 1979).

Once background information has been presented in the form of either tentative or trial proposals, Japanese negotiators present much more detailed information, especially if requested, but they expect technical experts to fill in the details later in negotiations. After a counterpart has made a presentation, Japanese negotiators ask many questions about the issues, interests, and proposals raised.

Japanese negotiators usually do not expect final concessions, bargains, or trades to occur during the early proposal making or information-gathering and exchange portion of negotiations. They usually have not laid out their own interests or final positions at this time, only tentative ones they want to test, so it is generally premature to move too quickly to problem solving.

Cultural Patterns of U.S. and Canadian Negotiators

Members of both mainstream and dominant cultures in North America (Canadian and American) carry expectations and exhibit ways of interacting when providing and soliciting information. Their approaches may or may not be totally compatible with those of negotiators from less direct-dealing cultures. At this stage North Americans may present and request information and not make any proposals at all or may use a positional negotiation approach and present information through their positions. Regardless of the approach, North Americans generally present considerable information and believe themselves to be quite open. In return, they usually expect a fairly straightforward and direct process with two-way communication and data exchange.

American and Canadian data presentations, in comparison to many other cultures (such as Brazilian, French, Japanese, Hong Kong Chinese, and Russian), tend to be explicit and concise (Hall and Hall, 1990). For members of the dominant cultures of North America, negotiations are seen as analytical and fact oriented, so facts and data are presented directly (Adair, Weingart and Brett, 2007). Presentations are also linear, rather short, and oriented toward finding pragmatic solutions. "Americans often prefer digests to long articles and detailed reports. They often announce at the beginning of oral presentations what they are going to talk about and when the discourse will end. Short, punchy presentations . . . are preferred" (Hall and Hall, 1990, p. 168). In addition, depending on the situation, North American presentations may also involve humor, not always common to other cultures, to build relationships and establish a lighter tone to information exchange (Hall and Hall, 1990).

Because Americans and Canadians are quite time conscious relative to most other cultures and expect negotiations of almost all types to be short and efficient, their presentations often provide less general background information, and often move more rapidly to discussion of potential options or solutions. Thus, their approach contrasts with German negotiators (Smyser, 2003), who often make long and encyclopedic presentations of information.

North American modes of presentation are often direct and assertive and provide explicit arguments or rationale for the views expressed. They also affirm the validity of the data, the strength of the results, the quality of a product, and advantages of the proposal. However, for some negotiators from other cultures, this style may be seen as bragging or exaggerating, and the approach may be neither compelling nor well received. A Mexican negotiator involved in commercial negotiations with Americans noted that "at times foreigners interpret the U.S. position [or manner of presentation] as simple bullying, and throwing weight around under a mantle of righteousness, but some of it originates in a competitive U.S. spirit which is often perceived as greed for money and power. Also U.S. weight in world politics had produced a big brother attitude of imposing principles" (von Bertrab, 1997, p. 42).

While Canadians are generally somewhat more moderate in their approach than that described above for U.S. negotiators, the general style is similar to that of their southern neighbor.

Many cultures approach information exchange by providing extensive background data and then, indirectly, request more, which they might need prior to moving toward discussion of possible settlement options or making proposals. However, in some contexts, such as interpersonal relationships between men and women or high-stakes political negotiations, North Americans often reverse this order. Americans, especially men, have been observed to begin an information exchange process by requesting or demanding information or making an initial proposal rather than providing background information themselves (Tannen, 1990). This pattern of making a demand without providing a rationale can be found in many North American opening statements that focus on positions. The lack of background information, logic, and reasons for conclusions is often disconcerting for members of cultures that expect information to be provided prior to discussing important issues or proceeding to problem solving.

However, in international commercial negotiations, but not necessarily political ones, U.S. negotiators may not be as direct in making demands for information or putting forth early positions. Positions are often only presented later, and are seen as the result, consolidation, and culmination of information gathering and exchange. In this context and approach, U.S. negotiators request information from their counterparts, make statements about their own preferences and priorities, engage in argumentation, and make relatively few offers (Adair, Weingart, and Brett, 2007). Information exchange is seen as a prerequisite for moving toward problem solving or development of proposals. Only after significant information is exchanged, or a counterpart has failed to provide adequate information or put forth a proposal that the U.S. negotiator believes requires a response, will they counter with an early offer.

Cultural Patterns from the People's Republic of China

Chinese negotiators emphasize establishing and building relationships in the context of sharing information and conducting discussions for political or commercial negotiations. Chinese negotiators typically want to negotiate from a principled position or a set of general principles to which subsequent detailed agreements will comply (Solomon, 1999). Before reaching any agreements, Chinese negotiators want to draw out information from a counterpart to "assess his or her motives and objectives, and to test out through a variety of facilitating maneuvers and pressure tactics the firmness of his or her position and degree of impatience to reach a settlement" (Solomon, 2001, p. 76).

Chinese negotiators frequently want their counterparts to speak first and provide a comprehensive and detailed overview of all issues and information, as opposed to partial or alternating presentations. Only later will they respond and share their views. This strategy is initiated to encourage the counterpart to reveal information that can later be incorporated into the Chinese negotiator's strategy for sharing information. Western and Japanese negotiators who have negotiated with representatives of the People's Republic of China have noticed their tremendous interest in collecting information. One American business negotiator remarked that after presenting several days of product and financial information, the Chinese team thanked him for his "opening statement," implying that they expected his company to present an even more detailed explanation later.

The motivation for seeking information comes from two sources. The first is curiosity. Chinese negotiators working on a specific problem or project are frequently interested in the subject at hand and want information about it to satisfy their curiosity. Second, Chinese negotiators are generally accountable to a range of superiors, who may or may not be at the table. By obtaining significant amounts of information, they can share it with their superiors later, demonstrate to those in authority that they have studied the problem well, avoid making either premature or disadvantageous concessions, and gain an element of protection if an agreement proves to be unpopular or unacceptable.

Chinese negotiators often use an interesting tactic that Solomon (2001) refers to as "projective-test diplomacy." This involves the presentation of a "vague but appropriate sounding phrase—much like a Rorschach inkblot—as part of an exchange, leaving their counterpart to give concrete meaning to it, thus maneuvering him to develop a specific interpretation to which the Chinese side can then respond" (p. 77). This process enables the Chinese team to assess a counterpart's views without having to disclose information or make any commitments themselves. Another common tactic is pretending to a lack of understanding. This strategy can be used to avoid dealing with an issue that they do not want to discuss or as means to elicit more information from a counterpart.

Cultural Patterns of Russian Negotiators

Researchers have found that negotiators from the former Soviet Union and Russia desire information, request it repeatedly, and carefully assess what they receive. However, they are often relatively reluctant to share information with their counterparts (Schecter, 1998; Smith, 1989), to the point of even being secretive (Rajan and Graham, 1991). Russian negotiators equate information with power and the ability to influence counterparts, so they frequently hold it and share it only when necessary or when compelled to do so. While this wariness is partly probably related to maintaining power, in other cases the information requested by a counterpart may not actually be known to a Russian negotiator. Social structures in Russia and other former Soviet Republics are extremely hierarchical and bureaucratic, with significant centralized decision making. Frequently, only people with high status are allowed to gain or reveal information or to approve communication of data by subordinates to counterparts. Thus, Russian negotiators often need time to obtain needed information or permission to release it from superiors, which can extend the information exchange phase of negotiations.

As members of a high-context culture, Russians often tend to communicate indirectly and holistically and provide only general information with few specific details. A negotiator may also share information in the form of critiques of a counterpart's proposals—that is, in expressing what he or she does not like about a counterpart's proposal, the Russian negotiator reveals information about his or her own needs and interests. Later in the process, the Russian negotiator may make general proposals. Frequently, specifics emerge only during the final agreement-making stage of negotiations, when Russian negotiators try to get a counterpart to provide detailed information on what they will or will not do, while preferring to leave their own commitments open and unspecified.

Brett and others (1998) noted that the information exchange patterns of Russian negotiators can influence the outcomes of negotiations in terms of both their own interests and those of their counterparts. In a study of negotiators from six cultures (Brazil, France, Hong Kong, Japan, Russia, and the United States), researchers found that Russians achieved the lowest level of joint gains in negotiations. One of several factors that influenced their findings was their low level of disclosure and information exchange.

Cultural Patterns of Egyptian Negotiators

Negotiations with Egyptians are likely to require extended time and incorporate a combination of two sometimes contradictory cultural patterns derived from Bedouin tribes and the *suk,* or market (Quandt, 1987; Cohen, 1997). Egyptians exhibit a relationship orientation to processing negotiation issues and may spend extended time conducting social conversations and exploring issues. During these conversations, the issue of face saving is crucial, along with the preservation of important principles. Conversations often circle and loop as information is gradually shared and drawn out of a counterpart. As relationships deepen, Egyptians are known to shift to the *suk* style of interaction, which involves proposing maximalist or exaggerated opening positions, presenting arguments, probing those of a counterpart, raising questions, sharing doubts, and suggesting options: in short, haggling. As the parties exchange information, a high value is placed on the way words are used, for the form of the language can be more persuasive than the content (Patai, 1983). Other characteristic patterns are articulate assertions, perceived exaggerations, at least in contrast to non-Arab cultures, and repetition of major points.

Cultural Patterns of North Korean Negotiators

North Koreans engage in highly ritualized positional bargaining. "Opening plenary statements by North Korean negotiators have generally consisted of expansive and rigid formulations of negotiating demands designed to gain maximum leverage for subsequent negotiations. The strategy of presenting the most uncompromising and maximally advantageous position possible is designed both to intimidate one's counterpart and to facilitate a settlement as close as possible to one's bottom line" (Snyder, 1999, p. 54).

After formal plenary sessions, parties often engage in informal sessions where working-level or technical team members meet to discuss issues. They may also participate in informal one-on-one conversations over meals and during breaks. Early phases of these meetings often involve probing and testing how committed parties are to positions presented in opening statements. If there is any flexibility, parties may explore possible compromises in the form of linguistic formulations that might be mutually acceptable (Snyder, 1999). This involves looking for a mutually acceptable framework, principle, formula, or agreement in principle and then developing the right language to articulate it. During these informal conversations, North Koreans may reveal more about their true negotiation position, explain their logic and thinking, and present opportunities for compromise. However, they may not adhere to these views once they return to plenary sessions.

Cultural Patterns of Indonesian Negotiators

Indonesia, the fourth most populous country in the world, has great diversity in cultural patterns for information exchange, ranging from quite direct approaches characteristic of Batak or Madura, to the much less direct approaches of Java. Indonesia is a hierarchical, rank-and-status-based culture (Brett, Shoemake, and Hale, 2006). Therefore, information generally is expected to be given and received from people in positions of authority and recognized as experts on the subjects under discussion. Indonesians, especially Javanese, as members of a high-context and indirect-dealing culture, tend to present information in fairly general terms and only gradually clarify issues through extended discussions. Often lots of information is left for a counterpart to deduce from what has been said. If questions are asked, they are framed in general terms and not stated in an adversarial manner.

Indonesian culture, like many other Asian cultures, emphasizes harmony. Therefore, most negotiations are conducted in a nonadversarial manner. In exchanges between parties that consider themselves to be peers, information is presented and received in an orderly and respectful way. The parties are likely to avoid posing questions or making comments until they have had an opportunity to analyze in private what they have heard. Questions about data may be asked informally or in private rather than in joint session. If parties explore information together, they generally do so in an amicable and nonconfrontational manner. However, if there are significant differences in the rank and status of the negotiators, those of higher rank may be much more assertive than subordinates.

Due to the Indonesian cultural orientation toward harmony and the tendency to suppress differences in negotiations, Indonesian negotiators often use *musyawarah,* or deliberation, as a means to search for *mufakat,* or consensus (Brett, Shoemake, and Hale, 2006; Moore and Santosa, 1995). *Musyawarah* is a general conversation about an issue with relatively little debate or overt disagreement. The goal of an effective *musyawarah* process is to identify where the truth lies and where people agree. Of course, the process can be manipulated, as one party might intentionally make a misstatement about what he or she sees as the emerging common ground that is a distortion of what the counterpart agreed to.

Cultural Patterns of Mexican Negotiators

Mexican negotiators in general are quite sensitive to issues of honor, respect, and position, which can influence the dynamics of information exchange. In Mexico, respect carries more emotional overtones than is common practice in the United States (Condon, 1985). Mexican negotiators automatically expect respect from their counterparts based on the social or political position they occupy. Issues of equality and superior-subordinate relationships are closely related to the concern for respect. Mexicans want to be treated as equals or recognized as superiors, a reflection of the relationship between a *patrón,* or boss, and a *peón* (Condon, 1985). Deference to people with status is important.

These fundamental patterns affect how Mexican negotiators receive and provide information. First, Mexicans expect counterparts to treat them as equals, not as subordinates or junior partners in talks, and to be reasonably forthcoming with information. A Mexican negotiator who senses that the counterpart is talking down to him or considers him less than an equal partner in talks or intimates that he will have difficulty understanding technically difficult information or issues will resent that counterpart and is likely to resist that person.

Second, Mexican negotiators, as members of a more risk-averse culture, are cautious about revealing information that could put them at a disadvantage. Negotiators often hold information quite close to their chests and reveal it only gradually, only after a counterpart has made significant disclosures (von Bertrab, 1997). If a relationship of trust and rapport has been established between parties, the Mexican negotiator will be more willing to disclose information. When such information is shared, it is often done by a senior negotiator or team member. Mexicans are also reluctant to share negative data, even if the data are very important (Condon, 1985). Negative information may be presented or reframed with a positive spin.

PROBING FOR ADDITIONAL INFORMATION

Presentations rarely completely fulfill all of a party's needs for information or understanding. Thus, negotiators need to pursue additional means for obtaining data. Negotiators have three alternative methods for obtaining additional information:

1. *Talking and observing:* Listen to and observe the counterpart or keep talking with the hope that the desired information will be intentionally or unintentionally revealed.

2. *Asking and answering questions:* Pose questions in a variety of different forms.

3. *Alternatives to questioning:* Engage in a range of other means for gaining information. Whether negotiators use any of these approaches is influenced by their cultures. In the sections that follow, we identify cultural patterns that determine whether any method for probing is permissible or relatively unacceptable.

Talking and Observing

Members of some cultures, especially high-context cultures, obtain information through talking and observing, and ask relatively few questions. People in these cultures understand information through their familiarity with the context, which gives meaning to information. The assumption in these cultures is that if a person does not know something, he or she can learn whatever is needed from careful observation. Also, by observing and not questioning, the person demonstrates deference to those who do have the information, refrains from interrupting a knowledgeable party with foolish questions, creates an opportunity to learn information at his or her own pace, and avoids losing face by showing his or her ignorance. How people deliver and receive information is also determined by issues of hierarchy, respect, age, and gender.

Information and Hierarchy. In hierarchical societies, subordinates tend to refrain from asking questions of superiors. The reverse may or may not be true. In some hierarchically oriented societies, a superior may feel free to ask subordinates questions regardless of the content or how embarrassing the answer might be. The subordinate is expected to answer immediately and to the point.

Information and Showing Respect. Cultures that value demonstrating respect for people (either superiors or subordinates) by not putting them in embarrassing situations may save face by refraining from asking questions. As noted in Box 8.1, high-context and indirect-dealing cultures value respect for relationships, many of which are based on traditional hierarchies and values of respect for age, position, and other status markers.

Other cultures consider it disrespectful if no questions are asked because posing questions demonstrates that the questioner has been listening and is interested. For example, Americans have a reputation for asking many

---

Box 8.1. Posing Questions with Respect

One of us and a colleague were training a group of government mediators for the Ministry of Justice in Sri Lanka. Although trainees acknowledged a status difference between the U.S. instructors and themselves, they accepted that American educational practices encourage direct questioning and discussion during the training process and readily engaged in active questioning.

At the conclusion of the training program, trainees were to meet with the secretary of the Ministry of Justice to receive their diplomas and learn about changes in their job responsibilities. Before the closing ceremony, the trainees acknowledged that they had many questions they wanted to ask the secretary, but noted that they could not request specific answers to their concerns. The U.S. trainers asked them why. They responded that in Sri Lankan society, individuals are reluctant to question someone in authority, for to do so risks not only their own face but that of the person in authority if he cannot answer.

The trainers asked the Sri Lankan trainees to describe a proper process for getting answers to their questions. They decided that the group could collect written and anonymous questions and present them to the secretary to answer at his convenience. That way the person in authority could select the ones he wanted to answer and find answers ahead of time. No single member of the group would be singled out as the questioner and no one's face would be tarnished by an ill-considered inquiry.

---

questions. Most public presentations are followed by a question-and-answer period. This American pattern is rooted in child-rearing and educational practices that encourage children and adults to ask direct questions and an egalitarian ideology. British higher education also promotes a practice of critical thinking and looking for flaws in an argument or logic—which can result in quite pointed, even aggressive, questioning. This British norm is supported in the most elite educational institutions as a demonstration of dominant intellect.

Information and Age. Age is a cultural variable that often affects whether questions will or will not be asked, and to and by whom. In most non-Western and more traditional cultures, age is granted significant status. In negotiation teams from these cultures, elder members engage in more question asking, and younger members may remain silent. Cultures that respect age are often affronted by questions from younger negotiators whose status or rank on their team is based on expertise and specific knowledge rather than age.

Information and Gender. Gender can influence questioning, depending on the culture. In her study of interactions between American men and women, Tannen (1990) noted that women are more likely to ask questions than men. She explained this phenomenon as a difference between men who see relationships in terms of hierarchy and status and women who see them in terms of making connections and finding common bonds.

When you offer information, the information itself is the message. But the fact that you have the information and the person you are speaking to does not also sends a meta-message of superiority. If relations are inherently hierarchical, the one who has more information is framed as higher up the ladder by virtue of being more knowledgeable and competent. From this perspective, finding one's own way or obtaining information without asking questions is an essential part of the independence that men perceive to be a prerequisite for self-respect:

> To the extent that giving information, directions or help is of use to another [as women see it] it reinforces bonds between people. But to the extent that it is asymmetrical, it creates hierarchy: Insofar as giving information frames one as the expert, superior in knowledge, and the other as uninformed, inferior in knowledge, it is a move in the negotiation of status [Tannen, 1990, pp. 62–63].

This pattern does not seem to hold in cultures where men and women have less egalitarian relations. In these cultures, women often ask fewer or no questions in mixed groups. Relations between women may be more open in these societies, but status and hierarchical relations also play a role in female-female relationships.

Cross-cultural and cross-gender negotiations can redefine the rules of inter-actions in negotiations. In the recent past, it has been reported that foreign businesswomen working in China have been very successful as negotiators and as questioners. Chinese negotiators in the business and diplomatic realms are predominantly men. They do not have a set of cultural guidelines for relating to foreign women and so treat Western women as a sort of a "third gender." They graciously respond to the women's questions, often more easily than if they were negotiating with a Western male. However, this dynamic does not hold true for all of Asia.

Generally women are not as readily accepted in key negotiator roles in Japan and Korea; some businessmen see the presence of women in negotiations as an example of cultural insensitivity. Women in Japanese companies are generally relegated to lower roles as "office ladies" and rarely rise to management. Some Japanese businessmen have difficulty taking a professional woman seriously. They only grudgingly do business with a foreign woman because they know that practices are different in the West.

Asking and Answering Questions

One of the key ways to obtain information from a counterpart is to ask questions—but not all cultures support the asking of questions, at least not by anyone or at any time. It is also clear that negotiators ask different kinds of questions to solicit information from a counterpart (Storie, 2003), including the following types:

- Open-ended questions elicit provision of more general information, avoiding any implication of a right answer.
- Closed or narrowing questions focus on specific desired information.
- Clarifying questions are aimed at increasing understanding.
- Broadening or expanding questions seek elaboration of an idea or point.
- Explaining questions intend to gain information about the logic or ratio-nale of a point.
- Interest-based questions probe the needs, desires, or goals of a counter-part, often asking, "Why is that important to you?"
- Challenging questions force more detail or demand evidence to back up a claim.
- Option-generation questions attempt to widen the scope of possibilities being considered for meeting interests: "Have you thought about X?"
- Consequential questions encourage a counterpart to consider the possible consequences of a decision or outcome

Table 8.1 illustrates the range of possibilities for questioning and provides additional information about which cultures may prefer specific types of questions. The use of specific kinds of questions, when they are asked, and by whom varies tremendously across cultures. Among the variables that influence asking and answering questions are these:

- *Degree of equality or similar status between parties.* Are the participants relatively equal in rank and status? Therefore, who can ask questions of whom? Can anyone ask questions, or only certain people designated by hierarchical rank?

- *Degree of tension or conflict between parties.* Is the context the development of a commercial deal with little or no tension, or is it a hot conflict among warring parties?

- *Timing and process of asking questions.* Are there norms that guide when questions can be asked? Do they permit questions only at specific times, or is interrupting at any time permissible?

- *Frequency and number of questions asked.* Does the culture support asking a lot of questions, or are negotiators expected to pose relatively few questions and obtain information in other ways?

- *Explicitness and language in questioning.* Are questions expected to be fairly general and indirect (high-context cultures) or direct and explicit (low-context cultures)? Are negotiators concerned with how questions are framed in terms of delicate language or artful phrasing?

The process of intercultural negotiation can challenge or change cultural norms and rules about asking and responding to questions, at least for the purposes of a specific negotiation process. Negotiators are not always familiar with each other's questioning practices and do not necessarily expect foreign counterparts to know what they consider proper behavior. If fundamental relationships are healthy, negotiators are often tolerant of counterparts who use an unfamiliar approach as long as it does not grossly offend them.

SUGGESTED STRATEGIES FOR COORDINATIING QUESTIONING AND ANSWERING

- Identify your own cultural norms for asking and answering questions before entering into negotiations (be self-aware). If possible, determine if your approach is compatible or complementary with those of your counterpart, or if they are very different.

- If cultural patterns are similar or complementary, proceed as you would in your own culture.

Table 8.1. Types of Questions and Cultural Orientation

Type of Question	Purpose or Goal	Example	Orientation of a Culture
Open-ended question	To encourage a respondent to talk more and share additional information To leave the focus or detail of the answer up to the respondent	"Can you say some more about that?" "Say more. I'd be interested in hearing your thinking on that subject."	Common in indirect-dealing cultures throughout the negotiation process Common in direct-dealing cultures at the beginning of negotiations or when a negotiator wants to elicit more general information and not narrow answers
Closed or narrowing question	To narrow the range of possible responses by a respondent and limit the kind of information that this person can give To get a respondent to be more specific To get a *yes* or *no* answer or pin a respondent down	"When exactly did the problem begin to develop?" "Did you disagree with the proposal?" "Did he or she follow through on the commitment?"	Common in direct-dealing cultures Common in legal negotiations where cross-examination is common May not be used as much in non-direct-dealing cultures
Clarifying question	To elicit more data when information is complex or a negotiator is confused To request additional data to clarify a point To confirm understanding To move from more general information to specifics	"We are confused about that point; could you clarify it for us?" "Could we get a bit more detail about your proposal so that we can better understand your thinking and goals?" "We understand that you have this goal, but confirm that we have heard you accurately." "Can you let us know whether we understand what you want?"	Used in most cultures; however, the degree of specificity requested in responses may be more explicit in direct-dealing cultures
Broadening or expanding question	To get a more complete picture of a situation or problem To encourage a respondent to elaborate on a point To expand possible issues, needs, or interests that can be used to find an acceptable agreement	"What else occurred that made you see the situation in that way?" "What other factors should be considered?" "What other interests are important to you and your organization?"	Used in most cultures

Table 8.1. (*continued*)

Type of Question	*Purpose or Goal*	*Example*	*Orientation of a Culture*
Explaining question	To elicit more information on the reasoning behind a respondent's perspective, view, or position To encourage greater introspection on the part of a respondent	"What makes this so important to you?" "How did you decide about what should be done?" "What questions did what happened raise for you?"	Used in many cultures, but may not be used as much in non-direct-dealing cultures because it may put a respondent on the spot to explicitly explain his or her views
Interest-based question	To elicit and clarify psychological and relationship interests To elicit and clarify procedural interests To elicit and clarify substantive interests	"What concerns do you have about...?" "How did you feel about what happened?" "How would you like to feel in the future?" "What kind of relationship do you want in the future?" "What about the process was a problem?" "What process would you like to use to settle this issue?" "What is most important for you to achieve in the settlement of this issue?"	Used in many cultures, but may be less common in cultures or situations where positional bargaining or negotiation is the norm, a search for or discovery of interests is not common, or less-direct means are used to identify interests
Challenging question	To challenge or confront a respondent's reasoning or logic To elicit or demonstrate contradictions in logic or intended outcomes To encourage a change of mind	"Can you explain to me what seems to be a contradiction between your past and current actions?" "Can you explain your thinking, because I just don't get it?" "Can you show me how this would really work and how it meets either of our interests?"	Common in direct-dealing cultures where overt conflict or disagreements are common and accepted, challenges and adversarial behavior are the norm, or protecting a negotiator's honor or face is considered to be less important

(continued overleaf)

Table 8.1. Types of Questions and Cultural Orientation (*continued*)

Type of Question	Purpose or Goal	Example	Orientation of a Culture
Option-generation question	To encourage a respondent to think about or develop multiple options To frame option generation in terms of meeting joint goals or interests	"What could be done to better achieve your goals and meet your interests?" "Do you see two or three ways that we might address our concerns, achieve our goals, and meet our interests? How might we do that? Can you think of some ways?"	Commonly used in many cultures, but is less common where parties spend more time on trial-and-error proposal presentation and advocacy as a way of generating possible options for agreement than asking questions to identify possible solutions
Consequential question	To encourage a realistic assessment of future consequences, costs, or benefits of an action or agreement	"What might happen if...?" "How might you or others feel about...?" "So what might happen if we do that?" "Are there any costs or downsides of that option in the future?" "Are there potential benefits of that option for either of us in the future?" "Do you really think that you can win [in court]?" "What will this option really cost?"	More common in direct-dealing cultures May be asked in less direct-dealing cultures but in a less pointed way

- If cultural patterns regarding questioning and answering are different, assess how tolerant you or your counterpart might be of these differences. Do you need to adapt your own style, or can you ask your counterpart to change?
- If you are from a direct-dealing culture and working with a counterpart from an indirect-dealing culture who expects primarily open-ended and nonpointed questions, ask multiple indirect questions as a means to triangulate information, and be alert for answers that may not be given directly, or ask questions informally or in private.

- When working with counterparts who are highly adversarial and confrontational and ask pointed, judgmental, or barbed questions, decide
whether reciprocation will be a beneficial strategy. On occasion, mirroring
their questioning strategy can be used to demonstrate strength, resolve,
and unwillingness to be taken advantage of. However, in other situations,
mirroring their approach will exacerbate differences and damage relationships. An alternative is to be direct but fair and neutral in asking and
answering questions.

Alternatives to Questioning

Negotiators who face barriers to asking questions or find that their questions
are not eliciting the desired response have several options:

- Make a statement that responds in some way to what a counterpart has
just said, and ask for confirmation or correction.

- Present a hypothesis of what you think a counterpart thinks, believes, or
proposed, and ask for confirmation or correction.

- Indicate nonverbally that you have heard what a counterpart has said, but
do not respond. Wait in silence to encourage them to say more.

Statements. Statements are verbal responses to information provided by a
speaker that generally attempt to reflect back what the speaker has shared.
When a listener makes a statement in reaction to a presentation, it often
prompts the speaker to share more or more detailed information—more even
than if a direct question were asked. Statements are especially useful in
cultures that do not make extensive use of questions, where questions may
lead to a loss of face, or where they may be seen as a challenge to a person's
knowledge, honor, or truthfulness. Dillon (1990) notes six kinds of statements
a listener can make:

✍

- *Declarative statements* are used to gain more information, much like a
question. These statements are direct responses to what has been presented.
For example, if a negotiator says, "The price that all other suppliers are
being paid is X." The respondent (knowing otherwise) may say, "It is my
understanding that there is a significant range in pay, and the average is really
not X, but Y." This declarative statement will elicit more information but
avoids the use of a question.
- *Reflective statements* essentially repeat information that was just spoken
to promote understanding. These statements can be verbatim (that is, in a

parroting fashion) or may be summaries that capture the general intent—which is usually more useful because it shows understanding. For example, a party might say, "We are unable to make the delivery at the time agreed on in the contract because of unpredictable labor problems." The listener might respond, "Unanticipated problems with the workforce and their ability to complete the work make it difficult for you to meet the terms of our contract." Generally reflective statements either confirm that what the listener heard was true or elaborate on the point, providing more information to clarify the statement. Another reflective statement may be no more than, "That sounds really interesting. I'd like to hear you elaborate on that a bit more." Indicating such interest may be all that is needed to encourage more information.

• *Statements of mind* describe a listener's thoughts or feelings after hearing the speaker. These statements may show a lack of understanding, such as, "I'm confused about that point," or "I do not understand why you see it that way." Other states of mind are distracted, such as, "I'm sorry, I was thinking about a previous point that was raised and didn't get your last point," or muddled, as in, "I just can't decide if option A is the better one or if it has more negative consequences than option B." Statements of mind might also affirm a relationship or progress, such as, "I really appreciate all the work of the technical teams, and I think the detailed proposals they have brought us are quite helpful."

• *Statements of interest* simply indicate that you have heard what has been said and would like to hear more.

• *Speaker referral* is a process of linking statements between two speakers to point out a similarity or difference, such as, "What Ali just said seems to be similar to what Mohan said a few minutes ago." Or, "Ishitani said X, and Raja said just the opposite." Pointing out a discrepancy between two speakers usually elicits more information to clarify both views or explain how they are the same or different. An alternative strategy is to request a speaker to compare ideas with another speaker.

• A *practitioner reddition* (*reddition* means *explanation*) involves the listener in recounting a personal experience, feeling, or knowledge of the issue. After a speaker presented his or her perspective, the listener might respond, "That's very interesting, but I see it differently. In my experience, the problem should be analyzed as follows..." and provide an alternate explanation for the situation. This kind of statement generally elicits additional information from the initial speaker. In this context, a listener could also respond by stating his or her own interests on a question raised. This would involve identifying a substantive, procedural, or psychological need the listener would like to address—for example, "I can understand how that solution and time frame meet your needs, but it does not meet my need to have a new plant in place and workers hired before the next election. I need to demonstrate new economic development in this region if I am going to maintain my credibility with my people." This type of interest statement usually elicits a response, so the interest can be discussed.

Responding to the Speaker. A request for reevaluation is intended to get a speaker to question what he or she has said. Dillon (1990) notes three variations. First, speakers can be prompted to ask themselves a question. To give a fairly assertive example, a listener might say to a speaker, "Now hold on a minute. Listen to what you just said. Doesn't that proposal raise any questions in your own mind about how difficult it would be to implement and get the division to accept it?" Second, the listener can open the topic to others present. For instance, the listener might say, "I'm sure what you have just proposed has raised some questions in the minds of some of the other people here. Maybe we should take some time to address those potential concerns." Finally, the listener can turn what the speaker has said into a topic for further discussion by stating, "That is an interesting idea that certainly merits further discussion by all of us. As a way to get us started, can you give us more insight into your thinking, and then we can share some of ours?"

Nonverbal or Verbal Signals. Signals are cues that indicate that communication has been received and can elicit more information, but they do not require the listener to make an extended statement. For example, a listener might make a brief pause and add a quick expression of feeling about what has just been said, such as, "That would really be beneficial!" or "That's interesting." This will often elicit more information. Signals do not have to be a content statement. In the United States, a negotiator might say no more than "hmmm." In India, Sri Lanka, and Bulgaria the listener might shake the chin and head in a figure eight pattern that says nonverbally "yes, I'm with you," or "I'm following what you say." The Japanese equivalent is a rapid nod of the head.

Silence is the last alternative to questions that often elicits more information. Holding onto silence or brief periods in negotiations when no one is saying anything often induces participants to provide more information. In U.S. culture, periods of three to five seconds during which nothing is said but attention on the speaker is maintained are acceptable nonverbal gaps in conversation. Beyond that, the situation becomes uncomfortable and people will usually begin speaking. Other cultures are more tolerant of silences and are comfortable waiting several minutes or more to center themselves, gather their thoughts, or formulate a response (Taylor, 1983).

Direct Request for Information. Direct requests, rather than questions, are another way of getting additional data. Fisher (1978) noted a hierarchy of requests, demands, or actions that one party can ask of another, as depicted in Figure 8.1. As one proceeds up the sequence of requests, each subsequent level

Demand for action,
with ultimatum

Demand

Request for conduct

Propose several alternative kinds
of conduct

Ask for a promise of conduct (for example, take
affirmative action; stop taking action now being
taken; refrain from acting)

Ask for a promise under some conditions

Ask for an offer

Ask for an idea or possible solution

Offer advice

Offer information

Ask for advice

Ask for information

Figure 8.1. Hierarchy of Requests or Demands in Negotiations
Source: Fisher (1978).

more narrowly defines the desired answer or response from a counterpart. In most cultures, the forms of request on the lower-left corner of the scale are considered to be less adversarial.

Participants in negotiations do use higher levels of requests or demands, especially if there is a significant power differential between counterparts, or if they are testing to determine what kind of hierarchical relationship exists between them. Negotiators are more likely to make demands at higher levels on the scale when the relationship is conflicted and parties perceive that risks are greater if they do not get the information they need or if the stakes are high for winning or losing.

CONCLUSION

By this point, negotiators have gained an understanding of the issues in question. Often they have clarified their own interests, concerns, and needs and have learned about those of their counterpart. By using a range of procedures for exchanging information and perspectives, they are now ready to engage in a problem-solving process. This will entail exploring positions that have already emerged during the process so far or generating additional options, the focus of the next chapter.

CHAPTER NINE

Problem Solving and Option Generation

The Timbisha Shoshone tribe has lived in what is now known as Death Valley in California since time immemorial, ranging seasonally over millions of desert acres. In 1933 much of their land was incorporated into Death Valley National Monument, which was later made a national park. The government neither paid compensation to the tribe nor provided a homeland—and ultimately the tribe brought a series of lawsuits against the federal government, including the National Park Service. During the 1990s, attempts to settle the land claims through negotiation were grinding along with little progress. Finally, the assistant secretary of the interior for fish, wildlife, and parks made a trip to California and observed the unproductive dynamics in the talks. He decided to visit the tribal president personally and sat with her for several hours under a tree outside her house, listening to her recount her life, the difficulties of her people, and their dream of a restored homeland. The assistant secretary then intervened to change the negotiation approach of the government team, instructing them to seek solutions rather than resist the claims. Within months, an agreement was reached that ultimately became law, providing over seventy-five hundred acres of land to tribal members, much of it within the national park.

The previous phases of negotiation set the stage for problem solving, which is the process for developing concrete solutions to negotiators' individual and joint issues, problems, or conflicts, with the following considerations:

- When do the parties engage in option generation or problem solving?
- Who generates options in what forums?
- How can parties cultivate attitudes of cooperation?
- What is the process for clarifying parties' issues, needs, interests, and concerns in preparation for problem solving?
- What is the purpose of joint problem-framing statements, and how is this accomplished?
- How do parties generate options and potential agreements?

CLARIFICATION OF TERMS RELATED TO OPTION GENERATION

Before examining these issues in detail, it will be helpful to review relevant terms. In Chapter Four we introduced the concepts of positional and interest-based negotiations and clarified the differences among a position, an interest, and a need. Because these terms are important in problem solving, we start by reviewing them briefly:

- *Needs.* Everyone has needs for food, sleep, shelter, health, security, friendship, community, and self-esteem (Maslow, 1954). Maslow's hierarchy of needs posits that the more basic needs for food, shelter, and safety take priority; if they are not met, people do not move up the hierarchy. Issues like respect, recognition, and creativity are important but do not take precedence over the more fundamental needs. Basic needs are triggered when a negotiation process touches on issues of survival and identity, which greatly raises the stakes for those who feel that their right to exist is in jeopardy (Mayer, 2009). Thus, the protracted peace process in the Middle East is made more difficult by the fact that both Israelis and Palestinians feel that their existence is threatened. Generally needs can be met in many ways, but their ultimate satisfaction in some manner is generally nonnegotiable for the party holding them. They must be addressed in some way for any durable agreements to be reached.

- *Interests.* Interests can be seen as the preferred means for getting needs met (Mayer, 2004). For instance, we all need shelter, but a returning refugee family that finds someone else occupying their ancestral home will not be satisfied by any house. They strongly prefer to regain their own home. Therefore, they have an interest in repossession of their old house. But even here, we can imagine multiple scenarios for meeting this interest in terms of timing, payment, conditions, compensation, and so forth.

- *Concerns.* Negotiators sometimes refer to concerns, a rather imprecise term that can capture a wide range of issues that hold a degree of apprehension or simply interest in the outcome. Normally, a concern does not rise to the level of deeper fear or true anxiety.

- *Options.* An option is one of multiple ways to satisfy the needs, interests, or concerns of one, both, or all parties to negotiations. The proposal of an option is different from a proposal of a position. Proposal of an option implies that there are other possible ways to address needs and interests. For example, a negotiator might say, "One possible option for addressing this problem is X." Usually unspoken but implied is the further statement, "There are probably other mutually acceptable ways to address the issue. I am open to considering any other approaches that you might suggest or that we can develop jointly as long as my interests can be met."

- *Alternative.* An alternative is one of two or more options. A negotiator can propose an alternative to a proposal by a counterpart to illustrate that there are other ways to meet individual or mutual interests. A negotiator might also present alternatives for consideration by a counterpart to demonstrate that there are multiple ways to address a problem, prod a counterpart to think of other ways of meeting mutual interests, or compare the merits and costs of the alternatives.

- *Position.* A position is a specific preferred option or solution to an issue, problem, or conflict advocated by a negotiator to satisfy his or her needs or interests. However, the stated position may not explicitly express the interests or concerns of a bargainer. In addition, positions, especially those presented early in negotiations, often fail to address the interests or needs of a counterpart. As we have seen, positions form the basis for positional bargaining.

- *Proposal or offer.* A proposal or an offer is an idea, intellectual framework, position, option, or suggestion made by a negotiator to a counterpart as a means to promote settlement of an issue, problem, or conflict. Proposals may present general or specific options, alternatives, or positions.

- *Concession.* A concession is a proposal or offer made by one negotiator to a counterpart that involves giving up something in exchange for an agreement. Concessions may be made unilaterally by one party or linked with trades or exchanges made by a counterpart on the same issue or another one.

- *Solution.* A solution is an alternative, option, or proposal that is acceptable to all concerned parties. It may be proposed by one party or developed jointly by all involved parties.

- *Agreement or settlement.* Similar to a solution, an agreement or settlement denotes acceptance by negotiators of a proposal, option, alternative, position, or solution. Agreements or settlements are generally reached when one of the elements of the proposal meets many, if not all, substantive, procedural, or psychological interests of the concerned parties.

TIMING OF OPTION GENERATION

In this book, we have presented negotiation as a fairly linear or phased process. However, negotiations more often follow a nonlinear path. (See Gleick, 1988, for a description of nonlinear systems.) Watkins (1998) notes that "observation of negotiation processes reveals: movement toward agreement tends to proceed in 'surges' rather than in an even flow. In particular, negotiations proceed through cycles in which protracted periods of inaction are punctuated by short bursts of substantial movement, until agreement is reached or breakdown occurs" (p. 246). Potential solutions to issues may be offered by the parties at virtually any time during negotiations. There does not seem to be a right time or single cultural pattern for developing solutions.

Cultures that are future oriented—that is, those that place a high priority on planning—may develop options prior to or at the beginning of negotiations, but may not actually propose them openly until later in talks. Cultures that are more present oriented are more likely to develop options as discussions progress rather than crafting elaborate proposals or logic prior to negotiations.

The overall approach parties take to the negotiation process—relational, positional, or interest-based—is the variable that most directly influences the timing of option generation and the presentation of alternatives to counterparts. Positional bargainers often propose potential solutions early in negotiations in the form of positions. These opening positions are generally high initial demands or very low offers that lay claim to the maximal gains a party wants to achieve or the most a party is willing to concede through participation in talks. Initial positions or demands also serve an educational purpose. They demonstrate how strongly a party feels about an issue, how important it is to them, and how far a counterpart will be expected to move to meet the party's goals.

Relational and interest-based negotiators are more likely to delay generating options, presenting potential solutions, or advocating any positions until a positive relationship has been established or parties have exchanged enough information about their interests that informed options can be generated. By delaying option generation until there is a clear understanding of the interests of all concerned, parties have a better chance of developing acceptable proposals that are responsive to critical needs. An exception are cultures like the Japanese, which in some contexts may present early trial positions or proposals as a means to sharing information about their views and interests, and potentially elicit information about a counterpart's from their response or presentation of a counterposition or proposal (Adair, Weingart, and Brett, 2007).

CONDUCTING DISCUSSIONS ON ISSUES

How parties conduct discussions is affected by their cultures. The form that such discussions take is influenced by three factors: the overall format selected by negotiators for talking, the ways they think and process information, and the means chosen to influence and persuade each other. We look at the first two of these factors in this chapter and persuasion strategies in the next one. Negotiators have a range of formats to choose from when discussing issues, including these:

- Social conversation
- Ritual talk
- Open, unstructured, informal, and substantively focused discussion
- Debate
- Dialogue

We discussed social conversation, ritual talk, and open substantive discussion in Chapter Eight. However, some clarification is needed on debate and dialogue.

Debate

Debate involves negotiators in a "culture of critique" that is characteristic of a broader "argument culture," which is a group, organization, or society that values argumentation as a way of discovering the truth or arriving at conclusions (Tannen, 1998). Cultures that subscribe to this approach often practice a cultural norm in which "conflicts are to be aired, vigorously pursued and contested and then," if agreement cannot be reached, "settled through legal or political means," which are either participatory democratic processes or a decision by a legitimate authority (Mayer, 2004, p. 46). Members of these cultures also believe that without in-depth debate, all sides of an issue and arguments for and against various views will not be adequately understood and that fragile or superficial decisions will result. Debate not only provides an opportunity for full expression of views, it also encourages intellectual prowess.

Such norms regarding argumentation are found in countries with strong connections to Anglo-Saxon culture or subcultures in former colonies, where public and parliamentary debate is the norm, including the United Kingdom, Australia, Canada, some Kenyan and Nigerian groups, New Zealand, South Africa, and the United States. Argumentation is also accepted or encouraged in Germany, France and many of its former colonies, Spain and subcultures in Latin America in which Spanish culture is influential, Italy, Greece, Russia and many former Soviet Republics (where a dialectical approach to education and intellectual interaction are still used), Armenia, India, Pakistan, Sri Lanka, Israel and people who maintain a strong Jewish culture, and Arab cultures in many Middle Eastern countries. Argumentation as a means to discover the truth is common to many religious traditions. Jewish, Islamic, and more fundamentalist Christian religious traditions use both verbal and written argumentation to interpret religious scriptures.

In this approach to the discussion of issues, interests are seen as polar opposites, as in the statement that "there are two sides to every question" (Tannen, 1998, p. 7). In negotiation parlance, issues are framed only in terms of distributive outcomes, in which for one party to win, the other must lose. Negotiators who see things in distributive terms find it hard to consider or conceive of integrative solutions in which all parties gain something (Thomas, 1983; Walton and McKersie, 1991). In the distributive bargaining process, each party takes a position on an issue and advocates for it. Such advocacy takes one of two forms: negative advocacy, in which the negotiator criticizes or attacks the view of a counterpart, and positive advocacy, in which the negotiator proposes a solution that meets his or her own needs. The negative focus is more common than the positive approach, and in some cultures, it is almost an automatic response. While in some circumstances, debate may be a helpful means for understanding an issue and active advocacy is absolutely necessary to achieve a desired end, debate and argumentation can also have negative consequences:

> When you are having an argument with someone, you're usually not trying to understand what the other person is saying, or what in their experience leads them to say it. Instead, you are readying your response: listening for weaknesses in logic to leap on, points you can distort to make the other person look bad and yourself look good. Sometimes you know on some back burner of your mind, that you're doing this—that there is a kernel of truth in what your adversary is saying. Sometimes you do this because you are angry, but sometimes it's just the temptation to take aim at a point made along the way because it is an easy target [Tannen, 1998, p. 9].

Conclusions of debates or arguments usually result when one or more negotiators (1) are persuaded to adopt the view or position of a counterpart; (2) agree to a compromise where gains or losses are shared (either voluntarily or by coercion); (3) become worn down and give up; (4) agree to drop advocacy of the issue in question and remove it from the agenda; or (5) reach an impasse.

Dialogue

Dialogue is an approach for discussing issues and interests that is used in a wide variety of cultures. Where debate is often focused on winning, constructing a stronger argument, or scoring intellectual points, dialogue is oriented toward exploration, striving to understand, and, in some cases, discovering a shared reality. Dialogue is useful for discussing issues, gaining a better mutual understanding of them, and developing solutions that meet the needs and interests of all parties. Dialogue also can be aimed simply at developing better understanding and improving relationships or actually solving problems.

Why do some cultures favor dialogue over debate? Some cultures or sub-cultures, such as the Religious Society of Friends (Quakers) and followers of Mahatma Gandhi, choose dialogue and consensus decision making because they believe that each person holds part of the "truth" and that an authentic solution can be developed only through sharing these truths. The Dutch have a tradition of more consensual, as opposed to adversarial, democracy due to an egalitarian class structure and historical dependence on each other to maintain structures to regulate rivers and hold back the sea (Mansbridge, 1983; Schama, 1988). The Japanese and Javanese (of Indonesia) see dialogue as a way to maintain proper social norms and relationships. The Thais also use dialogue to maintain proper relationships between subordinates and superiors (Mulder, 1992). Village societies value dialogue as means for preserving harmony within the community, as members will continue to live with each other long after a specific disagreement or conflict has been resolved (Von Benda-Beckmann, 1984; Slaats and Portier, 1992). When rural indigenous groups in Latin America deal with a strong and powerful Ladino counterpart, they may choose dialogue as a way of avoiding the risk of offending the stronger party, who might harm them in retribution for being directly challenged.

Although there are many formats for dialogue, most exhibit common principles. The first is embracing nonduality and rejecting dualism, a belief that there are only two possible views or positions on any issue problem or question. A nondualistic approach automatically assumes that there are many possible views of problems or conflicts and many possible answers or solutions to them. For example, the traditional Chinese view of a problem sees polarities as "complementary and necessary partners, interacting to form a higher synthesis rather than as irreconcilable and eternally warring opposites" (Derk Bodde cited in Tannen, 1998, p. 219).

This viewpoint has also been described by Lederach (1995) as the ability to embrace paradoxes: "A paradox is the interplay of two opposite ideas or energies that seem to create an irreconcilable contradiction. The irreconcilable nature emerges from a tendency to understand contrary ideas in an either/or frame of reference in which one must be chosen over the other. A paradoxical approach suggests the energy of the ideas is enhanced if they are held together, like two sides of a coin" (Lederach, 1995, p. 19, with reference to Smith and Berg, 1987). By embracing an approach of nonduality, a negotiator avoids the trap of looking only for contrasts and missing areas of overlap.

In terms of principles, negotiators also engage in dialogue to develop integrative solutions in which all parties gain and there is neither a winner nor a loser. The motivation for this approach can be pragmatic and self-interested. A negotiator might think, "If there is a winner and a loser on this issue today, there will be a winner and a loser on other issues in the future. Rather than getting into a win-lose cycle, it would be better to develop a solution with joint gains." Or, "I've got to relate to this guy, and we have to implement this agreement; better not take unfair advantage now at the risk of headaches in the future."

When conducted well, dialogue avoids personal attacks or equating the person with the problem (Fisher and Ury, 1981). Individuals who feel put down, disrespected, or devalued are likely to return to a dualistic or positional approach or to refuse to engage in dialogue. It should be noted that separating the person from the problem does not imply a lack of emotion or passion about an issue. Depending on the culture, dialogue can allow the expression of emotions, but the focus is on the problem and not the parties.

GENERATING OPTIONS

Many individuals or groups may be involved in generating options for consideration and possible inclusion in a deal, settlement agreement, or larger accord:

- Individual negotiators, who may represent themselves or a larger group or team
- A spokesperson for a team or group, designated to engage with the counterpart party, with varying degrees of authority
- A leader or decision maker who may be directly or indirectly involved in negotiations
- An entire team or a subgroup
- A mixed subgroup, with members from both teams, often with a technical assignment
- A negotiator's constituents, who may be consulted regarding their ideas or asked to provide feedback about active options
- Internal or external experts, engaged by a single party or jointly by both or all parties

- Intermediaries, such as brokers and mediators, who may also assist the parties in option generation

Options are generated in a number of settings or forums, with the choice partly determined by who is participating. The forum is also influenced by the issues to be addressed, the degree of tension between the parties, the expertise needed, team structures, the decision-making authority of the negotiators, and, of course, the cultures of the parties. We now explore typical forums for option generation and the cultural variables that influence which one is used.

Formal Joint Sessions

Forums of this type are preferred by members of cultures that value face-to-face deliberations, direct discussion of issues, and where at least some authority for decision making is given to the people who participate in them. These cultures may also be willing to form mixed subgroups in which members from each team can generate options for presentation to the larger group. Negotiators from Great Britain, the United States, Canada, France, Mexico, and Brazil are more likely to use joint sessions where mutual give-and-take and debate can occur, or mixed subgroups, to develop options.

Many traditional societies, such as the Maori of New Zealand and Native American tribes in the United States, also value face-to-face in-depth dialogue, use norms and rituals that prescribe where and how talks will be conducted, and help parties avoid loss of face or escalating conflict.

Private Team Meetings or Caucuses

A single party to negotiations may use internal meetings to generate options for strategic or tactical reasons or as a regular part of an organization's negotiation and decision-making procedures. An in-team meeting, or caucus, is a private discussion that can be held at various times during negotiations (Moore, 1987). A caucus may be conducted to assess the direction of talks, develop new strategies, create proposals, generate options, develop positions to present to a counterpart, evaluate options presented to them, break deadlocks, or make a final decision to approve agreements. A negotiator or negotiation team may choose to develop options in a private meeting or caucus—as opposed to joint sessions—for a number of reasons:

- They prefer to explore possible options without being observed by a counterpart.
- They find it easier to conduct more free-flowing discussions and consider the full range of team member views and opinions.
- Discussion of the risks, opportunities, and implications of a full range of options, including more creative alternatives, is easier out of public view.

- Private sessions avoid undue pressure or influence that might be imposed by the presence of a counterpart, audiences, or the media.
- They wish to avoid premature commitments.

In addition to in-team meetings, negotiators may need to consult with other parties, organizational authorities (executives or boards, for instance), or key constituencies. These sessions may be required to gain input on options, build a consensus on potential proposals, or secure final approval for a proposal to a counterpart.

It is not unusual for key organization leaders to remain outside direct negotiations with other parties for cultural or tactical reasons. Therefore, in the process of generating options or considering actual offers from counterparts, it will often be necessary to consult with leaders. Leaders and their negotiation teams may want to (1) maintain or preserve the distance between senior and final decision makers and counterparts for status, reputation, power, or political reasons; (2) protect them from direct pressure exerted by counterparts; (3) ensure their input without having to reveal it to a counterpart, (4) enable negotiators who are directly involved in negotiations to preserve positive personal relationships with counterparts by not having to personally own unpopular options or proposals decided on by senior leaders who are not directly involved; (5) avoid direct confrontations or expression of differences of opinion in the process of option generation; (6) share responsibility for decisions or avoid individual or team blame for a proposed solution if it should fail; or (7) use leaders as arbiters of last resort if an agreement cannot be reached at the table and a decision needs to be made.

Russian, Chinese, Japanese, and Indonesian negotiators often, but not always. prefer to generate potential settlement options away from the table rather than through direct dialogue with counterparts. Depending on the culture, joint sessions involving all members of each team may be used for information exchange and the presentation of options or positions rather than for direct development or modification of proposals.

Mixed-Interest Subgroups or Working Groups

This setting is a valuable venue for the generation of options. Small working groups representing all parties are one of the most effective ways of engaging in problem solving because they:

- Provide an opportunity for open and informal discussions
- Allow parties to try out ideas on each other without having to make binding or premature commitments
- Enable negotiators to refine proposals and build group consensus

- Offer a setting to develop appropriate framing of proposals, so that they are more likely to be accepted by all parties

Technical Working Groups

Technical working groups are quite similar to subgroups or working groups, except they are usually given a specific substantive assignment and usually include appropriate experts—either members of the negotiating teams or others brought in from the outside. People with special expertise can develop sophisticated options for the consideration of individual teams and all parties. For example, in water negotiations over the management of the Missouri River, which involved diverse cultural groups in the United States, including several Native American tribes, technical groups of hydrologists worked together to develop a range of options for consideration by the sixty-eight members of the full multiparty negotiation group.

Informal Meetings Between Individuals or Team Members

Informal meetings can be used to reduce pressure from the option-generation process and allow more creative exploration of possible solutions. They also provide opportunities for informal discussion of possible solutions, without making premature commitments or losing face by formal rejection in a joint meeting. Parties can gain constructive feedback on promising proposals, which allows them to make modifications for greater acceptability or drop those that a counterpart considers totally unreasonable.

Informal Conversations Between Spokespersons or Leaders

Key leaders or decision makers are known to engage in talks apart from their teams or other external influences. Such meetings generally involve only senior decision makers from each party and possibly their most immediate aides. Talks are usually held in private places where those involved will feel comfortable getting to know each other, exchanging views, and discussing potential options.

Mixed and Sequenced Venues

Most negotiations, regardless of the cultures involved, use a combination of the approaches identified. However, the correct combination and sequencing may be important. For example, direct-dealing cultures hold extensive in-team meetings prior to and during talks, but conduct significant option generation and modification in joint sessions.

Less-direct-dealing cultures may sequence meetings and forums differently. They may first hold extensive in-team meetings and informal talks with counterparts prior to beginning formal joint talks. Parties meet formally to define general goals and parameters for negotiations, and then delegate responsibility for generating options to internal groups from each side. Members of these internal groups then conduct additional informal meetings or mixed interest groups with counterparts to explore ideas generated internally or to build consensus. If agreement is reached in smaller groups, these ideas are brought back to individual teams for consideration and approval. If teams approve proposals, they will be presented to joint sessions for further consideration and approval.

SUGGESTED STRATEGIES FOR COORDINATING OPTION-GENERATION FORUMS

- Identify the forum that will be most comfortable for you and your team and for your counterparts for developing options.

- If the forums are the same, make the arrangements for their use.

- If the preferred forums are different, determine if there are approaches that would be acceptable to both or all parties and the possible sequence for using them. For example, consider holding informal discussions and then allowing time for in-team meetings before presenting options in joint session. Schedule frequent breaks as appropriate to allow individual negotiators or teams to consult with other members of their organization or constituents.

CULTIVATING ATTITUDES OF COOPERATION

Before engaging in specific option-generation procedures, negotiators sometimes initiate activities that promote greater openness to cooperation and collaborative problem solving. A number of these strategies were proposed by Fisher and Ury (1981).

Separating the People from the Problem

In many negotiations, it is often helpful to "separate the people from the problem" (Fisher and Ury, 1981). In other words, rather than focusing on the motives, actions, or demands of the "other side," negotiators are encouraged to focus on the problem as a joint task of all parties. Negotiators together can identify the key interests of all concerned and then accept the mutual task of trying to meet as many of those interests as possible. By shifting attention away from personal styles and personality issues, parties can better prepare themselves to focus on what is important to them. Richard Holbrooke, the U.S. negotiator involved in developing the Dayton Accords to end the civil war in the former Yugoslavia, used this approach when he separated President

Milosevic of Serbia and his actions, which Holbrooke found to be abhorrent, from the long-term goals he was striving to achieve (Holbrooke, 1999).

While this approach can be valuable in promoting greater cooperation, it does have a cultural bias. It assumes that people can be separated from a problem, a Western way of thinking: the ability to compartmentalize factors. Thus, negotiators from the West believe that people, issues, and interests can be separated and addressed in isolation (Salem, 1997). Negotiators from many Asian, Middle Eastern, or Latin American cultures, who depend on relationships to develop mutually acceptable options, do not generally separate the people from the problem. In their cultures, the counterpart and their relationship with them are inextricable from the problem and the solution—they are bound together. Because of the linkage of the person and the problem, members of these cultures may pursue several alternatives. They can work to improve the relationship and build a positive bond to promote problem solving, try and ignore the problematic behavior, or explore whether the counterpart can be replaced by a more amenable and less problematic partner.

SUGGESTED STRATEGIES FOR SEPARATING PEOPLE AND PROBLEMS

- A negotiator who decides to separate the people from the problem being addressed can do so indirectly or directly. Indirect application of this principle involves systematically ignoring the irritating personal attitudes or behaviors of a counterpart, focusing on the substantive issues and interests to be addressed and encouraging the counterpart to do the same simply by setting an example of the desired attitude and behavior. This is a modeling approach to behavior change.

- One direct approach to separating the people from the problem involves a more explicit acknowledgment of attitudes and behaviors that each party finds difficult or unacceptable, and, at the same time, a direct suggestion that all parties set these aside and focus on the key issues and interests that need to be addressed. Generally, such a direct approach to gaining parties' cooperation to separate the people from the problem will work only in direct-dealing cultures and countries. In almost all others, an indirect-modeling approach is more likely to be successful.

Finally, a more consequential direct approach is to explore ways to change counterparts, either directly or indirectly.

Attitudes Toward Winning and Losing

All cultures carry attitudes regarding whether it is possible to develop joint gain solutions in which all parties win. While some cultures accept the possibility of win-win outcomes, others tend to believe that one party will likely win at least some more than the other party—or one party will actually lose. These attitudes reflect beliefs described earlier as integrative versus distributive solutions, which influence the approach that parties select for negotiations and option generation.

Those with win-lose or distributive orientations are likely to use positional negotiation procedures throughout the negotiation process, including during option generation. One of us, when working in Haiti, noted a strong cultural orientation toward win-lose outcomes. Many Haitians have to struggle to obtain the basic necessities for survival. Several Haitians interviewed about their approach to dispute resolution indicated that a significant number of members of their culture resent someone getting ahead and see advancement by one person in relation to another person's getting stuck or falling behind.

Negotiators with win-win or integrative orientations are likely to use interest-based approaches. Japanese bargainers represent a good example: they seek integrative solutions and are likely to use interest-based approaches to option generation to achieve them.

SUGGESTED STRATEGIES FOR COORDINATING ATTITUDES TOWARD WINNING AND LOSING

- See Chapter Four for extensive material on coordinating different approaches to winning and losing.

Aspiration Expectations: Setting a Goal of Integrative Solutions

Aspiration expectations refer to the goals and expectations parties have for the outcomes of negotiations. These expectations relate to both the quantity and quality of benefits expected by a negotiator. Research on negotiations has found that when negotiators set high aspiration targets and strive to attain them, they usually achieve greater benefits than when they set lower expectations (Thompson, 2001; Galinsky, Mussweiler, and Medvec, 1999). Similarly, negotiators who focus on attaining the ideal do better in increasing benefits to be shared by all than focusing on just what they ought to get (Galinsky and Mussweiler, 2000).

These research results apply equally to the development of integrative versus distributive options. When parties state explicitly that the goal of option generation is to develop integrative solutions in which all parties' needs are addressed, they are more likely to attain that goal than when this outcome is only assumed or unstated. By leaving this goal unstated, parties leave the door open for beliefs about win-lose or distributive outcomes to prevail. Of course, making an explicit goal statement will work well only in direct-dealing cultures. More subtle means will be necessary in indirect-dealing cultures.

The Value of Generating Multiple Options

In general, the more options parties have to assess for their ability to satisfy interests, the better. Obviously parties can also generate too many options, which can create coordination problems itself, but this is relatively rare. More commonly parties fail to generate enough options to permit comparisons among them regarding their ability to satisfy individual or joint interests. This creates a difficult situation—even deadlock—in bilateral negotiations, when the parties are using positional bargaining and have only two options on the table. Typically, to overcome this barrier, one of the parties has to push the others to develop a wider array of possible solutions.

Separating Option Generation from the Evaluation of Options

In the heat of negotiations, parties tend to propose alternatives and then almost immediately evaluate them, one at a time. There is a risk with this practice that parties will start a pattern of tit-for-tat rejection, in which one party proposes an option and the counterpart immediately judges and rejects it. Subsequently the counterpart makes another proposal and the other negotiator repeats the pattern of assessment and rejection. The parties may then repeat this pattern in multiple rounds of option proposal and rejection, making little progress toward a settlement.

In the experience of many negotiators and the authors, a more productive process is to generate as many options as possible without any commentary or judgment (either positive or negative), until the parties have exhausted their imaginations and cannot come up with any additional ideas. Only then do the parties assess the options, using the parties' stated interests and needs as the criteria for evaluation.

The challenge for negotiators is to recognize that a negative dynamic is occurring and to find a way to change to the more productive pattern. Usually one of the negotiators needs to call attention to the unproductive dynamic and suggest that all parties separate the generation of options from their evaluation.

SUGGESTED STRATEGIES FOR CHANGING THE OPTION-GENERATION DYNAMIC

- In a direct-dealing culture, it is usually possible to call attention to the negative dynamic and suggest that the parties generate multiple options before any one of them is evaluated—for example: "It appears to me that we have been going around in circles. Each of us is rejecting all options out of hand. Why don't we try coming up with as many ideas as we can without any comments from anyone—and then we can see how the options or a combination of them might meet each of our needs."

- In an indirect-dealing culture (or if one party is strongly indirect dealing), it will be more acceptable to model the desired behavior rather than point out the difficult pattern. Thus, the party who wants to change the dynamic might say, "You have suggested several interesting options, and we have offered several alternatives as well. I would like to hear more of

your ideas and present a couple of more options myself. As we do this,
I am going to refrain from commenting on any of the ideas until we have
heard them all.''

- Suggest that all of the options (even ones previously rejected) be assessed
  based on how they meet the interests of all parties.

- Change the dynamic in a pattern in which one party makes a suggestion and the other immediately rejects it. This is a difficult dynamic to
  break and takes discipline. Even if the parties have all agreed to generate
  options without immediate judgment, they may slip back into the negative
  pattern. Someone will have to monitor the process and remind the parties
  about the agreed change in pattern.

- If a party suggests a position and wants or demands your immediate
  response, a form of evaluation, acknowledge the position as one possible
  way to address the issue or interests and request that at least two more
  options be developed or presented before any one of then is assessed.

Clarifying Issues, Needs, and Interests in Preparation for Problem Solving

By this point in negotiations, the parties should have developed a clear
understanding of the issues that must be addressed and the needs and interests
that have to be met for a satisfactory outcome. A listing of issues and the
associated needs and interests forms the agenda for problem solving.

A common negotiation problem concerns how directly and explicitly issues
and interests are articulated and understood at this phase of negotiations,
regardless of whether discussions are happening within or between cultures.
As we have seen in relation to other factors and phases, how needs and
interests are expressed is influenced by three factors: whether negotiators come
from low- or high-context cultures, are direct or indirect dealing when it
comes to processing issues or conflicts, and are using relational, positional, or
interest-based approaches to conducting negotiations.

Low- or High-Context and Direct and Indirect Negotiators. Negotiators from
low-context cultures who are also direct dealing are likely to make their issues,
needs, and interests more explicit prior to shifting to problem solving than
will negotiators from high-context and indirect-dealing cultures. Low-context,
direct-dealing negotiators value a significant level of detail regarding issues,
needs, and interests because they believe that a clear statement of these factors
will increase the probability that acceptable options to meet them will be
developed and that negotiators will not be trying to solve the wrong issues
or problems.

Direct-dealing and low-context negotiators are also more likely to restate explicitly what they have heard from a counterpart and to summarize what they have concluded from the exchange of information conducted in the previous phase. Such a summary typically includes a brief review of relevant background information, a restatement of the issues that need to be addressed, a listing of the interests that must be met, and, possibly, a direct request from a counterpart to confirm the accuracy of their perceptions and statements. On occasion, they will want issues, needs, and interests to be written down in briefing or position papers, particularly in more formal or protracted negotiations.

Negotiators from indirect-dealing and high-context cultures are less likely to articulate their understanding of issues, needs, and interests so explicitly because they assume that their counterpart already understands them or can intuit them. Negotiators from these cultures prefer general and diplomatic framing of topics and interests rather than specific or detailed statements that might put a negotiator on the spot, cause unnecessary discord, or make the party proposing them appear self-centered. They are likely to use subtle techniques for framing issues, such as allusions, indirect suggestions, or metaphors, so as to preserve relationships and keep the option of settlement open for a more auspicious time.

Relational, Positional, or Interest-Based Negotiators. Relational negotiators at this stage of the negotiation process usually begin to shift toward a positional or interest-based approach to problem solving. The relational orientation, in combination with preferences for direct or indirect dealing, often determines whether they will shift more toward positional or interest-based approaches for developing possible settlement options.

Indirect-dealing and relational negotiators may choose to shift to a positional approach if they believe that everyone understands the issues and interests in question, and all that remains is to make concrete proposals or present positions that address them to the greatest extent possible for all involved parties. They may also shift to a positional approach if they are more powerful than their counterpart and believe they can dictate at least the broad parameters of settlement, if not the details. Finally, they may shift to a positional approach if their substantive and procedural interests are so important that they are willing to risk a positive future relationship for a desired outcome, or they are pushed into the process by an aggressive and positional counterpart. These negotiators may shift to an interest-based approach if tensions between negotiators are low, maintenance of a positive working relationship with a counterpart is deemed critical, or they want to be sure to develop solutions that meet the needs of all concerned.

Direct-dealing and low-context negotiators, who, up to this point, have been positional bargainers, may either continue to use this approach or shift to a more interest-based strategy. If they remain in a positional mode, they may forgo any restatement of the issues or interests to be addressed and proceed directly to making proposals for settlement or presenting positions. If they have shifted to a more interest-based approach, they may explicitly restate the issues and interests to be addressed. Interest-based negotiators almost always restate issues and interests before engaging in option generation.

SUGGESTED STRATEGIES FOR COORDINATING THE CLARIFICATION OF ISSUES AND INTERESTS

For Negotiators from Direct-Dealing and Low-Context Cultures Working with Counterparts from Indirect-Dealing and High-Context Cultures

- Begin by understanding that a counterpart's reluctance to directly articulate issues, needs, or interests is not necessarily an indication of bad faith. He or she may be reluctant to make these topics explicit for a variety of reasons, some of them culturally based.

- Determine whether it is necessary for you to have a clear articulation of issues and interests. Also determine whether you believe that both you and your counterpart understand the general gist of the situation and can proceed to generate options to meet individual and joint concerns without having them clearly stated.

- If a clear and explicit articulation of issues and interests is needed, decide how detailed it has to be to meet your needs and, at the same time, accommodate your counterpart's expectations and norms. They may not have to be as explicit as would be the case in your culture for you to proceed.

- If clearer and more explicit articulation is needed, determine if this can be done in an indirect manner in a plenary session, an informal or off-the-record meeting with your counterpart, or a side meeting with one member of your counterpart's team with whom you have a positive relationship and where confidences can be more easily shared.

Strategies for Negotiators from Indirect-Dealing and High-Context Cultures Working with Counterparts from Direct-Dealing and Low-Context Cultures

- Begin by understanding that a counterpart's tendency to articulate issues and interests directly and explicitly and provide lots of details is not necessarily motivated by a desire to cause embarrassment or to be rude. This person's motivation is usually to present clearly what he or she is concerned about and understand what you are interested in.

- Determine if it is possible for you to be more explicit about your issues and needs without creating additional tensions, unnecessary disagreement, embarrassment, or slights to the personal honor of any of the parties.

At times just a bit more disclosure will satisfy your low-context counterpart and will create greater trust, allowing negotiations to proceed with more comfort and confidence.

- If necessary or appropriate, communicate your understanding of your counterpart's and your own issues and interests in private, informal, or off-the-record meetings with either your individual interlocutor or a member of his or her team with whom you have confidence. This approach allows more candid disclosure of information about delicate topics and informal discussion of issues without prematurely locking parties into positions, and it permits a party to save face in situations where more formal and public disclosure of views might be difficult.

- Consider conveying information to your counterpart through an intermediary if direct articulation of your views is uncomfortable.

DEVELOPING JOINT PROBLEM STATEMENTS

We introduced the concepts of framing and reframing in Chapter Four as important tools for negotiators. In addition to restating issues and interests, negotiators may decide to frame a joint problem statement before proceeding to option generation. Joint problem statements set out the interests of all parties as a way of declaring, "This is the problem we need to solve together." Through the subsequent process of option generation, the negotiators strive to develop solutions, viewing the stated interests much as an inventor, engineer, or builder would see design criteria or specifications.

One-sided framing of issues is quite common in negotiations regardless of the cultural context in which they are occurring. In the heat of trying to resolve a conflict, negotiators often conceptualize their goals in ways that either dismiss the concerns and interests of their counterpart or do not acknowledge them. This is a particular problem for positional negotiators, but is also common for interest-based bargainers.

These are examples of one-sided framings of issues and interests:

A. "The refugees cannot return to their original communities. There are other people living in their houses now, and there will be no place for the returnees to live."

B. "We do not want your nuclear-powered or nuclear-armed ships to visit our ports. Their visits put the safety of our people at risk and are politically unpopular."

C. "We have production quotas to meet! Whether it is a religious holiday or not, we expect your people to work on that day."

Each of these statements defines an issue to be addressed and includes reference to interests, but only the interests of the party making the statement. The needs and concerns of other parties are not included in the statements. We can imagine their counterparts making equally one-sided statements of their own positions and interests:

A. "Everyone has a right to return to their home communities and to regain their houses from the illegal squatters."

B. "Our nations have been allies for decades against common enemies. The alliance means nothing if you refuse to allow our ships in your ports and force us to sail thousands of miles for basic servicing!"

C. "This is our most important religious holiday of the year. We demand our religious rights!"

Unilateral framing of issues and interests inhibits collaborative generation of proposals for settlement. It fails to recognize the validity of all parties' interests, which should become the criteria for developing potential solutions. Framing joint problem statements can help overcome this problem. These statements describe topics for discussion and the focus for option generation in terms of meeting all parties' needs and interests.

How do negotiators develop joint problem statements? The previous section explored the process of clarifying issues and associated interests. Once interests have been identified and acknowledged, explicitly or implicitly, one or both parties are in a position to attempt a joint problem statement. Often the process starts with a negotiation team stating or restating their own interests and their best understanding of the interests of their counterpart—just to be sure that he or she has heard correctly. At this point, someone articulates a joint task that includes both or all parties' interests, similar to the statements above. There are several general patterns for joint problem statements:

• "How can we [address X problem] in a way that meets your needs for [A] and our interests in [B]?"

• "We are looking for a solution that does X to meet your interests and Y to meet mine."

If we take the one-sided framing of the statements above and expand them to contain the interests of both parties, they might look like this:

A. "We need to find a process for the orderly return of displaced people that accommodates the needs of those who remained behind, as well as returning families."

B. "How can be met the need to service the nuclear fleet and at the same time not create unnecessary political problems or raise health and safety concerns of the local population?"

C. "We are jointly looking for a solution whereby the company can meet its contractual delivery deadlines to customers and at the same time respect employees' religious values and enable them to celebrate their religious holidays at the appropriate times."

Each of these statements contains the interests of both parties. To develop this kind of statement and have it accepted by all concerned, the needs and concerns of all negotiators must generally be understood. A party does not necessarily have to agree with or support a counterpart's needs or interests for them to develop a joint problem statement and engage in option generation. It is necessary only for a negotiator to recognize that the counterpart's interests are important to him or her and to be willing to explore how to address them.

This process is illustrated in Figure 9.1, in which both parties' interests are identified separately and then combined into a statement of common interests.

Two illustrations of the process for developing joint problem statements follow:

Example 1

- *Party A's framing of issues:* "We are the 'little people' in this community, and many of us are from indigenous groups. We demand control over situations that could have bad impacts on our lives. The mine is going to pollute the river, which will definitely affect our lives and health. We want to be listened to and demand to have something say about water quality monitoring."

- *Party B's restatement of party A's interests:* "You are concerned that local people have direct influence over what happens in their community. You want to be consulted with and heard by the company and involved in

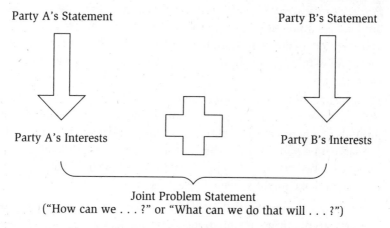

Party A's Statement   Party B's Statement

Party A's Interests   Party B's Interests

Joint Problem Statement
("How can we . . . ?" or "What can we do that will . . . ?")

Figure 9.1. Framing a Joint Problem Statement in Terms of Multiple Interests

some way to make sure that the water quality of the river is monitored and protected.''

- *Party B's framing of issues:* "We agree we must have accountability in development of the mine, but it is hard to involve people who may not understand technical or scientific information and cannot read and write.''

- *Potential framing of party B's interests:* "While you agree there needs to be accountability, you are not sure how to involve people with various levels of education.''

- *Framing of a joint problem statement (by either party A or B):* "We need to develop ways for local people and representatives of the company to work together to prevent any negative impacts on the community that might result from mining activities. We also need to explore how community members, regardless of their education, can be involved in monitoring and ensuring protection of water quality.''

Example 2

- *Party A's framing of the issue:* "Just because someone looks as if they might come from the Middle East or Pakistan, we insist that they should not be discriminated against by racial profiling when boarding airplanes.''

- *Party B's restatement of party A's interests:* "You want airline and security personnel to refrain from targeting people, treating them differently, or violating their civil rights because of their appearance or possible national origin.''

- *Party B's framing of the issue:* "We do not want to take any risks. Our nation has already suffered enough. We must check anyone whose background is questionable to help guarantee the safety of the flying public, as well as people on the ground.''

- *Party A's framing of party B's interests:* "Safety of passengers in the airplane [as opposed to on the ground] and people on the ground is your major concern. You want to be sure that you have taken adequate measures to minimize risks and increase the probability of safety for all concerned.''

- *Framing of a joint problem statement (by either party A or B):* "How can we find ways to ensure the safety of the flying public, check the backgrounds of any passengers whose intentions may be questionable, and at the same time uphold civil rights and refrain from discriminating against passengers because of their appearance or possible national origin? How do you think we might achieve these joint goals?''

A classic international conflict in which reframing was critical in seeking solutions occurred during negotiations between Israel and Egypt over the disposition of contested territory in the Sinai Peninsula resulting from the 1973 war. The Egyptians initially framed the issue as a position: "We demand that the Israelis withdraw their troops from the Sinai. The land is ours!" The Israelis responded with an equally positional statement: "We will never leave! We need the land for our defense and to ensure we will not be attacked in the future." Eventually issues were reframed as a problem representing both parties' interests: "How can Egypt regain political sovereignty over the contested portion of the Sinai, and at the same time ensure that Israel can have secure borders, protected from any future armed invasion?" This framing allowed the Israelis and Egyptians to trade sovereignty and political control of land for its demilitarization and security for Israel.

GENERATING OPTIONS OR POTENTIAL SOLUTIONS

Options are frequently developed using positional or interest-based bargaining procedures, as described in Chapter Four. In the positional process, negotiators generally alternate the presentation of positions and counterpositions that meet their individual and, ideally, mutual needs and interests. Positions are considered and debated by parties until such time as one or more parties is convinced of the merits of a position and accepts it, a compromise is reached, or there is a convergence of opinion on a mutually acceptable proposal. At best, the proposed positions are informed by parties' understanding of each other's interests and needs. Interest-based procedures focus on the identification of parties' individual and joint issues, uncovering and making as explicit as possible all parties' interests and needs and then searching for options that will address them. (As noted in Chapter Eight, some cultures, such as the Japanese, may also use a positional approach for information sharing about their interests. Early positions are illustrations of solutions that will meet their interests and are presented to elicit responses that present information about a counterpart's interests. At this point, Japanese negotiators are not locked into their position, but are using it as a vehicle for information exchange.) Within the larger framework of positional and interest-based negotiations, practitioners can turn to a range of option-generation procedures for either approach. A number of these are detailed below with guidance regarding cultures that frequently use them. We have divided the procedures into three categories:

- Procedures for producing additional ideas or options
- Procedures for addressing particular kinds of factors
- Procedures for linking and packaging proposals on multiple issues

Procedures for Producing Additional Ideas or Options

Negotiation parties often need to develop new ideas as part of a problem-solving process. At times, they have become stuck using other processes or have simply become deadlocked and need to explore other possibilities. If they are engaged in integrative negotiations and attempting to address the needs and interests of all parties, the generation of multiple options is a normal part of the process. Parties typically use one or more of the procedures described next to expand the proposals on the table.

Brainstorming. This procedure helps parties generate a range of possible ideas to consider without requiring an agreement to any of them, at least during the initial brainstorming process. Assuming that the parties have agreed to the need for producing as many possible options as possible to address a common issue or problem, one of them will propose a brainstorming process as a way to generate a lot of ideas quickly.

A brainstorming process has five guidelines:

1. Options are presented in brief using only headlines or key words. They may be fleshed out later if necessary.

2. The goal is to generate as many potential options as possible, so parties should continue to offer ideas quickly for a specified period.

3. Parties agree to refrain from critiquing or evaluating any proposal until a complete list has been developed.

4. Parties are encouraged to suggest innovative and even "wild" ideas and should not be constrained by concerns for practicality at this stage. The goal is to get as many creative ideas on the table as possible.

5. The suggestion of an option or idea does not commit anyone to it, including the person proposing it. The idea becomes one of the possibilities on the table for discussion.

Once a list has been developed, parties may ask for clarification on some of the proposals or ideas that have been raised. Questions of clarification are allowed so that parties can learn more about the idea and determine if they want to pursue it further, but in-depth discussion, critiques, or debate is curtailed until several ideas are selected for further elaboration.

Once everyone has a basic understanding of the range of options, they may narrow the number that will be developed and analyzed in more detail. Two methods for narrowing the range of ideas for further development are to identify several proposals that parties jointly consider promising, and focus on those, or ask each party to identify options they consider to be unacceptable and eliminate them, thus narrowing the list to those that both parties wish to discuss further.

Brainstorming is commonly used in cultures where option generation is a fairly structured procedure, the parties accept a focus on group process, and issues are often divided into smaller parts as a way to develop solutions. This and other problem-solving processes are common in the majority cultures in North America, northern Europe, and Australia and in the business sectors of many African countries. As we have seen, other cultures favor more holistic approaches to option generation and prefer to develop integrated packages and work on all issues simultaneously. Members of those cultures are likely to resist structured solution development procedures, including brainstorming.

Fractionating. Negotiators have often found it useful to break an issue down into its parts and then negotiate the pieces. For instance, in a commercial deal regarding purchase of manufactured goods, negotiators might focus on the question of the price per item and get stuck there, unable to find a price that falls within the bargaining range of both sides. However, if they manage to break the problem down, looking at issues of quality, quantity, specifications, time of delivery, transportation costs, communication, and length of contract, the two parties might find it possible to negotiate on these issues separately and come to substantive agreements on most—or discover that they have quite different needs in relation to the subissues, allowing them to come to agreement. Perhaps the seller has been balking on the question of price per piece because he was concerned about his ability to produce the quantities demanded in a timely manner. By looking at that question separately, they might discover that the buyer is more concerned about price and less about time of delivery, allowing them to come to agreement on a package deal that meets each of their needs.

Trial-and-Error Option Generation. This process can be used to generate multiple options fairly rapidly and get feedback on them prior to selecting or agreeing on one. Parties can use it in conjunction with either positional or interest-based approaches to negotiations.

In a trial-and-error process, a negotiator presents an option—or perhaps several options—without asking a counterpart for acceptance of them. Rather, after this initial presentation of the idea or ideas, the negotiator asks for feedback from the counterpart—what he or she likes or dislikes about the option. Counterparts can also be asked to compare options and indicate which they prefer over others. There is often a lot of give and take in these discussions, and talk may be quite free-flowing. Ultimately the negotiators can use the information exchanged to modify an option to make it more acceptable to the other party or develop one or more additional options for consideration. As the negotiator listens to the feedback from a counterpart, he or she will receive crucial information about the other party's needs and interests, which then becomes helpful for adapting proposals.

In general, effective negotiators propose many more options for counterparts to consider than do ineffective bargainers (Moran and Stripp, 1991). The trial-and-error approach supports the generation of multiple options.

Hypothesis Testing. In hypothesis testing, the negotiator develops a detailed hypothetical solution to a problem, proposes it to a counterpart, and asks that person to suspend judgment on its elements until it can be fully explored. Hypothesis testing generally allows a broader and more in-depth analysis of a potential solution than the trial-and-error approach. This approach can be used by either positional or interest-based negotiators.

The issue or issues addressed in the hypothetical solution can be quite narrow or more comprehensive in nature. As in the trial-and-error approach, a counterpart may be asked to indicate the strengths and weaknesses of the hypothetical solution, areas that are acceptable or need to be changed, and possible modifications. Also, two or more hypothetical solutions may be compared and contrasted with respect to how well they satisfy interests. None of these are eliminated until the end of the analysis process.

Hypothetical option development works best in cultures or situations where people are able to work at a level of abstraction and are capable of holding judgments in abeyance. In some conflicts or cultures, parties are unwilling to consider hypotheticals for fear that they will pushed into adopting them. Members of these cultures are generally very concrete thinkers and prefer to consider a tangible proposal that is a genuine offer.

Elaboration. In this process, a key element of an agreement is identified and agreed on by the parties, and then gradually components are added until a final acceptable settlement is elaborated. For example, the U.S. Army Corps of Engineers was negotiating with American Indian tribes on the Missouri River regarding management of water and releases from dams to meet agricultural and environmental needs, while also protecting Native American burial grounds that might be seriously affected by raising and lowering reservoir levels. The parties started with the key agreement that measures needed to be taken to prevent the exposure of or theft from grave sites. They then explored how lake levels could be maintained at acceptable levels, so that graves that had been covered by water would not be exposed by excessive releases. Next they considered what would happen if water levels did recede and how burial sites could be identified and protected in those circumstances. This discussion led to preliminary agreements on investigation and survey strategies. Subsequent discussions focused on specific monitoring methods and protection procedures to be used by law enforcement officials. The process used to address this series of issues was an expanding add-on of options and solutions.

Elaboration is primarily used by interest-based negotiators and is a common practice by Japanese, some Middle Eastern and African, and many traditional cultures where agreements evolve from a series of ongoing discussions.

Group Conversation or Dialogue. This process is a continuation of conversational information exchange. In this approach, negotiators engage in conversations about issues of concern and raise options that might be mutually satisfactory. Participants often present options in a tentative manner, in combination with other options, or as trial or hypothetical solutions, to avoid deadlocks or premature commitments or to allow a party to save face if a proposal is objectionable.

Group conversations may be informal and unstructured or given more form and order, depending on the desires or cultures of the participants. Settlements often flow from agreement on common principles or frameworks or from a process of circling or elaboration of key issues until an accord is reached. Such processes are common in many Middle Eastern societies, some African, and many traditional or indigenous cultures.

Model Agreements. This process borrows solutions developed by parties in similar situations or predicaments, adapting them as potential settlements for the issues at hand—taking whole solutions, selected components, or broader frameworks. For example, models for political autonomy and federal arrangements have been negotiated in several settings to address interethnic and interreligious conflicts (Harris, Ansty, and Reilly, 1998). Negotiators have used these models to inform themselves about possible solutions and serve as frameworks for negotiations.

In international negotiations between the United States and Russia after the collapse of the Soviet Union, there was a lack of institutional mechanisms for addressing foreign policy issues and negotiations previously handled by the International Department of the Central Committee of the Communist Party. In response, the United States and Russia established a strategic stability dialogue among senior officials at the deputy level from both countries who met on a regular basis in Washington and Moscow to discuss long-term issues such as peacekeeping, expansion of the North Atlantic Treaty Organization, and strategic defenses. The United States established a sophisticated interagency structure for communication and coordination among the U.S. participants, which served as a model for the Russians that they ultimately replicated (Schecter, 1998).

The Single Text. This process is a variation of model agreements and the elaboration process described above and package agreement that will be described later. In the single-text process, one party (or a third party) listens to all sides, identifies the key interests, drafts a working memorandum of understanding that outlines the issues to be agreed on, and then either lists potential options for agreement on each or incorporates them into a single comprehensive agreement. The resulting draft text is presented to all parties as a working document for discussion and revision. The text is circulated and discussed, and modifications are suggested, explored, incorporated, or dropped. After multiple iterations and changes to the draft, the document may achieve a form that the parties can accept or agree to.

The strength of this process is that it provides parties with a tangible document with possible options that they can examine and experiment with to develop options, changes, or agreements. It enables them to visualize a complete agreement, see where links and trades could be made, and focus on resolution of specific individual issues that are difficult to resolve. This process for option generation is valuable when multiple parties or individuals are involved in negotiations. It was used to help facilitate agreements in the negotiation of the Camp David Accords and the Law of the Seas (Carter, 1982; Princen, 1992; Caminos, 2001).

Building on a Vision. A range of procedures approaches problem solving and option generation from a different perspective: articulating the ideal and using that as the basis for discussions. Vision-oriented procedures start from the premise that parties often hold similar views about the way things should be in an ideal world: how a relationship should function, how society should operate, and how resources should be shared, among many other examples.

Negotiation and conflict resolution experts have discovered that it is often possible to engage disputing parties in a preliminary process in which the parties (two or more) identify the specific elements of a desired future with regard to important issues. For instance, labor and management teams have identified how they would like the relationship between their two groups to function, including issues of behavior, attitudes, and communication. Typically the visions of the two groups overlap to a large extent, and it is not too difficult to meld them into a common picture of the future direction of the relationship. The vision becomes the frame for identification of barriers to achieving the ideal and problem solving on those barriers. This process was elaborated by Blake and Mouton (1984).

Vision building can be used in other ways too. One of us worked with a government commission in Rwanda that had a mandate to prevent a repeat of the genocide there and build national unity and reconciliation. The commission represented a diverse cross-section of Rwandan society, with people from the two main ethnic groups, different religions, men and women, and so forth.

As the group worked to develop a viable strategy, first it was important to articulate a specific vision of what a healthy future Rwandan society might look like, including how ethnic groups would relate to one another. As a second step, they identified factors that represent obstacles to that vision, which then became the focus of problem-solving processes and the development of program strategies for reconciliation.

Vision-building processes are particularly useful for working on relationship issues, but they can also be used to address other kinds of factors. Relationship-oriented cultures will appreciate the focus on relationships, but might not be attracted to explicit discussion of such matters, as many relationship-oriented cultures are also indirect dealing and high context. But if relationships are in serious trouble, this more systematic and deliberate approach might prove useful.

Procedures for Addressing Particular Kinds of Factors

Over time negotiators have developed methods for discussing specific kinds of issues. For instance, material goods (houses, lumber, oil, food assistance, land, and so forth) are usually handled differently from issues of pride, respect, apologies, and acknowledgment.

Expanding Resources. This approach is really an attitude and an intention based on the principle that one way to meet the needs of multiple groups is to expand the pie (Fisher and Ury, 1981). Rather than engage in a fierce struggle over what is perceived as a scarce resource, parties look for ways to create additional resources, to the benefit of all. If the parties can do this, they are more likely to develop integrative rather than distributive solutions. For example, the parties to the Middle East conflict—Israel, Jordan, and Palestine—are currently engaged in talks sponsored by the Middle East Desalination Research Center, part of the broader peace process and facilitated by one of the authors. They are exploring ways to expand the amount of usable water in the region by desalination of seawater and brackish water in the Jordan River Valley. Increasing water will be of benefit to all parties and can potentially reduce conflicts over a scarce resource.

Reallocating Resources. Negotiators search for methods to manage or reallocate existing resources in creative ways in order to better accomplish individual or joint goals. The process requires parties to reexamine their resources and determine if different management approaches will increase the options. This could involve, for instance, redeployment of personnel, reorganization of a corporate or political structure, or conversion of capital into a different form. This kind of effort may be related to efforts to expand the pie.

Compensation for Loss or Inconvenience. This process begins with parties acknowledging that one party has or will suffer losses as a result of a past or future action by the other. Negotiators try to define and quantify the loss by looking for commonly accepted standards and criteria to apply. Once these are identified, parties search for options that will compensate the harmed party for past losses or to mitigate any future ones. This approach has been used to address environmental justice issues and develop appropriate compensation or remedies for minority communities that have experienced negative impacts to health, quality of life, or their communities due to industrial operations.

Formulas for Addressing Different Appraisals of Risk or Impacts of Time. Parties often have difficulty developing acceptable settlement options because they have different assessments concerning the potential impacts of risks or time. For example, Company A from a developed country is negotiating a long-term contract for the purchase of manufactured parts for its product with Company B from a developing country. Company A needs a predictable and long-term supply of the components on a just-in-time basis and is willing to agree on a midrange fixed-price contract for a relatively large purchase made over a long period of time. The company believes that the price that it is offering to Company B will more than compensate that company for any fluctuations of price in raw materials needed to manufacture the component. Company A also believes that there will be only minimum changes in the price of the raw materials over the life of the contract, and in fact the price could drop due if new sources come on line. However, its need for just-in-time delivery means that predictability is the highest priority, and it does not want to look for new suppliers and negotiate new prices constantly.

Company B appraises the situation very differently. Its management has studied past price fluctuations in the raw materials and believes them to be volatile. Although other suppliers may develop, all are in politically unstable parts of the world. Therefore, although raw material at a lower price might be obtained, this is not assured. In addition, other manufacturers need the materials, and demand could drive the price up to the extent that the price offered by company A might not cover costs, and it would have to supply the component at a loss. Company B fears getting locked into a low price for materials, seeing the price rise sharply at some time in the future, and thereby incurring significant losses. Both parties want to make a deal, but they are deadlocked on the price to be paid for the raw materials because of their different assessments of risk over time.

To handle this problem, the parties could create a formula that ties the price for the component to the cost of the raw materials to produce it. If the price went up, the purchase price would automatically increase according to the formula. In fact, there could also be a provision addressing a significant drop in the price of the raw material. Formulas can be guided by such variables as the consumer price index (in the United States), the inflation rate, or other independent external measurements or criteria that are acceptable to the involved parties.

Procedural Solutions to Substantive Problems. Parties are not always able to assess the likely impact of an agreement—that is, they are not sure what will happen if they agree to a proposed solution because there are too many unknowns or unpredictable elements. This can present an obstacle to reaching an agreement. In this approach, the parties identify a mutually acceptable procedure to arrive at an acceptable substantive agreement. For example, a family that has been internally displaced during a civil war might return to their village and find a neighbor who remained during the fighting occupying both their house and farmland. They demand that he leave. He refuses. He says the house had been destroyed and that he had put all of his savings and lots of labor into rebuilding it. He refuses to walk away and give the house back without receiving adequate compensation. Also, after clearing the fields, he has planted a crop that will be harvested in two months, and he certainly is not going to give up all the labor that went into the clearing and planting without compensation.

In spite of extensive talks, the parties cannot reach agreement. Ultimately they decide to ask for help from a third party but cannot agree on who this should be. Finally, they agree that each of them will select a person whom the other person also accepts. Each will pay these people an equal amount to provide them with advice and an independent appraisal of the value of the materials and labor that went into rebuilding the house and the cost of the seed and labor for cultivating the land. The parties will use these financial determinations as the basis for negotiations; if they still cannot reach an agreement, they will average the estimates and settle at the resulting number. In either case, the agreed procedure results in an option they can use as the basis for further talks or provide them with a final agreement.

Linking and Packaging Proposals on Multiple Issues

The procedures outlined next are mechanisms for working with multiple issues, recognizing that a settlement can emerge by balancing gains and retreats on different questions. These mechanisms can be used in conjunction with some of the other procedures already outlined, as the linking and packaging processes do not generate additional options, but look for ways to develop workable combinations of existing options, usually by balancing the needs and interests of the parties involved.

Links and Trades. This approach has a number of variations. First, an issue and an associated settlement option, if considered alone, may be hard for one party to agree to because of unacceptable losses, inadequate benefits, or the potential sacrifice of important interests. However, if this issue and settlement option is linked with another issue and options that provide significant positive benefits or concessions by a counterpart, the two together may make an acceptable trade. If this approach is used, parties often have to conduct trial-and-error combinations of issues and options to determine which ones can be linked to form acceptable trade-offs. In a variation, the parties agree to link two or more issues and mutually unacceptable options, and drop them from the negotiation agenda. This is a perfectly acceptable trade so that neither has to deal with undesirable issues or options.

For example, an international mining consortium might enter negotiations with local tribal leaders and local government administrators regarding the terms of resettlement for local farmers who will be displaced by a new mining operation. At issue are compensation for the farmers' land, provision of new housing, costs of relocation, possible compensation for crops lost (depending on the timing of the move), and services and amenities (water, schools, health care) in the new location. The company is concerned about the total cost of the resettlement program and the schedule for relocation, which could seriously delay mine development. After preliminary discussion of all issues, wrangling continues for some time regarding the method for compensation of land: whether there will be cash payment or replacement of land, the quality of the new acreage, the need for clearing and preparation, and so forth. Eventually the lawyer representing the farmers suggests that the two teams address other issues and set aside the land compensation predicament for the moment. The company agrees, and the two parties engage in a series of discussions on the other issues in technical subgroups. The subgroups report back to the full teams, and it becomes apparent that by making more generous provisions for new housing and services, the farmers will accept more modest compensation for their land. The two teams construct three potential combinations of options for further discussion with the full farmer group and with company officials. Ultimately one package of linked options emerges as most acceptable to the company and community.

Managing the Timing of the Receipt of Benefits. This approach involves links and trades of items that the parties value differently, using time as a variable. Imagine that representatives of the same international mining company in the previous example are negotiating with officials of the national government over rights to mine a valuable mineral. The national government is interested in a fairly rapid return of funds to use for economic development and other immediate priorities, while the mining company is interested in long-term returns. An agreement might be reached in which a higher return on mining revenues is paid to the government in the early years of the mine's operation in return for lower returns later. In this case, parties are able to trade items that they valued differently—revenues and time—and ultimately reach an agreement.

Trading Items Valued Differently or Trading in Different Currencies. In these processes, parties educate each other about their needs and interests and explore whether it is possible to trade items that each values differently to satisfy each party's interests and, at the same time, make no sacrifices of important needs. Lax and Sebenius (1986) suggest that negotiations are often possible because people value items ("currencies") differently and desire different outcomes, thus allowing trades.

An example at the community level involved a small village in Lebanon that wanted a new water system, including pumps installed in various neighborhoods. The community was relatively poor and lacked the resources to buy the pipes or pumps. An international development agency wanted to help, but lacked adequate resources to pay for labor to install the water system. After extensive discussions, the men in the village agreed to provide their labor free of charge if the development agency would supply the excavation equipment and materials. This agreement depended on exchange of items that parties valued differently. The villagers concluded that they could contribute the labor free of charge when they did not have to work in their fields; the development agency wanted to avoid paying high prices for labor. Conversely, the development agency had the means for purchasing the pipes, but it would have been prohibitively expensive for the villagers.

Trading in different currencies sometimes involves making exchanges in different forms than would normally be expected but that have some equivalency—which can increase the parties' flexibility regarding possible options.

Conditional Agreement. Often during the course of negotiations, parties develop options for settlement that they believe will be viable but wish to avoid reaching final closure on them until they can consider the settlement of other issues or assess a comprehensive agreement that covers all topics of concern. Conditional agreements are often proposed as tentative accords to promote progress in talks. Occasionally conditional agreements are the only way that negotiators can move toward closure because of unknown factors on other issues or changing circumstances outside the negotiations. A warning: all parties need to explicitly acknowledge when they are making a conditional agreement versus one that is final. Significant problems will arise later if there are divergent views regarding the degree of closure on an issue or package of issues.

Contingent or Reciprocal Agreements. This procedure links the acceptance of a potential solution with the outcome or occurrence of a future event, or a reciprocal action or exchange by another negotiator. For example, a government and private mining companies might negotiate agreement on a windfall profit tax. The parties might agree that when the international price of a mineral reaches a specified level, companies would pay a higher tax on their profits, and when it sinks below this price, a lesser amount would be paid. Execution of the contingent agreement is tied to an external variable—in this case, the international price of the mineral.

An example of a contingent agreement involving the sequential exchange of multiple options or actions is a peace agreement designed to achieve disarmament and demobilization of armed forces. A government might agree to confine its troops to barracks if an insurgent force reciprocates by moving soldiers to a defined containment area. Next, the government might propose an option for demobilization and integration of former insurgents into current government forces or reintegration into society at large. The proposal might specify payments or financial support to help former fighters find new jobs, gain additional training, or secure agricultural land. Once some of these options are in place, the insurgents will reciprocate and turn in their arms. In the sequence, each further element is contingent on fulfillment of the previous item. This procedure is particularly useful when warring parties do not trust the other party to comply with the agreement. By making each element contingent on implementation, the party avoids making large concessions absent compliance from the other party.

Package Agreements. Package agreements are comprehensive settlements that combine solutions on multiple issues into one mutually acceptable package. Such packages typically depend on a series of smaller links and trades. Package agreements often involve a multiplicity of links and trades, any one of which alone might be unacceptable. However, in a combined package, the gains and losses as a whole are satisfactory enough that all parties can agree. The North American Free Trade Agreement is a good example of how negotiators from Canada, Mexico, and the United States put together a package agreement, with some additional side agreements, that was acceptable to the parties and ultimately approved by the three governments. In that accord, single-issue agreements on a number of topics would have been impossible, but they became politically acceptable when included in a package.

Package agreements are usually assembled by negotiators very late in the negotiation process, once significant information is available about all parities' interests, a number of conditional agreements have been developed, or possible links and trades have been identified. Package agreements can be developed and proposed by one party or may be developed through concerted joint efforts by multiple parties.

One variation of a package agreement, which is influenced by the positions a party has taken and the timing of its presentation, is a proposal for a comprehensive settlement with a "jump to agreement," described by Zartman and Berman (1982). This brinksmanship approach is common when a party has held an unyielding position throughout negotiations and decides to present a take-it-or-leave-it proposal—forcing either a decision or an end to negotiations: "Such a position either assumes that agreement is only worthwhile at a certain fixed point, since the security position is not very costly, or it assumes that negotiations can continue for a long time, until the other party agrees, because there are no time costs. Usually too, there is a moral stand attached to this position, enabling the party to hold out even when it hurts. Revolutionary and, lately, developing countries often adopt this tactic, benefiting from a sense of righteousness in conditions where things cannot get much worse" (Zartman and Berman, 1982, p. 174).

CONCLUSION

The generation of potential options is a key negotiation activity regardless of the approach used. Negotiations seldom move to a successful conclusion without a range of possible solutions on the table. Although each culture has a preferred style, most accept one or more of the various methods described here. In the following chapters, we move toward the later phases of negotiation, looking first at how parties attempt to persuade or influence each other and then at the process of coming to closure.

CHAPTER TEN

Influence and Persuasion Strategies

If you haven't fought with each other, you do not know each other—Chinese proverb

The second word [the answer] makes the quarrel—Japanese proverb

Good silence is better than a bad dispute—Russian proverb

Do not remove a fly from your neighbor's face with a hatchet—Chinese proverb

The friend of my friend is my friend. The enemy of my friend is my enemy. The friend of my enemy is my enemy. The enemy of my enemy is my friend—Arab proverb

It is best to let an offense repeat itself three times. The first may be an accident, the second a mistake, only the third is likely to be intentional—Kongo proverb

The one who forgives gains the victory—Yoruba proverb

The one who throws the stone forgets; the one who is hit remembers forever—Angolan proverb

[Augsburger, 1992]

The exercise of influence and persuasion begins the moment parties decide they will negotiate to achieve their goals. Although we present persuasion strategies and tactics at this stage of negotiations, efforts to influence views, attitudes, and behavior occur from the first moment negotiators come in contact with each other and sometimes even before—and they continue through the entire negotiation process. At times, persuasion efforts continue long after a formal agreement has been reached. In the context of negotiations, persuading a person, team, or group to change their minds depends on how each negotiator has defined or framed the purpose, goal, or outcome for talks; how well options on the table satisfy each party's interests; the approaches to influence used by the parties—and how those approaches interact with each other; and the effectiveness of selected strategies in achieving persuasion.

By this stage in negotiation, parties may have been able to identify each other's interests and generate a range of reasonable options to address them. If so, little persuasion may be required to reach an agreement. Parties may simply need to refine a proposal, make final trades, or polish a reasonably acceptable option. However, if options, proposals, or positions on the table are not acceptable to one or more negotiators, they have several possible choices for how to proceed:

- Try to modify an existing—so far unacceptable—option or proposal to make it more acceptable to all parties

- Continue to generate new options or present new proposals that more clearly meet all parties' interests

- Try to change each other's views about one or more of the options or proposals on the table

The previous chapter explored the process of generating and adapting options, corresponding to the first two approaches above. We now turn to an examination of the last approach: persuasion.

NEGOTIATOR POWER AND INFLUENCE

The power and influence of negotiators—and their ability to persuade a counterpart to meet their interests—is ultimately determined by their ability to act unilaterally to satisfy their own needs without depending on the cooperation of the counterpart at all. There are two variations of this form of power: the ability and willingness to exercise coercion and possession of a good alternative to a negotiated agreement.

Parties with significant coercive power over a counterpart may not have to negotiate at all to get what they want. They can break off talks or impose their will in negotiations without incurring significant costs. For example, the Allied Powers essentially dictated the terms of the Treaty of Versailles to the Central Powers at the end of World War I (Macmillan, 2003).

Negotiators also gain power through the ability to walk away from the table due to a viable alternative way to get interests met—an alternative that is equal to or better than those that could be gained through negotiation with the parties currently at the table. This is a party's best alternative to a negotiated agreement, or BATNA (Fisher and Ury, 1981). A party's BATNA might involve an alternative negotiating counterpart, who might be more respectful, trustworthy, generous, or better positioned to meet key needs. Or a BATNA might refer to alternative procedures for attaining a negotiator's goals, such as going to court and obtaining a favorable judicial decision, appealing to public opinion to encourage cooperation, or engaging in nonviolent direct action, such as boycotts, strikes, or sit-ins.

While the ability to act unilaterally, coerce compliance from a counterpart, or have a good BATNA may be ideal, negotiators do not always have this luxury. They may not have, or may not know whether they have, adequate coercive power to force a counterpart to comply. They may not be willing to take the risk or endure potential negative impacts that often result from the exercise of coercion. Or a party may want a healthy relationship with a counterpart, and the use of coercion, while facilitating the attainment of some interests, may inhibit satisfaction of others.

Parties' culture and normative practices affect the use of persuasion strategies and tactics in intercultural negotiations. Much like the information-exchange procedures described in a previous chapter, negotiators choose strategies based on what they consider to be persuasive and behaviors that are culturally acceptable for changing a counterpart's views. For example, while one culture might value direct-dealing debate and logical arguments, another might prefer an approach that focuses on building a trusting relationship and indirect talk and persuasive tactics. Negotiators must be attuned to these differences in cultural preferences for influence strategies.

Researchers have identified common preferences for the tactics that members of specific cultures consider to be persuasive or compelling and use on their counterparts. For instance, Graham (1993) conducted a laboratory study of verbal negotiation tactics commonly used by members of executive education programs and business classes from ten cultures: Japanese, Korean, Taiwanese, Chinese (northern and southern), Russian, German, French, British (U.K.), Brazilian, and American. He found that paired negotiators used specific methods in the percentages presented in Table 10.1.

Table 10.1. Verbal Negotiation Tactics

Bargaining Behaviors and Definitions	Cultures (in each group, n = 6)									
	Japan	Korea	Taiwan	China[a]	Russia	Germany	France	United Kingdom	Brazil	United States
Promise: A statement in which the source indicated his intention to provide the target with a reinforcing consequence, which the source anticipates the target will evaluate as pleasant, positive, or rewarding.	7*	4	9	6	5	7	5	11	3	8
Threat: Same as promise, except that the reinforcing consequences are thought to be noxious, unpleasant, or punishing.	4	2	2	1	3	3	5	3	2	4
Recommendation: A statement in which the source predicts that a pleasant environmental consequence will occur to the target. Its occurrence is not under source's control.	7	1	5	2	4	5	3	6	5	4
Warning: Same as recommendation, except that the consequences are thought to be unpleasant.	2	0	3	1	0	1	3	1	1	1
Reward: A statement by the source that is thought to create pleasant consequences for the target.	1	3	2	1	3	4	3	5	2	2

Punishment: Same as reward, except that the consequences are thought to be unpleasant.	1	5	1	0	1	2	3	0	3	3
Positive normative appeal: A statement in which the source indicates that the target's past, present, or future behavior was or will be in conformity with social norms.	1	1	0	1	0	0	0	0	0	1
Negative normative appeal: Same as positive normative appeal except that the target's behavior is in violation of social norms.	3	2	1	0	0	1	0	1	1	1
Commitment: A statement by the source to the effect that its future bids will not go below or above a certain level.	15	13	9	10	11	9	10	13	8	13
Self-disclosure: A statement in which the source reveals information about itself.	34	36	42	36	40	47	42	39	39	36
Question: A statement in which the source asks the target to reveal information about itself.	20	21	14	34	27	11	18	15	22	20
Command: A statement in which the source suggests that the target perform a certain behavior.	8	13	11	7	7	12	9	9	14	6

Note: The numbers in the table body show what percentage of respondents used the bargaining behavior.

[a]Northern China and environs.

Source: Graham (1993, pp. 126–127).

The range of persuasive tactics used across cultures was remarkably similar, with questions and disclosures being the most frequent. However, the frequency of each tactic varied significantly. For example, Japanese negotiators, in comparison to other national groups, were the most reticent to engage in self-disclosure and provide information. Chinese and Russians used significantly more questions than did other cultures. Brazilians, Koreans, and Germans used more commands.

PERSUASION TACTICS OF SELECTED CULTURES

The remainder of this chapter looks in more detail at the persuasive tactics of eleven cultures. Similar information was presented in Chapter Eight with regard to the information exchange stage of negotiation.

As with all such discussions regarding cultural tendencies—and as already stated elsewhere in this book—it is difficult to generalize about cultures without falling into false stereotyping or other unfair characterizations of members of cultures. As with any other average, there are many members of these cultures who deviate from the norm for many reasons, such as personal temperament, education or profession, international experiences, or membership in a subculture with its own behavioral norms. That said, the observations that follow are based on research and informed observation by members of the cultures themselves or people who have had considerable contact with these cultures.

French Influence and Persuasion Strategies

French negotiators frequently use a combination of relationship and logic as their primary means of influence. In an interview with Cogan (2005), Alain Lempereur, a researcher on negotiation style, notes that French negotiators are midway between Chinese and Americans in their orientation to creating a relationship prior to beginning substantive negotiations and the initiation of influence. Chinese stress the creation of a relationship with a counterpart prior to beginning substantive talks, while Americans are more likely to leap into discussing content almost immediately, without establishing firm and trusting personal relationships.

French negotiators seek to establish a minimum degree of confidence that there will frankness, fair dealing, and trust as a prerequisite for substantive talks. Relationship influence can be built through social conversation, bantering, or sparring as participants explore different views while attending common social functions or sharing meals (Fisher, 1980; Barsoux and

Lawrence, 1990). Meals are often used as a place to test ideas informally, before formal presentation in more structured negotiations (Barsoux and Lawrence, 1990). For the French, social conversation is used to create connections between participants. The content and process is designed to link people together through an exchange of ideas and emotions, commonly through the brilliant use of words and language.

Once French negotiators begin substantive presentations, they are likely to make proposals with logic to back them up as their primary means of persuasion in what might be called "the power of a good argument." French negotiators try to be the first to discuss substantive issues in order to gain the advantage of laying the foundation and principles on which further talks will focus (Cogan, 2005). The persuasive process begins with a confident, assertive, and often bold presentation of a general principle, which is proposed as a frame and guide to discussions that any solutions or details of an agreement will fit. The general principle is followed by deductive reasoning in which a chain of causality is deduced: "A implies B which implies C and on to Z and sometimes beyond" (Gerard Araud, cited in Cogan, 2005, p. 122). Facts bolstering the proposition are added incrementally throughout the process until the final summary of the argument and the conclusion. Often the main point of the argument is identified only at the end of a long and exhaustive dissertation (Cogan, 2005). This final conclusion is often presented in a concise and blunt manner, in which little room is allowed for disagreement. The French mode of argumentation in negotiations emphasizes as much the form and style of delivery as the content; the articulateness and brilliance of the speaker and his or her style are seen as significant means of persuasion.

Once the French negotiator has made the initial argument, a counterpart may make a presentation, but often the French interlocutor seems not even to be listening. The goal of French negotiators is to express their point of view, gain acceptance by their counterpart, and avoid being persuaded themselves. Because the French are reluctant to compromise, especially on matters of principle, they tend to return to previous arguments in the middle phases of negotiations, embellishing them or delving more deeply into a point but basically maintaining the same conclusions. Gilles Andréani, the head of the Analysis and Forecasting Center at the French Foreign Ministry, notes, "During a negotiation, the important thing for the French is to be right, and to demonstrate this by disquisition rather than by compromise and bargaining. Unlike many others, they do not feel a compulsion to compromise. They consider that it is to the overall benefit of negotiation to have a party present who is disinterested, who has a different point of view, and who therefore can be of service" (cited in Cogan, 2005, p. 137).

This pattern of discourse, holding the line and repeating earlier arguments, often holds true until negotiations seem to have reached a deadlock or their very end. It seems that these advocates believe that by continuing to make the same argument, their counterpart will ultimately see the light and agree with them. Two responses to the French reluctance to change positions are setting deadlines and developing a one-text procedure (Cogan, 2005). However, if a deadline is not important, it will commonly be ignored. The one-text process can be used to develop a comprehensive solution to multiple problems. However, this too may be rejected if it is not written in French, or if the French-language draft is not considered as the final authoritative and guiding text.

Final agreements between and with French negotiators often seem to be reached at the last moment, when it appears that talks will break down unless one or more parties moves. Shifts in position are often motivated by new instructions from superiors or development of a new logic or rationale that is presented articulately, provides a reasonable argument for a shift in position, or provides a practical solution to a problem—and does not violate the original principle.

RECOMMENDED APPROACHES FOR WORKING WITH FRENCH NEGOTIATORS

- French negotiators, especially in the context of doing business, want to build positive relationships with counterparts prior to engaging in substantive negotiations. Therefore, engage in social conversations, bantering, and verbal sparring as appropriate, and attend social functions and meals to build rapport and trust.

- Listen to and consider the initial French proposals. Strive to understand the principles and logical framework that underlie them, and assess whether they are acceptable to use as a foundation for future talks.

- Remember that French negotiators generally use deductive reasoning or logic for problem solving and persuasion. In this approach, they try to get an agreement on a principle and then use it to develop subsequent options or proposals. If you are comfortable with this approach, use it. If not or if you do not agree with the initial premises, propose an alternative principle and associated options that might meet both parties' needs. Be prepared to present your logic.

- Do not be deterred if your counterpart does not seem to listen to or accept your counterlogic. It is probably too early for him or her to do so.

- Expect repetitions of arguments from your counterpart.

- Recognize that early compromises are not the norm for French negotiators. These usually come only toward the end of negotiations, after
major efforts to persuade a counterpart to accept their view have been
unsuccessful.

Japanese Influence and Persuasion Strategies

While many cultures use direct and assertive communications as means to
persuade each other, Japanese tend to use communications to transmit information that they hope will be compelling to their counterpart. Mizutani (1981)
believes that the average Japanese does not place a high value on overtly
persuading others to change their minds or actions, and in fact may actively
avoid it. In place of direct persuasion, Japanese are more likely to use personal
relationships, information exchange, and a number of less-direct means of
influencing counterparts (Graham and Sano, 1979; Hodgson, Sano, and Graham, 2000; Blaker, 1977a, 1977b; March, 1990; Gudykunst and Nishida, 1994;
Blaker, Vogel, and Giarra, 2002).

Japanese may use different means when negotiating with insiders and
outsiders, based on Japanese perceptions that non-Japanese do not understand
or follow the prescribed norms for hierarchical relationships that are determined
by rank, status, and power. Japanese negotiations, whether with members of
their own culture or outsiders, often begin with the Japanese negotiator
trying to determine the hierarchical relationship of the parties. In Japan,
interactions between people are defined according to vertical and horizontal
relationships and hierarchies. Vertical ranking between people has developed
to a significant extent and great emphasis is placed on seniority (Nakene,
1972). The parties' hierarchical power relationships, whether symmetrical or
asymmetrical, determine patterns of communication, deference, obligation,
and influence strategies.

Like negotiators in many other cultures, when Japanese bargainers believe
that they are in a hierarchically superior position or perceive that they have
more power, they behave in a manner befitting their rank and expect def-
erential behavior from lower-status or weaker counterparts. They are also
likely to be more direct and explicit in their influence tactics. However, their
communication and influence strategies are generally less explicit than those
used by members of more direct-dealing cultures when they are in a similar
power position.

Japanese negotiators with significant status and power often prepare detailed
and explicit information to share with their counterparts and potential defensive
arguments to support their views, with little consideration of strategies that

might be needed to convince other negotiators to accept their thinking. They assume that the information presented will be compelling in itself, requiring little argumentation or advocacy to defend. In trying to influence counterparts in this manner, they also seem to ignore any concessions that they might have to make and give little consideration to what the other party might want or have to concede to reach an agreement (March, 1990). Japanese negotiators tend to use this influence approach because they wish to avoid direct disagreements, argumentation, horse-trading, or potential loss of face for either party that could result from having to back down or change a proposal (March, 1990; Graham, 1985).

To develop information for presentation, Japanese negotiators often spend extensive time working within their organization or team to build an internal consensus on the data and conclusions. Once a consensus has been reached, it is difficult for Japanese negotiators to change their options or proposals without going through another internal deliberative process.

The patterns of explicitness and seemingly one-sided presentation of information may be modified when Japanese negotiators are in a weaker position relative to counterparts or when they are conducted in the context of traditional negotiations within Japan, such as in buyer-seller relationships in which the buyer is seen as the more dominant—a major difference between Japanese and other cultures. Domestically, Japanese negotiators who are more powerful or of higher status, such as buyers, are expected by weaker counterparts to seek solutions that consider the interests of all parties, although the weaker party's needs may be satisfied to a lesser extent. On occasion these Japanese expectations may also carry over to international political and economic negotiations, where Japanese perceive themselves to be in a weaker position. For example, many negotiators and researchers have noted this pattern in Japanese-U.S. negotiations (Blaker, 1977a, 1977b; Blaker, Vogel, and Giarra, 2002; March, 1990). However, Japanese negotiators have learned over time that outsiders do not always understand their values, norms, and reciprocal relationships. As a result, Japanese negotiators, who in the past have been taken advantage of by foreign counterparts, do not always defer to a stronger party.

Japanese negotiators, regardless of whether they are in a superior or subordinate or stronger or weaker position in relation to their counterpart, use a number of additional means of influence beyond the provision of information. Central among these is cultivation of positive, trusting, and long-term working relationships. "The Japanese are not accustomed to the Western system of communicating and negotiating, which lets both sides present conflicting interests and ideas before reaching a conclusion. They prefer to reach a solution as amicably as possible, and there is a tendency to compromise with others by laying groundwork, referred to in Japanese as *nemawashi,* before reaching final agreement" (Davies and Osumo, 2002, p 159). In this process, "much time is spent getting to know one another. Since the Japanese would prefer not to depend on a legal system to iron out conflicts, a strong relationship of trust must be established before business can begin" (Hodgson, Sano, and Graham, 2000, p. 28).

Beyond cultivating relationships as means of influence, Japanese often use a range of defensive strategies to achieve their goals. Unlike more assertive or challenging approaches that involve argumentation or debate used in other cultures, these strategies focus on reinforcing information presented previously, presenting data again, clarifying or reiterating important points or conclusions, or describing information in a different manner that may be more acceptable. Defensive strategies are used to avoid direct disagreement or confrontation, circumvent the need to rebut proposals or conclusions presented by a counterpart, save face for all concerned, and prevent the need to back down from their own conclusions.

Other defensive strategies commonly used by Japanese include deflecting conversation about topics that they do not want to discuss, avoiding talk about anything that may be perceived as negative, commenting indirectly about a counterpart's points rather than making their own, or engaging in circular discussions that do not seem to reach a conclusion. They may also give illustrative examples of problems that might arise from an option in a manner that is not likely to be seen by their non-Japanese counterpart as direct criticism of their views (or if challenged, can be easily dismissed as merely examples) (Yamada, 1997). *Amai,* or ambiguity, is commonly used in Japanese communications and negotiations to prevent unnecessary or undesirable commitments, create vagueness that allows more freedom of action, or save face in difficult situations (Davies, 2002).

Because Japanese value their reputation and what people think of them, they may use indirect or direct appeals to give or save face or avoid shame, following widely accepted cultural norms, or request that a party recognize their duty or mutual obligations to encourage agreement or compliance. Hirokawa and Miyahara (1986), in comparative studies of strategies used by Japanese and North American managers to gain the cooperation of tardy workers, found that the Japanese managers often appealed to the employees' sense of duty to their firm, whereas the Americans preferred to give ultimatums or make threats of negative consequences, such as docking pay or firing. Japanese also often make appeals to the common or joint good, typical in more collectivist cultures, to obtain cooperation. Japanese managers and negotiators often ask for cooperation for the good of the long-term relationship and the company, to avoid tensions, or to achieve long-term benefits for all.

When more cooperative strategies of influence do not work, Japanese negotiators turn to a number of stalling tactics in order to wear down resistance to an idea or proposal and persuade a counterpart to have a change of mind or lower resistance to addressing the Japanese negotiator's interests. These tactics include engaging in circular and convoluted discussions in which multiple ideas and views are embedded in a single long statement, engaging in "stretch talk" in which a negotiator stretches out the sounds of words to indicate that the points being raised are difficult to address, or lowering the level of his or her voice to indicate problems (Yamada, 1997).

Japanese negotiators resist public expression in negotiations of negative feelings or the use of direct coercion, by themselves or others, as a means of influence. Japanese value *wa*, or harmony, in interpersonal and intergroup relationships and are reluctant to express emotions that will disturb smooth interpersonal relationships or escalate tensions. When uncomfortable, they may begin to smile a lot or drop into extended periods of silence.

RECOMMENDED APPROACHES FOR WORKING WITH JAPANESE NEGOTIATORS

During direct negotiations by non-Japanese with Japanese counterparts, Hodgson, Sano, and Graham (2000) recommend the following approaches:

- Ask lots of questions as a persuasive tactic to elicit more information, clarify the counterpart's thinking, and indirectly, and in a nonthreatening manner, uncover weaknesses in their arguments. Negotiators can also claim not to understand what the other has said or their views on issues or proposals as a way to gain more data or understanding of the logic behind an option.

- Be explicit and self-disclosing, but not overbearing, in presenting your views, needs, and interests.

- Use as many positive influence tactics as possible, including making credible promises, identifying solutions that will result in positive benefits, appealing to commonly accepted or reasonable standards or norms, and providing incentives and rewards for cooperation.

- Remain silent to allow space for Japanese counterparts to consider their views and develop more positive responses.

- Change the subject to other issues if an impasse occurs, returning to the contested issue later.

- Take breaks to allow time for reconsideration of options or proposals in private.

- Change offers or concessions or make firm commitments that make offers or proposals more believable.

If progress cannot be made in joint session, negotiators may move to private meetings where other strategies can be used—for example:

- Delay talks to allow the Japanese counterparts to explore their options, discuss alternatives, and build an internal organizational consensus for a new proposal.

- Indirectly imply that alternative routes may be pursued to meet interests, rather than continuing negotiations with the current counterpart, if adequate progress toward agreement cannot be made.

- Bring in more senior executives of each party to promote a new look at issues in question, break a deadlock, or encourage more cooperation.

- Ask for the help of a *shokai-sha* (the party that introduced you to your Japanese counterpart) or *chukai-sha* (a mediator) to facilitate discussions. (Often the *shokai-sha* can perform both functions.) The *shokai-sha* typically facilitates by shuttling between parties and conducting private meetings with each until an accord is reached.

In general, negotiators working with Japanese counterparts are advised to avoid aggressive or disruptive tactics, such as emotional outbursts, public derogatory remarks, or overt threats or confrontations that risk damaging harmony or *wa* or might cause a counterpart to lose face.

U.S. Influence and Persuasion Strategies

American negotiators generally view negotiations as a technical, businesslike, and linear problem-solving process. "U.S. negotiators have a distinctive style: forceful, explicit, legalistic, urgent and results-oriented. Although these traits vary according to personalities and circumstances, a recognizably pragmatic American style is always evident" (Quinney, 2002, p. 1). These were the conclusions reached by thirty seasoned U.S. and foreign diplomats and scholars as they examined U.S. involvement in diplomatic negotiations. However, most of these behaviors are also found in a range of other intercultural negotiations involving Americans in the economic, business development, and even tourism sectors.

In general, Americans view the major task of negotiations as solving a problem or dispute. (Note that the term *dispute* is often preferred over the word *conflict*. The former indicates a limited disagreement involving a limited number of parties whose components can be resolved, while the latter implies more intractable differences or violent actions involving broader social or political questions and a wider range of parties.) In American dispute resolution, a problem is identified, options to address it are generated, and then effort is exerted to persuade a counterpart of the best way to resolve the issues in question. Persuasion is often based on following accepted rules, following the logic of facts and figures, and appeals for give-and-take rather than appeals to relationships, emotions, aspirations, or traditions (Quinney, 2002). If a solution can be found that addresses the interests of multiple parties and offers joint gains, this is all well and good. If not, assertive efforts may be made to persuade, push, and, on occasion, coerce a counterpart to accept an agreement favorable to the American negotiator. This approach to persuasion holds true for both transactional business negotiations and efforts to resolve conflicts.

For Americans a major goal of communication is persuasion: "U.S. negotiating behavior is fundamentally forceful and pragmatic. Individual negotiators may be genial or moralistic, or pushy, but ultimately all share a businesslike concern to achieve results in the shortest time" (Quinney, 2002, p. 1). To achieve this end, U.S. negotiators use a range of patterns of persuasive arguments and tactics.

"Cordiality is welcome but not necessary" (Quinney, 2002, p. 5). Because Americans generally see negotiation as a technical problem-solving process, they generally place less emphasis on the establishment of firm relationships as a primary influence strategy. Instead, they focus on procedures for problem identification, option generation, and substantive agreement making. Americans do value positive relationships, but they expect that agreements are more likely to be reached and observed because pragmatic interests are satisfied rather than due to affective bonds between the parties. They may spend some time building relationships and creating a positive climate for talks, but this will probably not extend for a long period—generally a day at most and more likely from five to thirty minutes.

In political, economic, and business negotiations, negotiators from the United States often use data-based or factual approaches as means of persuasion. This is particularly true in negotiations that seek agreements on problems of mutual concern rather than to resolve conflicts. Thus, Americans present substantive information they believe is relevant to the issues under discussion and that will create a basis or rationale for acceptance of their ideas, options, or proposals (Glenn, Witmeyer, and Stevenson, 1977). Substantive data and the implications that can be drawn from them are seen by Americans as more persuasive than the detailed or elegant logical arguments or philosophical discourse commonly used by French negotiators. However, U.S. negotiators also use argumentation to support the data they have presented.

American negotiators also use direct comparisons or cost-benefit analyses of options or proposals to demonstrate the merits of their preferred solution. Comparisons may be conducted through questioning, making statements, or drawing conclusions. Questioning is often used to reveal flaws in a counterpart's logic or to uncover possible future implications, costs, or risks of an option.

In addition to the various strategies described, American negotiators often use a variety of positive influence tactics. These include revelation of information about their own proposals, and the interests and reasons behind them, as a way to induce a counterpart to address their interests or reciprocate with more information about their interests; an appeal to adhere to commonly accepted standards or norms; offering of mutually beneficial proposals; and provision of tangible incentives or rewards for cooperation or compliance. Americans are also "particularly adept at creating 'linkage,' making agreement on one issue dependent on progress on other issue areas" (Quinney, 2002, p. 8).

Depending on the circumstances, Americans may shift to more assertive argumentation strategies in which explicit conclusions are drawn and advocated based on information that has been presented. Argumentation approaches appeal to practicality, flexibility, utility, efficiency, cost-effectiveness, quick outcomes, and rapid receipt of benefits that will result from agreement. If argumentation does not work, Americans are not averse to exercising more aggressive or coercive tactics. U.S. culture accepts assertiveness and a degree of aggressiveness. In negotiations with non-Americans, U.S. negotiators often have significant coercive power at their disposal. This is true in political, economic, and business negotiations. A study conducted by the Kellogg School of Business at Northwestern University of U.S. business negotiators noted that Americans are open to issuing warnings, explicitly pointing out when a counterpart has violated a norm, making demands for change, threatening explicitly if a counterpart does not comply with their wishes, or using sanctions or more coercive means if their interests are not met (Hodgson, Sano, and Graham, 2000, p. 112).

In *U.S. Negotiating Behavior* (2002), Quinney reported that non-U.S. diplomatic negotiators and informed observers note that since the end of the Cold War, when the United States became the only remaining superpower, American negotiators bargaining in "high" politics (such as security issues) and "low politics" (such as environmental and trade issues) can be "domineering, insistent, and uncompromising. They are less concerned to negotiate, in the sense of exchanging views and exchanging concessions, than to dictate terms or to persuade their counterparts of the rightness or potency of the American position. Unilateralism has become both a policy and an attitude. Even cordial and conspicuously polite U.S. representatives tend to adopt a take it or leave it position" (p. 3). Furthermore, he writes, this status as a global hegemon "has aggravated a long-standing U.S. trait: namely the inclination to moralize, treat negotiation as an opportunity to reveal impeachable truth rather than to respect the other side's worldview" (p. 3).

RECOMMENDED APPROACHES FOR WORKING WITH U.S. NEGOTIATORS

- Anticipate a brief period of time for building relationship and fairly rapid movement to focus on substantive issues, problems, or disputes to be addressed.

- Expect a linear and problem-solving approach to negotiations, often with time for resolution of specific issues.

- Expect a results-oriented attitude from American counterparts and a belief that every issue can be addressed and resolved.

- Be prepared for a presentation of information in a direct, concise, and clear manner and the expectation that you will reciprocate with a similar level of detail.

- Be open to articulating your interest and probing for theirs.

- Avoid being vague, nonspecific, or focusing on philosophical principles; seek practical and pragmatic solutions.

- Expect to be pressed to clarify points, explain your logic or rationale, and explore the impacts of various options that you or Americans present.

- Consider linking issues and building packages that are mutually acceptable.

- Expect that Americans are likely to engage in direct back-and-forth bargaining, development of options at the table, and reaching compromises (if they are necessary) through direct talks rather than through internal private meetings or caucusing.

- Do not be surprised by being pushed to reach a timely and rapid settlement of issues.

- Expect that persuasion will be undertaken through substantive argument, a marshaling of what they believe to be compelling facts, or an explanation of how the preferred solution will be beneficial, rather than the expression of strong emotions, bullying, or direct intimidation.

- Explore your counterpart's potential time constraints and the potential impacts they may have on the negotiation process.

- Anticipate being pushed in a heavy-handed way if solutions you propose or that are on the table do not meet your American counterpart's interests.

Chinese Influence and Persuasion Strategies

Negotiators and researchers have long studied the approaches of Chinese negotiators toward influence and persuasion in the political, economic, and business realms. Beginning in the 1960s, the focus of analysis was on political negotiations (Iklé, 1964; Lall, 1968; Young, 1968; Solomon, 1995, 1999). Later, with the economic opening of China, a wide range of research, studies, and popular books on negotiation focused on Chinese economic and business interactions (Pye, 1982; Macleod, 1988; De Mente, 2004; Seligman, 1989; Hu and Grove, 1991; Adler, Braham, and Graham, 1992; Schneiter, 1992; Blackman, 1998; Fang, 1999; Chen, 2003; Lam and Graham, 2007).

Negotiation practitioners and researchers have identified a number of persuasion tactics commonly used by the Chinese. One means of influence is the determination of where negotiations are conducted and the psychological impact this can have on both Chinese negotiators and their counterparts (Pye, 1982). Negotiations with interlocutors from the People's Republic of China (PRC) and overseas Chinese are often conducted in China or at the Chinese party's venue. Control of the place for negotiations enables negotiators to manage the environment and ambience of talks. Although China has become both more developed and Westernized, at least in outward appearance, during the past twenty-five years, it is still unfamiliar territory and an alien environment to many foreign negotiators. Unfamiliar surroundings, manners, food, banquets, and meeting arrangements, as well as jet lag, all contribute to a sense of disorientation. Chinese negotiators are capable of using these factors to gain advantage and "maximize the sense of gratitude, dependence, awe, and helplessness" of a counterpart due to the unfamiliarity of surroundings and procedures (Solomon, 1999, p. 61).

Chinese negotiators often want counterparts to recognize that they have come to China to satisfy their interests and that the needs and expectations are not necessarily reciprocal (Pye, 1982; Solomon, 1999). The non-Chinese counterpart is placed in the position of a supplicant requesting negotiations. This creates a dynamic in which the Chinese are in a superior position from the start.

Chinese negotiators, whether from the PRC or based in other locales such as Hong Kong or Singapore, frequently cultivate friendly and trusting relations with counterparts prior to beginning substantive negotiations.

> The Chinese negotiating style is shaped by the fact that the process involves two levels of negotiations: 1) the manifest level of bargaining about concrete agreements and 2) the latent level at which they are trying to strike "emotional bargains." At the manifest level, there are discrete issues calling for agreement or non-agreement; at the latent level there is a continuous flow of emotions as the Chinese seek to build up ever more complex webs of sentiment. The rhythms of the explicit negotiations may have little relationship to the pace at which the personal and human bonds are being nurtured [Pye, 1982, p. 87].

Friendship (*youyi*) and the obligations that it implies for the Chinese extend far beyond what is expected of a bargaining relationship in other cultures. While positive connections help Chinese negotiators determine whether a counterpart is trustworthy, whether business can be conducted with them, and whether agreements are likely to be honored, they also have another influence function: the creation of reciprocal obligations. By developing friendships and positive interpersonal bonds (*guanxi*), Chinese negotiators strive to create feelings of interdependence and implied or explicit obligations between parties (Chen, 2003; Lam and Graham, 2007). Chinese negotiators assume that counterparts will avoid risking relationships if differences arise over procedural or substantive issues, and will make concessions to preserve valued connections. Thus, the cultivation of friendships becomes a major strategy and tactic for influencing counterparts and extracting concessions for Chinese negotiators.

Connections may be nurtured by providing for a counterpart's creature comforts (accommodations, entertainment, banquets, and so forth), gift giving, taking them on field trips and to cultural events, or even playing a counterpart's favorite music. Chinese negotiators may also foster relationships by self-deprecating behavior or statements about both themselves or China, which, even though they go against a desire to project strength, are designed to encourage sympathy, empathy, or compliance with Chinese desires or wishes. Chinese often note that China is an underdeveloped country that needs help and assistance. Later appeals are made to "old friends," thus expressing the Chinese party's desire to maintain the friendship that has been created and indicating that uncooperative or compliant behavior by a counterpart puts the relationship at risk.

When negotiations begin, whether in economic or political realms, Chinese negotiators try to influence their counterparts by deferring to them and encouraging their "guests" to speak first (Pye, 1981; Solomon, 1999). Qiao Guanhua, the deputy foreign minister of China, once said during talks with Henry Kissinger, the U.S. national security advisor, over the establishment of relations between the People's Republic of China and the United States, "We have two sayings: one is that we are the host, we should let the guest begin; the other says that we are guests, we should defer to the host" (Solomon, 1999, p. 77).

In his research on Chinese commercial negotiations, Pye (1982) noted that "it is basic to the Chinese negotiating style to insist that the other party reveal its interests first while the Chinese mask their interests and priorities" (p. 35). This tactic can demonstrate hospitality and openness to hearing what a counterpart has to say. It can also encourage an interlocutor to reveal information about his or her views before the Chinese negotiator is required to do so, thus avoiding premature disclosure of interests. Or it can be used to feign disinterest and encourage more concessions from a counterpart, or may provide the Chinese negotiator with time to think about a response before revealing his or her own proposals. This tactic also enables a Chinese negotiator to critique what the counterpart has said rather than make a proposal.

Another Chinese approach to persuasion, and a major characteristic of Chinese negotiating style, is to propose a set of general guiding principles, standards, objectives, or "concrete arrangements" fairly early in talks. Principles are advocated by Chinese negotiators to help create friendly and trusting relationships, symbolically define the spirit of agreements, clarify where parties stand on general issues, affirm common understandings, and create a framework for future talks (Pye, 1982).

The principles proposed may help define the parties' intentions regarding the relationship that is being established between them, their organizations, or their countries. Later, Chinese negotiators may advocate the application of principles to advocate for agreements on procedural and substantive matters or issues. This process is in sharp contrast to the approach of some other cultures, such as Americans, who believe that "progress in negotiations is best facilitated by adhering to concrete and specific details, avoiding debates about generalities, which can easily become entangled in political or philosophical differences" (Pye, 1982, p. 40).

Principles proposed early in negotiations are often used in later discussions in a very rigid manner as agreed-on goals, standards, and criteria to which all future agreements must conform, or they may merely provide a general direction within which Chinese negotiators may be very flexible. If the former strategy is pursued, Chinese negotiators may consistently point out contradictions between what counterparts agreed on earlier and their later proposals, or accuse them of violating the spirit of a prior agreement and shame them into compliance (Pye, 1982, p. 43).

Later in negotiations, Chinese negotiators use other influence or persuasion tactics, which range from gentle and indirect tactics to more assertive and aggressive measures. Researchers have identified the more subtle and less directive tactics (Pye, 1982; Blackman, 1998; Seligman, 1989; Fang, 1999; Solomon, 1999, Chen, 2003; Lam and Graham, 2007):

- Asking lots of questions to gain information or force counterparts to show their hand or reconsider their thinking on a proposal
- Waiting for counterparts to make concrete proposals while refraining from doing so themselves
- Requesting more specifics or indicating that more benefits will have to be offered to get their attention
- Bringing up their problems and asking counterparts to address them without providing any suggestions themselves
- Requesting that counterparts take more risks because of their leadership position in the world, wealth, or political power
- Claiming hurt personal or national feelings

- Indicating that opinions of the Chinese people or masses are being adversely influenced by the lack of cooperation on the part of an interlocutor

- Using indirect communications and subtle loaded language that imply negative consequences for failure to agree

- Signaling a fading opportunity or time limits on reaching agreements

- Indirectly criticizing a counterpart by criticizing a similar party

- Playing dumb or feigning lack of understanding or misunderstanding to draw out the views of a counterpart

- Stalling and using time pressure, saying that it will take an undetermined amount of time to consider a new idea or proposal

The same researchers have identified these more direct pressure and influence tactics:

- Changing negotiators and requiring a counterpart to start over with relationship building or a discussion of principles previously agreed on

- Using diversionary measures, such as bringing up false issues or irrelevant clauses, identifying a minor issue and raising its importance to an unexpected level, making a seemingly unrealistic demand about a small point to take the focus away from controversial issues, avoiding describing what they really desire, or gaining a minor concession before they have to make an offer that results in fewer benefits for them than originally expected or desired

- Pushing to reopen closed issues as a way to delay settlement or gain more concessions

- Asserting either that they lack the authority to decide or the responsibility to implement agreements (which is often true because these two areas are often separated in Chinese bureaucracies) or that they must defer to senior leaders for decisions

- Claiming that agreements cannot be implemented because of regulations, which may or may not actually impose the claimed restrictions or that a solution proposed by a counterpart is "not the way it is done in China"

- Playing negotiators off against each other by indicating that another party is in the wings and wants to negotiate with the Chinese counterpart on the same issues

- Beating up on "old friends" by playing on guilt or maintaining that the Chinese negotiator personally or China itself is in serious trouble and needs help (concessions) to address the situation

- Indicating that the Chinese negotiator will lose face if a favorable agreement is not reached

- Raising expectations that an agreement is possible but then not following up on the point, or asserting that internal dynamics make it impossible to follow through without receiving additional benefits

- Requesting quid pro quo exchanges that are claimed by the Chinese to be equal but are not so perceived by a counterpart

- Making last-minute demands and claiming they are required to reach a final agreement

- Threatening potential loss of the relationship or consequences of non-agreement

- Attacking directly and personally or publicly embarrassing a counterpart in the press

Chinese negotiators also bring pressure by identifying mistakes that have been made by a counterpart, claiming serious offense, and asking for correction for what has been done. They also use the good guy/bad guy or "hard" or "soft" negotiation ploy, and have been known to exploit differences of views within a counterpart's team (Solomon, 1999).

RECOMMENDED APPROACHES FOR WORKING WITH CHINESE NEGOTIATORS

Negotiators and researchers have offered the following advice concerning persuasive strategies for negotiating with Chinese counterparts (Pye, 1982, Blackman, 1998; Seligman, 1989; Fang, 1999; Solomon, 1999; Chen, 2003; Lam and Graham, 2007):

- Think in the long rather than the short term. Use persuasive strategies that will promote long-term relationships and benefits rather than merely short-term gains.

- Spend the time necessary to create positive interpersonal and intergroup relationships, which can help develop reciprocal expectations and obligations.

- Consider agreement on general principles regarding relationships, procedures, or substantive issues, and take them seriously. However, take care that principles will not be interpreted to your disadvantage at some time in the future or narrow what can be discussed, requested, or offered.

- Take the time necessary to educate your Chinese counterparts. Explain your ideas about issues, interests, options, and proposals fully so they will be able to explain and defend them to superiors and do not feel rushed into premature decision making.

- Ask lots of questions to gain information and persuade Chinese counterparts to reassess their views, interests, or positions.

- Avoid creating unrealistic expectations of what can be exchanged or given in negotiations, as this risks disappointment, irritation, and resentment.

- Steer clear of offers by the Chinese, such as gifts or expensive entertainment, that create a sense of indebtedness and may require offering concessions in the future.

- Maintain patience, and recognize that negotiations and decision making in China often take longer than in other countries.

- Avoid strategies that could result in loss of face or shame for your Chinese counterparts, their organization, or China in general.

- Do not express anger or mutual recriminations if problems arise, even though the Chinese may do so, because they see these actions as indications of insincerity in a counterpart. Consider smoothing over differences by stating that there was a misunderstanding and that everyone might have a right to be upset about it.

- Use coercive tactics only as a last resort, or if you are in an unquestionably superior power position; such tactics may cause irreparable damage to harmony and relationships and result in failed talks.

- Bring in an intermediary (*zhongjian ren*) or, if necessary, higher-level leaders or executives, to help break impasses.

Russian and Former Soviet Republics' Influence and Persuasion Strategies

Negotiators and researchers have long studied the persuasion strategies and tactics used by bargainers from the Soviet Union, Russia, and other former Soviet republics (Dennett and Johnson, 1951; Craig, 1972; Pipes, 1972; Gartoff, 1977; Hingley, 1977; Jönsson, 1979; Whelan, 1979; Kapleman, 1985; Slocombe, 1986; Sloss and Davis, 1986; Stoertz, 1986; Binnendijk, 1987; Kennan, 1987; Sloss and Davis, 1987; Harris and Moran, 1989; Smith, 1989). Since the major political changes in the late 1980s and 1990s, there have been fewer studies on negotiation behaviors of members of these cultures in the post-Soviet era.

An interesting exception examines whether a more collaborative negotiation culture has emerged from the top-down governing and other social structures in a number of countries in the Caucasus: "A negotiation culture is a framework . . . composed of two pillars—the institutional dimension and the relational dimension. The institutional dimension of a negotiation culture refers to institutional arrangements conducive to deliberation among and between individuals, interest groups, social organizations and governance structures. The relational dimension of a negotiation culture embodies sociocultural patterns at the individual level, targeted toward the 'basic means of getting what you want from others'" (Ohanyan, 1999, p. 85). The author concludes that a more collaborative negotiation culture has not been rapidly forthcoming in the region. Rather, a number of elements have persisted: centralized and top-down institutional structures and authority at the state, industry, and enterprise levels; clientelism, that is, extensive networks of hierarchical and dependent relationships between patrons and clients, many with roots in the positions of superiors in state institutions; and the newly rich entrepreneurs who took over privatized state companies and connections built up by membership in or family involvement in the former Communist Party. These institutional and relational patterns have led to a significant continuation of hierarchical, top-down, command-oriented negotiations dynamics among parties negotiating within these cultures and in interactions with outsiders.

Richmond (1992) and Schecter (1998), in their research on Russian society and negotiation practices, found similar continuities in institutional structures; interpersonal relationships, especially between those with and those without power; approaches to negotiation; and influence and persuasion strategies and tactics from earlier times. Russian negotiators commonly use a number of approaches in the political and economic sectors to influence counterparts. Many of these are also found among negotiators from former Soviet Republics who grew up during the final years of the Soviet Union.

Smith (1989), in his review of Soviet negotiating and persuasion strategies, noted that "authoritarianism, risk avoidance and control" were key determining factors in Soviet approaches and behavior in negotiations. Although the political and economic structures of Russia and many post-Soviet republics have changed significantly from those of the Soviet Union, the essential approach to negotiation is embedded deeply in the cultures and appears to have persisted (Richmond, 1992; Schecter, 1998).

Hingley (1977), in his analysis of Russian psychology and interpersonal and interorganizational relationships, noted that members of this culture seek to establish superior and subordinate relationships with friends, colleagues, counterparts, or adversaries—whether the other party is a fellow Russian or a foreigner. Smith (1989) applied this analysis to Soviet and Russian relationships in negotiations. In his experience and that of other non-Russian negotiators, Russians usually begin the process of direct talks by engaging in overt attempts to gain a superior position in relationship to counterparts. Thus, negotiators from the former Soviet Union and Russia usually initiate their persuasion strategies with one or more of several tactics. The first approach is to begin with a general presentation on the broader implications or meanings of the negotiations and efforts to define the situation in favorable terms for the Russian negotiator. By establishing the parameters of talks, Russian bargainers hope to define what and how issues will be talked about and thereby control the agenda.

In the second approach, which is more risk avoidant, the Russian negotiator makes a positive statement about upcoming negotiations, asks the counterpart to explain his or her views first, and then aggressively criticizes what has been said, but without offering a counterproposal (Schecter, 1998). Russian negotiators believe that early engagement in argumentation is a way to test the views, strength, commitment, and resolve of a counterpart. A party that bends or gives in during this early phase of talks is likely to be perceived as weak, subordinate, and subject to efforts of exploitation later (Gorer and Rickman, 1950; Deane, 1947).

In a related alternative opening, Russian negotiators advocate the adoption of a set of principles that will guide negotiations, a tactic similar to the approach of Chinese negotiators. Russian negotiators advocate for the acceptance of proposed principles, believing this will place them in a superior position in later bargaining.

A third approach is to start by proposing a maximum position that sets out excessive demands (Cohen, 1991; Smith, 1989, Schecter, 1998) that many counterparts perceive as unreasonable. In this approach, both the tone and content may be relatively extreme (Schecter, 1998). The proposal is usually followed by assertive and, on occasion, aggressive arguments about why the Russian proposal should be accepted by the counterpart. Unbending advocacy of the position may continue for a long time, into the middle stages and even to the end of negotiations.

Each of these four openings is designed to place Russian negotiators in a dominant position relative to the counterpart and give them significant control over the negotiation process itself and the substantive issues that will be discussed. The argumentation tactics used are those that are persuasive to Russians themselves: compelling data, credible opinions of experts whom they respect, and the views of respected allies (Schecter, 1998).

There are other common Russian influence strategies during early phases of negotiation as well (Jönsson, 1979; Smith, 1989; Schecter, 1998):

- A "red herring" technique, in which a negotiator makes a startling or outrageous demand and, once it has stirred up emotions, withdraws it while demanding a concession in return

- Presentation of information that is very much in their favor, often stretching the truth, and on occasion distorting accuracy

- Expression of anger as a means of intimidation

- Efforts to personally put down or demean the counterpart
- Lengthy repetition of arguments in favor of the Russian case

All of these strategies serve to test a counterpart's views toward the Russian team and its own positions, determine its level of resolve to maintain the position, uncover inconsistencies, assess weaknesses and strengths, and identify points that can be exploited in later talks.

Russians use emotions much more frequently than negotiators from other cultures, especially those from Asia, Latin America, or North America, where maintenance of smooth interpersonal relationships and avoidance of negative feelings in negotiations is a priority. During the Soviet period, observers saw Russians using anger and demeaning behavior to intimidate counterparts and force them to give in. More recently, Russians have used more positive emotional appeals, including emphasizing that negotiators are in similar positions or are equals, requests for sympathy or assistance for their country in its current situation, or appeals to help them deal with superiors in the bureaucracy by giving them a more favorable offer.

While emotional expression is common in Russian negotiations, rapid mood shifts are also not unusual. Tactics of abuse or extreme hostility can rapidly shift to more respectful relations and acts of friendliness, and then, just as quickly, shift again to the previous hostile mode without any explanation or even embarrassment on the part of the Russian negotiator (Whelen, 1979). If an extreme position is put on the table and rejected soundly by the counterpart, Russian negotiators may shift negotiations to a more realistic basis. Rejection generally needs to be expressed with strong feelings (but not necessarily negative ones), real conviction, or a credible principle to be convincing. However, if rejection of the Russian position is not convincing, the Russians are likely to reinforce their position and continue to push hard for their proposal. In general, former Soviet and Russian negotiators expect their counterparts to stick to their position as steadfastly as they do. They expect a counterpart to raise a position or issue repeatedly if it is important to them.

If Russian negotiators cannot gain agreement on the parameters of negotiations, persuade their counterpart to make an acceptable offer, secure an agreement on principles, or achieve a concession on their initial high demand, they may respond by trying to create a relationship of equality—in their view, the only viable alternative to being a subordinate. "In all relations which are not defined as leader and led, superordinate and subordinate...Russians...demand the most absolute equality in their personal relationships. It would appear that Russians do not conceive of any intermediate positions: there is either complete equality or complete subordination" (Gorer and Rickman, 1950, p. 177). Russian negotiators may also shift to other persuasion tactics and become less aggressive, including more collaborative means of persuasion such as creating more respectful relationships (but not necessarily agreement on issues), emphasizing interactions among equals, and identifying commonalities, such as being important players in the world scene.

At this time in negotiations, Russians may also begin to make informal contacts with members of a counterpart's team with either positive or more controlling goals. On the positive side, they might explore potential points of agreement or where the counterpart might make concessions. On the controlling side, they might identify individuals whom they believe to have views more favorable to their position and to be more pliant—and then attempt to split those individuals off from their team to create disorganization and dissention. They may also use humor and tell tall tales, *vranyo*, to pull a counterpart's leg (or as Russians commonly say, "hang noodles over a person's ears" or "lift the gloom and pull back the darkness") but not necessarily to gain advantage (Smith, 1989, p 43).

During the middle phases of negotiations, Russians are often unwilling to entertain compromises. During the Soviet era, compromises were seen as making concessions to a class enemy or giving up important principles, honesty, or strength. Russian negotiators also seem to fear that if they offer to compromise, their counterpart will become more aggressive and take advantage of them on later issues—all consistent with Russian assumptions about negotiating behavior. Conversely, offers of compromise by a counterpart may also be seen as an indication of the other's weakness and an invitation for exploitation. During this phase, if agreements are reached at all, Russian negotiators are likely to offer small, incremental concessions (which they resist framing as compromises) or propose linkage of issues to allow mutually beneficial trades.

In the end game of negotiations, Russian negotiators may continue to repeat arguments presented in earlier stages. They apparently do this to make a final effort at persuading a counterpart to accept their proposal, convince their superiors that they have made their best effort to promote their case, and as a psychological prerequisite for shifting to a new position. It also appears that a counterpart must repeatedly reject their proposals to be believed.

If desired agreements are still not forthcoming, former Soviets and Russians today may resort to stalling tactics. "Frequently Russians refuse to answer letters or telephone calls, announce that they are not available, and insist on postponing or changing dates.... Stalling is a deliberate effort to wear down an opponent and force concessions, especially from a goal oriented opponent" (Schecter, 1998, pp. 82–83). Stalling may also be used to raise the stakes in negotiations. Negotiatiors who need a settlement and for whom time is important may be induced to give in and make concessions to their Russian counterpart.

If Russian negotiators discover that they do need to change positions, they have several alternatives. Often they have only one fallback position for their counterpart to consider, and they may offer it at this time. If this option is also not acceptable, the Russian negotiators may have to go back to their superiors for clarification, new instructions, or a new mandate or use more indirect means to induce their counterpart to provide them with a more acceptable option. For example, in the Strategic Arms Limitation Talks, when Soviet negotiators wanted to avoid making an unacceptable commitment or returning to their superiors for new instructions, on occasion they gave their U.S. counterparts a "nonpaper" with off-the-record options for them to consider. However, the Russians stated explicitly that if the ideas in the paper were publicly attributed to them, they would adamantly deny it. If Americans had questions of clarifications about issues raised in the Russians' nonpaper, they could reciprocate with a nonpaper of their own to explore other options. If the ideas in the nonpaper were acceptable to the United States, their negotiators could propose them back to the Russians as American proposals. These in turn would be taken by their Soviet counterparts to their superiors for consideration. Russian negotiators believed U.S. proposals that met indirectly identified Russian interests would be more acceptable to their superiors, and posed less risk to them, than if they sought similar new instructions directly (Rowney, 1992).

During the end game, Russian negotiators may claim that they lack the authority to make a binding decision, which may be true (Schecter, 1998). However, in the past, it appears that Russian negotiators used this claim as a tactic for pushing a counterpart to reconsider whether to accept an option on the table rather than risk time delays or the unknown decision of a superior who is not at the table. When a position does change, former Soviets and Russians commonly believe that

> you do not lose by finally changing your position. You win by demonstrating your seriousness. Your adversary will have contempt for you if you give in easily, respect if you have fought hard. Of equal importance, your superiors upon whom you are totally dependent for a position of enormous prestige and practical benefits in the Soviet [or Russian] context, are most unlikely to reprove you for being too tough in your negotiations with the class enemy. Moreover, the longer you hold out, the more likely it is that the other side will make a move that you can use advantageously [Smith, 1989, p. 36].

In the final phases of negotiations, a Russian negotiator will try to convince a counterpart that a concession made requires an equivalent from their counterpart. Matching concessions one-for-one may be expected, even if the concession made by one party is not equal in amount or importance to that made by the other party.

RECOMMENDED APPROACHES FOR WORKING WITH RUSSIAN NEGOTIATORS:

Negotiators and researchers have developed the following recommendations for negotiating with Russian counterparts (Richmond, 1992; Schecter, 1998):

- To the greatest extent possible, try to negotiate with a counterpart who has significant authority and, if persuaded at the negotiation table, will be able to make major decisions. Given the structure of many Russian negotiation teams and the delegation of authority, this may be difficult to achieve.

- Avoid offending Russian sensitivities about their country, its strength, or its technical prowess in comparison to others. Unintentional creation of one-up/one-down dynamics can make a Russian counterpart defensive, with negative impacts on talks.

- Do not depend exclusively on personal relationships to motivate offers or concessions or promote final agreements. For Russians, the basis for final agreement tends to be tangible benefits, agreements in which they did not lose, or settlements that conform to a valued principle.

- Demonstrate strong resolve, be consistent, and persistently and repeatedly advocate for and show unbending commitment to ideas, principles, or options that are nonnegotiable, or where there is only marginal movement. Russian negotiators respect commitment to proposals or positions that are important to the counterpart. A counterpart who gives in too easily is vulnerable to being exploited, to the Russians' advantage.

- Avoid surprises and the presentation of entirely new ideas in formal sessions without providing a Russian counterpart with adequate notice in informal meetings. Whenever possible, use informal meetings to explore and refine ideas, options, and proposals before bringing them to a formal setting.

- Be willing to extend the time frame for discussions and persuasion. Recognize that often a significant amount of time is needed for bureaucratic decision making or approval by a negotiator's superior who may be risk avoidant. Demonstrate where possible that time limits either are not so important or that the opportunity for a favorable agreement is fading. Avoid being pushed into a situation where a deadline or time dictates a settlement or requires undesirable concessions.

- Link any agreement on one issue to an agreement on another issue—or, if necessary, link a concession to a counterconcession from the Russian negotiator. Later concessions by Russian negotiators on other issues, in exchange for a concession made earlier by a counterpart, generally will not be forthcoming. Also, make sure that exchanges are of similar magnitude or value and not just one-for-one.

- Consider developing packages as a way to address multiple issues. Packages avoid making concessions on linked issues, obscure overall gains and losses for any one party, and help save face when a concession has to be made on a specific issue. On some occasions, packages also seem to be more easily sold by Russian negotiators to their superiors.

- Be clear and explicit about consequences for all parties if agreements are not complied with. Consider using both positive incentives and negative consequences for compliance.

Egyptian and Arab Influence and Persuasion Strategies

The persuasive approaches used in Egypt and a number of other Arab countries are built on four common cultural patterns: relationship building, positional bargaining (the market or *suk* approach), traditional tribal approaches, and significant emphasis on the language used and the way that viewpoints are presented (Quandt, 1987).

Relationship building and positional negotiations are common in Egypt and many other Arab cultures as means for influencing counterparts. Quandt (1987) equates this style of negotiation and persuasion to the process that is used to reach agreements in local markets or *suks*:

> There should be a preliminary period of discussing issues that go well beyond the transaction that is contemplated. This involves a ritual of establishing a personal relationship. Once that has been accomplished, often after endless cups of coffee and tea, the actual bargaining can begin. The seller will start with a much higher price than he expects to achieve, and part of the game is to work toward a compromise solution. Both parties know how much of a compromise is acceptable to them at the outset, but neither wants to reveal his final position too soon. Typically haggling will go on for some time, both may threaten to break off the process, both will engage in a whole series of maneuvers to find out the real bottom line of the other party, and in the end a deal is likely to be struck that will allow both parties to feel satisfaction. Alternatively, the process may seem to drag on indefinitely, a sign that the Egyptian side is not ready for a deal but does not want to bear the onus of breaking off the negotiations [p. 119].

Egyptian or other Arab negotiators do not consider making a high demand at the start of negotiations as an act of insincerity, bad faith, or a way to delay reaching an agreement. Rather, it is a ritual that emphasizes that the negotiator is strong and has the authority or status to ask a high price for agreement. This does not mean that they will not modify their initial demand later in negotiations, once deeper personal relations have been established and more information is exchanged about each party's interests.

Observers of Egyptian negotiators and those from other Middle Eastern countries have noticed three persuasive patterns that are used later in negotiations, especially in conditions where the *suk* approach to bargaining is being followed: never taking a direct no for an answer, extreme persistence in encouraging a counterpart to come up with a solution that is acceptable to them, and an appeal to assuage personal feelings that are being ignored or harmed (Johnstone, 1989). Johnstone noted that Egyptian students, when negotiating with non-Egyptian counselors, would never take no for an answer. They continued to advocate for their position repeatedly, pushing for a more favorable response. If a proposal was ultimately rejected by their counterpart and no other acceptable one could be developed, Egyptian negotiators were likely to charge that they were being ignored or hurt and demand that their personal needs or interests be addressed.

A second approach to negotiations in the Arab world is that commonly used among tribes. Quandt (1987) has called this a Bedouin model for talks. This approach is commonly used in serious disputes, often where blood has been shed and issues of face and honor are at stake. This persuasion process, like that in the *suk*, begins with one or more parties engaging in posturing, making high demands, and possibly issuing threats. These may be presented in ritualized settings, such as conferences or meetings between representatives of key parties (as it is often dicey to bring the two protagonists together in a face-to-face meeting). Negotiators may use highly emotional, heated language and sarcasm and lose their temper (Patai, 1983).

High demands and later dynamic moves used for persuasion are influenced by whether the counterpart is from the same or a different culture. Because Egypt is predominantly a Muslim country, the counterpart's status and relationship with Islam is important:

> Islamic thought recognizes the inevitability of struggle between Islam and other religious communities, and, at the same time, stresses the need for resolution within the Muslim community itself.... This suggests a dichotomy between how Muslims regard their relations with the greater world community, and how they perceive life within the community of believers. In the former, basic differences in religious creed color the entire relationship; in the latter, an equally strong religious commitment drives all believers toward harmony. The concept of continuous struggle with external forces flows naturally from a belief in religious absolutes. It presumes the existence of substantial and irresolvable differences among peoples and, in contrast, a consistency of belief among those who profess a single religion [Murray, 1997, p. 45].

The cultural-religious view of continuous struggle in certain circumstances may encourage Egyptian negotiators to use persuasive strategies oriented to the restoration of harmony when differences arise within their own community. However, when dealing with external parties, they are often willing to engage in protracted competition and refuse to accept the views of a counterpart. Contests that are framed in terms of struggle involve upholding honor, dignity, or religious commitments and thus make participants reluctant to compromise. Some negotiators believe that disputes of this type cannot be resolved and that ongoing contradictions will remain until one or another party can prevail against the other. More often, however, the confrontation is not so drastic and relationships are not so badly damaged—and they can request the assistance of a trusted third party or mediator (*wasīt)* to assist them in finding a solution.

Because issues of honor are at stake, haggling over solutions as in the *suk* approach is seen as entirely inappropriate. The involvement of a mediator is used to provide a door that parties can walk through individually or together, reach an agreement, save face, and preserve honor (Patai, 1983). Instead of haggling, the mediator helps parties exchange "gestures of generosity [that] are relied upon to change the atmosphere of negotiations, and it is the job of the intermediary to be sure that if such gestures are made, they will be reciprocated" (Quandt, 1987, p. 120). In addition, the mediator, rather than looking for compromises, may help the parties discover principles to which all agree, which can shape detailed agreements and save face for all concerned. This may involve sacrifice in which "one side willingly gives up something that it legitimately thought it should have (or promises something it legitimately thought it was not required to promise) in order to achieve a greater good. The sacrifice may be for reasons of high principle, common friendship, or personal moral values, but it is definitely not a concession or a compromise" (Murray, 1997, p. 52). Mediators commonly ask parties to reach an agreement for the sake of a valued principle or person, such as peace, restoration of harmony, restoration of honor, harmony of the village, or respect for one's brother or father (Patai, 1983).

Egyptian and other Arab negotiators take great care in their language of persuasion. The Arab American historian Phillip K. Hitti (1943) observed, "No people in the world has such enthusiastic admiration for literary expression and is so moved by the word spoken or written as the Arabs.... The rhythm, the rhyme, the music produce on them the effect of what they call 'lawful magic'" (p. 21). Johnstone (1989) has called this approach to influence "presentational persuasion." This method is "based on the assumption that being persuaded is being moved, being swept along by a rhythmic flow of words and sounds in the way that people are swept along by poetry. The goal of presentational persuasion is to make one's claim maximally present in the audience's consciousness, by repeating it, paraphrasing it and calling aesthetic attention to it" (pp. 147–148).

"Eloquence is emphasized and admired in the Arab world far more than in the West, which accounts for the 'flowery' prose in Arabic, both in written and spoken form. *Instead of viewing rhetoric in a disparaging way, as Westerners often do, Arabs admire it.* The ability to speak eloquently is a sign of education and refinement" (Nydell, 1987, pp. 102–103). Thus, in negotiations, whether over political questions, intergroup relations, or commercial transactions, Arab speakers emphasize the way that something is said, as well as substantive content. Arab speakers vary the volume of speech for dramatic effect and to demonstrate commitment to a view. They may also on occasion exaggerate or overassert, make unqualified promises or issue threats, repeat slogans, or quote poetry, proverbs, blessings, or quotations from religious texts to make an important point (Patai, 1983; Nydell, 1987). Persuasive arguments are often repetitious and appear to be circular as negotiators try to persuade their counterparts to the validity of their views.

Eloquent language may also be used to obscure meanings, cloud commitments, or protect a counterpart from direct criticism. When an Egyptian or Arab counterpart says that a proposed option or solution "is difficult" or "might be difficult," he is often signaling that it is either not acceptable or will be impossible to implement (al-Omari, 2003).

RECOMMENDED APPROACHES FOR WORKING WITH EGYPTIAN AND MANY ARAB NEGOTIATORS

- Be prepared for an extended period of time and conversation focused on relationship and interpersonal trust building. This often occurs over tea or a meal. This phase of negotiations is generally a critical precondition to moving on to substantive discussions.

- Recognize that the way negotiators from these cultures communicate is often as important as the substance. Expect and tolerate long and elaborate speeches or comments, which may be framed to evoke your emotions or persuade you to your counterpart's views.

- Do not be surprised by initial high or low demands or initial positions. Your counterpart expects that bargaining will occur to move toward a positive settlement range. If appropriate, you may also use a similar strategy to illustrate the importance of your issues or interest.

- Expect that your counterpart will not initially take no for an answer and will try various arguments, many of which may be circular or repetitive, to persuade you to his view. After an extended period of talk or argumentation, he may be more open to exploring options that you might suggest.

- References to God, religion, or honor may be common. Avoid making any questionable statements about religion or that call a counterpart's honor into question. Also avoid talking about women in your counterpart's organization or family.

- If negotiations stall, consider using a mediator to break the impasse or preserve face or honor.

Indian Influence and Persuasion Strategies

Like most other multicultural countries, India comprises a wide variety of social groups and diverse cultural patterns of persuasion. In negotiations, the divide between political and economic or business negotiations is often critical. Political negotiations are usually handled by members of the government bureaucracy, who may or may not have final decision-making authority. Thus, means of persuasion must be not only effective for parties at the table but also compelling for their superiors. The means of persuasion will differ depending on the level of officials involved and the power relationship they have to counterparts.

In international relations, Indians often have a dominating style when dealing with parties they consider to have less power, such as those from Nepal and Sri Lanka, but may be much less forceful and are more likely to pursue a more defensive strategy when relating to a powerful nation such as the United States (Cohen, 1997). Economic negotiations are more likely to be carried out by parties who have decision-making authority.

A number of negotiators, both Indian and from other cultures, have noted that Indian negotiations are characterized by initial distrust between parties. Dunung, an Indian national herself, remarked that "Indians tend to trust each other only when it is convenient" (1995, p. 383). Cohen (1997) found that mutual suspicion is the norm in bureaucratic relations. However, "At the heart of business in India is the trust factor. Establishing a personal relationship of trust and respect is important and expected.... It is mutual trust and understanding that allows for the flexibility in conducting the business transaction, particularly if problems occur" (Trade Media Ltd., 1991, p. 35). For this reason, parties need to spend time at the beginning of negotiations to build trust before agreements can be reached. However, the length of time for relationship building is generally not as long as required in other Asian countries such as Japan and China; Indian negotiators prefer to begin substantive talks fairly rapidly. Therefore, social relationships and trust may be cultivated over time and through repeated social and business meetings. Indians tend to be process oriented and wish to follow an orderly sequence for discussions. They expect data or facts to be presented in a clear and precise manner by a counterpart and try to do the same themselves.

Indian negotiators are significantly more competitive bargainers in comparison to negotiators from some other cultures, and they negotiate agreements in many areas of their lives (Druckman, Benton, Ali, and Bagur, 1976; Carment and Alcock, 1976). They use a more deductive style of reasoning, more like the British and American negotiators, and base decisions on empirical data or, on occasion, ideology. They can use an argumentative style for persuasion, but generally do so in a respectful, nonantagonistic manner (Moran and Stripp, 1991). Indian negotiators generally dislike public displays of emotion and value impulse control, so they may mask their emotions and hide their views on issues. These behaviors may stem from their colonial experience of British officials who felt that showing emotions was bad form or the Hindu tradition of abjuring desire (Cohen, 1997).

Many Indian negotiators are risk avoidant, especially if they are from government bureaucracies. Some negotiators have noted that Indian bureaucrats are more likely to find reasons for inaction than action. They are concerned about their personal reputations, requirements to follow bureaucratic rules, perceptions of them by their superiors, or, in some situations, the views of the public at large. For this reason, "Officials are bound to conform to 'culture-bound' behavior or risk 'social disapproval'" (Cohen, 1997, p. 128). However, after exploration of options, formal rules can be overcome by the development of pragmatic informal practices. When this approach does not work, Indian negotiators refer decisions to their superiors—or at least say they will have to do so—as a means of influencing their counterpart.

One study found that Indian negotiators tend to be less compromising than counterparts from the United States and Argentina and more frequently reject their counterpart's offers (Druckman, Benton, Ali, and Bagur, 1976). If deadlocks do occur and a negotiator believes that an Indian counterpart either does not have the authority to make a decision or is reluctant to do so, the negotiator may need to contact a superior who can decide. However, this influence tactic should be used judiciously, as it is likely to irreparably damage the relationship with the counterpart whose personal authority has been circumvented.

Indian negotiators have a more flexible view of time than do typical negotiators from the West. They tend to bargain longer than negotiators from the United States and Canada (Cohen, 1997, p. 117), especially when older males are involved (Druckman, Benton, Ali, and Bagur, 1976), and they allow periods of silence during talks, both for deliberation and to encourage a counterpart to bring forth new ideas or proposals. They are willing to wait for extended periods of time—much longer than foreign counterparts—if a favorable agreement is not forthcoming. Timing of agreements may be delayed due to the bureaucratic time necessary to make decisions.

RECOMMENDED APPROACHES FOR WORKING WITH INDIAN NEGOTIATORS

- Expect that building trust will take some time. Make efforts to demonstrate sincerity.

- Speak clearly and directly about issues being negotiated, and avoid excessive expression of emotions, especially negative ones.

- Be prepared for fairly assertive, competitive negotiations in comparison to those of many other cultures. Positional bargaining, extensive argumentation, and strong adherence to positions are common, and negotiations often are more protracted than in Western cultures.

- Be predictable. Follow through on promises or commitments.

- Look for solutions that are predictable and lower risk, especially in negotiations with counterparts from the governmental sector.

- If impasse occurs, explore whether it is possible to talk with a counterpart's superior.

Indonesian Influence and Persuasion Strategies

Indonesia is the fourth largest country in the world and contains diverse cultures on its 13,677 islands, 6,044 of which are inhabited. However, most Indonesian subcultures have similar negotiation styles, being fairly indirect dealing, with the possible exceptions of the Batak in North Sumatra and Madurese from the island of Madura, where the populations are much more direct dealing, explicit, and, according to many other Indonesians, even blunt in their communications.

Indonesians place a high value on building positive and smooth interpersonal relationships before beginning substantive talks as a means for later persuasion. This may be built through social activities, such as taking ritual tea and eating snacks, informal relationship-building conversations, and formal opening sessions that demonstrate respect between counterparts.

Indonesians use relatively indirect means of influence and avoid expressions of negative emotions or raising their voices in negotiations (Harris and Moran, 1987; Dunung, 1995). They typically begin persuasive activities by circumventing subjects that may be controversial, and when they do begin to talk about them, they do so indirectly to avoid overt disagreements or making any parties feel *malu:* embarrassed, ashamed, or ill at ease (Harris and Moran, 1987). Direct questioning is generally not used as a means of persuasion, as Indonesians are reluctant to put counterparts on the spot. When questions are used, they are usually relatively indirect (Dunung, 1995). Any disagreements are discussed in informal settings, where issues can be explored without any of the negotiators risking the loss of face.

Like many Japanese negotiators, Indonesians often seek consensus on agreements, or *mufakat,* to develop solutions that all can accept. Persuasion occurs through informal discussions or the *musyawarah* process, in which all parties indirectly try out potential solutions, without actually committing to them, until a favorable one is developed (Moore and Santosa, 1995; Dean, 2000; Noel, Shoemake, and, Hale, 2006).

Generally Indonesians do not pressure each other to reach agreements and do not like to be pressured themselves. Time is seen as much more flexible and unlimited than in many other countries, especially North America, Europe, Singapore, and Hong Kong. Because Indonesian society is highly stratified, especially in Java, whose population makes up about 45 percent of the nation, Indonesians are persuaded by opinions of higher-status negotiators. These individuals are usually men over forty years of age who have high-status positions and a university education. Opinions expressed by these negotiators are more valued than those of younger individuals, women, or people with lower status or levels of education (Dean, 2000). Having the interest or support of senior decision makers is often believed by Indonesians to be persuasive to counterparts. Their presence often indicates the seriousness of talks.

Persuasion is often based on finding solutions that are right intuitively rather than those based on a principle or process of logic. "Westerners should be careful not to assume that this implies poor decision making on the part of Indonesians. On the contrary, Indonesians need to feel that the basis of a business interaction is that it feels 'right' and is for the greater good" (Dunung, 1995, pp. 230–231).

Indonesians, especially when addressing difficult or tension-provoking issues where face may be involved, often use informal intermediaries to sound out counterparts on possible solutions and carry messages on possible options or proposals. Intermediaries help both to avoid direct disagreements and confrontations and are perceived as able to deliver messages to counterparts, which will be more persuasive than if a party directly involved delivered them.

RECOMMENDED STRATEGIES FOR WORKING WITH INDONESIAN NEGOTIATORS

- Be prepared to spend a significant amount of time building positive working relationships and trust. This may involve engaging in social activities.

- Avoid expression of negative emotions or direct or coercive means of influence.

- Avoid establishing superior-subordinate relationships in circumstances where negotiation counterparts are peers.

- Begin the discussion of substantive questions in a fairly indirect and general manner. After relationships, trust, and rapport have been built, specifics can be addressed.

- Be self-disclosing, but not overbearing, in presenting your views, needs, and interests.

- Consider discussing difficult issues in informal settings, and without an audience, with individuals who are the decision makers or have direct access to decision makers. Use private forums so that neither you nor your counterpart loses face. Explore options and develop solutions that can be brought back to formal talks for approval.

- Use as many positive influence tactics as possible, including making credible promises, identifying solutions that will result in positive benefits, appealing to commonly accepted or reasonable standards or norms, and providing incentives and rewards for cooperation.

- Change the subject to other issues if an impasse occurs, returning to the contested issue later.

- Take breaks to allow time for reconsideration of options or proposals in private.

- Ask for the help of an intermediary to shuttle between parties and conduct private meetings with each until an accord is reached.

Mexican Influence and Persuasion Strategies

"Mexicans, like members of other collectivist cultures, place a high value on building positive personal relationships as means to persuade counterparts in negotiations. They also emphasize saving their own face, with somewhat less concern for their counterpart's. Their goals are to nurture mutual confidence, engage in unpublicized, informal discussions, and seek solutions to particular problems" (Grayson, 1987, p. 133). This is true in commercial negotiations from large business deals to haggling in a market.

Status is an important Mexican value, and it can be used by a counterpart to encourage cooperation. Acknowledgment of a counterpart's formal position, academic achievements (an M.D., Ph.D., J.D., or engineering degree), or other important accomplishments can make a counterpart feel more at ease, feel respected, and be more cooperative (Kras, 1989). Regardless of the values placed on personal relationships, Mexican negotiators are not averse to making initial high demands or taking hard positions as strategies for convincing a counterpart to move a significant distance to meet Mexican needs or interests (Grayson, 1987). This is true in bargaining over political, business, and other commercial matters.

While Mexicans often use more passive and conflict-avoidant strategies, especially in contrast to their North American counterparts, they are also competitive bargainers and are willing to deliberate on issues for long periods of time without reaching agreement (Kagan, Knight, and Martinez-Romero, 1982; Cohen, 1997). Intractability and delayed agreement making have been identified as major strategies of Mexican negotiators (Grayson, 1987). Mexicans are willing to talk and negotiate at length before reaching agreement. This strategy may be based on a number of factors. First, they may assume that through extended talk, their counterpart may be worn down and will ultimately present a more favorable proposal. A second factor is that many Mexican negotiators often seem to perceive negotiations as "a 'zero-sum' rather than an 'expanding-sum' game—if one side wins, the other must loose" (Grayson, 1987, p. 143). This is especially true when Mexicans negotiate with Americans. If negotiations are seen purely in win-lose terms, there is no need to rush to be taken advantage of (Grayson, 1987).

Verbally persuasive strategies include advocacy of general principles, as well as arguments advocating specific solutions to particular problems as means to persuade counterparts (Kras, 1989; Moran and Stripp, 1991; von Bertrab, 1997). Using rules or laws as guidance for problem solving is often less important than examining the specifics of a particular situation and finding customized solutions to address them ("Mexico: Let's Make a Deal," n.d.)

Mexicans use a combination of emotion, description of personal experience, gradual revelation of information, and appeals for respect, dignity, and national honor as means of persuasion (Moran and Stripp, 1991). Emotional expression is used to indicate the degree of importance of issues and interests and how specific solutions will affect different parties. Emotions expressed in negotiations may include efforts to build friendly and trusting relationships through being a good host and providing a range of enjoyable social activities; dramatic and, on occasion, exaggerated appeals to signal to a counterpart the importance or seriousness of the issues at stake; measured expression of anger, especially when negotiations are with a more powerful party; appeals for consideration or compassion regarding critical interests or needs; and requests for concessions to Mexicans, who often present themselves as a supplicant or weaker party, especially when negotiating with the United States (Fisher, 1980; Pastor and Castañeda, 1989; Cohen, 1997).

Other common Mexican means of persuasion are appeals to and respect for preservation of their dignity, independence, and autonomy (Harris and Moran, 1989; Cohen, 1997) and to promote just and fair agreements. "Mexicans are extremely sensitive to the world around them and have a marked capacity to empathize with the people with whom they interact.... They are also extremely sensitive to criticism, due to a deep emotional response to everything that affects them personally. For this reason they try to avoid situations which show them in a negative light or involve them in conflict'' (Kras, 1989, p. 34). When persuasive strategies are used by counterparts that offend this sensitivity, the response may be a surprise verbal and aggressive assault (Cohen, 1997). Mexicans prefer private and off-the-record negotiations, where personal relations can be built and brought to bear on difficult topics or problems. More public forums are likely to be used to present more hard-line positions or posturing.

RECOMMENDED STRATEGIES FOR WORKING WITH MEXICAN NEGOTIATORS

- Be prepared to spend time building a positive personal relationship with your counterpart. This may involve social activities such as meals, going to a nightclub, visiting their family, or going to local historical or cultural sites.

- Directly recognize your counterpart's status or position, and use his or her title. Avoid any actions that may result in a slight to this person's honor, a loss of face, or an indication that Mexicans are not your equals.

- Be prepared for long and sometimes intractable negotiations in which your counterpart may try to wear you down to gain concessions.

- Advocate for principles that will result in mutual gain.

- Avoid direct criticism or confrontation. It will result only in greater resistance to your ideas or impasse.

- Develop and present concrete proposals that will result in mutual benefits as means to overcome views about zero-sum outcomes.

- Use appeals to respect, honor, dignity, independence, and autonomy as influence strategies.

Nigerian and Common African Influence and Persuasion Strategies

While the description in this section focuses on Nigerian negotiating behavior, many of the same characteristics can be found in other African cultures despite their extreme variety. Nevertheless, it is difficult to generalize about African peoples because the continent is huge and the diversity of peoples vast.

Nigeria has the largest population in Africa, more than 270 language groups, and many cultures within one national state: Yoruba, Ibo, Hausa, Fulani, and many others (Richmond and Gestrin, 1998). Like other Africans, Nigerians place a high value on building sincere, trusting, and respectful relationships before they begin substantive negotiations. Their early persuasive strategies are often designed to establish relationships of trust between a counterpart, an individual, or a group (family, firm, organization, or tribe).

First meetings generally have both ritual and social purposes. The goal of first contacts is to put the parties at ease for a social conversation. "Normally before a meeting begins, there is general talk about events that have little or nothing to do with the business at hand. This can go on for some time. If the meeting involves the coming together of people who have never met, but who are trying to strike a deal (an African and a foreigner), the African will try to reach out for friendship first" (Harris and Moran, 1989, p. 484).

Nigerians enjoy talk, discussions, and argumentation. For them, experience, emotion, and intuition form the basis of persuasive argument. In contrast to members of many other African cultures, Nigerians, especially from the southern part of the country, are very direct dealing. In Nigeria itself, southerners are seen as hustlers and hard negotiators, possibly because of their long history as traders (Richmond and Gestrin, 1998). Direct dealing translates into low-context communications when it comes to persuasion. "Nigerians . . . will tell you exactly how they feel about everything. In contrast to other African countries, in Nigeria yes is more apt to mean yes, and no, no, and you are more likely to be told straight away . . . when you are doing something wrong" (Richmond and Gestrin, 1998, p. 178).

Positional bargaining as a means of persuasion and reaching agreements is expected in Nigeria. For example, "Yorba market transactions are a lively test of wit involving seller and buyer. . . . Since prices were seldom fixed, the understanding was that the seller would ask a price higher than he or she would accept, and the buyer was free to see how low he or she could bring the seller" (Owomoyela, 1988, p. 179). In general, the African and Nigerian approach to negotiations, while pushing hard for a good deal or agreement, is done in a manner that preserves decorum and face. Neither the parties nor the issues being discussed are demeaned. Nigerians focus on finding solutions in which each party will have at least some needs and interests satisfied, and all parties leave negotiations believing that they have engaged in a positive social interaction and gained something substantive (Richmond and Gestrin, 1998). At times the buyer may even recognize the seller's needs and make the first significant offer so that the seller does not lose face.

A wide variety of means of persuasion can be used in this positional bargaining context. One is explaining the logic and rationale for a proposed offer. If it is reasonable, it may be accepted. Another means of persuasion common in Nigeria is appropriate recognition of a counterpart's rank or status, often due to formal position, age, gender, or education. Demonstration of respect for a counterpart can go a long way in forming a positive relationship and increasing influence, as there is a belief that "the position of the individual is above the concerns of business, and [a strong] . . . emphasis on personal loyalty and trust in business relationships" (Moran and Stripp, 1991, p. 207).

In formal meetings, respect can be demonstrated by how and what is said, such as a smooth voice level and acknowledgment of a counterpart's importance or position, and also how and where one sits, with lower-status people generally sitting in a lower position than higher-status people. In formal meetings, people of higher status do not want to be challenged or embarrassed. Thus, proposals need to be made in a manner that takes this factor into consideration. However, parties with higher status may criticize the views of a counterpart as a means of persuading them to change their minds.

Persuasion, if it is not carried out by the actual decision maker as a participant in negotiations, may be exercised by a subordinate negotiator who says that he must return to his superior, often "Big Man" in a tribal community, to gain approval for an agreement. This strategy may be based in fact: the direct negotiator may not have the authority to decide and may need to consult in order to reach an accord. If this is the case, Richmond and Gestrin (1998) advise that negotiators should not embarrass a counterpart by belittling his lack of authority to make a decision on the spot.

Nigerians view a rapid task or substantive focus in negotiations with skepticism and are not likely to use time pressure as a means to influence agreement making. They often want to discuss issues fully and at length. Due to their experiences of colonialism, Nigerians are sensitive to being treated as equals, especially by Europeans and Americans, and they resist foreign attempts to dominate them (Richmond and Gestrin, 1998).

RECOMMENDED STRATEGIES FOR WORKING WITH NIGERIAN AND SOME OTHER AFRICAN NEGOTIATORS

- Begin negotiations with non-task-oriented social conversations. Get to know your counterpart personally. Discussion of family and business is common.

- Nigerians are generally direct dealing, but many other African cultures are not. With Nigerians, it is acceptable to be direct, put forth both issues and interests for discussion, and engage in argumentation, debate, or dialogue.

- Expect that your Nigerian counterpart will engage in strong positional negotiations over an extended period of time. Protracted discussions are used to fully understand issues in question and to push for the best settlement. If you want to use an interest-based approach, consider strategies presented in earlier chapters for making a transition.

- It is acceptable to show emotion, although strong expression of negative feelings can have an adverse impact on your relationship with your counterpart.

- Use logic and enhancement of a counterpart's position or status as means of influence.

GENERAL PERSUASION STRATEGIES

The following list offers general approaches for coordinating persuasion strategies and tactics. Obviously the particular approach depends on the people, cultures, and situations involved:

- Clearly identify your own interests. Make sure you know which substantive, procedural, and psychological interests are the most important to you.

- To the best of your ability, identify the interests of your counterparts, and speculate about what may be important to them based on the situation, issue at stake, or their culture.

- Review your best alternatives to a negotiated agreement—your BATNA—and speculate on that of your counterpart.

- Consider whether your counterparts are resisting your proposals or options—and why that might be so. Are they objecting to the substance, or are you creating resistance due to your own persuasion strategies, personal style, or behaviors that might be normal and acceptable in your own culture but not in theirs?

- Consider whether you are resisting their proposals, and why. Similarly, is the problem with the substance or their negotiating behavior?

- Have your counterparts been able to change your mind—or you theirs? Why or why not?

- Speculate on alternative means of persuasion or influence that you are willing to try and might be effective with your counterparts.

- Is there a culturally appropriate way that you can signal to your counterparts that their persuasion tactics are not working? Is direct confrontation needed or desirable, or will it create more resistance or loss of face?

- Determine if a better relationship is needed to develop trust and respect. If so, undertake appropriate strategies to enhance your relationship.

- Consider whether and what forms of data or logic are most likely to be persuasive to your counterpart and the approach to present it that may be compelling.

- Consider how to create more benefits for your counterpart (and yourself) for agreement.

- Assess the potential positive or negative impacts of using coercive influence, and determine if this is appropriate, necessary, or the best way to achieve your goals. Consider using the minimum amount of this form of persuasive power to avoid a backlash or escalation.

CONCLUSION

By the end of the problem-solving phase of negotiations, negotiators commonly have developed a level of rapport with each other, and perhaps a modicum of trust. They will have developed and begun to consider a range of potential options, proposals, solutions, or positions about which they can agree or will at least consider, and begin to engage in earnest to initiate persuasive strategies and tactics to move them toward agreement.

In the next two chapters, we consider a range of possible outcomes to relationships and issues in negotiations and the final steps toward reaching agreements.

CHAPTER ELEVEN

Assessing Options

More than forty negotiators engaged in a policy dialogue to develop recommendations to the State of California legislature a growth management plan—and they had done well. Representatives of large industry, homebuilders, municipal leagues, environmental groups, and minority and environmental justice advocates had negotiated recommendations to address growth management issues in the state, including urban sprawl, highway construction, commuter miles driven, economical policies for homebuilders, water use, protection of ecologically sensitive areas, and assurances that minority communities would not suffer adverse impacts from development.

Now came the hard part. Before submission to the state legislature, each negotiating group had to secure the approval of the proposals by their own organizations, which represented differing organizational cultures, decision-making processes, and criteria for assessing proposals. Industry and homebuilders sought approval from trade associations concerned about possible negative economic impacts. The Municipal League, concerned about local planning rights and tax revenues, had to wait for its annual meeting. Environmental groups and social justice representatives submitted the proposals to their boards, members and legal teams (author's experience as facilitator).

⁓

Negotiators must assess potential outcomes throughout the negotiation process and certainly during the final phases. The outcomes of negotiations

327

typically include agreements regarding the parties' interests with respect to relationships, substantive matters, or procedures. The final phase of negotiations may be quite extended, depending on the cultures of the parties, the difficulty of the issues, and the ability of the parties to communicate and engage in problem solving.

As with many of the other approaches and procedures explored in earlier chapters, the outcomes of negotiations are influenced by culture. In this chapter, we examine:

- Satisfaction of interests in negotiations
- Cultural considerations in developing and assessing potential outcomes
- Some general procedures for assessing options, proposals, positions, and potential outcomes
- Standards and criteria that guide decision making

SATISFACTION OF INTERESTS IN NEGOTIATIONS

During the negotiation process, parties put forward alternatives, options, proposals, or positions. Such solutions need to satisfy, at least minimally, all parties' substantive, procedural, and relationship and psychological needs and interests to be acceptable. (See a full description of interests in Chapters Two and Four.) To review:

- *Substantive interests* are tangible outcomes or benefits a party wants to have satisfied, exchanged, or received as a result of negotiations.
- *Procedural interests* pertain to parties' preferences regarding the process by which problem solving, negotiations, or dispute resolution occurs and ways agreements are reached or implemented.
- *Relationship or psychological interests* focus on how individuals or groups are treated, both in the negotiation process and outside it. They also include how participants feel or want to feel about themselves and their counterpart, and how relationships are valued and shaped through deliberations.

Awareness of these potential outcomes can help parties set the goals they want to achieve. We have provided an extensive list of possible outcomes at the end of this chapter.

CULTURAL CONSIDERATIONS IN ASSESSING OUTCOMES

Awareness of cultural factors or standards that influence parties' satisfaction with potential solutions can assist negotiators in developing outcomes that are culturally acceptable. When parties develop proposals or consider the acceptability of offers, they use culturally influenced criteria regarding reasonableness, appropriateness, fairness, and justness. Although parties from the same culture may apply either similar or different criteria to assess a proposal or weight such criteria differently, the situation becomes more complicated when people from different cultures or countries negotiate with each other. Because of dissimilar backgrounds, experiences, education, religions, and ideologies, parties may apply diverse standards to assess the viability of an option, proposal, offer, concession, or solution.

In this section, we present several conceptual frameworks for understanding how cultures perceive outcomes and some factors to consider when assessing proposals.

Who Assesses Outcomes?

Negotiation outcomes can be assessed by individuals or by groups. For some issues and in some situations or cultures, only the principal party or parties are involved in evaluating potential outcomes, especially in individualist cultures. In collectivist cultures, numerous people—extended family members, a kin group, business colleagues, or various levels of superiors or subordinates in a private firm or government organization—may be consulted or actively involved.

A central concept in collectivist cultures is the self, which affects how decisions are made. Riesman, Glazer, and Denney (1953) note that "the tradition-directed person...hardly thinks of himself as an individual" (p. 33). Collectivist societies see individualism as selfish and inconsiderate of the interests of the group. In traditional societies decision making is oriented toward the group or collectivity, and individuals get their needs met in the context of satisfying group needs.

One potential indicator of a culture's orientation toward who should be involved in decision making is the structure of families. Members of many traditional cultures tend to live in extended families with important kinship networks. Some families have fairly centralized patriarchal decision-making procedures; this is often the case in Mediterranean, Middle Eastern, and a number of Latin American cultures. Others require consultation, direct engagement, or approval by members of an extended network of potentially concerned parties, or use a combination of a central decision maker with extensive input from others. Models of family social structure and decision making are often expanded and applied to decision making in broader social institutions.

Japan, China (especially in more traditional and governmental sectors), and Indonesia are three cultures where group decision making is clearly the norm.

In Japanese corporations and governmental agencies, decisions are developed through an elaborate consensus-building process, the *ringe* system, in which numerous vertical and horizontal consultations and approvals are conducted before an agreement is reached (Hodgson, Sano, and Graham, 2000). In traditional Chinese culture, the concept of an individual personality distinct from a social group does not exist (Hsu, 1971). Because individuals are viewed as part of larger social groups and their environment, multiple parties must be considered before taking decisions.

Indonesians also emphasize group decision making, practicing the traditional *musyawarah* consensus-building system and variations on it throughout the archipelago (Moore and Santosa, 1995). Other cultures that emphasize the involvement of groups in decision making are Colombia, Pakistan, Peru, Taiwan, Singapore, Mexico, the Philippines, Greece, Turkey, Brazil, and Argentina (Hofstede, 1984).

Another factor in cultural orientation toward individualism or collectivism is the degree to which the society is bureaucratized and has organizations with procedures that require consultation with multiple parties or levels before agreements can be reached. This has been noted in negotiations with Russian or Soviet teams in the past. Before agreements could be reached, numerous communiqués were exchanged between the Russian negotiating team and the Moscow bureaucracy (Smith, 1989). Similar patterns have been observed in India, which has a long tradition of a bureaucratized civil service.

In contrast to collectivist cultures, other cultures emphasize the individual. In general, these societies are more urban and industrial, and the social structure of families has shifted from extended kinship structures to the nuclear family, individual autonomy has increased, and there is a greater likelihood that decisions can be made by individuals with less consultation with groups. Examples of these cultures are those in the United States, Australia, Great Britain, Canada, the Netherlands, and New Zealand. To a somewhat lesser degree, the cultures of Italy, France, Sweden, and Germany are also individualist. Israel, Spain, and India fall into a middle range, with a combination of individualist and collectivist tendencies (Hofstede, 1984). As noted, Japan is a highly urbanized society but also a collectivist-oriented culture.

While the individualist orientation is found most frequently in North America, northern Europe, and countries settled by people from the British Isles, there seems to be a small but significant worldwide trend in this direction. China, for example, has witnessed rapid industrialization, development of the private sector and individual entrepreneurs, and migration of large numbers of people to cities in East and South China, where they have become disconnected from local traditions, clans, and families. Those trends have led, at least in some sectors of the society, to greater individual autonomy and decision making (Hessler, 2006).

International negotiations involving counterparts from individualist and collectivist cultures may have trouble reaching agreements due to their different approaches to evaluating options and outcomes. Graham and Sano (1979) note this pattern in U.S.-Japanese business negotiations: Americans tend to send smaller teams with more flexibility and authority over direct decision making, while Japanese negotiators work in larger groups and require extended periods of time for consultation and consensus building within the team and in the organization.

Variations in Emphasis on Relationship, Procedural, or Substantive Outcomes

Tensions often arise between negotiators from different cultures when the involved parties do not understand that cultures place more or less emphasis on either substantive or relationship and procedural outcomes.

Outcomes can focus on clarifying or defining relationships between parties and the norms or procedures that will guide future interactions, or substantive agreements, or a combination of all three. Outcomes that are relationship or procedurally oriented seek to promote goodwill among the parties, define how they will interact in the future, and, in many cases, detail substantive benefits in more general terms. For example, in negotiations between parties from the People's Republic of China and foreigners (frequently Westerners), early rounds of discussions conclude with primarily relationship-oriented outcomes that establish fraternal relations between the parties. Historically, Chinese emphasize such outcomes because they allow them to gain a sense of the trustworthiness and sincerity of the negotiation partner, affirm that positive connections have been created, and establish principles that will guide future relations and deliberations.

In contrast, many outcomes focus on substantive issues, such as specific exchanges of materials or performance (money, commodities, land, and reciprocal actions). Agreements that emphasize substance might address the sale of fruit in a transaction between a U.S. buyer and a Mexican seller operating under the North American Free Trade Agreement, or determine agreements about the reduction of nuclear arms between Russia and the United States.

Distributive Versus Integrative Outcomes

Depending on the people, issues, general situation, power relations, and the cultures involved, parties will seek either distributive or integrative outcomes. Some parties prefer procedures that result in win-lose settlements (distributive) or outcomes where benefits or losses are shared (integrative). Cultures that see the parties or issues in either-or terms are likely to strive for solutions in which one party dominates another. Conversely, members of other cultures who are in similar situations seek outcomes where benefits are maximized for all parties or differences are equalized or minimized. They try to avoid solutions where one party must bear extreme losses. These outcomes are often termed *integrative solutions* because they strive to satisfy the needs of all parties to the greatest extent possible. However, an integrative solution does not require that all parties' interests are totally satisfied in the same manner or to a similar degree. Integrative solutions combine options and trade-offs adequately to meet all parties' substantive, procedural, and relationship interests. Several years ago, two staff members of CDR Associates worked with the governments of the United States and Japan on the design of procedures to resolve conflicts arising from construction contracts. The U.S. team proposed arbitration as the preferred dispute resolution procedure. The Japanese, not wanting to directly reject the American proposal, said that this procedure would be "very difficult" (read "impossible") for them to accept. When probed for their reasoning, the Japanese responded that an arbitration decision was likely to result in a direct confrontation between the involved parties and a distributive win-lose outcome, and it would not allow the parties to save face. They preferred mediation, in which a mutually respected third party would shuttle between disputants, helping them to develop mutually acceptable solutions and, if necessary, privately proposing possible settlement options. The Japanese believed that this approach was more likely to result in integrative settlement options in which all parties could win, and everyone could save face.

Agreement in Principle Versus Resolution of Component Parts

Some cultures strive to develop general frameworks of agreements, or a set of broad guiding principles, prior to working out details regarding tangible outcomes. This approach to the development of substantive outcomes is found in cultures influenced by deductive reasoning found in continental European philosophy or educational systems, such as France and many of its former colonies. Other countries where this pattern is found are Russia, China, and many former communist countries that have been influenced by Marxism-Leninism, another form of logic with roots in European philosophy.

Other cultures tend to break problems into smaller component parts (or building blocks), seek agreements or resolutions for each component, and then combine them into a master settlement. Negotiation researchers have noted that cultures with empirical philosophical systems or whose educational systems value pragmatic subjects and practical applications are more likely to pursue this approach to outcomes. The dominant cultures of the United Kingdom, Ireland, the United States, Canada, Australia and New Zealand, and India are cases in point.

Clearly there are variations in these two approaches in all cultures, and a number of societies use both. For instance, Germany and the Scandinavian countries often incorporate both agreements in principle and building-block approaches and outcomes.

Similar or Different Standards of or Concepts of Justice

Concepts of justice or fairness, which are culture dependent, become the criteria on which the quality of relationships is judged and the acceptability of substantive outcomes is based. Concepts of justice frame the kinds and content of outcomes that will be acceptable. In order to survive and avoid descending into a state of anarchy, all cultures must reach a common understanding regarding broadly accepted standards of justice and fairness. However, the numerous cultures espouse diverse definitions of justice.

By examining many negotiations, we can identify orientations toward justice and fairness. For instance, the concept of retributive justice defines the kinds of punishments or coercive outcomes considered to be appropriate in specific situations. Thus, the orientation toward retributive justice determines what reprisal can be taken for specific actions, such as a murder in a blood feud between clans in Albania (Hasluck, 1967) or what form of punishment should be imposed by the international community on Iran or North Korea for their pursuit of nuclear programs. In the first case, the interclan feud, the extraction of blood money may be both culturally appropriate and acceptable. In the second case, economic or political sanctions may be considered—at least by many non-Iranians—to be reasonable outcomes.

Another concept is competitive justice, in which each party seeks to maximize gains and minimize losses using whatever means of power or influence are available. While many theorists reject brute power as a basis for just solutions, many parties to negotiations or disputes readily adopt this approach.

Distributive justice is another viewpoint. In this approach, each party gains an outcome or division of desired benefits, based on an agreed-on principle, such as entitlement, equity, or quality. Justice based on entitlement allocates benefits according to a person's or group's qualifications, such as status, rank, role, class, or prior ownership of a resource. For example, in the traditional culture of the Tswana of South Africa and Botswana, the criteria for the resolution of disputes depend on the status of the parties—and higher-status parties are given special consideration and may receive more in any settlement due to their position in the community. This principle is generally accepted by parties of both higher and lower status (Comaroff and Roberts, 1981).

Equality justice allocates benefits in similar proportions to all parties, regardless of other factors. For example, parties might agree that all future employees of an international relief or development project will be evaluated based on their expertise and skills, not on their race, religion, or national origin; or that relief supplies will be distributed in a war-torn zone regardless of whether recipients are refugees or residents who did not leave during the conflict and independent of ethnicity. Another example might be an agreement to share gains or losses in a business partnership, where each has contributed roughly similar assets, albeit in different forms, on a fifty-fifty basis.

The third kind of distributive justice is equity, in which the parties agree to distribute resources, benefits, or losses based on a commonly agreed standard of fairness. For example, an international donor might agree that labor contributed by members of a community to construct a local water system will be considered equal to the financial contribution for materials by a donor.

A final form of justice is social welfare justice, in which resources or benefits are distributed according to a standard of the common benefit. An example is the Marxist principle of "from each according to his ability, to each according to his need." In Muslim countries, richer members of society are expected to take the poor into consideration and tithe to ensure that they receive welfare. Finally, in negotiations with international companies involved in extractive industries, local community members in developing countries often expect that companies should provide financial assistance or a fair and reasonable percentage of profits from the operation to promote sustainable development.

If negotiating parties can agree on a common standard of justice to guide agreement making, so much the better. However, in intercultural disputes, a common standard may not exist. Fortunately, when dealing across cultures, it may not always be necessary for the parties to agree on a common standard of justice; rather, each must find the outcome acceptable according to their own standards, if perhaps for different reasons.

Acceptance of Uncertainty Versus Predictability

Uncertainty is a fact of life. Some cultures are comfortable with uncertainty and risk and have developed coping mechanisms to effectively manage it, if and when it occurs. Other cultures are not comfortable with uncertainty and may not have explicit ways of managing it. Individuals, institutions, societies, and cultures can be placed on a continuum from risk averse to risk taking. Parties who are risk averse tend to avoid outcomes that are unpredictable, could result in potential loss, or are hazardous or dangerous. Losses may be material or involve loss of face, respect, or status. Conversely, risk takers and cultures that are more prone to risk taking are willing to accept, and may even revel in, exposing themselves to situations where losses are possible, because they believe in the possibility of high gains

Hofstede (1984) compared management behavior in thirty-nine national cultures around the world and ranked them according to their orientation toward avoidance of uncertainty. Members of cultures with high uncertainty avoidance often felt uneasy or threatened by uncertainty in all aspects of life and tried to control its impacts; defined achievement in terms of personal or organizational security (that is, low risk of harm or loss); viewed conflict and competition as sources of aggression that should be avoided; resisted change and wished to maintain predictable patterns or solutions; sought consensus decisions as a means for increasing safety; and preferred written rules or regulations that would provide predictability.

Hofstede also found that cultures that were experiencing modernization and a high rate of social change; were younger democracies (post–World War II); had religions that stressed absolute certainties, the hereafter, and sin (Catholicism, Orthodox Christian, and Islam); had a high mean age for leaders in their population; and had large bureaucracies tended to try to avoid uncertainty. Some of the cultures that fell into this category (orientations toward avoiding uncertainty) were Greece, Portugal, Belgium, Japan, France, Turkey, Israel, Italy, Pakistan, Spain, and almost all Latin American countries. Conversely, cultures that were in a stage of advanced modernism—were older democracies, had more tolerant religions, had younger mean ages of leaders, had multiple smaller organizations, and relied more on negotiation to resolve conflicts—tended to be less uncertainty or risk averse. National cultures that are more likely to take risks include Singapore, Denmark, Sweden, Ireland, Great Britain, India, the Philippines, the United States, Canada, Australia, New Zealand, Norway, the Netherlands, Switzerland, and Finland.

How does the question of uncertainty avoidance and risk aversion relate to negotiations and outcomes? Orientation toward risk taking is often related to the issues in question, how important they are to a party, the power relations of those involved, and what will constitute an acceptable settlement. For example, Blaker (1977a, 1977b), in his studies of Japanese negotiating behavior, noted a tendency of the Japanese government negotiators since the end of World War II to pursue risk-averse strategies in diplomatic situations. However, Japanese businesses have pursued a more confident and risk-taking strategy when operating abroad. Blaker argues that the reasons for these variations within a single society are related to the perceived amount of power and influence that the particular Japanese entity has in relation to its negotiation counterpart. Japanese businesses enjoyed more perceived or actual power, resulting in more risk-taking behaviors and strategies.

GENERAL PROCEDURES FOR ASSESSING OPTIONS, PROPOSALS, POSITIONS, AND POTENTIAL OUTCOMES

Taking into consideration some of the cultural variables described, how do parties assess outcomes and decide if they are acceptable? Culture does make a difference. Assessment may be a highly deliberative and cognitive exercise, or it may be much more intuitive or based on strong feelings. This section explores both more deliberative and cognitive approaches, as well as more intuitive methods.

Structured Cognitive Procedure

Negotiators ofen use the following general cognitive process to assess options, proposals, or outcomes to negotiations. A negotiator or negotiation team:

1. Reviews the initial interests and goals as identified at the beginning of negotiations and considers how these have evolved or completely changed as result of exchange of information and dialogue. Interests may need to be redefined or clarified.

2. Identifies measures or standards and criteria to use to decide if and when an interest has been satisfied or a goal has been reached.

3. Assesses how well any of the options on the table, including a counterpart's proposals, or other potential outcomes satisfy their interests or promote achievement of goals.

4. Determines whether the options offered for the satisfaction of individual issues are acceptable and whether the options, proposals, or trades intended to satisfy all or multiple issues and resultant benefits or costs are acceptable.

5. Decides if there are important outstanding questions or concerns, considers whether modifications to options or proposals to address individual issues or components of a settlement package might make them more acceptable, and identifies potential changes to explore with the counterpart.

6. Determines if other possible benefits might be gained by continuing negotiations.

7. Reviews the BATNA (best alternative to a negotiated agreement) to determine if there are alternative procedures or negotiating parties that might produce superior results and better satisfy interests.

8. Assesses the total costs and benefits of either reaching a negotiated agreement or breaking off negotiations.

The process looks remarkably detailed, linear, logical, and structured. In fact, most individuals or teams—even those from the most logical and cognitive cultures—skip steps, take them out of order, or repeat steps as needed. The core element is making interests explicit and then using them as the primary measure to determine the acceptability of an option or proposal.

Intuitive Procedures

The application of logical and cognitive processes in decision making and the assessment of options are far from universal; many people depend on intuition and are guided by their feelings. Researchers have found that negotiators from a number of cultures use a rapid intuitive process to evaluate options and outcomes (Buchannan and O'Connell, 2006; Gladwell, 2005; LeBaron, 2002; Matsumoto, 1988). Gladwell (2005) describes the process by which people make rapid intuitive decisions as "thin-slicing," in which decision makers use information that their mind is continuously consciously and unconsciously taking in (which individuals are usually not even aware of) to make decisions or conclusions in not much more time than it takes to blink. Wilson (2002), one of the major researchers on the "adaptive consciousness," notes that this mode of thinking developed in humans as a way to make quick decisions when they were under stress and needed to respond quickly, often for their very survival. The process continues to be used today for making many routine judgments or decisions in negotiations. While some might question the wisdom of rapid, intuitive decision making, especially when contrasted with a more analytical and structured decision-making process, it works quite well in many circumstances and can result in better outcomes than more deliberative reasoned judgment. Reason can often become bogged down with too much information that can be contradictory or inconclusive. The intuitive process of thin-slicing filters available information and applies both conscious and unconscious frameworks to draw conclusions about it.

Intuitive decision making is valued in many cultures. For example, Matsumoto describes a process in which Japanese negotiators, almost exclusively male, use their *hara*, which is both a primordial center of man in his body and connection to nature, as well as an internal process for communicating with a counterpart. It does not rely exclusively on intellect, emotion, or the five senses. A professor at the International Christian University in Tokyo states that *haragei*, the use of *hara*, "is the least confrontational form of negotiation" (cited in Matsumoto, 1988, p. 23).

Haragei in communications is a way to rapidly understand a situation, assess the intentions of a counterpart, determine if an agreement or working relationship is possible, and communicate this information. Interestingly, use of feelings or intuition is more widely practiced in many more cultures than might be expected. In a survey of business leaders and executives in the United States, respondents noted that they used both analytical abilities and intuitive skills when making important decisions. However, instinct was credited for 80 percent of their successful decisions (Buchannan and O'Connell, 2005).

LeBaron (2002), a researcher in the field of dispute resolution, supports the inclusion of intuition in decision making and dispute resolution processes: "Intuition is enhanced by concentrating less on the particulars of a situation and the agendas we may have for them and more on the present moment. Intuition is less about interpreting body language or expressed ideas as facts, and more about sensing them on the symbolic level, listening for the language that speaks directly to our symbolic receptors" (p. 130).

An important factor in intuitive decision making has been identified by Nobel laureate Herbert Simon (1983). He stresses the importance of decision makers' ability to chunk and organize information, so they can store and retrieve it for decision making at a moment's notice. Chunking and organizing information involves the identification of patterns of information that can be easily recalled when facing similar situations in the future. The new situation is rapidly scanned and analyzed according to past stored knowledge and patterns, and then conclusions are drawn. Hayashi (2001) notes that "various studies of experts in diverse fields—parole officers predicting which criminals are likely to break the law again, doctors making diagnoses, school admissions officers predicting which students will succeed, and so on—have concluded that professional judgment can often be reduced to patterns and rules" (p. 63).

Although many negotiators use intuition in decision making—many quite successfully—there is no guarantee that it is more effective than using some form of rational or structured approach. In fact, there are instances in which either an intuitive or a rational approach would suggest a particular decision, but the negotiator later regrets it.

So how can and do negotiators avoid making intuitive decisions that might be wrong or result in less than satisfactory negotiated outcomes? Hayashi (2001) identifies several strategies that are common among business executives who use more intuitive processes. First, decision makers should avoid "revisionism," the tendency to "remember when we didn't trust our gut and should have, while conveniently forgetting when we were fortunate to have ignored our instincts" (p. 64). Second, negotiators should avoid self-fulfilling prophesies in which an individual makes a decision and then proceeds to make the situation come out the way he or she wanted by use of extra knowledge, effort, or activities regardless of whether the choice was a good or bad one. Third, negotiators should avoid overconfidence or overestimation of their wisdom concerning past or current decisions. Numerous research projects have demonstrated negotiators' tendencies to overestimate their wisdom or ability to accurately predict outcomes (Thomas, 2001; Williams, 1983). Finally, decision makers need to check on whether past intuitive decisions have been accurate or correct. If they are, then a negotiator may feel freer to rely on his or her intuition in deciding on current or future issues. If not, a negotiator may want to be more cautious about following his or her intuition.

Rational and analytical, and intuitive, approaches are part of the same mental processes; the difference is how much weight a negotiator places on one or the other. Peter Senge, the author of the *Fifth Discipline* (1994), notes that "people with high levels of personal mastery do not set out to integrate reason or intuition. Rather they achieve it naturally—as a by-product of their commitment to use all resources at their disposal. They cannot afford to choose between reason and intuition, or head and heart, any more than they would choose to walk with one leg or see with one eye" (p. 168). To maximize their effectiveness, negotiators must use both their intellect and their intuition.

External Assistance, Advice, and Assistance in Decision Making

While some negotiators exclusively use their own intellectual or intuitive resources to assess and make decisions about outcomes, others consult external authoritative sources that provide additional perspectives. Others perform rituals that might lead to desired outcomes. Whether a negotiator considers an external source to be valuable depends on culture.

Scientific or Technical Advice. Members of cultures that value the use of the scientific method often consult scientists or technical experts—engineers, biologists, chemists, ecologists, and so on—for information before making decisions in negotiations. For example, a multiparty negotiation our organization mediated involved over twenty parties, including U.S. federal agencies, municipalities, hydropower resellers, water conservancy districts, farmers, and conservationists, and addressed flows for the ecological preservation of a national park hydropower generation, and agriculture. Participants consulted modelers, individuals with expertise in statistical projections, before trying to make final water allocation decisions. The modelers provided information regarding river flows on a seasonal basis and the effects of different options for water allocation and use. In international arms control negotiations, the national teams have consulted arms experts who evaluate the viability of various control regimes, estimating whether it would be possible to ensure compliance based on available surveillance systems.

Legal or Financial Advice. Some cultures place a high value on reaching decisions that comply with legal, financial, or standard accounting laws, standards, or norms. Negotiators from such cultures may insist on consulting with lawyers or financial advisors before reaching decisions. These experts review settlement options to confirm that they are legal, parties' rights are protected, and ensure that a settlement is financially fair and advantageous. Members of other cultures do not subscribe to these norms and often find it odd that their counterparts consider them so important.

Prayer or Meditation. In certain cultures, religion plays an important role. Members of those cultures may not make decisions regarding the outcomes of negotiations before seeking the advice of a higher power. Prayer or meditation, in many forms, is a means for obtaining this guidance. Prayer may involve either individual or group acts of supplication, meditation, or communing with higher powers. For example, in Malaysia, village mediators, who are often imams, commonly use prayer as part of the dispute resolution process (Wall and Callister, 1999).

Ancestors. Some past-oriented cultures perform rituals and consult with ancestors to gain their input, approval, or support when assessing options or making decisions. Ancestral input is often attained through prayer or other specialized rituals, the outcome of which indicate the inclinations of a party's forebears. The Guatemalan example presented at the beginning of this chapter illustrates this approach.

Rituals to Promote or Ensure Desirable Outcomes. Members of some cultures or subcultures believe that performing specific rituals will increase the probability of desirable outcomes. Such rituals may involve pilgrimages; chants of songs or repetition of specific words; or performing specific culturally prescribed acts, often at sacred or religious places. Mulder (1992) has described the role of ritual acts in Thailand as a means of making decisions and ensuring desirable outcomes.

Divination. This process for obtaining advice involves consulting with a wide variety of external persons or performing specific acts that people believe will give them insight into positive or negative external forces that may affect an event or action. Divination has a long history in many cultures. For example, cultures in the Philippines, Indonesia, and Sri Lanka value astrology, the reading of an individual's chart or the interpretation of astrological signs, to determine auspicious or inauspicious times to make decisions or carry out actions. Even high political leaders in some of these cultures have used astrology to guide decision making on major efforts. Of course, use of astrology is not confined to non-Western cultures. In the recent past, it was reported that a U.S. first lady used astrological predictions and shared this information with her husband, President Reagan, to guide him in making international policy decisions (Regan, 1989).

In China and in some overseas Chinese communities, some negotiators use the I Ching to help them assess outcomes. While the I Ching generally does not give specific answers to a petitioner's questions, it is expected to reveal patterns that will enable them to find the answers to the questions they have asked. Examples of other divination methods include practices such as voodoo *wanga* rituals performed by houngans or mambos, priests or mediums, in Haiti; chiromancy or palmistry; haruspicy, the inspection and reading of the entrails of slaughtered animals; the use of peyote or sweat lodges by Native Americans to induce trances; and smoke scrying, or reading messages of smoke from a fire. In Tibet, some citizens consult with Buddhist monks to divine the future and conduct rituals of giving them food or alms to gain merit, increase the latent positive potential of a supplicant's karma, and encourage the desired outcome (Tseten, 1995).

STANDARDS AND CRITERIA TO GUIDE DECISION MAKING

The cognitive and intuitive processes we have described identify procedures for evaluating options, proposals, positions, or outcomes. We now turn to standards or criteria that negotiators can use to make these assessments.

Clearly the wide diversity of issues, problems, disputes, or conflicts requires different measures to determine how well they satisfy a negotiator's interests or needs. The following provides a long (but nevertheless suggestive!) list of factors that negotiators use to evaluate options, proposals, positions, or potential outcomes of negotiations. These factors are not valued equally by all cultures and individual negotiators, and some cultures place significantly more weight on some factors than on others.

Diverse negotiators and cultures value different factors presented here—or weight them differently. This is not intended as a checklist, but rather as a resource to inspire negotiators to reflect on what factors they consider important in assessing options.

In most cases, we have used the general term of *option* in the description of the criteria rather than constantly repeating all of the different forms: *option, proposal, position,* or *potential outcome.*

1. *Basic satisfaction of interests, concerns, and needs.* Does the option, proposal, or potential outcome satisfy the substantive, procedural, and relationship or psychological needs of both parties?

2. *Personal decision-making process or style.* How does the option fit with the individual decision-making style of the process or the parties? Does

it require an immediate decision, or will it allow time for more considered deliberation? Can the decision maker's process be adapted so that a conclusion can be reached?

3. *Cultural congruity or fit.* Is the option congruent with the cultural values, norms, or expectations of the parties?

4. *Relationship.* Does the option promote the desired relationship and meet the psychological interests of both parties? Will anything be gained or lost in maintaining a relationship with the other party if a settlement is not reached?

5. *Kinship network.* Will the option appear fair, reasonable, and acceptable to the kin or associates of the parties?

6. *Organizational culture.* Is the option congruent with the organizational standards, criteria, and culture of the negotiators?

7. *Constituent approval.* Will a party's constituents, supporters, superiors, or the public approve of the most likely option or final settlement package?

8. *Political dimensions.* Does the option satisfy political values, norms, or goals?

9. *Justness and fairness norms.* Is the option fair and reasonable? Does it conform to the norms of the community or standards common for addressing issues of this type?

10. *Traditions or precedents.* Is the option congruent with the way that similar issues have been handled in the past?

11. *Religious or moral values.* Is the option congruent with religious values and beliefs or widely held social values regarding morality?

12. *Adequate information.* Is adequate information available to make a wise and informed decision? If information is unavailable because of a lack of research or unknown future consequences, how can a decision be made with the best available data?

13. *Monetary or resource exchange.* Does the option satisfy the financial or other tangible benefits (as opposed to wishes or desires), goals, and objectives of both parties?

14. *Alternatives to a negotiated agreement.* Are there other ways to achieve goals or interests instead of continuing to negotiate with this counterpart? Would the outcome be preferable through those alternative means?

15. *Cost-benefit analysis.* Does the option offer benefits that outweigh any actual or potential costs for both parties?

16. *Risk and predictability.* Does the option reduce or increase risks? Are any increased risks acceptable? Are specific options more predictable than others?

17. *Leverage and influence.* What means of influence are available to persuade or coerce the other party to reach an agreement on desirable options or outcomes? Is there the will to use these means of influence to achieve desired ends? What are the benefits and costs of using these means? Will the projected benefits outweigh the costs to relationships or other factors?

18. *Effort in relation to benefits.* How much effort has already been expended to resolve the issues? How much more may be required to conclude the negotiations—and is this effort worthwhile?

19. *Equality factor or relative advantage.* Does the option result in an equal or mutually acceptable distribution of benefits or provide an acceptable balance of advantages between parties? Is either of these two factors important to the parties in reaching an agreement?

20. *Optimization.* Has the best potential outcome been achieved for all parties, given available resources, leverage and influence, personalities, and so forth? Can the outcome be improved on to the benefit of all or one of the parties without any additional adverse impacts on another?

21. *Timing.* Is the timing right to agree on this option or settlement package? Can more benefits be gained by a timely settlement or delaying agreement? Are there costs associated with settling now or delaying agreement?

22. *Future relationship ("shadow of the future").* Does the option bode well for the future relationship of the parties, or will it create potential problems?

23. *Precedent.* Does the option establish an important precedent or avoid creating an unwanted precedent?

24. *Transaction costs.* Will the implementation of this option be achieved with the lowest possible transaction costs (time, money, personal emotional involvement) relative to the benefits of the result? Can transaction costs be minimized by a rapid agreement or other measures?

25. *Feasibility of implementation.* Is the option feasible? Can it really be implemented (technically, financially, in time, emotionally)?

26. *External dynamics.* Is there a likelihood—indicated by trends, cycles of change, similar events, or analogous events—that a better option will present itself in due time because of external, environmental, or structural factors that are outside the negotiations? Cultural or other factors external to negotiations can influence decision making: organizational

restructuring, new elections, or a specific ceremony or ritual could result in different attitudes toward agreements.

27. *Saving face and honor and avoiding shame.* Does the option allow all parties to save face and protect their honor, as perceived by themselves or important audiences, or will one or more parties lose face?

28. *Harmony.* How important is it to the parties that the agreement promotes or restores harmony between them? Are they willing to live with unresolved feelings or tensions, or do they want to improve interpersonal relationships?

29. *Guilt.* Does the option avoid assigning guilt, absolve a "guilty" party, or determine guilt as a component of decision making?

30. *Intuition or gut feelings.* Does the option intuitively feel correct?

31. *Restitution or revenge.* Does the option adequately compensate a damaged party for harm, provide restitution, or make the party whole? Does the option address a psychological need for exacting revenge or inflicting negative consequences on the other, enabling one or more parties to psychologically end their attachment to the conflict?

32. *Intangible benefits.* Does the option result in intangible benefits, such as parties feeling good about themselves or each other, providing a model for other parties, or gaining satisfaction in living out values?

33. *Added benefits.* Will a small amount of additional time or effort result in significantly greater benefits for one or more parties, or is the additional time and effort not worth the possible rewards?

34. *Unintended consequences.* Are there any unintended consequences, positive or negative, that can be foreseen and might result from agreement or nonagreement on this issue? How are these consequences to be avoided or encouraged?

35. *Auspicious time, will of the gods, and so forth.* Are there factors or forces beyond the control of the negotiators that indicate that agreement is favorable?

SUGGESTED STRATEGIES FOR COORDINATING THE ASSESSMENT OF OPTIONS

In assessing the viability or acceptability of options and proposals that have been developed through intercultural negotiations, parties should consider the range of possible outcomes and apply criteria appropriate to individual or cultural norms. Ultimately all parties have to make their own judgments about the options on the table and decide whether to accept an overall agreement.

As we have seen, the assessment process depends on the negotiator's situation and culture. As a negotiator:

- Identify who in your culture or organization has the authority to assess options, proposals, positions, or potential outcomes. As best you can, identify how the other party or parties will assess options. In particular, determine whether the parties are more individualist or collectivist. If all parties have similar orientations for assessment, use commonly accepted procedures. If one party has more of an individualist orientation and another a more collectivist approach, expect that negotiations may take longer than if both parties were individualistically oriented.

- Learn more about who will be involved in decision making and what the decision-making path will be, including how a decision will move from person to person in the organization or community, criteria that will be used to make a decision, and the time projected to reach an internal agreement.

- If negotiators are from individualist cultures, prepare for more rapid evaluation and response, immediate flexibility to change options or solutions, and more authority by counterparts at the table to make decisions.

- Determine whether you or your counterpart will need to consult external advisors or experts or perform specific rituals before making decisions on potential or specific outcomes. Allow time for appropriate consultation or ritual acts to be performed.

- Assess the orientation of you and your culture toward integrative (joint gain) or distributive (win-lose) outcomes on the issues in question—and do the same for the other party or parties you are working with. Determine if distributive outcomes are the only possible result of negotiations, or whether integrative solutions are feasible. If it seems that there is potential for integrative solutions, develop a strategy to help attain this goal and a way to educate the other party about your preferred procedures and outcomes.

- Analyze the emphasis you place on building relationships, establishing procedures, or concluding tangible substantive agreements, as well as the orientation of the other party or parties. (Some of this is influenced by culture but is also affected by the specific issues and interests involved.) If the approaches are different, decide how much you can or will need to accommodate the different expectations concerning relationships, procedures, and substantive outcomes. Develop strategies to educate other parties about your cultural preferences and methods to persuade them to meet your needs and preferred cultural approaches to these questions.

- Consider possible standards of justice that are important to you or other members of your culture that might guide settlement. Assess whether your counterpart uses the same or different standards. Try to identify objective criteria or standards that you might hold in common. Determine if you have to hold the same standards to reach agreement, or whether settlement is possible, even if the parties are applying different standards.

- Identify your orientation and that of your counterpart toward producing agreements in principle or more detailed settlements on smaller issues or components of the problem or conflict. Determine if you must adhere to your preferred approach or whether you can accommodate the preferences of your counterpart.

- Evaluate options, proposals, positions, or outcomes against any other relevant standard or criteria identified as being important.

CONCLUSION

By the end of this phase of negotiations, negotiators will have reached at least tentative conclusions as to whether it will be possible to reach a settlement or agreement on all or individual remaining issues, and determine whether potential outcomes will be mutually acceptable. They may decide to continue negotiations to seek a mutually agreeable settlement on specific issues, for which they will have defined acceptable parameters, a bargaining range, or potential options that will address their interests. For some issues, they may have determined that linkage or packaging, in which gains and losses are combined in a generally acceptable solution, may be the only way to resolve them. They may also realize that it will be difficult to resolve some issues at this time. Finally, for a number of reasons, they may decide to drop some issues from their negotiation agenda.

After engaging in an option assessment process using intuitive or cognitive approaches (or a combination of these), negotiators are ready to see if they can reach closure on a full agreement in the final phase of negotiations. In the following chapter, we explore the strategies typically used to bring negotiations to a close, including the cultural dimensions.

CHAPTER TWELVE

Reaching Closure and
Developing Agreements

Diplomats and other high-level officials of the United States, Russia, and a third country were engaged in negotiations over a treaty covering military and environmental issues of common concern. They had used large-group discussions with simultaneous translation to reach general agreements on principles and procedural agreements on actions to implement them. They now had to refine the terms of settlement and put them in writing.

Discussions up to this time had been fairly free-flowing. While notes had been taken on conclusions and agreements by members of each team and the two facilitator/mediators (one American and the other Russian) in their own languages and on their own laptop computers, reaching a final accord would require a high level of precision to capture the appropriate tone, intent, common understanding, and precise wording in the text of the treaty. To facilitate the drafting process, two computers, projectors, and screens were set up in the negotiating venue. One would record agreements in English and the other in Russian. As each party stated his or her understanding of what had been agreed on, it was repeated by simultaneous interpreters. At this point, the computer and projector system failed, and negotiators had to gather around the laptop of one of the facilitator/mediators who recorded the gist of what was said in English. Once the computer projector system was up and running again, translators with expertise in precise language and drafting wrote up the agreements and put them on the screens for all to see. Actually seeing the terms led to further discussions, clarifications, and refinement. Interestingly, during the refinement process, negotiators switched from simultaneous interpretation to consecutive interpretation (a process in which one person speaks and his or her words are translated after finishing a thought or phrase). Although this slowed the process, this procedure enabled participants to engage in greater dialogue about the precise terms and wording to be used in the document (Bernie Mayer, facilitator/mediator, as told to the authors).

∞

Negotiators from different cultures view the concluding phase of negotiations in diverse ways. This phase involves a wide range of activities and outcomes. In some cases, the emphasis is on tying up loose ends from previous discussions and reconfirming what has already been agreed on. In others, there is a shift to intense bargaining over contentious issues, the development of possible links and trades, or a decision to drop a particular claim as a means to reach agreement. In yet other situations, the parties shift to assembling a package agreement in which gains and losses are shared or creating a truly integrative solution that all parties perceive to be a win.

In some circumstances, this phase of negotiations completes discussion of the issues in question and triggers immediate implementation of terms of settlement, in which the substantive terms are of primary importance. In others, at the conclusion of this phase, the parties have merely reached a plateau in talks, or a round of discussion has been completed that will be followed by a successive series of deliberations, either with higher-level officials or to work out details of a general agreement. This last pattern for the "end" of negotiations is common in cultures whose members believe that the future is unpredictable, the parties' circumstances or information for a wise decision is likely to change, or that further discussions will always be needed to refine previous agreements. Such cultures also consider the parties' ongoing relationships to be of primary importance—hence, the expectation of further talks and refinements.

Agreements reached during this phase of negotiations may satisfy the involved negotiators' interests, enabling them to reach a settlement, or the negotiators may be dissatisfied with the terms, forcing them to consider breaking off talks and seeking other means to achieve their goals. To reach an agreement, the elements of a proposed agreement have to match or exceed each party's best alternative to a negotiated agreement, or BATNA (see Fisher and Ury, 1981) in terms of both substantive provisions, procedural satisfaction, and future relationships.

Negotiations can changes parties' relationships, feelings toward each other, and individual emotional states. They may bring a difficult relationship to a close. Alternatively, parties may decide to continue to interact despite continuing tension or mistrust. Negotiations can also mark the beginning of a new phase of a positive friendship or business relationship, a beneficial partnership or joint venture, or renewed respect, trust, and reconciliation.

Regardless of the substantive, procedural, or relationship issues that remain for negotiators to address at this phase of negotiations, culture can again have significant impacts. In this chapter, we examine the following aspects of the final phase of negotiations:

- Who is involved in final negotiations
- A range of views about the end of negotiations and the degree of closure that the parties expect
- Approaches for handling remaining issues and negotiation tasks
- Common problems that occur in the final stage of negotiation
- Acknowledgment of agreements and future relationships
- Variables in the form and content of agreements across cultures.

VIEWS ABOUT THE END OF NEGOTIATIONS: ENDINGS, CLOSURE, AND FINALITY

Culture shapes negotiators' views about what constitutes the end of negotiations, including the kind of relationship that they want to result from their deliberations, whether contractual and time limited, or more holistic and unbounded by a specific period of time.

Negotiators from contractually oriented cultures, such as mainstream North American and northern European, assume that agreements and outcomes that result from negotiations will focus primarily on substantive and procedural issues. They might discuss relationship issues during talks, but these are generally not included in agreements unless they are delineated in terms of a working relationship (Blake and Mouton, 1984). Relationships are also seldom relied on to ensure future cooperation or compliance. Rather, the written contract itself is seen to secure compliance.

In contrast, members of cultures who subscribe to holistic relationships, including negotiators from many Asian, Middle Eastern, and traditional societies, assume that relationships and agreements are works in progress and that there may not be a definitive moment when either is completed. Given this assumption, no settlement is considered final because agreements are always being refined or modified to address changing circumstances. The parties to agreements work together over an extended time—perhaps their entire lives. Therefore, they may identify the need for additions, deletions, or modifications to the original terms of an agreement to better meet their individual or joint needs. An agreement is always considered open for renegotiation.

Most negotiators from contractually oriented cultures prefer permanent and binding agreements. If terms are to be renegotiated, the process is expected to be conducted according to preagreed conditions, triggers, or schedules. For instance, most labor-management contracts contain clauses specifying when and how changes can be made and when the entire contract will be renegotiated. Contractually oriented negotiators are uncomfortable with the loose terms and constant renegotiating that are characteristic of agreements by members of holistic cultures. When placed in a holistic relationship environment, contractual negotiators will sometimes feel that no agreement is solid, conditions and requests are always changing, and nothing is predictable. This may lead them to question whether their counterpart is negotiating in good faith, trying to take advantage of them, or manipulating the situation in their favor. Conversely, negotiators from cultures that are more holistic often see contractually oriented counterparts as unfeeling, untrusting, rigid, inflexible, and presumptuous regarding their ability to know what will happen in the future and their ability to control it.

An illustrative clash between these two views occurred a number of years ago between Japanese managers of a new automobile plant that was opening in the United States and representatives of its North American labor union. Japanese executives, from a culture that values holistic-oriented relationships and who were officials of Mazda, negotiated a new working relationship with American labor and management during the creation of a new automobile manufacturing plant in Flat Rock, Michigan. The Japanese wanted to create a new and innovative relationship between management and labor than would normally be the case in the United States, and have flexible contracts with less rigidity. They believed that any current or future differences between management and labor could be resolved, and the terms of the contract revised, in the context of ongoing working relationships.

Although the Americans were initially skeptical of this informal agreement, they decided to go along with it and see how it would work. Over time, some permanent agreements were reached, but many workers and managers began to desire a more formal contract that explicitly spelled out the relationships, expectations, roles, and responsibilities between Japanese managers and the U.S. workforce. The Japanese too were not entirely satisfied with the loose holistically oriented contract, because the Americans did not behave like Japanese workers. The Japanese managers noticed that Americans did not subscribe to the same management-labor relationship expectations that were familiar to the Japanese and instead resorted to more adversarial means to resolve disputes (Fucini and Fucini, 1990).

Americans working with Arab executives during earlier oil boom days in the Middle East noted similar problems with final agreements and closure processes. American managers complained about unclear terms, an inability to get specific details, lack of performance criteria or schedules, and so forth.

Soviet negotiators were also known for making general agreements that lacked specific terms, especially during the Cold War (Smith, 1989). The philosophy behind this approach, as it was applied in negotiations between representatives of communist and capitalist societies, was based in Marxism-Leninism: that there will always be contradictions between communist and capitalist societies, the ends justify the means, and agreements between countries with Marxist and capitalist ideologies are temporary truces until more favorable objective conditions allow revision of the terms—that is, to terms more favorable to communist interests. This worldview led Soviet negotiators to strive for only general agreements, the terms of which could be interpreted quite differently depending on future circumstances, and with the expectation that modifications could be made as needed.

Similar dynamics and assumptions—in perhaps exaggerated form—have been demonstrated in negotiations among North Korea, China, and the United States over nuclear issues, in which the North Koreans have taken strong general positions that can be used to their advantage. This pattern has also appeared in negotiations between representatives of the People's Republic of China and the West, albeit to a lesser extent, especially in more recent times.

Although the political and economic regimes in many former communist countries in Eastern Europe, the former Soviet Union, Central Asia, and Vietnam have changed significantly, the desire for general and vague agreements and somewhat adversarial relationships with outsiders from old capitalist countries in the West on occasion still seem to persist. Although this cultural pattern may result from lags between old and new philosophical systems, or possibly tensions between more holistic and contract-oriented cultures, they may also arise from historical patterns of distrust of outsiders, fear of being dominated by foreigners, and a desire to maintain flexibility to preserve advantage.

SUGGESTED STRATEGIES FOR COORDINATING VIEWS TOWARD ENDINGS AND CLOSURE

- Identify the cultural norms for you and your own culture—and those of your counterpart—regarding endings and closure in the context of the particular type of negotiations underway.

- If you share common understandings, pursue either self-ratifying and self-executing agreements (for contract-oriented cultures) or agreements that will be developed over time in the context of your ongoing relationships (for holistic-oriented cultures).

- If you and your counterpart do not have the same understandings regarding closure, consider using one of the following strategies.

For the Negotiator Who Prefers or Wants More Closure

- Explain why you want full closure: predictability, not wanting to reopen negotiations later, ease of implementation, peace of mind, or something else.

- Describe the kind of agreements you would like to see to illustrate the degree of closure that you desire.

- Listen to the views and concerns of your counterpart, and see if there are ways that you can adapt to or accommodate to them.

- Be clear about what you can and cannot live with. If flexibility is possible, accommodate to your counterpart's needs and concerns. If not, clearly describe what you can and cannot do, recognizing that your stance may prevent an agreement.

- If your counterpart resists a greater degree of closure, explore including procedures in the agreement that will contribute to predictability, such as promises to discuss specific issues in the future and procedures and time lines for these conversations. If the situation warrants, provide explicit consequences for failure to discuss or reach agreements on unsettled issues.

For Negotiators Who Prefer Less Closure

- Proceed as above, and explain, if it is culturally appropriate, why you want more flexibility in the agreement and do not need the degree of closure requested by your counterpart or what degree of closure you can and cannot live with. Explore ways that you might accommodate to your counterpart's needs.

COMMON PROBLEMS IN THE FINAL STAGES OF NEGOTIATIONS

Unforeseen difficulties are quite common at the end of negotiations, but particular issues arise in intercultural negotiations. We list the most frequent dilemmas and offer possible strategies for responding to them:

- *"We don't understand the agreement (or what we are agreeing to)."* This dilemma takes place when the parties do not speak the same language, have different levels of language skills and sophistication when working in a foreign tongue, or have different conceptions of what the proposed agreement means or the terms being used to describe it. Some parties may also use purported misunderstanding as a tactic for encouraging a counterpart to reveal more, a means to force a counterpart to be more specific, or to delay agreement. Strategies for addressing this problem include continuing to talk until mutually understood terms can be agreed to, asking what part of an agreement is unclear and then addressing this specific problem, or obtaining better language interpretation so that all parties can work in their native tongue.

- *"We do not understand the wording/interpretation/translation."* Working across languages is not always easy. Even among people who share the same language and culture, differences in accents, wording, idioms, or colloquial expressions may cause barriers to understanding. When working across cultures where participants speak different languages, problems are magnified, because people may not be working in their native tongue or are using words for which there is no translation or commonly understood meaning (Moore, 2004). For example, "Arabic has no word for 'compromise' in the sense of reaching agreement through struggle and disagreement. But a much happier concept, *taarradhin* (tah-rah-deen), exists in Arabic. It implies a happy solution for everyone, an 'I win, you win.' It's a way of resolving a problem without anyone losing face" (p. 69). In China, people get things done through *guanxi*. This concept entails building good relationships by giving gifts, sharing meals, granting favors, and developing a norm of reciprocity. In Japanese, the term *yoko meshi* is a combination of the words for "boiled rice" and "horizontal" and literally translates as "eating boiled rice horizontally." "This is the how the Japanese define the peculiar stress induced by speaking a foreign language: *yoke* is a humorous reference to the fact that Japanese is normally written vertically, whereas most foreign languages are written horizontally" (p. 87). In Swahili, the language of much of East Africa, the word *bado* is used to say no, but exclusively when "it is theoretically possible that the action may occur in the future" (p. 78). For example, a person who is asked whether it is possible to execute specific terms of agreement may answer *bado*, meaning "not at this time, but it might be possible in the future." Similarly, the Swahili term *sasa havi* translates literally as "right away," but immediate action for the speaker may not mean the same thing to the listener.

The use of language and particular wording is an important issue in intercultural negotiations. We have participated in negotiations in which the parties engaged multiple interpreters and translators to good effect; often each interpreter has a different native tongue but is a professional translator in another language. For instance, in negotiations between Russian and American officials, each side brought an interpreter—the American a native English speaker who was expert in Russian and the Russian a native speaker of that language who was a professional translator of English. In these situations, the translators can discuss meanings, vocabulary, and word use in order to assist the negotiators. Before sessions, negotiators can also provide their interpreters with a list of terms they will be using in upcoming talks, and ask the interpreters to agree on the terms that will be used by all concerned to convey the same information and meaning.

Confusions over terms and their meanings, written translations, and interpretations of working documents or, especially, final agreements can be disastrous. A classic example is the different wordings in the English and Maori texts of the 1840 Treaty of Waitangi in New Zealand. The treaty, signed between British colonists and a number of indigenous Maori clans, defined the legal relationships between settlers and local people. Unfortunately, there were significant differences in the English and Maori translations and understandings. The British colonists generally proceeded to expropriate Maori land, while the Maori understood the treaty as protecting their rights. The variations in wording and interpretations allowed British colonists to gain full control of the islands and the land. It was not until the mid-1970s that the different interpretations of the treaty and resultant impacts on the Maori began to be addressed through the establishment of the Waitangi Tribunal (Yenson, Hague, and McCreanor, 1989; Treaty of Waitangi, 1840).

To overcome such translation and interpretation problems, all parties should use translators who are native speakers of their own languages and expert in that of the counterparts to draft and review all documents for consistency of meaning. Ideally, all drafts and final documents should be read, edited, corrected, and approved by multiple translators and readers to ensure accuracy and similar intent.

- *"We need more time."* or *"We will have word from our superiors within the next week/month/year."* This request is common among negotiators from cultures that do not make decisions rapidly or where time and speed are not as critical. It is also typical of collectivist cultures, where approval or ratification of an agreement must be obtained from multiple individuals, groups, or levels in a bureaucracy before a decision is final. Negotiators working with counterparts from Native American tribes in the United States, First Nations in Canada, the bureaucracies in the People's Republic of China, India, Japan, and many Latin American countries have often reported this kind of request.

Note that the plea for more time can also be a tactic to avoid ratifying an agreement that is less than satisfactory or is displeasing to a negotiator's superiors, or it might be used to obtain time to see if a better deal can be obtained from a competitor. Some negotiators seek delays while internal organizational dynamics change or until external developments allow a more favorable outcome. Delays have also been used as a way for a party to say,

''No. no deal,'' without ever having to reject a proposal directly, clearly a preference of an indirect-dealing negotiator.

Negotiators facing a request for more time first have to figure out if the demand is valid and needed, a stalling tactic, or an indirect rejection of the settlement. Sometimes this can be determined through off-the-record informal talks with counterparts at various levels in an organization, discussions with third parties, or more indirect sleuthing. If the added time is truly required to obtain approval for a final agreement, the negotiator must decide how long he or she is willing to wait for a response. If a settlement is time limited, competitive advantage is lost, or there are other options, a negotiator may not want to wait. However, if agreement seems likely with just a little more time, it may be desirable to agree to more time. Extensions can even be made with the negotiator's stipulation that if more time is allowed, the expectation is for a favorable decision.

- *''What you did/said earlier offended us. We expect an apology/a new offer/a concession from you to make it right.''* This request may be valid or a ploy for gaining additional concessions. Before responding, the negotiator must consider the issue from the point of view of the counterpart (that is, not based on what would be difficult, uncomfortable, or offensive in your own culture). If the claim is valid (something said or done really was uncomfortable or offensive to the other party), he or she will need to decide what can be done to address the problem in a manner that is culturally, politically, and ethically appropriate for all parties. A third party might be able to help to sort this out. (See Chapters Fourteen and Fifteen.)

If the claim of offense seems spurious or designed merely to gain advantage, the negotiator may want to adhere to his or her original view or position and avoid making any apology, offer, or concession. However, this strategy needs to be executed carefully, for even if the claim is a bluff, unless it is in the interest of the counterpart to settle, he or she may use its rejection as an excuse to terminate negotiations. Note that apologies can be quite effective and do not necessarily require any additional concession on a matter of substance.

- *''By the way, we have one more issue. We need one additional thing from you in order for us to close the deal.''* This is one variation on the doorknob strategy: parties employ it when the end is in sight and the parties are literally about to walk out the door together, having reached an agreement. (This is slightly different from the next tactic.) Psychologically, the parties have come to substantial agreement, perhaps after a difficult series of exchanges. In this circumstance, one party uses the positive prospect of a deal to bring up one more issue in the belief that the lure of the almost completed deal will induce their counterpart to make additional concessions.

This kind of move can be interpreted in several ways: the party knew about this issue all along, and is just bringing it up now as a way of forcing the other party's hand on a relatively minor matter; the counterpart did not know about the issue, or it was raised by a superior in the process of obtaining approvals; or this was, in fact, one of the most important concerns in the negotiations, but the counterpart was unable to raise it earlier for whatever reasons—and at this point, you might start "real" negotiations on a core issue. Faced with one of these possibilities, the negotiator must decide if this is an important or minor issue for both parties. He or she must also determine if the other party is bringing this up now as a tactic for forcing a concession or for scuttling the negotiations, or if they have been bargaining in good faith, and this issue has really just emerged.

- *"Well, we are not getting anywhere. I am leaving."* This is the more classical doorknob strategy or doorknob close in which a party says, "We will walk out the door if you do not give us what we want." Parties exercise this threat of a total breakdown in negotiations unless they get their way, often when talks are not going well or they are not getting their way. (Note the contrast with the previous tactic, which specifically uses the fact that things are going well as a lever.) This is a common tactic among North American negotiators engaged in negotiating labor contracts, and in some negotiation sectors internationally.

The response should be governed by the perceived legitimacy of the move, the risk its use poses to the breakdown of negotiations, and the negotiator's willingness or capability to respond. If it appears to be a bluff, the negotiator may want to refuse to give in. However, he or she must be willing to risk the entire settlement if the threat is genuine. If the threat appears to be real, he or she must decide how far to go to meet the concrete demands to salvage a deal.

- *"Isn't there just a little bit more?"* This is a common bargaining tactic in many intercultural negotiations for all levels of interactions between individuals, groups, businesses, or national governments. It is particularly common when the requester is from a lower-power or lower-status group than the counterpart. The tactic is often coupled with requests for fairness, righting of past wrongs, or claims that what the person is asking for is very little in comparison to the resources of the more powerful counterpart. Interestingly, the tactic works, especially if the party to whom the request is being made can be made to feel guilty or obligated in some way to the person making the request. We saw this tactic in practice in India. Whether it was the rickshaw driver or a businessperson, everyone seemed ready to ask for "just a little bit more." It has also been a common practice in negotiations with diplomats from the Peoples' Republic of China.

- *"A sweetener for me/my boss/the organization would help get this approved in a timely manner."* In some cultures, this would be called a bribe, but in others, it is common practice to promote agreements. In considering such requests, negotiators need to be clear that they are not violating ethical standards or laws. For example, when negotiating with government officials to start an infrastructure initiative in a Middle Eastern country, one of us was asked by a counterpart to give a small research contract to another government official who was not directly involved with the project. The counterpart suggested that the proposed recipient official could perhaps be "given a little money to do a token research project that might in some way be of assistance to the project"—which, by the way, would secure his support for the initiative. After assessing the request, finding that the proposed official did not have any of the research skills that would justify a research grant and that the request was really for an illegal bribe, the author and his colleagues rejected the request.

- *"Don't you trust us?"* This statement often relates to issues regarding compliance to an agreement and reflects resistance to clear compliance mechanisms. The question can be used to secure a concession based on real or claimed emotional bonds, without any tangible assurance of goodwill or mechanisms to ensure compliance by the counterpart. It can be used in both good faith and in bad and as a way to strengthen emotional commitments or gain advantage over a counterpart. Of course, even posing the question exposes a lack of trust in the relationship: if there is true trust, the question need not be asked; if there is a lack of trust, asking the question invites a false assurance or an acknowledgment that trust is missing.

  Negotiators from relationship-oriented cultures are likely to rely on personal relationships to ensure commitments to agreements. Negotiators from contractually oriented cultures will probably want more tangible assurances. The dilemma is how to ask for clear procedures or mechanisms without damaging relationships. As was said in the 1990s in international negotiations between the United States and the Soviet Union over nuclear arms control, "Trust but verify." (The issue of compliance mechanisms is addressed more fully in Chapter Three.)

- *"I want my lawyer (or legal team) to review our agreement."* While seeking legal assistance may be normal and acceptable in many cultures, it is not in others. The desire to involve lawyers may be perceived by negotiators from some cultures as an indication of mistrust, unnecessary adversarial behavior, or nit-picking. More will be said later in this chapter about the involvement of legal counsel, the roles they can play, and how to overcome barriers related to their participation.

- *"This would be very difficult."* or *"No (niet), it is not possible!"* These communications have been discussed earlier in this book. The first is common in indirect-dealing cultures where it is difficult to say no directly. The second is common in Central and Eastern Europe where, at least in the past, saying yes was riskier than saying no, because someone who said no could not be held responsible by superiors for a problematic decision.

When encountering a no in intercultural negotiations, negotiators must first determine what no means in the counterpart's culture. If a counterpart from Indonesia or Japan says that something is "very difficult," the negotiator will have to decide how hard to push the issue, and if the decision is to pursue it further, find a way to explore it indirectly. However, if the counterpart saying no is from a direct-dealing culture, the negotiator can ask why, probe the logic and rationale, and explore what it would take to change the no to yes (or from *niet* to *da*) (Richmond, 1992).

ACKNOWLEDGMENT OF AGREEMENTS

Assuming that negotiators overcome any of the problems outlined above and any of the myriad other barriers that are common toward the end of negotiations, they now move to acknowledging agreements and articulating the terms of settlement and the shape of future relationships:

∽

- *Articulating the agreement.* Assuming that negotiating parties have the authority to finalize an agreement without additional approvals, they can proceed to articulate a proposed settlement by creating a formal or informal verbal or written summary statement. This statement generally includes the agreed terms, which may be developed only during this end stage, or it may be a summary of points raised and agreed along the way. Informal verbal statements may be made by one of the parties or by both, with subsequent comparison of the two statements to clarify any possible differences. If a third party is involved (mediator or facilitator), he or she may make a verbal statement regarding the points of agreement—to test those with the parties prior to attempting to draft a formal statement.
- *Affirming the agreement verbally.* After the final agreement is restated verbally or read aloud, it is usually acknowledged by a verbal affirmation. A direct verbal affirmation is especially important in cultures that do not rely on

written agreements, because both parties want to hear that the other party will honor the agreement.

- *Affirming the agreement through silence.* Sometimes cultural differences make direct affirmation of the agreement difficult. Indirect-dealing cultures may be reluctant to disagree explicitly and may make a noncommittal statement, such as, "It will be difficult," or remain silent, assuming that everyone understands the silence to mean disagreement. (This is especially true in Japan and other Asian countries.) Sometimes silence indicates agreement or at least not outright opposition. For example, a party may want to agree but cannot speak up without losing face or position or the possible support of constituents. By remaining silent and letting an agreement be approved without formal assent, he agrees by not actively disagreeing. In other cultures, negotiators proceed according to the norm of silence meaning consent.

- *Affirming the agreement nonverbally.* In South Asian cultures (India, Pakistan, Sri Lanka, and others), bobbing the head and chin in a figure eight pattern can denote a straightforward yes as well as a more ambiguous and noncommittal "I hear you" or a nonverbal greeting or acknowledgment. It is readily misinterpreted by other cultures as being closer to the nonverbal signal of shaking the head from side to side to mean no (which in Bulgaria also means yes). Because of cultural confusion regarding nonverbal signals, parties should be cautious and research the culture of counterparts to determine commonly understood nonverbal signals for indicating approval or disapproval.

If a party is primarily verbally oriented and accepts oral agreements ("a person's word is his bond"), stating and finalizing an agreement in some manner may suffice. However, if one or more of the participating cultures is oriented toward written agreements, they may expect a written settlement that summarizes the terms that parties have agreed to. The next two sections examine the form and content of agreements and the variety of procedures for drafting them.

STRATEGIES FOR ACKNOWLEDGING AGREEMENTS

- Identify the cultural norms for you and your culture for how agreements are recognized and acknowledged, and do the same for your counterpart.

- If you and your counterpart follow different norms, determine the extent to which you can accommodate your counterpart and still satisfy your own procedural and psychological needs.

- Determine if allowing silent affirmation is acceptable to enable your counterpart to save face or protect him- or herself from criticism.

FORM, CONTENT, AND TERMS OF AGREEMENTS ACROSS CULTURES

Agreements reached through negotiations vary in terms of their form, content, and terms. Some are simple verbal promises made privately between parties. Other forms include public announcements, letters (or e-mails) exchanged between parties, Memorandums of Understanding (MOUs) or Memorandums of Agreements (MOAs), formal legal contracts enforceable in a court of law, or treaties signed and ratified by recognized legitimate authorities. Regardless of the form that agreements take, there are a number of variables regarding the degree of closure, levels of agreement, explicitness, and so forth that members of different cultures prefer as they codify their agreements. Table 12.1 details a number of factors, each of which is stated as a continuum between two extremes. Generally the variables on the left side of the table are components of more explicit, defined, and enforceable agreements, while those on the right are broad, loose, and voluntary in nature. Most agreements include components of all of these variables, but where the agreement falls on the continuum depends significantly on the issues being settled, the parties, and their cultural norms regarding the terms of settlement.

Most of these variables have been discussed already in this chapter or in previous chapters. Elements associated with ratification, implementation, and compliance are discussed in the next chapter.

DRAFTING WRITTEN AGREEMENTS

Negotiators from different cultures have varying attitudes toward written agreements. Assuming that the parties have agreed to the need for a written agreement, they will have to harmonize their approaches to this task. We examine several dimensions of developing written agreements: the different forms, when they are drafted, and who drafts them.

Forms of Written Agreements

Human beings have been producing written records of settlement outcomes for centuries. These have taken many forms, including these:

- An informal written statement of agreement
- A letter or e-mail exchanged between negotiators
- An MOU or MOA
- A legal contract, rule, regulation, or law

Table 12.1. Dimensions of Agreements: A Continuum

Contract-oriented relationship	⟷	Holistic and affective relationships
Impersonal relationship, less self-disclosure, more business-oriented discussions	⟷	Personal relationships among parties, more self-disclosure, discussion of a wider range of issues
Written agreement	⟷	Oral agreement
Limited duration	⟷	Long duration or undefined time frame
Substantive content	⟷	Procedural, psychological, relationship content
Comprehensive settlement, address all issues	⟷	Partial settlement addressing some issues or some open for later process
Detailed agreements on all issues	⟷	Agreement in principle
Tightly defined terms or specific details	⟷	Loosely defined or general terms
Agreement considered binding	⟷	Agreement considered nonbinding: discretionary compliance
Self-executing agreement (in effect on signing)	⟷	Non-self-executing agreement (requires continued performance or ongoing exchanges)
Unconditional implementation	⟷	Implementation is contingent on performance of predetermined actions
Implementation is unilateral; can be executed by one party alone	⟷	Implementation is mutual; requires joint action to execute
Revision is not expected or is nonnegotiable	⟷	Revision is expected or is negotiable
Agreement is self-ratifying and considered approved by parties at the table	⟷	Agreement requires further approval or ratification by parties away from the table
Explicit consequences for noncompliance	⟷	No explicit consequences for noncompliance
Compliance compelled by compulsory or coercive measures (contractual obligations or administrative or judicial decisions)	⟷	Compliance by voluntary commitments or incentives (pledges of honor, public statements, and rituals)

- A pact, covenant, or compact
- A convention, entente, or treaty

Depending on the intent and proposed use, agreements can be informal or formal, use common language or legal terms, and contain substantive, procedural, or affective components. If the agreement is to be legally binding in the courts of one or more of the negotiators or an international venue, the settlement will usually have to be a legal document—contract, law, or treaty.

When Written Agreements Are Developed

Written agreements can be developed incrementally during the course of negotiations or at the conclusion of discussions. Drafts can draw on the individual or collective notes of the parties, or on a record kept by a neutral recorder or third-party mediator or facilitator. It is useful to keep official notes throughout the negotiation process and to read and correct summaries of agreements that have been reached to avoid reopening issues at a later time due to disagreement about previous discussions.

Who Drafts the Document

Drafting can be done by one party, jointly by all parties, or by subcommittees—consisting of the parties' representatives or subordinates. A neutral third party, such as a mediator or facilitator, or one or more legal representatives of parties can also draft texts.

Single-Party Versus Multiple-Party Drafting. If only one party drafts an agreement, there will be consistent language, and cross-party committee coordination problems may be avoided. Sometimes, there is also a greater possibility of drafting proposals with jointly acceptable benefits that the other party or parties will readily agree to (Fisher and Ury, 1981; Fisher, 1976).

However, there are psychological disadvantages to single-party drafting. The party drafting the document may feel a psychological investment in the document and may later resist making changes desired by counterparts. The other party may also feel no ownership and may be willing to challenge the form or content more readily than if he or she had been involved in its creation. Language is another issue. There is a greater possibility of unacceptable or biased language or unequal exchanges if only one party writes the document.

If all concerned parties write the draft, either directly or through representatives, there is a higher level of commitment, and therefore the potential for greater ownership and a more thoughtful check for fair and accurate language.

Subcommittee Drafting. Sometimes a group is too large to work together as a committee of the whole, especially for drafting a document. Therefore, a subcommittee composed of representatives of the key stakeholders may be appointed to produce a draft agreement for consideration by the full teams. Subcommittees can be composed of people who have experience working together or have particular writing skills. They are also able to resolve language differences and interpretations that may cause difficulties later on during ratification.

Drafting by Intermediaries. One benefit from the use of mediators, facilitators, recorders, and other third parties is that they free the parties to discuss substantive issues without having to focus so much on the process. They can do the same for drafting documents. Such intermediaries can be sensitive to the psychological issues of negotiators. They can also control the use of negative and positive terminology, as well as the ordering of topics and framing of the balance of exchanges.

The process of drafting a tentative settlement can be an important part of the agreement-making process. A single-text negotiating document, which contains possible settlement language and a range of options, can be developed by an intermediary and used as the basis for future discussions and deliberations (Spencer and Spencer, 1992; Fisher and Ury, 1981). However, if this approach is used, all parties must be clear that the single-text document is a draft and open to total revision or even rejection if it is not found to be helpful.

Drafting by Lawyers. Lawyers are often engaged when the final agreement is a legal document or a party has a cultural orientation toward the use of lawyers as drafters or reviewers of settlements. However, members of some cultures, especially those that are more oriented to holistic relationships, may object to the presence of lawyers in negotiations or even in the drafting process. In these circumstances, members of cultures that value lawyers' involvement in drafting may do well to keep their legal advisors in low-profile positions throughout the process. While lawyers may be involved in final drafting, it is important that key decision makers or chief negotiators, who have built the personal relationship between the parties, be seen as the final arbiters in terms of the form and content of the agreement.

The Power of the Pen and of Language. A common maxim in negotiations is that the party who drafts an agreement has significant influence, if not actual control, over the framing and wording of its content. For example, French negotiators almost always insist on drafting final agreements or, in the diplomatic arena, resolutions. They are motivated in part by pride in language, the role that France has historically played in international relations, and the desire to keep their nation in the public view. However, French negotiators also want to frame the content of the agreement in a manner that, if necessary, can be interpreted in their favor and ensure that the binding language of the final document, which would guide any future interpretations of the accord, will be in French (Cogan, 2003). For these reasons, parties may struggle to determine who writes settlement agreements and what language will be binding if any future issues arise over interpretation.

Negotiators can encounter difficulties ensuring that a written agreement has the same meaning and intent in all relevant languages. Cross-cultural agreements are frequently written in one language and then translated into the others. It is crucial that the translations express identical meanings so that they cannot be interpreted differently by people reading them in different languages. As we have suggested, multiple translators, representing each party, can cross-check the documents for accuracy and congruity of intent.

We can cite one additional example from the business realm. A legal colleague represented an entrepreneur in negotiations between the People's Republic of China (PRC) and a New Zealand shrimp farm. The bargaining process resulted in a deadlock, because the term *technology transfer* was misunderstood. A New Zealand attorney created an agreement that specified that the PRC would "transfer technology" to the New Zealand firm so shrimp could be raised using the Chinese techniques. When the terms of the agreement were translated to the Chinese, they balked, refusing to have a "technology transfer" from the PRC to a foreign nation.

The New Zealand team argued that a deal was not possible unless the transfer occurred. After more than an hour, the translators of the two teams took a break and tried to figure out why the Chinese representatives were resisting implementation of this crucial component of the settlement. As it turned out, the translation of "technology transfer" had two very different meanings. For the New Zealanders, it meant sharing information, but for the Chinese, it meant giving away their technology so that they would no longer control it. Once the differences in terminology were clarified, the parties moved on to devise an acceptable translation that allowed them to conclude the negotiation.

SUGGESTED STRATEGIES FOR HANDLING WRITTEN AGREEMENTS

- The parties should discuss and decide the form that the record of negotiations will take and how decisions will be memorialized. Consider the future use of the document and who will use it, the level of formality required, and whether it needs to be written in legal form.

- Determine the appropriate timing for agreements to be drafted: as they occur during negotiations, at the end of each negotiation session, or at the conclusion of the negotiation process. If drafting is deferred until later, ensure that all parties keep accurate notes and periodically check them against each other verbally during discussions (or appoint an official recorder and ensure that the parties confirm the accuracy of meeting records).

- The parties should decide together who will be involved in drafting agreements.

- Determine who will translate the agreement and which document and language will be the final word if there are differences in interpretation in the future.

CONCLUSION

Once the parties have articulated the content of an agreement, made oral commitments to adhere to it, or drafted a written settlement, the accord may require review, approval, and ratification by other concerned parties. Additionally, steps for implementation may need to be developed and put in place. These are covered in the next chapter.

CHAPTER THIRTEEN

Implementing Agreements

In an Asian country, three local ethnic groups engaged in open warfare, killing a number of people from each group. Local government officials lacked sufficient security forces to control the situation and found themselves unable to manage the problem. The governor asked for assistance from the central government—and the minister of the interior flew to the remote area to settle the matter. Upon his arrival, a lengthy series of rituals and ceremonies took place, all serving to honor the high official.

A representative of each party then presented their case. It concerned landownership and access, which had worsened with the arrival of farmers transplanted from densely populated areas to this relatively sparsely populated area. The transmigrants were clearing ancient rain forests, where local tribes had eked out a sustainable existence in a balanced relationship with forest resources for thousands of years. Their habitat was fast disappearing.

Eager to return to the capital, the minister made a pronouncement regarding the land issues and demanded that the tribes all pledge to refrain from further violence. The tribal representatives readily agreed and signed a written agreement that the minister had quickly drawn up. After a final ceremony to celebrate the agreement and the end of the dispute, the minister got in his plane and flew away. Within three days, fighting resumed. (This is an actual experience told to us.)

The parties involved in this situation all engaged in good faith. The local people appreciated the effort of the minister to make the long trip to address their problem. The minister thought he was providing a real service, sacrificing his own comfort and convenience as well. But why did the agreement fail? Everyone agreed to a settlement, but somehow it was not implemented. The following sections look at implementation strategies and steps.

REACHING AGREEMENT AND IMPLEMENTING IT

Development of implementation and monitoring plans and steps can happen during the course of negotiations as progress is made and agreements are reached on individual issues, or confirmed when a formal agreement is confirmed. In general, agreements can be self-executing (implemented immediately on an accord being reached) or non-self-executing (settled in a manner that requires ongoing performance monitoring or additional exchanges over time).

In general, self-executing agreements are less problematic in intercultural negotiations than those that are non-self-executing, as clear arrangements for implementation are made by the end of negotiations. However, non-self-executing agreements can result in significant differences in expectations and behaviors. Exchanges (of material, funds, statements, and so forth) or performance (actions) may not be carried out in the form, quantity, quality, sequence, or time frame expected. Delays, explanations for lack of performance, or ignoring implementation problems can strain relationships and lead to irritation, frustration, misperceptions, and stereotyping.

There are widely divergent cultural perspectives regarding the connection between reaching agreements and actually implementing them. Members of contractually oriented cultures generally view agreement making and implementation as one process. Negotiators from these cultures include elaborate details about implementation (specific performance, exchanges, process, timing, who will do what) in agreements. An agreement is not considered final until these details have been worked out and captured in a formal written document that becomes the record for terms of settlement. Because details about implementation are in the settlement document itself and all parties have participated in developing and approving them, the expectation is that parties will follow through on agreed-on terms, and they generally do. Of course, there are many contract disputes in contractually oriented cultures. However, most disputes arise over differing interpretations of compliance or the execution of a particular component; they do not usually concern problems in implementing the broader settlement itself.

Members of cultures that are less contractually and more relationship oriented may hold one of several views regarding the connection between agreement making and implementation. First, members of some cultures, while claiming to equate agreement making with implementation, do not always follow through on agreed settlements, especially to the level of detail that more contractually oriented cultures expect (Patai, 1983). In those cases, implementation often requires continuous follow-up, monitoring, and often further negotiations to ensure that agreements are accomplished.

Another view is that agreements are only general statements of principle and that implementation should be worked out in the context of the parties' ongoing relationship. Some cultures believe that the future cannot be predicted or controlled, and therefore they find it hard to conceive of workable implementation agreements that are developed ahead of time. Others prefer general agreements, believing that implementation steps can be generated only as the parties begin to work together, come to know each other better, and then jointly develop how an agreement will be implemented. This pattern has been observed in some Japanese negotiations.

A third view is that reaching either general agreements or agreements in principle is one phase of negotiations. Then, after a brief or extended hiatus in talks, separate follow-up negotiations are initiated to work out the implementation steps.

Members of many cultures assume that if a clearly defined substantive agreement is reached and agreed to by all concerned parties, the settlement will be implemented in good faith, in a timely manner, and according to both the sprit and the letter of the settlement. Unfortunately, the equation of agreement making and the intention to implement it is not universal. A number of cultures make agreements easily but do not necessarily intend to implement them, for a number of possible reasons.

In some cultures, senior leaders or officials who negotiate initial general agreements are not responsible for actual implementation; these tasks are delegated to others. Implementation may falter because implementing agencies, officials, or subordinates of senior negotiators lack understanding of the agreements; because there is no explicit or detailed implementation plan; because negotiators fail to assign individuals to manage follow-through; or because implementers lack commitment to the terms of the settlement. In addition, some cultures that are more present oriented may never get around to implementing agreements. Pressing immediate problems take precedence over implementing agreements reached in the past. Cultures that believe that individuals or groups have less control over the future often take this view (al-Omari, 2003). They say, "If God wants it to happen, it will happen."

Cultural values toward progress, harmony, and face-saving may also influence whether agreements reached are ever implemented. Agreement making, in and of itself, may be seen as beneficial, which gives face to negotiators, their superiors or constituents, and other concerned external parties. Agreement making implies that some action is being taken to address an issue and progress is being made. However, the desire of a negotiator or negotiation team to create and maintain an image of effectiveness may induce them to make agreements that they may not really want or have the ability to implement. Parties may reach agreements for image or publicity value, even if both parties know that they will never abide by the agreement. This was the case in a development dispute in postcommunist Poland (Olszanska, Olszanski, and Wozniak, 1993) between a national park and a local government concerning ownership of rights to a parcel of land. The parties reached an agreement because each saw it as a gain over the other, but neither expected to break implement it.

In addition, people from a number of societies and cultures are uncomfortable with overt disagreements. They do not like to deliver or receive negative messages. In certain circumstances, negotiators from these cultures may agree rapidly to almost any terms in order to avoid an unpleasant situation. This cultural pattern has been found in the cultures of indigenous tribes and bands in North America and in a number of Asian and Latin American cultures. In these cultures, it is not uncommon for all, rather than only one party, to collude in agreement making that no one expects to be implemented. The story presented at the beginning of this chapter is an illustrative example.

SUGGESTED STRATEGIES FOR HANDLING DIFFERENT VIEWS OF IMPLEMENTATION

- Assess whether your culture and that of your counterpart have similar expectations or cultural norms regarding implementation of agreements. If they are different or if there is any question as to whether the agreement will be executed according to agreed-on terms, make the implementation process as explicit as possible.
- Determine if agreements on implementation and monitoring procedures on steps should be agreed on prior to formalizing an agreement or after settlement. If there are differences of views, discuss them and see whether an accommodation of these views can be reached. Often an agreement on some implementation and monitoring steps, usually those that are the most predictable and not subject to external influences beyond the perceived control of one or more parties, can be agreed on. Others can be left until later.
- Determine the degree of detail desirable or necessary in an implementation or monitoring plan.

- Determine together what will be implemented and monitored, when actions will be completed, who will perform the monitoring functions, and what standards and criteria will be used to measure compliance.

- Reach agreements, if possible, regarding what will be done if there are breaches in the agreed implementation plan (consequences, steps to be taken, legal action, automatic losses, or something else).

- Decide what you will do if your counterpart is reaching an agreement on implementation that he or she has no intention to comply with—to save face, avoid conflict, for political reasons, or to gain later advantage.

ENSURING COMPLIANCE

How can parties ensure compliance with agreements? What kinds of problems can be anticipated and addressed? If disputes arise in the course of implementation, how will they be resolved? A major divide between approaches is once again based on contractual (low-context) versus holistic (high-context) orientations. The relative power of the parties is also an important factor. Can one party force the other to comply by threatening consequences or providing powerful incentives?

Contract-oriented negotiators commonly believe that the best way to avoid future disagreements is to clearly spell out the terms of the agreement or relationship in a written settlement document. The clearer the obligations, rights, or responsibilities of the parties are, the less chance there will be for a disagreement over the meaning of the settlement, and the more likely it is that parties will adhere to its terms. Members of these cultures take this approach to compliance for a number of reasons.

Contract-oriented negotiators often represent highly mobile groups or organizations that undergo constant changes. To ensure predictability and continuity of an agreement over time, address the fact that the individual with whom the agreement was concluded may not be around to implement it, members of contract-oriented cultures want to create clear, comprehensive, and iron-clad agreements that will endure independent of the people who negotiated them.

Additionally, contract-oriented negotiators also often come from cultures with developed legal systems that are widely perceived to be fair and impartial by the public and parties. These systems use analysis of documents such as contracts as part of their resolution process. A party from a culture of this type who believes that there is a contract violation is likely to seek legal redress for noncompliance and to enforce agreements. Disagreements about the terms of a contract or performance are often turned over to third-party advocates or decision makers—fact finders, dispute panels, arbitrators, or judges—who rely on a clear set of facts to resolve contract differences. Accuracy, clarity, and explicitness of contracts can also be persuasive to third-party decision makers should a dispute arise in the future. Because contract-oriented negotiators believe that the best way to protect their rights and interests is through a detailed contract, they often use the services of lawyers to draft agreements and formal contracts.

Holistically oriented negotiators use different approaches to encourage compliance with agreements and enforce settlements. Because many members of these cultures value harmony, long-term and smooth interpersonal working relationships, and face saving, they are often reluctant to use more adversarial procedures to manage and resolve differences. Compliance and enforcement strategies are typically less specific than those used by contractually oriented negotiators or in formal written agreements. They rely more on informal discussions, joint problem solving, or negotiations in the context of the ongoing relationship rather than on third-party judgments or enforcement. They also emphasize finding solutions in which no one is designated as being right or wrong and each of the involved parties is allowed to save face.

In addition to these factors, some holistically oriented cultures do not have access to well-developed and impartial legal systems—at least in comparison to many contractually oriented cultures. Legal systems in their societies are often distrusted, use unfamiliar procedures, or are perceived to be corrupt. As an alternative to legally enforced contracts and courts, members of holistically oriented cultures often rely on:

- Direct or indirect negotiations
- Third-party facilitation or mediation
- Pressure from the parties' families, peers, or associates
- Shaming, embarrassment, or threatened damage to an individual or group's reputation if a party does not comply with commonly accepted norms or terms of agreements

Only if these procedures do not work, if a dispute occurs between parties who do not have an ongoing personal relationship, or if a conflict involves issues of honor are parties likely to go to court or use other more coercive means to gain satisfaction (Nader, 1990; Von Benda-Beckman, 1984).

Compliance with terms of a settlement can also be induced by offering parties positive benefits for following through on agreements or threatening or imposing some form of negative sanctions. Positive inducements include measures such as lower fees for faster performance, promises of increased foreign aid for compliance with agreed-on international standards, or personal visibility or recognition for outstanding performance. Negotiators from some cultures view such positive inducements favorably and as a goal to strive for.

Negotiators from others see these measures as coercive and offered only to help a counterpart to achieve his or her own goals.

Depending on the cultures, issues, circumstances, situations, and people involved, negotiators may want to articulate potential negative consequences for noncompliance with the terms of an agreement. This approach ensures that all parties know what will happen if any parties fail to abide by the settlement and provides inducements to comply in order to avoid negative sanctions. In this approach, parties usually write consequences for noncompliance into their agreements: penalties, additional fees, reductions in payments, or even cancellation of a contract or an agreement.

This approach to noncompliance may seem quite normal in Western and some business cultures, but will be anathema to cultures that depend on relationships, respect, and personal trust to achieve compliance. For these cultures, even the suggestion of sanctions for noncompliance indicates that the agreement might be breached and may be enough to scuttle a settlement. One way to include negative consequences, if they are deemed necessary, is to require each party to perform according to the terms of the agreement and write in both positive and negative consequences for all parties based on their performance.

SUGGESTIONS FOR COORDINATING COMPLIANCE

- Determine whether positive or negative inducements to achieve compliance are necessary. Generally parties are more likely to look favorably on positive inducements and may resist including negative or coercive ones.

- If negative inducements are to be used, frame them in clear, explicit terms that will not be contested later, while at the same time protecting all parties' dignity and avoiding exposure to criticism from superiors or constituents.

FINAL APPROVAL AND RATIFICATION PROCEDURES

The approval process for negotiated agreements is bound by tradition, institutional structures, and what are perceived to be commonly accepted procedures for ratification. The approval process also depends on the issues that have been addressed and the context of the negotiations themselves. Finalization of a commercial sale will be treated quite differently from a labor-management contract or an international treaty.

Negotiators who have reached agreements may or may not have final authority to ratify and formalize it. They may have to submit the proposed settlement to others for final consideration and approval: superiors, legitimate authorities, constituencies, members of organizations, coalitions or communities, legislative bodies, or, on occasion, a judicial body. For instance, the representative of an environmental movement might be involved in negotiations regarding the cleanup of an industrial site—but will have to return to the larger community of environmental groups that selected him or her as a representative to ask for their confirmation of a proposed settlement.

In best circumstances, negotiators or other individuals at the table have kept these parties informed about the discussions and negotiation progress, so the final proposed settlement will not be a surprise and can be approved readily. In Japan, for example, it is expected that each representative in negotiations will regularly update colleagues who are not at the table and build consensus of their views in support of agreements that are emerging. This process, called *nemawashi*, is a common business practice that is considered an important leadership skill (Hall and Hall, 1987; March, 1988; Hodgson, Sano, and Graham, 2000). It involves the use of influence but should not involve coercion. Rather, it is about setting expectations and reconciling and integrating differing interests within one's own organization. When done well, *nemawashi* prepares negotiators to suggest mutually beneficial proposals and helps to prevent unwanted surprises during talks or negotiations. It is conducted throughout the negotiation process, including prior to the start of talks, as agreements are being developed, and at the conclusion of discussions prior to formal agreement.

The process for obtaining final approval of an agreement may involve securing the consent of one single powerful individual or may require the endorsement of many individuals or parties. In some cultures, negotiators informally or formally circulate a proposed agreement to the right people to gain final concurrence. These may include, among others, family leaders or members of negotiators' kin groups; tribal members, citizens, elders, religious leaders, or the public at large within a community; superiors in a business; administrators, politicians, or legislators in government; or members of a union or formal or informal opinion leaders in an organization. These people may read an agreement and provide input before it is officially approved, or they may be required to give final approval. Often the difference between a negotiated agreement that is approved and implemented, and one that is not, is the the failure of negotiators to consult appropriate people with the authority to ratify the final terms throughout and especially at the end of the process.

Agreements can be approved in a number of ways—for example:

- Individual approval, either unilaterally or with consultations, by a person with institutional authority to make decisions or speak for a group
- Vertical or horizontal negotiations and approval by superiors or constituents within an organization or broader community
- Bureaucratic approval

- Hierarchical consensus building
- Voting
- Approvals at mass meetings
- Religious sanctions

All of these procedures are culturally influenced. Let us examine some of these procedures in more detail.

Unilateral Approval

Unilateral approval is practiced in some traditional societies where elders have a recognized right to make decisions for the group. The process can also be found in patriarchal, autocratic, or dictatorial cultures or organizations, or situations where an individual, such as a judge or president, has been delegated the authority to decide difficult issues or resolve disputes. Unilateral approval may or may not involve consultation with other parties before a decision is made or announced. Some cultures that use this decision-making method also provide procedures for appeal to allow reconsideration of a unilateral decision that is unpopular, incongruent with widely accepted norms or values, or unlikely to be implemented.

Vertical or Horizontal Negotiations

Vertical or horizontal negotiations occur when a negotiator is representing superiors or constituents who are not at the negotiation table. Negotiators should maintain contact with superiors or constituents and conduct formal or informal internal bargaining with them to reach agreements on settlements that are being proposed at the negotiating table. This bargaining may take place throughout the negotiations; as part of in-team and vertical or horizontal discussions to identify issues and interests, generate settlement options, or assess and prepare offers.

In most organizations, some internal discussion and give-and-take are necessary to reach a final agreement that will have institutional approval or buy-in. In fact, such vertical or horizontal negotiations within the organization of one party can represent some of the most difficult bargaining that occurs in an agreement-making process. Often members of an organization who are asked to approve proposed agreements have not had the experience of their negotiators or negotiating teams of working with counterparts, building a working relationship, developing an understanding of the issues and interests, and solving problems together. These decision makers, who have been outside the direct negotiation process, do not always understand in a visceral way the logic and rationale for why specific decisions have been reached or the trade-offs that had to be made in order to arrive at a proposed settlement. Superiors and constituents who have not had the advantage of meeting with the other side must make their decisions based on the information provided by their negotiator, spokesperson, or team. In fact, it is not unusual for a negotiator or negotiation team to be accused of "selling out" to the other side or having been "corrupted" by constant contact with a perceived enemy. This is often referred to as the "hero-traitor" dynamic (Blake and Mouton, 1984).

Due to these dynamics, the representatives or spokespersons need to communicate constantly with superiors, constituents, or others who will be involved in a final approval to promote realistic expectations and boost the likelihood of final approval.

Bureaucratic Approval

Bureaucratic approval is a systematic process of institutional agreement making and ratification. In this procedure, agreements reached at lower levels of the organization must be approved in sequence by individuals in higher positions of authority. Generally there are rules to be followed, a predictable decision-making path, and formalized procedures for indicating approval or disapproval. Often a decision can be stopped anywhere in its vertical climb if a person in the hierarchy does not approve of the tentative settlement. In some bureaucratic organizations, significant negotiation takes place between levels, especially in cultures where individual initiative and perspective are valued.

In bureaucratic cultures, such as those in countries that formerly had communist systems in central and Eastern Europe, the current People's Republic of China, and some former colonial countries such as India, little negotiation may be involved in the approval process. Approval may be no more than a check-off process in which bureaucrats at various levels in an organization indicate that they have seen the settlement document and that appropriate laws, regulations, and procedures have been followed. Settlement documents are then forwarded to the top decision makers for final approval.

Often in these systems, bureaucratic approval indicates centralized control over a wide range of decisions, even ones of little significance, by senior decision makers. In these systems, initiative by people of lower rank is stifled, creating reluctance or fear to take responsibility for a decision that they may be held accountable for or may result in a reprimand in the future. Unfortunately this system creates significant bottlenecks and delays as prospective decisions waiting to be signed languish on the desks of senior decision makers. For individuals who are used to working in more flexible decision-making environments, their first encounter with a highly centralized bureaucracy can be quite unsettling and frustrating.

In the 1990s, two foreign businesspeople working in Poland met a British flower buyer who was trying to ship flowers to Sweden. They shared a taxi to the center of Warsaw. During the ride, the flower merchant lamented over the slowness of the Polish bureaucracy. He had purchased flowers at a private farm and, after negotiating a fair price, tried to ship them to Sweden. However, the export itself, as well as packaging and shipping, needed approvals from several agencies and ministries. By the time all the bureaucratic approvals were secured, he was worried that the flowers would be wilted or dead.

In this case, it was the approval process within a bureaucratic culture, rather than direct negotiations, that was the problem. Today, Poland has made significant progress in adapting to Western European commercial practices, and inclusion in the European Union has made doing business much easier. However, the case does illustrate some of the frustrations when bureaucratic approval is required for agreement or implementation of settlements.

Hierarchical Consensus Building

Hierarchical consensus building is an interesting variation on bureaucratic approval. This process is commonly practiced in Japanese corporations and government agencies. The *ringe* process involves circulating proposals and ideas up and down the bureaucratic organizational ladder for comments, development, or approval. Executives approve a proposal by placing a chop, a stamp with a *conji* character on it, on the document. If an idea or proposal is questioned or rejected, a chop may be denied or stamped upside down, indicating a problem.

After a proposed agreement has been circulated up and down the hierarchy, often multiple times, and all reviewers, or at least the critical ones, have indicated approval, a consensus is stated by a person in a high position and of respected authority in the organization. With this articulation, the proposed agreement is considered approved, and the parties can move forward to rituals and ceremonies that celebrate joint approval.

Variations of hierarchical consensus are commonly practiced in businesses, governmental agencies, and other institutions or communities in Asian, African, and Latin American cultures, where kinship or network approval is necessary to approve a decision, although the approval process may be less formal than the Japanese procedure described above. A negotiator or authority figure may visit respected members of the group for consultations and advice and to get a sense of how much support exists in favor of or against a proposed agreement. Consultation may also take the form of consensus-building meetings, practiced by the Maori in New Zealand, family councils in the Middle East, and traditional Tswana decision-making meetings in South Africa and Botswana (Comaroff and Roberts, 1981). All of these forms require consultation with family or village members before a respected elder announces a consensus decision or approves a new law or ruling.

Voting

Voting, another way to approve agreements, is most commonly used in cultures and situations where a decision reached by an individual negotiator or team must be approved by the other members of an organization, such as members of a labor union. Voting can also be used when a constituency, such as a community group, has appointed representatives to negotiate on its behalf but has not given them final authority to approve an agreement. For example, in negotiations between a Native American tribe and local government officials over interjurisdictional issues, if the tribe does not use traditional decision-making methods, a proposed settlement may have to be approved by a vote of its tribal council. Similarly, treaties, especially if reached by nations with democratic governments, may have to be approved by a majority or supermajority vote by a legislature or parliament.

Voting is generally used in cultures that value individual involvement in decision making, or where common procedure is to poll and gain approval from a broad group of parties or constituents. Individuals from cultures that are highly centralized or bureaucratic and where decision making is accomplished by a series of approvals by individuals in a hierarchy, are often amazed and confused by approval processes that require democratic involvement of a large number of people or parties. Several years ago, the Dushanbe (Tajikistan) Sister City Program presented its sister city of Boulder, Colorado, with an unusual gift—an original Central Asian tea house, which had been painstakingly crafted by skilled artisans and packed in multiple crates for shipment to the United States. Exchanges of visits and small gifts between the two sister cities had been going on for several years, but the gift of the teahouse, and the probable expectation for a reciprocal exchange, was quite large. The Tajiks were astounded when Boulder city officials delayed the reassembly of the tea house, because they had to go through a democratic process, which involved voting to approve the siting, financing, and construction of the facility. Ultimately, the siting was approved, the teahouse assembled, and it became a popular restaurant in town. Later, the Boulder Sister City Program reciprocated the gift with a cyber cafe for Dushanbe. Ironically, that city too had to go through an elaborate bureaucratic approval process to site the cafe, which include multiple negotiations with its sister city about the size of the donation.

Mass Meetings

Mass meetings can be used to approve agreements by submitting a proposal to an assembled crowd, where it is either accepted or rejected by popular acclaim. While this method can be an example of direct democracy, it can also be manipulated by organized and vocal minorities who may not represent the interests of the majority. Those who can shout louder or dominate deliberations may overpower weaker voices, or peer pressure may stifle the expression of minority views.

An example of this form of decision making occurred in South Africa as its institutions were emerging from apartheid. The University of the Western Cape in South Africa is composed of an ethnically diverse student body and administration. A mass meeting was called by leaders of a student group, who predominantly represented members of one racial group, to approve a student boycott of classes to protest increased student fees. The students had tried to negotiate with the administration and received several offers, all of which they considered unacceptable. The students called the mass meeting to win support for their demands and to approve a boycott aimed at forcing the administration to change its position. A large number of students attended the meeting, and it appeared, by a mass voice vote, that most of them approved both the demands and boycott. However, several days later, the university was still holding classes and many students were crossing picket lines to attend. A group of students called for a referendum to determine if the student body was behind the boycott. The referendum was held and overwhelmingly indicated little support for the boycott: the opinions expressed at the mass meeting did not represent the student body at large. The boycott ended, and the students returned to classes.

Religious Sanctions

Religious or spiritual approval commonly involves consulting a spiritual leader, holy text, or deity as part of a process for making a decision. History is replete with examples of leaders praying before reaching various kinds of agreements or even deciding to go to war. Traditional societies often perform religious ceremonies with chanting and dancing to obtain guidance for decision making. Societies that rely on scriptures or holy texts may consult these written works or knowledgeable holy people for interpretation or advice prior to making decisions. Spiritual approval in some cultures is also obtained by consulting astrologers or individuals knowledgeable in spiritual matters.

SUGGESTIONS FOR COORDINATING APPROVAL PROCEDURES
- Determine for yourself and your counterpart how formal approval of the negotiated agreement will be accomplished. Explore with them, if appropriate, the ratification process that they are using or will use, and explain yours.
- Remain open to means of ratification and consultation with individuals or groups that are not the same as yours if they will accomplish the same goals.

- Seek agreements on the steps that each of you will take and a projected time line to achieve the support and ratification from your respective decision makers.

- Discuss procedures that you will use if decision makers request modifications to the terms that had previously been agreed to.

CEREMONIES AND RITUALS FOR CONCLUDING NEGOTIATIONS

Almost all human cultures engage in ceremonies and rituals to recognize and celebrate transitions: the beginning or end of relationships or the conclusion or start of collective ventures. We can see this in the range of rituals practiced around the world related to births, baptisms, birthdays, saints days, coming of age, weddings, funerals, and other occasions. Similarly, virtually all cultures practice ceremonies to recognize, confirm, and induce compliance with negotiated agreements. Ceremonies or rituals may be brief and informal, such as gestures (a handshake or bow), or they may be elaborate and formal.

Oral promises and the signing of written agreements are often part of formal ceremonies, but parties may also engage in additional rituals to conclude the negotiations. Such rituals symbolically begin implementation of an agreement, or they may involve a tangible process that officially ends the dispute or formalizes the agreement and the new relationship. More elaborate rituals may be conducted at the end of negotiations—for example:

- Formal signing ceremonies at the conclusion of a labor contract, a business deal, or approval of a piece of legislation or treaty

- Verbal commitment ceremonies and rituals, including public meetings or press conferences, or making TV or radio announcements of a new relationship, settlement, or joint venture

- Ritual slaughter of an animal (common in the Middle East, Africa, and parts of Asia and the Caribbean), lighting lamps (Sri Lanka), burning incense (many cultures), or saying prayers (the Philippines)

- Mutual exchanges of gifts, either tokens or ones of significant symbolic or monetary value (practiced in many countries for a variety of occasions, from the conclusions of negotiations over a bride-price or dowry to the conclusion of major commercial deals)

- Eating or feasting together (common in almost all cultures, and practiced in an elaborate form in China)

- Drinking various beverages together (vodka in Russia and parts of Eastern Europe, sweetened coffee in Haiti, spirits in Korea, and *pulque* among indigenous groups in Mexico)
- Ceremonial dances or balls
- Religious ceremonies and rituals (joint attendance at a house of worship in highly religious societies; receiving a blessing from a religious authority; praying together; and smoking peace pipes in Native American and First Nation cultures)

Some ceremonies and rituals involve formal approval of substantive agreements, such as signing ceremonies, whereas others are affirmations of relationships. For example, in some cultures, the formal signing of documents is seen as a ritual to affirm a legal agreement and to commit to follow through with all terms of the settlement. A signed document is considered binding on all signatories among the dominant cultures of North America, northern Europe, and others that have strong legal traditions. In other cultures, signing indicates an intention to follow through, and ritual verbal promises are considered to be more important.

Psychological Closure and the Ritual Exchange of Apologies

In some disputes, the process of ending differences and reaching closure requires acknowledgment of the past, regret, wrong behavior, and a ritual exchange of apologies. In some situations, the parties themselves develop their own statements; in other situations, they ask for the help of an intermediary. For example, in traditional Chinese negotiations,

> the mediator can . . . engineer a ritualistic statement of regret with each party to be presented in the joint session. This mediator-instigated regret allows parties to save face ("I am not apologizing, I am offering this regret because I am obligated to the mediator"). At the same time, it gives the other party a reason to deescalate the conflict ("Well, at least he or she is willing to admit that some of his or her conduct is wrong"). Through this mechanism, both sides are able to interpret the act in their favor and thus be more conciliatory and constructive at collaborative problem solving [Chia, Lee-Partridge, and Chong, 2004, p. 461].

A formal signing ceremony is a ritual that takes place in cultures with strong written and legal traditions. The written word and a signature of a person in a position of authority demonstrates serious commitment to an agreement. Public international and intercultural signing ceremonies conducted in recent decades include the Camp David Accords signed by President Sadat and Prime Minister Begin, and mediated and witnessed by President Carter the signing of nuclear disarmament treaties involving Presidents Reagan and Bush and Gorbachev, the General Secretary of the Communist Party of the Soviet Union;

agreements reached between Nelson Mandela and President de Klerk in South Africa; the Dayton Peace Accords that ended war in parts of the former Yugoslavia; the North American Free Trade Agreement; and the Kyoto climate change agreement.

A signing ceremony widely seen as demeaning involved former President Suharto of Indonesia and Michael Camdessus, managing director of the International Monetary Fund. In a meeting concluding a settlement over measures to stabilize Indonesia's economy after the Asian financial crisis of 1997 and 1998, "as Suharto drew his pen to sign the agreement, Camdessus stood over him, arms folded, eyes cold, in an angry-father pose that was later to appear in the pages of a thousand newspapers" (Mallaby, 2004, pp. 189–190). Indonesians and others throughout the world, regardless of their feelings about Suharto and the accusations of corruption that had been aimed at him and his associates, saw this ceremony as an indication of domination of developing countries by the West and global financial interests.

Each of the signing ceremonies noted involved key leaders who signed the documents, with colleagues, observers, and, on occasion, the press in attendance. The signing confirmed the agreements and publicly committed the leaders to follow through on their terms. To ensure the success of such signing ceremonies, negotiators need to:

- Consult with all parties about the protocol and sequence of events, so that they feel involved in and committed to the ceremony.
- Determine what greeting and ritual affirmative gestures will be made.
- Agree on the ceremony site. Choose a neutral site or one that all parties agree on. One party may host the ceremony with the agreement of the other party.
- Consider the location and physical setup for the room, ensuring equal treatment for all parties.
- Establish procedures that ensure equal treatment, recognition of status, and prestige of key signatories and their delegations. If individuals of different ranks from each of the parties are involved, treat them in a manner befitting their status.
- Provide an opportunity for ritual speeches, tributes, and commitment statements. When parties are equal in rank and stature, they may speak in sequence.
- If the agreement involves the potential loss of face or position on the part of one or more parties, ensure that opportunities to save face, often presented in a favorable logic and rationale for the agreement, should be provided. This may entail rituals of respect by the dominant party for a weaker one, statements of appreciation or acknowledgment of willingness to work together, or avoiding any reference to delicate issues.

- Create two or more copies of the final document to be signed, one or more in each language, with the terminology already checked for accuracy and congruence.

- Decide on the document signing procedure to avoid confusion. This can include who signs first, or leaders can sign duplicate documents simultaneously and then exchange them for the other to sign. Or both parties can sign a single document and have it duplicated so that each party has a copy.

- Provide interpreters for key spokespeople and arrange their seating close enough to leaders to support their conversations.

- Establish an agenda for after the signing so events are clear to the participants. Consider including public statements, press conferences, receptions, banquets, religious ceremonies, and an exit procedure for the parties who signed the agreement.

Social closure rituals are common either beforehand, to lay the groundwork for formal agreements, or as part of ritual completion ceremonies. Some social closure rituals have been identified above. Below we provide more details about some of these ceremonies.

Eating and drinking, meals, and banquets are almost universal ceremonies practiced at the conclusion of negotiations. Their roots are probably based in ancient traditions of sharing food as a symbol of closeness, unity, and survival with close kin or associates. The formats for meals and banquets include large, fairly informal gatherings such as those at a Maori *marae,* a New Zealand venue and ritual where people circulate and eat with groups of family and friends; long, formal dinner parties typical of Western Europe; or community dining. Banquet halls are used in most countries for entertaining large groups. Banquets are particularly favored by the Chinese of the People's Republic for business and political entertaining. Chinese banquets are elaborate functions with a series of courses and toasts that are formally used to cement a relationship and honor the parties present (Seligman, 1989).

Exchanges of gifts, tokens of the relationship, or ritual objects are common in cultures that see initial agreements only as the preamble for future negotiations. These may be pictures, art, or an antique representing the giver's culture. For example, parties in East Timor who are concluding negotiations often exchange specific kinds of cloth or, in the case of marriage, old Dutch coins as symbols to indicate that transactional talks or a conflict are over.

Other Types of Outcome Rituals

For some cultures, conclusion ceremonies and rituals are seen as the major means to promote voluntary compliance to an agreement. For example, during the *intifada* in the occupied territories of the West Bank and Gaza, many

Palestinians did not want to use Israeli courts to resolve differences between them. Instead, they used mediation by a respected community or political leader to reach voluntary agreements. At the conclusion of the negotiations, the mediator would often convene a public meeting attended by the parties, other members of their families, and respected community leaders. At this meeting, participants would publicly announce the terms of their settlement. The expectation was that the public verbal commitment to the terms of settlement in front of witnesses engaged the parties' honor, providing strong social pressures to keep their word.

Commitment rituals confirm the commitment of parties. For example, in Islamic cultures, oaths and vows based on the premise of "if God wills it" (*inshallah* or *in shā' Allāh*) "are more acceptable than other utterances about the future, perhaps because the responsibility for carrying out the action is laid on God" (Alon and Brett, 2007, p. 67). Making such a statement with no intention to carry out the agreement is punishable (Shafi'I, 1983, vii, 65, as cited in Alon and Brett, 2007). As is said in the Koran (2:225), "Allah will not call you to account for thoughtlessness in your oaths, but to the intention in your hearts."

Yet another purpose for outcome rituals is to gain psychological completion of one phase of negotiations, a conflict, or relationship, and mark the beginning of a new phase of negotiations or relationship building. In negotiations involving the Chinese, the establishment of fraternal relationships between the parties is commonly followed by a banquet, which is in turn followed by additional substantive negotiations. Among some groups of Maoris in negotiations both among themselves and with non-Maoris, meals and ritual speeches are used to confirm progress and reaffirm the next steps or the future of the parties' relationships with each other.

A final purpose of outcome rituals is to enable parties to release a sense of injury and conflict from the past. Activities designed to achieve this involve public acknowledgment of past wrongs and roles parties may have played in perpetrating them, requests for forgiveness, affirmation that the conflict has been adequately addressed, and commitments to better future relationships among the individuals involved, their families, organizations, ethnic groups, or nations. For example, in East Timor, former disputants in traditional communities exchange such promises in public meetings in front of their extended families.

Among some South African groups, conflicts are ended by each disputant washing the hands of his or her counterpart, indicating that the dispute has been washed away and the involved individuals have been made clean by a valued resource, water. In Thailand, a blood feud between groups was brought to completion by the Buddhist monk who mediated the negotiated settlement by engaging the former adversaries in a ritual that had been used by an ancient Thai king to end a war. All parties were asked to bring a disabled weapon—a broken knife or a gun without its cylinder or bullet clip—and place it in a wooden box. The box was then filled with water and passed from person to person as everyone drank to symbolize the end of the conflict (Songsamphan, 1996).

SUGGESTIONS FOR COORDINATING THE CONCLUSION OF NEGOTIATIONS

- Consider what kinds of ceremonies or rituals are desirable, expected, or necessary for both your culture and that of your counterpart to conclude agreements or terminate conflicts over the issues in question.

- Think about the kinds of ceremonies or rituals that will help affirm or improve relationships.

- Consider what ceremonies or rituals will promote psychological closure or reconciliation, especially if issues have been hotly contested.

- Identify rituals that will encourage compliance to the terms of settlement.

- Discuss with your counterpart what ceremonies will best meet your individual and joint goals and interests.

- If negotiations conclude in the venue, locale, or country of your counterpart, be open to using and participating in closure rituals that are common there.

- If negotiations conclude in your venue, locale, or country, discuss with your counterpart whether you will jointly use your rituals, theirs, or a combination of both. Reach as many common agreements as possible, but do not be afraid to add some of your rituals to the process if they are not likely to be offensive to your counterpart. Often negotiators from other cultures greatly appreciate the opportunity to participate in the rituals of another culture.

- Determine who will have what roles and responsibilities in executing the ceremonies and rituals and, if appropriate, divide roles in a culturally acceptable manner.

CONCLUSION

By the end of this phase of negotiations, parties have reached mutually acceptable agreements, as well as procedures to implement and monitor them. Ideally the parties then engage in culturally acceptable ceremonies that affirm their relationships, confirm agreements, and induce them to comply. In circumstances where parties have been in conflict, they may engage in rituals of reconciliation where apologies are given and substantive exchanges made so that they can let go of old hurts and move on with their lives.

At this point, all that remains is to implement their settlement. If the agreement was self-ratifying or self-executing, this goal will have been accomplished at the conclusion of negotiations or in a subsequent ceremony or ritual. If it was non-self-executing, required continued performance, or details need to be worked out in the future, parties will need to continue to make agreed-on exchanges or continue their discussions and negotiations to refine and deepen their relationships or work out details on open or ongoing issues.

ASSISTED NEGOTIATIONS AND THIRD-PARTY ROLES

Part Three addresses how parties from different cultures approach the use of outside assistance in the negotiation process. Chapter Fourteen identifies a wide range of potential intermediary roles used in support of negotiations in various cultures. Chapter Fifteen examines the roles of mediator and facilitator, drawing a distinction between the two roles, and providing guidance about what experience and expertise to look for in a prospective intermediary.

Assisted Negotiations

T he manager of a forest products company assigned to administer the enterprise's grievance mechanism to resolve community complaints against the
company was concerned. He had received a grievance from a local farmer
against one of the company's truck drivers. The complainant charged the
driver with driving a logging truck off the road, breaking the farmer's fence,
and damaging some of his crops. In addition, the driver simply drove away
and never reported it. Knowing that the company wanted to be seen as a
good citizen, responsive to complaints and having a positive relationship with
members of the local community and its employees, the manager conducted a
systematic investigation of the complaint.

He first talked with the driver, who admitted that he had driven his truck
off the road and damaged the fence and crops, but he said it was not his fault.
He had swerved to avoid hitting a goat that jumped in front of the truck, which
he assumed belonged to the farmer who had lodged the complaint. The driver
said he did not try to find the farmer and tell him about the accident, because
his truck got stuck in the mud and made him late for the delivery of his load.
He offered to make an apology.

Next the manager set up a meeting with the claimant at his farm. However,
before he went, he considered how the community might view the talks if
he went alone or with the truck driver and negotiated a private settlement of
the claim. He was concerned that the farmer might ask for an unreasonable
amount of compensation or later claim that he was coerced to agree to an

unfair settlement by two "company men." To address these concerns, the company representative approached a group of respected local community leaders and requested that they attend and observe the negotiations. He asked that they witness both the fairness of the process and outcome, and if requested, report back to the broader community about what had occurred. He also asked them to provide advice, on an as-needed basis, to both him and the farmer, regarding what might normally be expected in terms of compensation for damages of the type that had occurred.

Ultimately, the driver's acknowledgment of responsibility for the accident, his apology, and the discussion—with the input of the community leaders—regarding fair compensation enabled all parties to reach an amicable settlement (Interview with a team member of an international company's grievance mechanism).

∽

Regardless of the culture, the vast majority of issues, problems, or conflicts between individuals or groups are resolved through informal conversations or more formal negotiations. Involved parties are able to make contact, establish forums in which to talk, and develop mutually acceptable agreements on their own, without the assistance of other parties. However, parties are not always successful. On occasion, there are issues or differences that participants are not able to resolve on their own, for a variety of reasons. In some cases, they are not able to get productive talks started, or they become trapped in circular and unproductive discussions. In other instances, they have started negotiations but reach an impasse. When these dynamics occur, negotiators have several choices:

- *Endure or "lump it."* Accommodate to or accept the status quo, without further attempts at resolution.

- *Pursue avenues other than talks or negotiations to meet their interests.* Explore ways to unilaterally attain goals through other means, or open talks with another party who is more amenable to establishing a positive working relationship and reaching an agreement.

- *Withdraw from negotiations and exercise coercion to achieve desired ends.* Withhold cooperation or support needed by a counterpart, publicly reveal information unfavorable to that person, or engage in litigation or other coercive tactics (demonstrations, strikes, boycotts, armed action) to force concessions.

- *Continue currently unproductive negotiations in the hope that the circumstances will change and talks will become more constructive.* Analyze why negotiations are not productive, and consider a range of strategies for transforming the nature of the discourse. Meanwhile, devote minimal energy to the process until it improves.

- *Ask a third-party decision maker to resolve differences or issues in dispute.* Take the case (or specific unresolved issues) to a judge or arbitrator who is empowered to render either a binding decision or an advisory opinion. An advisory opinion may carry weight with the parties or the public because of the decision maker's reputation, expertise, or perceived fairness.

- *Seek assistance from a skilled external party who can help parties negotiate and reach voluntary agreements.* They may include mediators or facilitators, or one of many other types of allies or third parties to assist the parties to communicate with each other, engage in productive problem solving, and reach a voluntary settlement of disputes or broader resolution of conflicts.

This chapter addresses the last two strategic choices for external assistance. In the rest of this chapter, we explore two topics: the sources of problems in negotiations and the forms of assistance available to negotiators from external parties to prevent or overcome such problems. The next chapter examines in detail two major forms of third-party assistance: facilitation and mediation.

PROBLEMS IN MEETINGS OR NEGOTIATIONS

Negotiations can founder for a wide variety of reasons. Some are related to specific characteristics of the parties, the issues they are facing, their competing interests, and the dynamics of the negotiation process. Cultural differences may also create challenges. There may be one central cause of difficulties or multiple interlocking and mutually reinforcing factors. Figure 14.1 identifies a range of difficulties that hinder the start of negotiations or produce deadlocks after talks begin.

A list of specific issues within each of the broad categories follows. Note that all of these problems are nested in the context of the cultures of the involved parties.

Relationship Problems

- Lack of adequate relationship establishing or building
- Different expectations regarding relationships and behavior
- Misperceptions or stereotypes
- Irritating personal habits or behavior, actions, or style

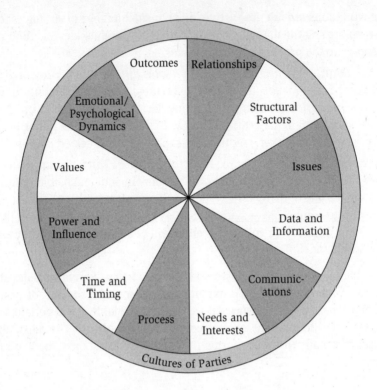

Figure 14.1. Potential Causes of Problems in Meetings or Negotiations

Structural Problems

- Unclear roles and responsibilities
- Different levels of authority or mandates
- Unclear, lack of, or dysfunctional organizational decision making or dispute resolution structures
- Inadequate or unequal control of needed resources
- Competing or mutually exclusive customary practices, rules, regulations, or laws
- Geographical or spatial proximity or distance
- Key parties excluded from talks or spoilers
- Adverse publicity or intense media attention on negotiations

Issues Problems

- Unclear or poorly articulated or framed issues
- Lack of mutual understanding of issues

- Unwillingness to talk about each party's issues
- Single problematic issue
- Too few issues for trades
- Too many issues to reach a comprehensive or implementable agreement

Data and Information Problems

- Lack of information
- Misinformation
- Diverse views on relevance of data
- Differences over methodologies for data collection and analysis
- Different interpretations or assessments of data

Communications Problems

- Preferences for direct or indirect talks
- Direct-dealing versus indirect-dealing cultural styles
- Low-context versus high-context cultural patterns
- Expression of strong emotions
- Lack of clarity or organization or too much specificity of ideas
- Difficulty listening
- Ineffective or inappropriate framing of issues or interests
- Circular or inconclusive talk

Needs and Interests Problems

- Lack of recognition or acceptance of basic needs
- Parties' lack of understanding of their own or counterparts' interests
- Lack of understanding of types of interests (substantive, procedural, relationship and psychological)
- Poor articulation or framing of interests
- Perceived or actual incompatible interests

Process Problems

- Lack of or unclear meeting or negotiation process or strategy
- Competing strategies and procedures
- Parties stuck in positions or positional bargaining
- Issue-sequencing problems
- Lack of or ineffective strategies for resolving specific issues

Time and Timing Problems

- Too little time or unrealistic deadlines
- Too much time or no deadlines
- Too little time to build relationships
- Too little time for information exchange or mutual education
- Premature offers
- Too little time spent on understanding interests or option generation
- Too little or too much time for decision making or external approval by superiors or constituents

Power and Influence Problems

- Lack of or ineffective use of means of influence
- Resistance to specific means of influence
- Lack of positive inducements or incentives
- Use of too much coercion

Values Problems

- Belief that parties must share the same values
- Lack of tolerance for diverse beliefs
- Perceived or actual incompatible or mutually exclusive values
- Inability to recognize superordinate or bridging values
- Definition of issues in terms of values rather than interests
- Difficulty recognizing, defining, and agreeing on spheres of interest
- Unwillingness to agree to disagree on some issues where values clash and reach agreement on others

Emotional and Psychological Dynamics Problems

- Lack of trust or respect
- Discomfort with disagreement or conflict
- Strong emotions (suppressed and not expressed)
- Win-lose mind-sets
- Desire for revenge or harm
- Feelings of hopelessness
- Lack of belief that a solution will be implemented

Outcomes Problems

- Lack of satisfactory settlement options
- Reciprocity or equal exchange problems

- Inability to develop acceptable links, trades, or packages
- Problems developing credible implementation or monitoring procedures
- Difficulties meeting psychological interests, addressing mistrust, and achieving emotional closure

ASSISTANCE TO ADDRESS PROCESS PROBLEMS OR IMPASSE

When negotiators, due to one or more of the problems described, cannot make progress in talks, they often need the help of external parties—often called allies, third parties, or intermediaries. They may also rely on services provided by a dispute resolution system, an institutionalized mechanism that provides assistance to help people resolve their differences. More will be said about such systems later in the chapter.

People Who Can Provide Assistance

People who help improve relationships and assist the parties to move toward agreement generally fall into two categories, distinguished by their relationship to the parties and the specific kinds of support they provide. They may be either allies of one or more parties who provide partisan or advocacy assistance or independent or impartial parties who help all concerned improve relationships or reach agreements. Table 14.1 identifies a range of functions and roles that external parties provide to address sources of impasse or conflict. The functions are arranged in sequence according to the time in talks when the assistance may be needed, although the timing of assistance is not entirely linear. It should also be noted that help may be informal or formal and provided in a direct or indirect manner, depending on the circumstances.

People in the first eight categories listed in Table 14.1 directly help negotiators reach voluntary agreements—that is, the the external party has no power or authority to impose a settlement on the parties. In the last category, assistance of third-party decision making, the intermediary provides assistance by rendering a binding decision or opinion.

When parties are stuck and cannot reach voluntary accords, they may need to submit particularly difficult issues—or, in some cases, all issues—to a third-party decision maker, such as a judge or arbitrator, for a binding or nonbinding decision. Binding decisions are those that parties have agreed to voluntarily or are compelled to accept, implement, or comply with. Nonbinding decisions constitute recommendations or advice by an authoritative third party that parties are free to accept or reject, but carry significant weight because of who has made them or the fairness of the process.

Table 14.1. People Who Provide Third-Party Assistance

Functions	People Who Can Provide Assistance
Assistance to initiate negotiations	• *Common friends, confidants, or associates:* Individuals or groups in close relationship with one or more parties who help open communications between them.
	• *Formal introducers or coordinators of ritualized meetings and related activities:* Individuals such as *shokai-sha* (introducers or go-betweens in Japan) or middlemen in other cultures who introduce counterparts or their representatives, and open talks between them.
	• *Conveners:* Individuals, groups, coalitions, organizations, or government agencies that advocate or sponsor talks and bring parties together (usually with some form of convening authority).
Assistance to promote procedural fairness and fair play	• *Witnesses:* Individuals or groups, such as community leaders or notables in some countries, who observe meetings or negotiations to verify their procedural and substantive fairness. (These individuals may not be entirely neutral regarding their relationship to the involved parties or impartial concerning issues in question.)
	• *Observers or monitors:* Impartial observers whose presence helps ensure procedural fairness, inhibit unethical behavior, encourage accurate reporting of events, and report observations to established authorities or broader publics if necessary.
Assistance to improve relationships or communications	• *Common friends, confidants, or associates:* Individuals or groups in close relationship with one or more parties, who may not be impartial regarding issues in question, and who informally give advice or act as go-betweens.
	• *Message carriers:* Trusted individuals who informally or formally shuttle between parties and carry messages aimed at improving relationships, trust, and communications.
	• *Social activity coordinators:* Initiators of social activities among parties, designed to promote positive relationships and greater trust but not to address substantive issues directly.
	• *Providers of good offices:* Go-betweens, often at the diplomatic level, who open communications between parties and subsequently may bring them together for face-to-face talks.

Table 14.1. (*continued*)

Functions	People Who Can Provide Assistance
	• *Interpreters and translators:* Individuals with knowledge and skills in the languages of the involved parties who can accurately interpret, translate, and convey accurate verbal or written messages. This can be a simple technical role or expand into facilitation.
	• *Conciliators:* Formal go-betweens with a specific focus on improving attitudes and the psychological readiness of parties to engage in direct talks or negotiations (confidence-building measures).
	• *Counselors or therapists:* Individuals who focus on improving insight, understanding, or changing the psychological mind-sets of an individual or group about themselves or a counterpart.
	• *Problem-solving group facilitators:* An individual or a team that provides forums and processes to improve parties' relationships, increase confidence, build trust, and increase common understanding of the parties' issues, concerns, interests, motivations, and fears.
	• *Spiritual mentors or guides:* Individuals who provide parties with spiritual or religious advice related to treatment of a counterpart or their common relationships.
Assistance to prepare for negotiations	• *Substantive advisors or coaches:* Individuals who help a party or parties develop a negotiation strategy or serve as reality testers on substantive issues in question.
	• *Trainers:* An individual or team that provides structured training for individual negotiators, a negotiation team, or multiple parties (either in parallel or jointly) to educate them about effective structures, approaches, and strategies for communications, problem solving, or joint-gain negotiations.
	• *Protocol officers:* Individuals knowledgeable about social and diplomatic protocol or customs and culture who advise parties on appropriate behavior and etiquette.
	• *Process advisors or designers:* An individual or team who advises negotiators on effective structures, approaches, and procedures for effective deliberations and negotiations.
	• *Spiritual advisors:* Individuals who prepare parties spiritually to engage in productive talks.

(*continued overleaf*)

Table 14.1. People Who Provide Third-Party Assistance (*continued*)

Functions	People Who Can Provide Assistance
Assistance through advocacy or support	• *Motivators:* Individuals who provide support and encouragement to enhance a party's psychological state and ability to participate effectively in talks. • *Emotional support persons:* Individuals who, by their presence behind the scenes or in negotiation forums, provide psychological support for parties. • *Verbal advocates:* Individuals skilled in verbal argumentation and logic who speak for or with parties. • *Fixers, go-betweens, or middlemen:* Individuals who work for a party and negotiate on their behalf to solve logistical or other problems related to working in another culture. • *Partisan experts:* Advocates knowledgeable about issues in dispute who present information (often technical, scientific, or medical) that supports one party's views or interests. • *Legal advocates:* Individuals or teams knowledgeable about the law who present legal arguments in favor of or supporting one party's views or interests. • *Spiritual advocates:* Individuals who provide religious justification for a party's views or positions. • *Supporters:* Parties not directly involved in negotiations who provide emotional, strategic, or tactical advice and support for a party, or through their public actions demonstrate a party's strength, resolve, and power to influence the outcome of negotiations.
Assistance with the negotiation process	• *Conveners:* Individuals, groups, coalitions, organizations, or government agencies that advocate for and sponsor talks and bring parties together (usually based on some form of convening authority). • *Process advisors or designers:* Individuals or teams who advise individuals, negotiation teams, or multiple teams on effective structures, approaches, and procedures for effective deliberations and negotiations. • *Logistics coordinators:* Individuals who arrange the time, venue, and logistics for talks and ensure distribution of important documents or other materials.

Table 14.1. (*continued*)

Functions	People Who Can Provide Assistance
	• *Moderators, chairpersons, or speakers:* Individuals who oversee the conduct of meetings and may have expertise and apply parliamentary procedures. (Can be an eminent or authoritative person from one of the parties or an independent person.)
	• *Facilitators:* An individual or team that provides process assistance to facilitate communication, information exchange, problem solving, and group decision making in meetings or negotiation sessions.
	• *Process or facilitative mediators:* An individual or team that provides independent and impartial process assistance to parties in conflict to improve how they negotiate.
Assistance with information or data	• *Sounding boards and reality testers:* Individuals whose judgment or advice is respected by one or more parties, who helps them think through proposals and options for settlement or assess their best alternative to negotiated agreement (BATNA).
	• *Witnesses or testifiers:* Individuals who provide firsthand information on behalf of one or more parties engaged in negotiations regarding what has occurred in the past.
	• *Partisan researchers or technical experts:* An individual or organization who collects, analyzes, and provides technical or scientific data to one negotiator or party.
	• *Independent researchers or technical experts:* An individual or organization—accountable to all parties and negotiators—who collects, analyzes, and provides technical or scientific data and makes this information available to all concerned.
	• *Neutral appraisers:* Independent experts whose services are secured by one or more parties to assess the value of tangible items (land, property, value of a company).
	• *Historical or cultural advisors or interpreters:* Individuals such as elders or other experts knowledgeable about cultural, historical, or customary traditions and procedures for addressing and resolving issues in dispute.
	• *Legal advisors:* An individual or firm that provides legal information or advice to an individual party or a group.

(*continued overleaf*)

Table 14.1. People Who Provide Third-Party Assistance (*continued*)

Functions	*People Who Can Provide Assistance*
Assistance with information or data	• *Investigators:* An individual or team that gathers information for use by one or more parties. • *Fact finders:* An independent individual or team that gathers information related to a dispute and often makes recommendations on how to proceed to resolve it or on ensuring fair outcomes in contested issues. • *Evaluative or advisory mediators:* Independent and impartial individuals who provide process mediation assistance and substantive advice to parties about the strengths of their arguments, legal cases, or technical information and make informed recommendations on possible settlement ranges or specific terms for agreement.
Assistance to memorialize, record, or draft agreements	• *Witnesses or testifiers:* Respected observers of negotiations, settlements reached, and promises made who will remember in the future what has been agreed on and may testify regarding terms of accords. • *In-team recorder:* Member of a negotiation team who keeps accurate notes on agreements reached or other points raised during negotiations. • *Public recorder:* An independent third party who takes public notes on a flip chart or computer/LCD projector, memorializes events or decisions at a meeting or during negotiations, and prepares an official record or minutes of the session. • *Stenographer or court reporter:* An independent third party who makes a verbatim transcript of deliberations or decisions made in a meeting or negotiation. • *Audiovideo technician:* An individual who makes audio or video records of activities or agreements in a meeting or negotiation session. • *Legal draftspersons, lawyers, solicitors:* Individuals who draft agreements reached through negotiations in formal legal language and documents. • *Drafting committees:* A group—either participants to negotiations, their representatives, or their lawyers—charged by all parties to draft a formal settlement document memorializing agreements reached through negotiations.

Table 14.1. (*continued*)

Functions	People Who Can Provide Assistance
Third-party decision-making assistance	• *Trusted individual:* A person respected and trusted by all parties to whom authority to make a decision is delegated. • *Traditional authority, elder, or religious leader:* Individuals empowered by tradition or the customs of a community to make a decision for parties involved in disputes, based on customary law or practice. • *Independent arbitrator:* An impartial individual or panel selected by parties to a dispute or appointed by a legitimate authority that is authorized to make a nonbinding or binding decision on issues in dispute, depending on the will of the parties. • *Administrative or managerial decision maker:* A representative of an organization empowered to make binding decisions on issues in dispute, usually based on administrative or managerial authority or organizational policies or rules. • *Judge, magistrate, or justice of the peace:* An official of a court who has legal authority to make judgments and binding decisions concerning the guilt or innocence of parties, merits of claims, and appropriate compensation for damages related to issues in dispute. • *Jury:* A body of persons authorized to judge and give a verdict on a contested issue. • *Legislature:* A legally selected and constituted body mandated to make policies and laws and settle conflicts commonly through voting and majority rule.

Third-party decision makers can assist negotiators in a number of ways. They can break deadlocks over "whether" questions (whether something was or should be done) or questions of merit (whether a party's claim or case has legitimacy and merit). They can also make decisions on "how" questions (what should be done to address a problem, right a wrong, make a claimant whole, or define the amount to be awarded to address a claim). Depending on what is requested by parties or required of the decision maker and the process, decisions on "whether" questions can break an impasse, and decisions on "how" questions can be referred back to parties for further talks and negotiations.

Dispute Resolution Systems

Dispute resolution systems are institutionalized mechanisms and procedures, including specific rules, processes, and designated personnel, that assist people to resolve conflicts. Systems have been established worldwide to resolve a wide range of issues, including:

- Labor-management disputes (Ury, Brett, and Goldberg, 1988; Costantino and Merchant, 1996; Westin and Feliu, 1988; Slaikeu and Hasson, 1998; Woodrow, 1998; *Guidelines for the Design of Integrated Conflict Management Systems*, 2000; CDR Associates, 2001; Lipsky, Seeber, and Fincher, 2003)

- Human rights conflicts (CDR Associates, 2006)

- Natural resource conflicts (Final Settlement Stipulation, 2003; Moore and Santosa, 1995; Atkins and Wildau, 2008; Moore and Brown, 2009)

- Company-community disputes (Wildau, Atkins, Moore, and O'Neill, 2008; Zandvliet and Anderson, 2009)

- Intense political or ethnic conflicts (Peck, 1996; Moore, 1993, 1994; Moore and Brown, 2009)

Systems may be quite simple and merely detail a process for resolving differences. An example is a contract clause in a business agreement that describes the steps the parties will take if and when a dispute arises (CPR Institute for Dispute Resolution, 2000). It may stipulate that when parties encounter a dispute, they will first try to resolve it through negotiation. If they are unsuccessful, they will try mediation, and if they still are not able to reach an agreement, they will submit the dispute to binding arbitration for a decision.

Systems can also be more complex and address a wide range of issues, problems, or disputes. Figure 14.2 describes an employee grievance mechanism that one of us helped design for a large international company. It details common components and steps for resolving these kinds of disputes.

Figure 14.3 presents a more complex grievance mechanism for resolving company-community disputes, which often occur in international development projects.

This system provides a range of possible dispute resolution procedures, including the company's suggesting a potential solution to resolve a complaint, capacity building and training of parties in effective negotiation procedures, third-party input or coaching, unassisted or assisted (mediated) talks, use of local customary procedures, or referral of contested issues to a third-party decision maker.

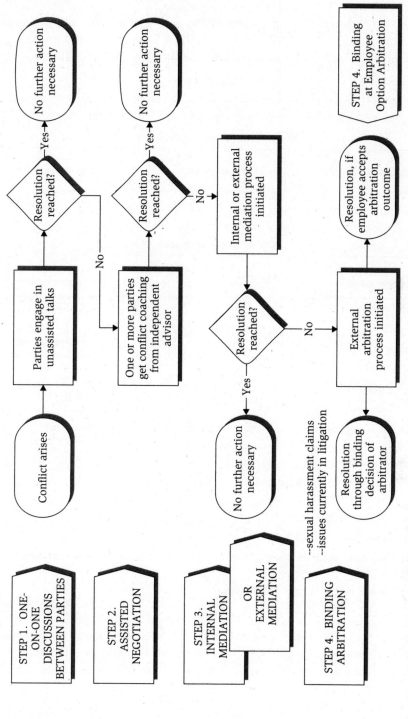

Figure 14.2. Labor-Management Dispute Resolution System

403

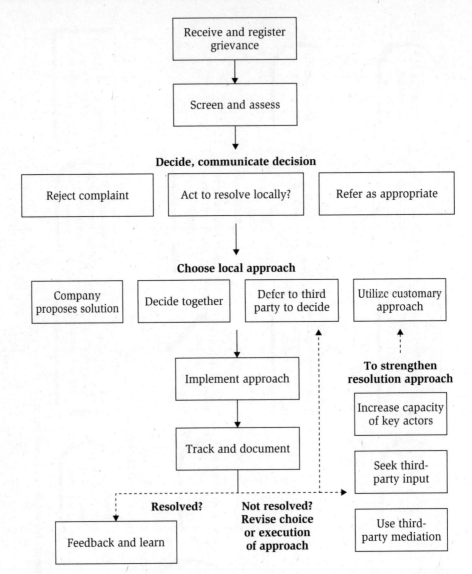

Figure 14.3. Grievance Mechanisms with Multiple Local Approaches to Resolving Complaints

Source: Wildau, Atkins, Moore, and O'Neill (2008).

For dispute or grievance resolution systems to be most effective, they need to be established before disputes arise. Procedures should be established and trained personnel prepared to assist disputants if and when they need them.

CONCLUSION

Negotiators who encounter difficulties or reach an impasse should consider whether help from one or more of the people described above or utilization of services of a dispute resolution system might help move talks forward. The kinds of assistance sought should be grounded in parties' assessment of the causes of problems to be handled and conform to cultural assumptions or norms regarding assistance. Once identified, appropriate people and roles can be determined and their involvement in talks secured. The next chapter looks at two of the most common forms of assistance, mediation and facilitation, in detail.

CHAPTER FIFTEEN

Facilitation and Mediation

The three parties had engaged in multiple violent conflicts in the past, but now they were willing to negotiate agreements that could result in joint benefits. The first negotiation meetings had established preliminary procedures and topics for future talks. The third meeting opened on a relatively cordial tone. However, shortly after the agenda review and opening statements, one of the parties insisted that their technical expert make a presentation that would outline the past harm and unfairness they had suffered, and continued to suffer, at the hands of one of the other parties. Although everyone agreed to hear the presentation, it did not take long for the spokesperson of the targeted party to explode and interrupt the presenter. "If I had known that I would be submitted to this rubbish and lies, I would never have come to talk. I'm ready to walk out!" he exclaimed. "Well, if you won't listen, we're leaving too!" retorted his counterpart who, fuming, stood up and moved to a table at the back of the room.

The mediator who was chairing the joint session asked the parties not to leave and requested a twenty-minute adjournment to allow him to talk with the parties separately. In each of the private meetings, he encouraged the parties to talk about what had happened. Both expressed how angry and frustrated they were with their counterpart's attitude and behavior. The intermediary then explored what their interests were about the presentation and its content. After talking with both of them separately, the mediator began to shuttle between them to explore what would be acceptable regarding continuing or discontinuing the presentation and under what conditions they would return to talks. With permission from each party, he shared the proposed conditions with the other. However, he made it clear that if they returned to negotiations, they would need to explain directly to each other why the issue was so important to them. Ultimately, the parties agreed to halt the presentation at this time, and a written outline of the presentation would be made available if any party requested it.

When the parties returned to joint talks, the spokesperson for the party that had made the presentation explained that it was important for their counterpart to recognize how much they had suffered and the unfairness of past arrangements between them. However, he agreed to move on to a discussion of issues that might result in mutual benefits and an agreement. In response, the other party acknowledged that it was hard to hear criticism that he did not believe was merited. However, they recognized that the past had been very hard for the other negotiator's people and indicated a willingness to develop agreements that would help address their concerns and result in future mutual gains. They also each thanked their counterpart for being willing to proceed with talks. With these exchanges, negotiations proceeded to a productive end (involvement of one of the authors in an international mediation process).

༂

In the previous chapter, we presented an overview of the range of assistance available to meeting participants and negotiators. We now turn to more detailed discussion of two key forms of third-party help: facilitation and mediation. We start with definitions of these terms.

AN INTRODUCTION TO FACILITATION AND MEDIATION

Facilitation is a process that enhances the effectiveness and outcomes of talks or meetings by promoting effective communication, information exchange, deliberations, and, when appropriate, decision making. It involves the assistance of a third party, a facilitator, who designs and conducts the meeting process but remains impartial regarding the substantive focus of the group's work. This form of intermediary has no decision-making authority regarding issues in question.

Facilitation is generally used to reach agreement on issues where there are only low or moderate levels of disagreement or tension among participants. It may also be used in high-conflict situations to solicit input or engage in preparatory or parallel dialogues on the issues, without a goal of reaching agreements. Effective facilitation can assist participants in achieving a variety of goals and outcomes. A facilitator can help build productive working relationships, clarify issues of concern, promote effective information exchange, increase mutual understanding, encourage discussion of important issues, focus parties on problem solving, and enable people to make consensus decisions (Ghais, 2005). Facilitators may be group members or independent external third parties.

Facilitators are often used in the context of meetings, retreats, workshops, training programs, and dialogue sessions—none of them aimed at a negotiated solution to problems, although some forms of decision making may be involved. Facilitators can also be used to assist a negotiation process—although at that point their role is often almost indistinguishable from that of a mediator. However, in some instances, parties may, for some reason, be sensitive about the term *mediator* and ask for the help of a "facilitator," thinking that they are establishing a distinctly different role. They may in fact limit the facilitator role in specific ways. For instance, during peace negotiations between 2002 and 2004, the government of Sri Lanka and the Liberation Tigers of Tamil Eelam decided to enlist the help of Norway and asked for a facilitation team. In doing so, the parties explicitly stated that for political reasons and their relationship with their constituents, they did not want the Norwegians to be very directive in terms of the agenda or facilitation process and did not want them to be directly engaged in the development of concrete proposals that could be explored with the parties.

Mediation is a conflict resolution process that helps negotiators resolve serious differences, disputes, or conflicts in a voluntary and mutually acceptable manner. It involves the assistance of a third party, a mediator, who has no power or authority to make a binding decision or impose any outcome on disputing parties. Mediators help negotiators effectively address contentious and difficult relationship, procedural, substantive, or structural issues.

Although the practice of mediation varies significantly across cultures (Lee and Hwee, 2009; Murithi, 2006; Moore, 2003; Goh, 2002; McConnell, 1995; Augsburger, 1992; Kellman, 1992), in general mediators assist negotiators to resolve conflicts through a variety of types of interventions—for example:

- Identifying or creating acceptable venues and forums for negotiations
- Bringing parties together and convening productive talks
- Providing the hope, security, and safety necessary for the discussion of difficult and often highly emotion-laden issues
- Helping parties acknowledge issues and problems from the past but focus on the future
- Assisting in rebuilding damaged working relationships, facilitating the establishment of positive new ones, and promoting reconciliation between parties

- Managing and improving communications
- Providing opportunities for appropriate expression of emotions
- Working with parties to design an effective process for negotiations and productive strategies for addressing specific issues
- Promoting information exchange and deeper mutual understanding of issues, needs, interests, and concerns
- Proposing effective problem-solving procedures
- Suggesting productive option-generation approaches, encouraging parties to suggest interest-based options, and helping invent creative solutions that address multiple interests
- Helping parties evaluate options and compare them to their best alternatives to negotiation (BATNAs) and worst alternatives to negotiation (WATNAs) away from the table
- Facilitating a process for adding, modifying, refining, or dropping options to make agreement more acceptable
- Identifying and building agreements on individual issues or packages of linked issues and agreements
- Providing (when appropriate and agreed to by all parties) substantive input or recommendations on potential solutions
- Recognizing, articulating, and confirming agreements on specific issues or broader sets of topics
- Drafting the language of agreements for further consideration by the parties and their advisors or superiors
- Helping parties reach psychological closure so that they can move forward on agreements, either individually or together
- Providing, on occasion, oversight and monitoring of the implementation of agreements

Negotiators often ask when it is appropriate to ask for the help of a facilitator or a mediator. The answer is: when parties are no longer able to make progress on their own toward achieving their goals or objectives. But how do you determine whether to select a facilitator versus a mediator? The answer depends on a number of factors: the level of assistance and amount of direction parties perceive they need to address their issues or conflicts; the degree to which relationships are strained or polarized; parties' level of adherence to positions and a positional negotiations approach (as opposed to interest-based procedures); and parties' expectations, needs and interests. These variables are detailed in Table 15.1.

Table 15.1. Comparison of Facilitation and Mediation

	Facilitation/Facilitator	Mediation/Mediator
Primary participants	Assembly of individuals, members of a group, or representatives of multiple groups	Primary individuals or parties to a dispute or conflict, negotiation teams, and possibly secondary or other concerned parties
Forums	Primarily meetings but can also be used in negotiations	Negotiation sessions
When used and issues or problems addressed	Used in situations where meeting participants have no, low, or moderate differences. In high-conflict situations, may be used to facilitate provision of information or solicit input, but not to make decisions	Used to resolve serious differences, disputes, or conflicts when parties are deeply divided over relationship, procedural, or substantive issues
Formats of meetings or sessions	Generally whole-group meetings or combination of whole- and small-group sessions, with a mix of individuals or interest group representatives in each	Joint sessions involving all key parties, private meetings of parties (caucuses) with or without involvement of the mediator, small problem-solving or work groups with mixed representatives of all parties, meetings of parties' spokespersons (with or without the mediator), meetings of parties and their superiors or constituents, and the mediator shuttling between private meetings with individual parties
Nature of participation	Participation in the process is generally voluntary	Participation in the process is generally voluntary, but under certain circumstances (such as in court-mandated mediation) may be compulsory. However, reaching agreement is totally voluntary

(continued overleaf)

Table 15.1. Comparison of Facilitation and Mediation (*continued*)

	Facilitation/Facilitator	Mediation/Mediator
Assistance provided	Relationship establishing and building and procedural assistance	Relationship establishing and building and procedural assistance, and possible (with the agreement or request of the parties) nonbinding substantive advice
Direction by the third party	Low to moderate regarding process; none on substantive issues	Moderate to high regarding process, and low, moderate, or high regarding substance, depending on the situation, will, request, or acceptance by the parties
Decision-making authority of the third party	Advisory regarding process, and none on substance	Advisory and nonbinding regarding process. None or nonbinding regarding any substantive suggestions on how to resolve issues in dispute depending on the will, request, or acceptance by the parties
Outcomes	Redefined or improved relationships between or among group members, greater understanding of issues, information exchange, and, if appropriate, consensus recommendations or agreements	Redefined or improved relationships and consensus agreements and decisions between or among parties concerning issues in dispute

Additional factors may be in play when parties are deciding whether to use the services of a facilitator or mediator, especially when they are in conflict. In more collectivist and indirect-dealing cultures, the use of an intermediary is embedded in the culture and is often an expected practice. Therefore, whether to use an intermediary, no matter what this person is called, may not be a question at all.

In direct-dealing and individualistic cultures, use of intermediaries is not as common as in collectivist societies. The parties expect to manage and resolve differences on their own without any external assistance (with the possible exception of lawyers) and often engage an intermediary only when talks have totally broken down, or conflicts have escalated to the point that the parties are polarized and costs and risks are escalating. Even then, the parties may be reluctant to engage the services of a mediator. It may be less threatening and more socially and politically acceptable in terms of the parties' self-image or the perceptions of outside observers to request the help of a "facilitator" to address "issues" or "differences," than to engage a "mediator" to help resolve a "conflict."

In addition, disputants who are not familiar with the voluntary nature of mediation, and the fact that control of all decisions ultimately rests exclusively with them, may be concerned that a mediator will be too directive, take sides, twist arms, tell them what to do, or force them to agree. (Mediator styles vary considerably. Some mediators provide process assistance, are not highly directive, and do not provide any input on substantive issues in dispute. Others may provide substantive suggestions in areas where they have expertise, if the parties request it. While no mediator has the authority to impose a decision, some do facilitate apologies to improve relationships, use logic and persuasion to encourage agreement, help parties conduct cost-benefit analysis of settlement options and may exert pressure, if they have it, to encourage parties to reach an accord. Note that coercive pressure—such as the possibility of sanctions or armed force—is usually only available to mediators from strong nations or international organizations.) Parties may also confuse mediation with arbitration where a third party is empowered to make a decision. For these reasons, some parties request the services of a facilitator, even when what they really need is the somewhat more directive help of a mediator. To overcome this barrier, some mediators agree to be designated as a facilitator, moderator, or provider of good offices to avoid a term or role that is emotionally or politically unacceptable to one or more parties.

A final factor in the selection of a mediator or facilitator is the level of confidentiality that can be assured to participants in a facilitated or mediated process. In many legal jurisdictions, including many in the United States, laws, rules, or regulations protect mediators and the confidentiality of mediated talks. These protections are generally not available to facilitators and facilitated meetings. These regulations recognize mediation as private settlement negotiations, and mediators cannot be subpoenaed to testify in a court of law about what occurred in the talks should negotiations fail and parties decide to pursue a judicial decision.

VARIATIONS IN THE PRACTICE OF MEDIATION

The practice of mediation differs significantly around the world. Negotiators should become familiar with the range of relationships intermediaries may have with disputing parties, their sources and forms of authority and influence, and variations in practice in order to make wise and informed choices about an appropriate intermediary. Moore (2003) identified five kinds of intercultural mediators:

- *Social network mediators*—trusted individuals who are part of the parties' social network, who may or may not be totally impartial regarding issues in question, but whom disputants believe can be of help

- *Benevolent mediators*—respected high-status and authoritative individuals whom disputants go to for advice and help in developing acceptable agreements

- *Administrative or managerial mediators*—persons who occupy formal positions in organizations and have the authority to make decisions about contested issues, but for a variety of reasons prefer to assist disputants to negotiate their own agreements within parameters prescribed by the organization

- *Vested interest mediators*—powerful individuals or parties who are not neutral toward disputants or impartial regarding issues in question, have a strong interest in the outcome of a dispute, and encourage, cajole, or coerce parties to agree

- *Independent mediators*—intermediaries who are neutral regarding their relations with parties and impartial regarding issues in dispute, who provide process assistance, and on occasion, at the request of the parties, independent substantive advice

Three cultural factors affect who serves in the mediator role and the functions they perform and how: whether one or more parties or the intermediary is from an egalitarian or hierarchical culture, prefers direct or indirect dealing and communication, and is oriented toward individualism or collectivism. Members of hierarchical cultures tend to prefer mediators with high status and authority based on their position in society or social or political institutions (Brett, 2007). Generally authoritative intermediaries are more directive and take control of both the process and the substantive issues in question. Although they do not have final authority to make a binding decision, they are likely to provide advice, instruct parties as to how they should resolve their differences, and apply personal or social pressure on the parties. For instance, Chinese mediators from the Peoples' Mediation Committee in the People's Republic of China and some commercial mediators from Hong Kong or Singapore are likely to follow this pattern of authoritative intervention. Similarly, community mediators in Sri Lanka are typically selected for their recognized position in society—and often strongly encourage or put pressure on one or more parties to accept a proposed settlement. Buddhist monks acting as mediators have used appeals based on a party's storing up merit and getting off the wheel of life (that is, getting to nirvana faster) for reaching agreements or reestablishing harmony.

Conversely, parties from more individualist cultures, such as the United States, northern Europe, Australia, and New Zealand, are more likely to select mediators with less positional authority or status, more substantive expertise, and experience resolving contested issues in question. Members of these cultures, both parties and intermediaries, also expect third parties to be less directive than in collectivist societies and to leave significant control over both the process and substantive outcome to the parties themselves. Even in the mediation of court cases in these cultures, where a mediator may be expected to evaluate the parties' legal cases and provide advice on settlement, negotiators expect to have a significant degree of control over the final outcome.

Members of direct-dealing cultures, where face-to-face communications, problem solving, and negotiations are the norm, are more likely to prefer mediators who are comfortable conducting most of the mediation process in joint session. (Possible exceptions are some lawyer-mediators and international mediators from direct-dealing cultures who are more comfortable working in separate meetings, or caucuses, with individual parties, rather than in joint session, or where there is the likelihood that expression of strong emotions may deadlock direct talks.) Conversely, members of indirect-dealing cultures, where saving face, preserving honor, and avoiding potential verbal or physical confrontations are high priorities, generally prefer intermediaries who are likely to shuttle between them and develop agreements through indirect exchanges and private meetings. As we have seen, members of the majority cultures in North America and northern Europe are more likely to be direct dealers, and members of some, but not all, Latin American and Asian cultures are more likely to be indirect dealers.

The cultural continuum between individualism and collectivism also influences the selection, procedures, and approaches of both parties and mediators. Members of individualistic cultures generally prefer mediators who focus exclusively on the issues and concerns of the primary parties. Broader parties and their interests are generally not deemed appropriate topics for talks, nor are they often involved. In collectivist cultures, parties often select mediators they believe will not only consider the primary parties' interests, but will also account for those of other potentially affected individuals and groups in a broader institution or community. The intermediary is expected to balance any outcome with its impacts on others who may or may not be directly involved.

The three variables noted above are the central factors that influence the desired qualifications and selection of mediators across cultures. However, a number of other factors influence the practice of mediation and selection of a mediator.

Membership in Any of the Parties' Cultures

If all parties, including the mediator, are from the same culture, they will likely share cultural understandings. For this reason, many parties prefer a mediator from their own culture because they believe this will help minimize the cultural noise that can interfere with productive talks. However, this is not always the case. Most cultures are made up of diverse subcultures, based on differences in gender, caste, class, social status, education, professional affiliation, religion, and so forth. Some of these factors often prove to be more influential on an intermediary's understanding of a party's culture than membership in the overarching common one. For instance, we have served as mediators in large multiparty environmental disputes in the United States, where the organizational cultures and decision-making processes of the business representatives are in stark contrast to the normal operating procedures of the environmental community, not to mention the bureaucratic cultures of state and federal representatives. Even when all participants are from the dominant U.S. culture, they come from sharply different subcultures, which often impede negotiations and provide cultural challenges for mediators. When Native American tribal representatives are added to the mix, cultural factors often become a primary concern.

Particular issues and dynamics may arise if a mediator shares the culture of one party but not that of another. There is a possibility that the intermediary will better understand the party from his or her shared culture than a person or group from the other. The mediator may also be seen by the party who is not a member of the mediator's culture as being more sympathetic to the counterpart's views and not totally neutral or impartial. One way to address this potential problem is to use comediators—one from each of the parties' cultures (if it is a two-party conflict). Another approach is to include a comediator who is not from any of the parties' cultures. This was an important factor in the selection of a mediation team involved in resolving a dispute among several African countries. The intermediary team included members who were not from any of the parties' cultures.

A final configuration occurs when the parties share the same culture and the mediator is from a different one. In this situation, there is the likelihood that the parties will better understand their own internal cultural issues and dynamics than will the third party. In this case, the mediator will need to work closely with disputants to understand their specific cultural perspectives toward negotiations and criteria for agreement making. Some mediators will also seek a cultural interpreter—a person whom the mediator can consult when he or she suspects that layers of meaning (linguistic, interpersonal, or political) are being missed. Such a person might be completely outside the negotiation setting but could also be someone in the talks. At times the language interpreter can play this role, depending on this person's temperament and political savvy.

Language Ability

Communications across cultures are never easy, and the difficulty is compounded when the parties or the intermediary do not speak each other's languages. Understanding meanings, nuances, and nonverbal communications is often critical for agreement making. For this reason, many parties prefer mediators who speak their languages, but this is not always possible.

When mediators and parties speak different languages, a host of potential problems in communications and relationships arise. If more than one language is being used and one of the parties and the intermediary share one of them, the party who does not speak that language may be at a disadvantage because of the barrier to direct communication with the intermediary. Mediators may also gravitate toward parties with whom they can easily communicate. Addressing this problem requires good and readily available interpretation. Ideally mediators should have their own interpreter to interpret directly what is being said by the parties or to verify the interpretation provided by parties' interpreters.

There are two choices for interpretation: consecutive or simultaneous. In consecutive interpretation, a speaker makes a series of statements (usually no more than a few sentences), and the interpreter subsequently repeats everything said in the second language. This process is repeated for chunks of information. Statements can be interpreted verbatim (more commonly) or in the form of a summary. Simultaneous interpretation occurs a split second after a message is spoken, and when it is done well, it provides as close to a verbatim statement of what has actually been said substantively as possible. Especially in large group sessions, simultaneous translation requires the use of complex and expensive audio equipment (headsets and microphones). Both interpretation processes can be effective in communicating the substantive content of what has been said. However, both may have difficulty communicating the emotional meaning or tone of messages, although much of that is transmitted nonverbally.

Some mediators and parties prefer consecutive to simultaneous interpretation because it allows them to watch the body language of speakers and have more time to think and reflect before responding, as they wait for everything to be repeated in another language. Other intermediaries and negotiators prefer simultaneous interpretation because it more accurately reflects the immediate flow and pace of the communication and what has been said.

Another language problem arises with respect to draft and final agreements if these are written in two languages. One of our CDR Associates Partners provided mediation services to several nations negotiating agreements on nuclear issues in the Arctic. Reconciliation of the final agreement in both

Russian and English took hours of painstaking and cooperative work among the two principal translators and the mediation team as they reviewed each word and phrase to make sure that the two documents had the same precise meaning.

Outsiders or Insiders

An important criterion for selection of a mediator is whether the person is an insider, quasi-ally, or an outsider in terms of his or her relationship to one or more parties or the issues in question (Lederach, 1991; Wehr and Lederach, 1996; Mason and Wils, 2009). Insiders are individuals or groups who are known and have an ongoing relationship with one or more of the involved parties. They may have been involved in providing advice or making decisions in the past and may be subject to reciprocal expectations or obligations. Government officials, managers, chiefs, and village elders often serve in this capacity.

Quasi-allies are individuals or groups who do not have a direct relationship with one or more parties and no or few reciprocal obligations, but they do share some of their views, concerns, and interests. They may also have some leverage or influence over one or more of the parties. In this sense, they are a potential ally of a party. In some circumstances, using insiders or quasi-allies as facilitators or mediators can increase trust and comfort for all concerned, especially if all of the parties are from the same culture or group and the intermediary is seen to be fair and objective. Interestingly, in some other situations, a party who is not from the same group as the counterpart may also prefer to use insiders or quasi-allies of the counterpart as facilitators or mediators because these relationships may provide more influence on the counterpart.

One example was when the United States approached Algerian diplomats in 1980 to mediate the release of American hostages being held by Iran. Algeria, whose diplomats were not close politically to the Islamic Revolution or Iran's leaders, was a Muslim country, a member of the anticolonial and nonaligned bloc, and it had often been critical of U.S. foreign policy. In spite of its commonalities with Iran, Algeria was seen by the United States as a viable intermediary because Algeria wanted to increase its political influence and stature in the world, be seen as an advocate for human rights and international law, and its potential to influence Iran.

Outsiders are individuals external to a dispute and disputing parties, who do not have a specific relationship or significant obligations to any of those involved. They typically have a more objective view of issues to be negotiated or resolved. In many conflicts, parties prefer an outsider, whom they believe will be more impartial and less likely to be buffeted by interpersonal or intergroup connections, obligations, or ongoing relationships than an insider.

Timing of Entry to the Process

Cultural differences influence the timing of when an intermediary actually enters a problem or dispute to provide assistance. Members of cultures that are indirect dealing invite intermediaries in earlier than those that are direct dealing—in fact, intermediaries may be involved throughout the process, from beginning to end.

On occasion, members of direct-dealing cultures are willing to use a facilitator early in a process to address problematic issues, but they often wait until they have been unable to start talks or they have broken down before engaging a mediator. Unfortunately, late entry of a mediator can cause challenging relationship and substantive dynamics for both the parties and the intermediary; these are not as difficult if assistance is provided earlier in the process. Increasingly justice systems and policy arenas in direct-dealing cultures require the use of mediation at specific stages of dispute resolution, especially when potential or actual litigation is involved. For instance, in some states and court jurisdictions in the United States and Canada, certain kinds of court cases must be taken to mediation before a judge will hear them.

Partial or Impartial Toward the Parties

In general, parties prefer mediators who are impartial and not biased for or against any party (Brett, 2007). Another way to look at this is that the intermediary has a positive commitment to help all parties address and satisfy their interests to the greatest extent possible. However, in some circumstances, especially in intercultural negotiations, the parties may select an intermediary who is not totally impartial or even leans toward the views or interests of one of the parties (Commaroff and Roberts, 1981). In selecting a mediator, parties need to determine whether trust and belief in fairness, even though the third party may not be totally impartial, is an adequate criterion, or whether they expect the mediator to be totally impartial.

Orchestrators or Deal Makers

Orchestrators and deal makers are two "ideal types" of mediators (Kolb, 1983). Orchestrators believe that mediation is an extension of the negotiation process with the procedural assistance, as necessary, of a third party. They are often referred to as process or facilitative mediators (Mayer, 2004). In general, orchestrators trust the parties to negotiate their own agreements. They believe that negotiators are well informed about the issues in question and that what parties need is assistance with the negotiation process—and they provide as much as the parties need or request. They provide limited advice or recommendations on the substantive issues in dispute. In this respect, they are similar to facilitators. Orchestrators often serve as catalysts for agreement making and may be asked to intervene only during difficult moments or when an impasse has occurred.

Deal makers have a very different orientation toward negotiations, mediation, and the mediation process. In general, mediators who take this approach believe that parties have only limited capacities to reach negotiated agreements on their own. They see the parties as ineffective bargainers, highly entrenched in their views and positions, and unable to break their deadlock without major changes in the negotiation process and direct intervention from the intermediary. Mediators with this orientation are directive both procedurally and substantively. They try to ascertain each party's bottom line and provide advice or recommendations on potential settlement options. They often encourage negotiators to make a deal and settle on a package crafted by the mediator. In general, most mediators are not totally one type or the other, but each has a tendency toward one orientation. More details about variations of each of these orientations follow:

∞

• *Substantively directive versus substantively nondirective.* Substantively directive mediators have extensive knowledge and experience regarding specific issues that the negotiators are addressing. In fact, their assistance is often sought by parties explicitly because of their expertise. Such mediators are frequently referred to as evaluative mediators because they typically assess parties' positions, analyze and question data that are presented, evaluate the merits of claims, give advice, and make recommendations or proposals for concrete settlement ranges or terms for agreement. For instance, in the United States, there are mediators in the environmental field who have become experts at assessing and allocating responsibility to multiple parties in environmental cleanup settlements.

• *Procedurally nondirective versus procedurally directive.* This variable refers to how directive a mediator is in terms of guiding or controlling the process for mediated negotiations. Some intermediaries provide only minimal direction and make few process suggestions, which parties are free to accept or reject. Other mediators are quite directive in terms of process, take control of the negotiations, and expect parties to accede to their decisions concerning procedures. A third group of intermediaries consults extensively with the parties and designs the process with them.

∞

Orchestrators and deal makers are found in almost all cultures and countries. In selecting a facilitator or mediator, negotiators need to be clear about how directive they want their intermediary to be in terms of substance and process.

Focus on Relationships, Task, or Both

Facilitators and mediators also vary regarding their focus on relationship issues or substantive issues or tasks. Some mediators, such as those who practice transformative or therapeutic mediation (Bush and Folger, 1994; Gold, 1994), place a high priority on improving the relationships among parties. Some advocate that this should be the primary goal for the process (Bush and Folger, 1994). Other mediators and facilitators focus principally on assisting parties to address substantive issues and spend little time or energy on relationship problems.

In real-life relations between parties and the mediator, there should not be a dichotomy between these two approaches. A good mediator should be able to focus on either relationship or substantive issues, depending on the circumstances, needs, or interests of the parties. In some cases, a relationship focus may be appropriate and needed to build trust and respect and move parties toward more productive problem solving. A concentration on relationships may be especially important if the parties are likely to engage in future interactions. However, improvements in a relationship are rarely sufficient to settle a dispute. Settlement of substantive or procedural issues will also be required for a sustainable agreement.

Where the Work of Negotiations Takes Place

This factor concerns where the work of negotiations takes place and where facilitators or mediators provide their assistance. At one extreme are intermediaries who work exclusively, or almost exclusively, in plenary sessions with both or all parties in the room working together on the issues (Friedman and Himmelstein, 2009). They prefer this forum because it encourages transparency in decision making, promotes direct communications, develops greater understanding, and fosters growth in trust (or avoids creating mistrust due to deliberations conducted out of sight). Plenary work also minimizes opportunities for the intermediary to manipulate information or the process or construct a solution that is not based on the participants' own efforts or desires. Finally, it encourages the parties to engage directly with each other in developing an agreement, thereby laying the foundation for future unassisted problem solving when an intermediary is no longer involved.

At the other extreme are mediators who conduct most of their work in private meetings with individual parties. They may begin in a joint mediation session but then rapidly transition to private sessions with each party, shuttling between them. Mediators who extensively use private meetings to forge agreements (variously called caucuses, pendulum, or proximity talks or shuttle diplomacy) exchange only information with parties that moves them toward agreement. Some intermediaries prefer this mode of operation because they can control communications, substantive offers, and the development of settlement packages that they can successfully "sell" to all sides. In some circumstances, mediators choose this approach due to concerns about extreme polarization on issues, rigidly held positions and highly divergent interests, or concerns about the expression of strong emotions or even the possibility of violence if parties were to meet in joint sessions. Some mediators use this approach because they are uncomfortable working in joint sessions, where substantive exchanges and emotional expression can become difficult or heated.

Once again, the two extremes are ideal types. Most mediators throughout the world use a combination of joint and private meetings as appropriate and required by the situation (Moore, 2003).

Knowledge About the Issues

An important issue in mediation (but less of an issue in facilitation) is how much substantive knowledge an intermediary needs about the issues under discussion. One school of thought argues that knowledge of group dynamics; communications skills; effective problem-solving and negotiation procedures; and mediation approaches, strategies, and tactics are all that is required for an effective intervention. The parties themselves or substantive experts brought in from outside are expected to provide content or knowledge needed to reach settlements—and a mediator's expertise, it is thought, will complicate the picture.

The countervailing view is that intermediaries should have specific substantive information and expertise relevant to the kinds of issues or disputes they are helping to resolve. Without this knowledge, they may not be as effective in their interventions as they could be, and they may slow coming to an agreement because the parties may have to educate the mediator about specialized language, technical issues, or standard practices. One of us once provided mediation services to the telecommunications sector, only to find that people in that field spoke to each other in a language that was ostensibly English but was completely incomprehensible to any outsider, including some of the other parties and the mediator! Here was a case where process expertise would not be sufficient. We obtained tutoring on the substantive issues in question to improve our effectiveness as an intermediary.

There is probably not a right answer to this dilemma. An intermediary who has only process expertise may not understand enough about the issues in question to provide effective process assistance. Conversely, a mediator who is a substantive expert in issues under discussion may have strong opinions about the outcomes and may fall into the trap of providing lots of advice, which may not be accurate or useful, represent only one view, and end up pushing parties to reach an agreement that is the mediator's rather than their own. In selecting a mediator, the parties must determine how much substantive knowledge the prospective intermediary needs to have about issues in question and whether they need to have this knowledge before entering negotiations or can learn as they work. In many cases, specific substantive knowledge may not be imperative if the intermediary has helped settle similar issues in the past and can learn content fairly rapidly through a situation assessment, interviews, or direct engagement with parties.

Local and Away Knowledge

Knowledge from "here" and "away" is a subset of substantive knowledge (Adler and Birkhoff, 2002). Local knowledge refers to ways of thinking and knowing things of importance, as well as cultural rituals and ways of behaving that are characteristic of a specific locale, community of people, or organization. Knowledge from "away" generally refers to information from communities or areas outside the locality of the dispute and is often defined in scientific, technical, legal, or economic terms. Knowledge from away is often seen as being more universal, as opposed to local knowledge, which is particularistic.

In selecting a facilitator or mediator, especially in intercultural problem solving or dispute resolution, it is often important for parties to determine if they need an intermediary who already knows their culture and customs or can acquire such knowledge quickly. In some cases, such expertise is necessary for understanding what is important to the parties and the issues in question. Mediators who rely on or are open to only one form of knowledge are likely to be handicapped in their ability to engage with parties who hold diverse worldviews. For example, in Ghana, an international mining company involved in resettlement of members of an affected community needed the assistance of a third party who understood the intricacies of customary land law and how local people valued property.

Authority to Decide Issues

A central variable in mediation (but not facilitation) is whether the intermediary has the authority to make or impose a decision on the parties in conflict if they cannot reach an agreement on their own. In the traditional practice of mediation, as opposed to adjudication or arbitration, the third party has no authority to make or impose a decision. Of course, mediators do have influence, but they lack the authority to make a binding decision on contested issues.

However, in certain circumstances and forms of mediation, the intermediary may have the power to make binding decisions for the parties if they cannot reach a voluntary settlement. This is common when people in positions of authority serve as mediators; have legal, administrative, or customary mandates or authority to decide contested issues; or are administrative or managerial mediators. Judges, magistrates, or justices of the peace; political, community, or religious leaders; and senior managers in the private sector or administrators in government agencies often serve as this kind of mediator.

Another situation in which an intermediary has the authority to settle irreconcilable differences is when parties voluntarily delegate this power to the mediator. In one such form, known as med-arb (short for mediation-then-arbitration), the parties agree before starting mediation that if they encounter a deadlock that they cannot break, they will accept a binding decision on the contested issue by their mediator (who on that issue becomes an arbitrator). In another form, arb-med, the intermediary hears parties' views on contested issues and makes a written binding decision. However, the decision is not immediately disclosed to the parties; they must first try mediation. If they reach a voluntary decision, theirs is implemented, and the intermediary's decision is never revealed. If they fail to reach an accord, they can request that the third party share his or her binding decision with the parties. Both procedures assure negotiators that there will be a decision on contested issues if a deadlock occurs.

Resources for Influencing Settlements

Mediators vary as to whether they bring resources to the table to influence settlements and the amount and kind of such resources. Most independent mediators, who focus exclusively on providing process assistance, do not have resources at their disposal to influence agreements or outcomes. However, other mediators are able to encourage parties to reach agreements based on their affiliation with a government agency, international organization, or an entity such as a corporation with assets and their ability to apply resources, such as financial assistance or incentives, loans, or other forms of aid. Mediators from the United States have exercised such leverage in various rounds of peace talks in the Middle East. Access to resources, to enlarge or sweeten the pie and encourage settlement, has also been a factor in the resolution of serious personnel or interorganizational conflicts.

Working Alone or as a Team

Some facilitators or mediators work alone. Others work with one or more colleagues as cofacilitators, comediators, or a team of intervenors. To some extent, the choice is based on intermediaries' personal preferences or styles, as well as perceived needs and dynamics of the involved parties. In many situations, a solo intermediary will be adequate to provide all requisite assistance. In other cases, such as those involving important intercultural dynamics, multiple parties, or difficult or technically complex issues, more than one intermediary may be needed. Some parties prefer a team of intermediaries that reflects, in its composition, the diversity of the parties themselves, based on ethnicity, nationality, gender, profession, and other characteristics. Other parties want to minimize attempts at political or economic influence on the intermediary and believe that such efforts are less likely with a mediation team. For example, the Mediation Boards of the Ministry of Justice and Law Reforms of Sri Lanka, in their community mediation program, moved to the use of mediation teams after several difficult years attempting to implement a single-mediator model, which they found that parties mistrusted and in which they were more susceptible to bribery or corruption.

Standards of Fairness

This variable refers to the standards and criteria the intermediary encourages parties to apply in deliberations. Some mediators, especially those in more closed or isolated cultures, encourage parties to apply local knowledge and standards when making decisions or evaluating options. These may be local laws or customs, traditional standards for agreements, or settlements determined through rituals. Other intermediaries encourage parties to consider broader standards, including national or international law, scientific research, technical or engineering solutions, or best practices.

On occasion, local and international standards will be at odds. This was a problem in relation to land law in East Timor after the popular referendum over independence from Indonesia and the violence that followed. Many local elders argued that customary law prohibited women from inheriting and owning land. International law, however, recognized equal rights to ownership regardless of gender. During the course of setting up a mediation system to resolve land issues, local mediators discovered that while women in some East Timorese cultures traditionally could not inherit land, they could inherit and claim ownership of all movable property: jewelry, household goods, foodstuffs, livestock, and their dowry. This realization changed the equation of power, and ultimately all parties were allowed equal claims on both land and movable property.

These two approaches to standards are not mutually exclusive; wise decisions are often grounded in both. However, the parties and the intermediary must accept that both local and external standards may provide valuable input into decision making.

Role in Monitoring and Implementation

Facilitator and mediator roles in monitoring implementation and ensuring parties' compliance with the terms of agreements vary across cultures and circumstances. In cultures where a party's word is his bond and verbal or written agreements are honored, intermediaries may have little involvement in implementation other than helping to work out details regarding roles, responsibilities, and timing. However, in other cultures, and especially in circumstances where it is expected that there will never be total closure of negotiations or on issues in question, or where agreements are expected to be worked out through ongoing interaction between parties, the involvement of a person who monitors implementation and compliance may be critical. In such cases, the intermediary may need to remain involved throughout the implementation process. This person's continued engagement and oversight can help encourage compliance and provide a forum for parties to address ongoing questions or new issues as they arise (Atkins and Wildau, 2008).

Training in Dispute Resolution

Many people serve as facilitators or mediators without any formal training. Their life experience, authoritative positions, network connections, reputations, personalities, and acceptability by concerned parties are all that is required for them to enter into disputes and be of assistance. In contrast, many facilitators and mediators are professional intermediaries with formal training and expertise in problem solving and conflict resolution. During the last thirty years, there has been considerable professionalization of the field of mediation and facilitation as intermediaries have participated in training programs, gained university certificates or degrees, undertaken internships, or worked in specialized mediation organizations. These professional intermediaries are guided by theoretical and practical knowledge, as well as experience in group dynamics, psychology, organizational development, problem solving, negotiation, mediation, law, and other relevant substantive subjects. The availability of professionally trained intermediaries provides parties with a range of qualified third parties from which to choose.

HIRING A FACILITATOR OR MEDIATOR

As they decide whether to ask for the assistance of a facilitator or mediator, and whom to select, the involved parties need to address several questions.

First, are the services of an intermediary needed, and why? Each party should reflect individually (and, ideally, together) on several questions to help them decide whether a third-party facilitator or mediator should be involved in the negotiation process:

- Have they encountered one or more serious relationship, procedural, substantive, or structural problems in the negotiation process that they are unlikely to be able to manage on their own? (See Chapter Fourteen for a list of potential problems.) If so, are these problems likely to damage relationships or the ability of the parties to work together and reach decisions?

- Are they currently not talking, or are there considerable barriers to getting talks started?

- Are any participants in negotiations from indirect-dealing cultures? Do any of the parties normally use third parties to assist them to reach negotiated agreements?

- When making decisions, do they usually rely on the assistance or advice of respected people in authority?

- Will they need to build a consensus among superiors or constituents, as commonly occurs in collectivist cultures, rather than relying on a decision by representatives directly involved in negotiations?

- Will differences in rank or status of the parties make it difficult for parties to talk directly or without assistance?

- Are strong emotions involved that will make it difficult for them to talk directly with each other?

- Is there is a risk of loss of face, damage to personal or group honor, or physical confrontation if they meet face-to-face or without the presence of a third party?

- Are administrative or judicial third-party decision-making procedures either unavailable or unacceptable to one or more of the parties? Do they prefer to come to a negotiated settlement, or would they rather a judge or arbitrator decide?

If any of the parties answer yes to most of these questions, involving a third party is probably appropriate. In the event that one party answers no to a number of the questions but the counterpart has said yes, the services of an intermediary will still probably be needed because of the perceptions, needs, or cultural orientations of the party requesting mediation assistance.

Second, what type of intermediary is required, and what assistance will they provide? If the parties decide that a third-party facilitator or mediator is desirable or needed, negotiators should consider the following questions to help them determine what kind of intermediary might be most appropriate:

- Based on answers to the questions in the section above, what are the major reasons that a facilitator or mediator might be needed? Consider specific problems, cultural norms regarding direct or indirect dealing, strong emotions, issues of face or honor, and the specific needs for third-party involvement in decision-making processes, for example.

- Are the manifest problems related mainly to communications and relationships, specific substantive issues, or the overall structure of the negotiation process? Are these generic problems—or is culture playing a major role?

- What is the focus of the negotiation process: straightforward issues (where a decision needs to be made, but there are not necessarily strong disagreements), difficult problems, specific disputes, or a broader conflict?

- How polarized are parties regarding their relationships, issues, or interests?

- Are the people involved part of an identifiable bounded family, group, team, organization, community, ethnic or religious group, or country? Such groups usually rely on internal facilitators or mediators for assistance in problem solving or dispute resolution.

- Do the parties want, need, or require an external third party to assist them?

- What kind of relationship between the intermediary and the parties is most likely to bolster positive working relationships and agreement making: insider, quasi-ally, or impartial outsider?

- Will a facilitator be more appropriate or acceptable than a mediator because the parties, issues, or interests are not highly polarized—or for other reasons related to the specific forms of assistance needed? (See Table 15.1.)

- To be effective, how directive will the third party need to be? Is relationship assistance enough? Will process assistance be adequate? Are substantive parameters or advice needed? Is greater leverage, pressure, or resources required?

Based on answers to these questions, parties will be able to make a decision regarding whether a facilitator or mediator is needed and the principal areas of focus for their assistance.

How to Find a Third Party and Select the Appropriate Person

The next step in the process is to secure the services of an acceptable and qualified intermediary. Facilitators or mediators enter disputes or conflicts a number of ways. They may:

- Enter the situation on their own initiative. This is difficult to do unless they have some connection with the parties or a good reputation.

- Be introduced to one or more disputants by someone associated with one or more of the primary parties who is concerned about the outcome or impacts of an issue, problem, or conflict on the parties themselves or a broader community.

- Respond to a request for help by one or more parties (but not necessarily all).

- Comply with a request of all parties who have talked with each other and mutually agree on the need for a facilitator or mediator.

- Be appointed by a legitimate leader, an organization, government agency, or intergovernmental body with legal or institutional authority to address conflicts and intervene in disputes. Examples include court-appointed mediators, diplomatic envoys, and special representatives of the secretary general of the United Nations.

Unilateral Intervention by an Intermediary

In some conflict situations, the relationship between the parties and their degree of polarization makes it difficult for them even to ask for the assistance of an intermediary. When this occurs, third parties may come forward on their own and offer assistance. Also, in tightly knit communities, mediators who are respected members of the social network of the parties may offer to provide assistance because they are concerned about the disputants, the dispute, and its potential impact on the community. For example, mediators who are part of the People's Mediation Committees in the People's Republic of China commonly enter unilaterally to assist in the resolution of disputes. Mediators from the U.S. Justice Department's Community Relations Service also take initiative and offer their assistance to communities to help resolve ethnic conflicts. In addition, mediators and facilitators from nongovernmental organizations frequently initiate processes of dialogue or reconciliation among conflicting parties on their own initiative. Sometimes these processes are conducted in parallel with official negotiations to provide support and address specific problems that may be impeding progress. At times, such talks begin informally and unofficially, but subsequently become associated with official processes. For example, the Italian religious Community of Sant'Egidio initiated talks among warring factions in Mozambique that evolved into official talks that played an important role in ending the protracted civil war in that country (Bartoli, 2001).

If an intermediary tries to intervene unilaterally, parties, individually or collectively, will need to answer the questions: Is the facilitator or mediator who is proposing to intervene the appropriate person to do so, and does he or she have the requisite expertise to help us? If the answers to these questions are yes and there are no serious disadvantages to accepting the intermediary's offer, the parties will have to decide how they will work with the facilitator or mediator to achieve their goals. If the answers to the questions are no, the parties will have to decide how to inform the intervenor, either directly or indirectly, that his or her services are not acceptable. Depending on the culture, the situation, or the status of the intermediary, this may be done indirectly by ignoring or not meeting with this person or agreeing to meet but not making firm commitments on next steps. In more direct-dealing cultures, rejection of an intermediary's services is more likely to be more explicit.

Unilateral Requests for Assistance by One or More Parties But Not All

On occasion, one party wants to use a facilitator or mediator but has not gained approval from his or her negotiation counterparts. If this is the case, the party who wants the help of an intermediary should consider the following possible approaches that might be acceptable or successful given the cultural sensitivities and other dynamics of the relationships with the other party or parties.

SUGESTED STRATEGIES

- Raise the idea in principle of using a facilitator or mediator, either indirectly or directly, with the counterpart before taking any initiative to contact one.

- Contact a potential intermediary directly and unilaterally, ask for assistance and request their help in contacting other parties to explore the idea of third-party assistance.

If the other party in a negotiation process has decided that he or she wants to use an intermediary and has made a unilateral contact with this person (that is, you are the party who is either reluctant or was not asked about use of a third party), you will need to decide if you have the option of refusing the use of an intermediary—either a specific proposed person or the general idea. You might also consider whether the use of a facilitator or mediator might be helpful, given the fact that your counterpart wants to use one. If the idea of using an intermediary is acceptable in principle, affirm your willingness to proceed, and explore the best way to select someone acceptable to all parties, perhaps including the person already contacted by your counterpart. If you are not interested in the assistance of a third party, explain your logic and rationale for declining and discuss how talks might proceed productively without assistance. If the specific proposed intermediary is acceptable, affirm your willingness to cooperate. If the third party is unacceptable, explain why, and consider how to secure one that is.

Requests for Assistance from All Parties

On occasion, either before a negotiation process begins or during the course of talks, parties decide that the assistance of a facilitator or mediator is desirable or essential. Once this decision has been made, parties need to work together to secure the requisite services. Prior to initiating a search, parties should address the following considerations:

- As already outlined previously: (1) What kind of assistance is needed: facilitation or mediation? (2) Will the focus be on relationship, process, or substantive assistance? (3) Is an individual intermediary or a team required? (4) How directive or prescriptive do they want the intermediary to be?

- What is the best process for finding and selecting a mediator or facilitator: recruitment, screening, interviews, selection, or some other process?

- Do the parties already know qualified candidates or organizations? Can one party conduct a search, or must all parties participate in the selection process?

- What will the interview and selection process be, and how will a decision be made, and based on what criteria?

- What will the parties do if they cannot reach an agreement on an intermediary?

Interviewing Candidate Facilitators or Mediators

During an interview, parties may want to ask potential candidates some of the questions set out in Box 15.1.

Appointed Facilitators or Mediators

In some conflicts, the parties do not have a choice over whether they have an intermediary or who will serve in that role. The decision to appoint a third party is made by an individual, department, or organization with the authority to intervene and promote the resolution of disputes.

The question of the choice of the intermediary and whether parties have a choice in the matter is an important one. In some cases, an organization may provide a list of recognized intermediaries for the parties to select from. In others, the intervenor may be appointed with minimal or no input or choice on the part of parties. For instance, the U.N. secretary general usually appoints his special representatives to conflict zones with some but not necessarily extensive consultation with the parties involved—although if a country or countries objected, he would take that into consideration. Similarly, the U.S. president frequently appoints special envoys for the Middle East peace process. These envoys serve at the president's pleasure, although they might be recalled if their credibility and acceptability with key parties in the region has deteriorated.

Defining the Role of the Third Party

Once a facilitator or mediator (individual or team) has been selected and depending on the context of issues to be addressed, parties often develop a clear contract, terms of reference, a Memorandum of Understanding, or a protocol for mediation that specifies the services and activities expected of the intermediary. This kind of explicit documentation is common in low-context cultures. In a high-context culture, the role of the intermediary would be culturally understood, and no one would need or expect an explicit contract. Where there is a mix of low-context and high-context participants, the need and form of an agreement with the intermediary should be negotiated among the parties.

Box 15.1. Potential Interview Questions for Facilitators or Mediators

- What is your understanding of the issues, problem, dispute, or conflict we are striving to address?
- Why do you want to work with us?
- Please give some examples of your experience in handling issues or problems that are similar to ours. What have been some of your successes and challenges? What have you learned about successful interventions or assistance?
- What is your general approach to designing an appropriate process?
- What substantive, procedural, or relationship knowledge or expertise do you have that might be relevant in providing us with assistance?
- Do you have any past, current, or future relationships with any of the involved parties that might influence your approach to intervention or issues to be discussed?
- How do you believe that your cultural background might influence your relationships with the parties or your assistance?
- What do you know about the cultures of the parties, and have you had any previous involvement with people from similar backgrounds?
- What is your approach to management of the facilitation or mediation process? How directive are you? How do you involve the parties in planning the process?
- Regarding our issues or dispute, what do you think might be most problematic? How might you help us address these problems?
- What kind of advice can you offer in advance of an assisted negotiation process?
- What questions do you have for us?

Assuming that some form of document or contract is needed, the parties and the facilitator or mediator should discuss and agree on the following issues:

- The scope of work and services expected
- The general process to be used by the intermediary, the degree of substantive input expected or desired by parties, and the level of direction or control delegated to the third party
- The projected time line for the talks, meetings, or negotiations
- Projected costs (either hourly rate, daily rate, by phases of the intervention, or a fixed price for the total process), and how and when services will be billed.

CONCLUSION

The presence and assistance of a mediator or facilitator contributes to the success of negotiations, especially if they involve difficult or sensitive subjects or conflicts. In some cultures, especially indirect-dealing ones, third parties are almost automatically involved to carry messages between parties, help people work out their differences, manage face-to-face meetings (if any), or engage in shuttle diplomacy. In other cultures, the involvement of third-party facilitators or mediators is more intentional and is a conscious decision and commitment on the part of involved parties to use an intermediary. In these cultures, parties choose whether they want assistance to address issues in relationships, process, or substance.

In still other cultures and situations, third parties are assigned or take the initiative to intervene, independent of the will of the parties. These intermediaries come from political, financial, or judicial institutions; the management of an organization; community elders; or other authoritative or powerful concerned parties. They often have the authority to establish parameters in which decisions or agreements will be made or have resources that can be used to reward or coerce parties to reach settlements.

The roles that facilitators and mediators play, the services they provide, and the interventions they make depend on the cultures of the parties and the intermediaries themselves. People or groups seeking to address important issues, problems, or disputes should consider whether the use of a facilitator or mediator is needed to handle negotiation problems or whether their involvement is necessary for cultural reasons.

REFERENCES

Adair, N., and Brett, J. "The Negotiation Dance: Time, Culture, and Behavioral Sequences in Negotiation." *Organization Science*, 2005, *16*(1), 33–51.

Adair, W., Weingart, L., and Brett, J. "The Timing and Function of Offers in the U.S. and Japanese Negotiations." *Journal of Applied Psychology*, 2007, *92*, 1056–1068.

Adler, N., Braham, R., and Graham, J. "Strategy Implementation: A Comparison of Face-to-Face Negotiations in the Republic of China and the United States." *Strategic Management Journal*, 1992, *13*(6), 449–466.

Adler, P., and Birkhoff, J. *Building Trust: When Knowledge from "Here" Meets Knowledge from "Away."* Portland, Ore.: Policy Consensus Center, 2002.

Albin, C. *Justice and Fairness in International Negotiation.* Cambridge: Cambridge University Press, 2001.

al-Omari, J. *The Arab Way: How to Work More Effectively in Arab Cultures.* Oxford: How to Books, 2003.

Alon, I., and Brett, J. "Perceptions of Time and Their Impact on Negotiations in the Arab-Speaking Islamic World." *Negotiation Journal*, 2007, *23*(1), 55–74.

Althen, G. *American Ways: A Guide for Foreigners in the United States.* Yarmouth, Me.: Intercultural Press, 1988.

Ardagh, J. *France in the 80s.* New York: Penguin Books, 1982.

Atkins, D., and Wildau, S. *Advisory Note: Participatory Water Monitoring: A Guide for Preventing and Managing Conflict.* Washington, D.C.: Compliance Adviser/Ombudsman, International Finance Corporation, 2008.

Augsburger, D. *Conflict Mediation Across Cultures.* Louisville, Ky.: John Knox Press, 1992.

435

Badillo, H. *One Nation, One Standard: An Ex-Liberal on How Hispanics Can Succeed Just Like Other Immigrant Groups.* New York: Penguin, 2006.

Barsoux, J-L., and Lawrence, P. *Management in France.* London: Cassell Educational, 1990.

Bartoli, A. "Mediating Peace in Mozambique: The Role of the Community of Saint Egidio." In C. Crocker, F. Osler Hampson, and P. Aall (eds.), *Herding Cats: Multiparty Mediation in a Complex World.* Washington, D.C.: U.S. Institute of Peace Press, 2001.

Bennett, M. "Towards Ethnorelativism: A Developmental Model of Intercultural Sensitivity." In R. M. Paige (ed.), *Education for the Intercultural Experience.* Washington, D.C.: Intercultural Press, 1983.

Bill, J., and Springborg, R. *Politics in the Middle East.* New York: HarperCollins, 1990.

Binnendijk, H. (ed.). *National Negotiating Styles.* Washington, D.C.: Foreign Service Institute, U.S. Department of State, 1987.

Blackman, C. *Negotiating China: Case Studies and Strategies.* Sydney, Australia: Allen & Unwin, 1998.

Blake, R., and Mouton, J. *Solving Costly Organizational Conflicts: Achieving Intergroup Trust, Cooperation and Teamwork.* San Francisco: Jossey-Bass, 1984.

Blaker, M. *Japanese International Negotiation Style.* New York: Columbia University Press, 1977a.

Blaker, M. "Probe, Push and Panic: The Japanese Tactical Style in International Negotiations." In R. Scalpino (ed.), *The Foreign Policy of Modern Japan.* Berkeley: University of California Press, 1977b.

Blaker, M., Vogel, E., and Giarra, P. *Case Studies in Japanese Negotiating Behavior.* Washington, D.C.: U.S. Institute for Peace Press, 2002.

Bodde, D. "Harmony and Conflict in Chinese Philosophy." In A. Wright (ed.), *Studies in Chinese Thought.* Chicago: University of Chicago Press, 1953.

Boss, W. Presentation on sources of power. CDR Associates Partner Retreat, 2003.

Brett, J. *Negotiating Globally: How to Negotiate Deals, Resolve Disputes, and Make Decisions Across Cultural Boundaries.* San Francisco: Jossey-Bass, 2007.

Brett, J., Adair, W., Lempereur, A., Okumura, T., Shikhirev, P., Tinsley, C., and Lytle, A. "Culture and Joint Gains in Negotiation." *Negotiation Journal, 14*(1), Jan. 1998, 61–86.

Brett, N., Shoemake, A., and Hale, C. "Conflict Resolution in a Non-Western Context: Conversations with Indonesian Scholars and Practitioners." *Conflict Resolution Quarterly,* 2006, *23*(24), 427–446.

Brigg, M. "Mediation, Power and Cultural Difference." *Conflict Resolution Quarterly,* 2003, *20*(3), 287–306.

Brook, T. *Vermeer's Hat: The Seventeenth Century and the Dawn of the Global World.* London: Bloomsbury, 1978.

Buchannan, L., and O'Connell, A. "A Brief History of Decision Making." *Harvard Business Review,* Jan. 2006, 32–41.

Burton, J. *Conflict and Communication: The Use of Controlled Communication in International Relations.* New York: Macmillan, 1969.

Burton, J. *Conflict, Resolution and Prevention.* New York: St. Martin's Press, 1990.

Burton, J. *Human Needs Theory.* New York: St. Martin's Press, 1993.

Bush, R., and Folger, J. *The Promise of Mediation: Responding to Conflict Through Empowerment and Recognition.* San Francisco: Jossey-Bass, 1994.

Caminos, H. *Law of the Sea.* Williston, Vt.: Ashgate Publishing, 2001.

Carment, D., and Alcock, J. "Some Psychometric Correlates of Behavior in India and Canada." *International Journal of Psychology,* 1976, *11*(1), 57–64.

Carroll, R., and Volk, C. *Cultural Misunderstandings: The French-American Experience.* Chicago: University of Chicago Press, 1988.

Carter, J. *Keeping the Faith: Memoirs of a President.* New York: Bantam Books, 1982.

CDR Associates. "Mediating Workplace Disputes." Unpublished manuscript, CDR Associates, Boulder, Colo., 2001.

CDR Associates. "Design of Dispute Prevention and Resolution Systems to Address Human and Minority Rights Issues, Problems and Conflicts." Unpublished manuscript, Boulder, Colo., CDR Associates, 2006.

Channock, M. *Law, Custom, and Social Order: The Colonial Experience in Malawi and Zambia.* New York: Cambridge University Press, 1985.

Chen, M-J. *Inside Chinese Business: A Guide for Managers Worldwide.* Boston: Harvard Business School Press, 2003.

Chia, H. B., Lee-Partridge, J., and Chong, C. L. "Traditional Mediation Practices: Are We Throwing the Baby Out with the Bath Water?" *Conflict Resolution Quarterly,* 2004, *21*(4), 451–462.

Cogan, C. *French Negotiation Behavior: Dealing with La Grande Nation.* Washington, D.C.: U.S. Institute of Peace Press, 2003.

Cohen, R. *Negotiating Across Cultures.* Washington, D.C.: U.S. Institute of Peace Press, 1997.

Comaroff, J., and Roberts, S. *Rules and Processes: The Cultural Logic of Dispute in an African Context.* Chicago: University of Chicago Press, 1981.

Condon, J. *Good Neighbors: Communicating with the Mexicans.* Yarmouth, Me.: Intercultural Press, 1985.

Coser, L. *The Functions of Social Conflict.* New York: Free Press, 1956.

Costantino, C., and Merchant, C. *Designing Conflict Management Systems: A Guide to Creating Productive and Healthy Organizations.* San Francisco: Jossey-Bass, 1996.

CPR Institute for Dispute Resolution. "CPR Institute for Dispute Resolution Model Contract Clause." New York: CPR Institute for Dispute Resolution, 2000.

Craig, G. "Techniques of Negotiating." In I. Lederer (ed.), *Russian Foreign Policy: Essays in Historical Perspective.* New Haven, Conn.: Yale University Press, 1972.

Craig, G. *The Germans.* New York: Penguin, 1983.

D'Amico, L., and Rubenstein, R. "Cultural Considerations When 'Setting' the Negotiation Table." *Negotiation Journal,* 1999, *15*(4), 389–396.

Davidheiser, M. "Harmony, Peacemaking, and Power: Controlling Processes and African Mediation." *Conflict Resolution Quarterly*, 2006, *23*(3), 281–299.

Davies, R., and Osumo, I. (eds.). *The Japanese Mind.* Tokyo: Tuttle Publishing, 2002.

De Mente, B. *Chinese Etiquette and Ethics in Business.* New York: McGraw-Hill, 2004.

Deal, T., and Kennedy, A. *Corporate Cultures: The Rites and Rituals of Corporate Life.* Reading, Mass.: Addison-Wesley, 1982.

Dean, G. "Doing Business in Indonesia." 2000. http://www.okusi.net/garydean/works/bizindo.html. (Originally appeared as a chapter in *Indonesia: Facing the Challenge*, East Asia Analytical Unit, Department of Foreign Affairs and Trade, Australia, 2000.)

Deane, J. *The Strange Alliance.* New York: Viking Press, 1947.

Dennett, R., and Johnson, J. (eds.). *Negotiating with the Russians.* Boston: World Peace Foundation, 1951.

CDR Associates. "Design of Dispute Prevention and Resolution Systems to Address Human and Minority Rights Issues, Problems and Conflicts." Unpublished manuscript, Boulder, Colo., CDR Associates, 2006.

Diamond, J. *Collapse: How Societies Choose to Fail or Succeed.* New York: Viking Penguin, 2005.

Dillon, J. T. *The Practice of Questioning.* New York: Routledge, 1990.

Dobson, T. *Aikido in Everyday Life: Giving In to Get Your Way.* Berkeley, Calif.: North Atlantic Books, 1994.

Doi, T. *The Anatomy of Dependence.* New York: Kodansha International, 1973.

Druckman, D., Benton, A., Ali, F., and Bagur, J. S. "Cultural Differences in Bargaining Behavior." *Journal of Conflict Resolution*, 1976, *20*(3), 413–449.

Dunung, S. *Doing Business in Asia: The Complete Guide.* Lanham, Md.: Lexington Books, 1995.

Embree, J. *Suye Mura: A Japanese Village.* Chicago: University of Chicago Press, 1939.

Etzioni, A. "The Gradualist Way to Peace." Presentation at the Fortieth Annual Meeting, American Orthopsychiatric Association, Washington, D.C., 1963.

Fagan, B. M. *Clash of Cultures.* New York: Freeman, 1984.

Fang, T. *Chinese Business Negotiating Style.* Thousand Oaks, Calif.: Sage, 1999.

Final Settlement Stipulation, *Kansas* v. *Nebraska and Colorado*, No. 126, Original, U.S. Supreme Court, Decree of May 19, 2003, 538 U.S. 720.

Fisher, G. *International Negotiation: A Cross-Cultural Perspective.* Yarmouth, Me.: Intercultural Press, 1980.

Fisher, G. *Mindsets: The Role of Culture and Perception in International Relations.* Yarmouth, Me.: Intercultural Press, 1988.

Fisher, R. *International Conflict for Beginners.* New York: HarperCollins, 1976.

Fisher, R. *International Mediation: A Working Guide.* New York: International Peace Academy, 1978.

Fisher, R. *Interactive Conflict Resolution.* Syracuse, N.Y.: Syracuse University Press, 1997.

Fisher, R., and Ury, W. *Getting to Yes.* New York: Penguin, 1981.

Friedman, G., and Himmelstein, J. *Challenging Conflict: Mediation Through Understanding.* Chicago: American Bar Association, 2009.

Friedman, T. *The World Is Flat: A Brief History of the Twenty-First Century.* New York: Picador, 2007.

Fucini, J., and Fucini, S. *Working for the Japanese: Inside Mazda's American Auto Plant.* New York: Macmillan, 1990.

Galinsky, A., and Mussweiler, T. "Promoting Good Outcomes: Effects of Regulatory Focus on Negotiation Outcomes." Working paper, Northwestern University, Evanston, Ill., 2000.

Galinsky, A. D., Mussweiler, T., and Medvec, V. H. (2002). "Disconnecting Outcomes and Evaluations: The Role of Negotiator Focus." *Journal of Personality and Social Psychology, 83,* 1131–1140.

Gartoff, R. "Negotiating with the Russians: Some Lessons from Salt." *International Security,* 1977, *4,* 3–24.

Geertz, C. "Suq: The Bazaar Economy in Sefrou." In C. Geertz, H. Geertz, and L. Rosen (eds.), *Meaning and Order in Moroccan Society.* Cambridge: Cambridge University Press, 1979.

Ghais, S. *Extreme Facilitation: Guiding Groups Through Controversy and Complexity.* San Francisco: Jossey-Bass, 2005.

Gilligan, C. *In a Different Voice: Psychological Theory and Women's Development.* Cambridge, Mass.: Harvard University Press, 1982.

Gladwell, M. *Blink: The Power of Thinking About Thinking.* New York: Little, Brown, 2005.

Gleick, J. *Chaos: Making a New Science.* New York: Penguin, 1988.

Glenn, E. S., Witmeyer, D., and Stevenson, K. A. "Cultural Styles of Persuasion." *International Journal of Intercultural Relations,* 1977, *1,* 52–65.

Goh, B. C. *Law Without Lawyers, Justice Without Courts: Traditional Chinese Mediation.* Aldershot, U.K.: Ashgate, 2002.

Gold, L. "Influencing Unconscious Influences: The Healing Dimension of Mediation." *Mediation Quarterly,* Winter 1994, 55–66.

Gorer, G., and Rickman, J. *The People of Great Russia.* New York: Chanticleer Press, 1950.

Graham, J. "The Influence of Culture on Business Negotiations." *Journal of International Business Studies,* 1985, *16*(1), 81–96.

Graham, J. "Japanese Negotiating Style: Characteristics of a Distinct Approach." *Negotiation Journal,* 1993, *9*(2), 123–140.

Graham, J., and Sano, Y. *Smart Bargaining: Doing Business with the Japanese.* New York: HarperCollins, 1979.

Grayson, G. "Mexico: A Love-Hate Relationship with North America." In H. Binnendijk (ed.), *National Negotiating Styles.* Washington, D.C.: Foreign Service Institute, U.S. Department of State, 1987.

Gudykunst, W., and Nishida, T. *Bridging Japanese/North American Differences.* Thousand Oaks, Calif.: Sage, 1994.

Guidelines for the Design of Integrated Conflict Management Systems within Organizations. Washington, D.C.: Society for Professionals in Dispute Resolution, 2000.

Gulliver, P. H. "Dispute Settlement Without Courts: The Ndendeuli of Southern Tanzania." In L. Nader (ed.), *Law in Culture and Society.* Hawthorne, N.Y.: Aldine, 1969.

Gulliver, P.H., *Disputes and Negotiations: A Cross-Cultural Perspective*, New York: Academic Press, 1979.

Hall, E. *The Hidden Dimension.* New York: Random House, 1990.

Hall, E. T. *The Dance of Life: The Other Dimension of Time.* New York: Doubleday, 1984.

Hall, E. T. *Hidden Differences Doing Business with the Japanese.* New York: Doubleday, 1987.

Hall, E., and Hall, M. *Understanding Cultural Differences: Germans, French and Americans.* New York: Doubleday, 1990.

Harrington, C., and Merry, S. "Ideological Production: The Making of Community Mediation." *Law and Society Review,* 1988, *22,* 713.

Harris, P., Ansty, M., and Reilly, B. *Democracy and Deep Rooted Conflict: Options for Negotiators.* Stockholm: Institute for Democracy and Electoral Assistance, 1998.

Harris, P., and Moran, T. *Managing Cultural Differences: High Performance Strategies for Today's Global Manager.* Houston, Tex.: Gulf Publishing, 1987.

Hasluck, M. "The Albanian Blood Feud." In P. Bohannon (ed.), *Law and Warfare: Studies in the Anthropology of Conflict.* Garden City, N.J.: Natural History Press, 1967.

Hayashi, A. "When to Trust Your Gut." *Harvard Business Review,* Feb. 2001, *79*(2), 58–65.

Hessler, P. *Oracle Bones.* New York: HarperCollins, 2006.

Hingley, R. *The Russian Mind.* New York: Scribner, 1977.

Hirokawa, R., and Miyahara, A. "A Comparison of Influence Strategies Utilized by Managers in American and Japanese Organizations." *Communication Quarterly,* 1986, *34,* 250–265.

Hitti, P. *The Arabs: A Short History.* Princeton, N.J.: Princeton University Press, 1943.

Hodgson, J., Sano, Y., and Graham, J. *Doing Business with the New Japan.* (3rd ed.) Lanham, Md.: Rowan & Littlefield, 2000.

Hoebel, E. "Song Duels Among Eskimo." In P. Bohannon (ed.), *Law and Warfare: Studies in the Anthropology of Conflict.* Garden City, N.J.: Natural History Press, 1967.

Hofstede, G. *Culture's Consequences: International Differences in Work-Related Values.* Thousand Oaks, Calif.: Sage, 1984.

Holbrooke, R. *To End a War.* New York: Random House, 1999.

Horowitz, D. *Ethnic Groups in Conflict.* Berkeley: University of California Press, 1985.

"Hostages Held at B'nai B'rith." *Greenbelt Interfaith News,* June 1, 1997. http://www.greenbelt.com/news/97/060116.htm.

Hsu, F. *Americans and Chinese: Passages to Differences.* Honolulu: University of Hawaii Press, 1981.

Hu, W., and Grove, C. *Encountering the Chinese: A Guide for Americans*. Yarmouth, Me.: Intercultural Press, 1991.

Hughes, R. *The Fatal Shore: The Epic of Australia's Founding*. New York: Vintage Books, 1988.

Iklé, F. *How Nations Negotiate*. New York: HarperCollins, 1964.

International Protocol Officers Association. *Protocol and Diplomacy*. Atlanta, Ga.: International Protocol Officers Association, 2002. http://www.protocolinternational.org/.

"Islamic Banking Making Inroads.' *Epic Times*, Dec. 27, 2004. http://english .epochtimes.com/news/4-12-18/25080.html.

Jarret, S. "This Is as Much as We Can Do: Aboriginal Domestic Violence." In G. Johns (ed.), *Waking up to Dreamtime: The Illusion of Aboriginal Self-Determination*. Singapore: Media Masters, 2001.

Johnstone, B. "Linguistic Strategies and Cultural Styles for Persuasive Discourse." In S. Ting-Toomey and F. Korzenny (eds.), *Language, Communication and Culture*. Thousand Oaks, Calif.: Sage, 1989.

Jönsson, C. *Soviet Bargaining Behavior: The Nuclear Test Ban Case*. New York: Columbia University Press, 1979.

Kagan, S., Knight, G., and Martinez-Romero, S. "Culture and the Development of Conflict Resolution Style." *Journal of Cross-Cultural Psychology*, 1982, *13*(1), 43–58.

Kahane, D. "Dispute Resolution and the Politics of Generalization." *Negotiation Journal*, 2003, *19*(1), 5–28.

Kaplan, R. *Surrender or Starve: Travels in Ethiopia, Sudan, Somalia and Eritrea*. New York: Knopf, 2003.

Kaplan, R. *Balkan Ghosts*. New York: Picador, 2005.

Kapleman, M. "Madrid Conference: How to Negotiate with the Soviets." In *Law and National Security Intelligence Report*. Chicago: American Bar Association, Feb. 1985.

Kapuściśnski, R. *Another Day of Life*. New York: Vintage, 2001.

Kapuściśnski, R. *The Shadow of the Sun*. New York: Vintage, 2002.

Kellman, H. "Informal Mediation by the Scholar/Practitioner." In J. Bercovitch and J. Rubin (eds.), *Mediation in International Relations*. New York: St. Martin's Press, 1992.

Kennan, G. "The Sources of Soviet Conduct." *Foreign Affairs*, 1987, *65*(4), 852–868.

Khuri, F. I. "The Etiquette of Bargaining in the Middle East." *American Anthropologist*, 1968, *70*, 698–706.

Klieman, A. "Israeli Negotiating Culture." In T. Wittes (ed.), *How Israelis and Palestinians Negotiate: A Cross-Cultural Analysis of the Oslo Process*. Washington, D.C.: U.S. Institute of Peace Press, 2005.

Kolb, D. *The Mediators*. Cambridge, Mass.: MIT Press, 1983.

Kopelman, S., and Olekalns, M. "Process in Cross-Cultural Negotiations." *Negotiation Journal*, 1999, *15*(4), 373–380.

Kras, E. *Management in Two Cultures: Bridging the Gap Between U.S. and Mexican Managers*. Yarmouth, Me.: Intercultural Press, 1989.

Lall, A. *How Communist China Negotiates.* New York: Columbia University Press, 1968.

Lam, N., and Graham, J. *China Now: Doing Business in the World's Most Dynamic Market.* New York: McGraw-Hill, 2007.

Lax, D., and Sebenius, J. *The Manager as Negotiator.* New York: Free Press, 1986.

LeBaron, M. *Bridging Troubled Waters: Conflict Resolution from the Heart.* San Francisco: Jossey-Bass, 2002.

Lederach, J. P. "Of Nets, Nails, and Problems: The Folk Language of Conflict Resolution in a Central American Setting." In K. Avruch, P. W. Black, and J. A. Scimecca, (eds.), *Conflict Resolution: Cross-Cultural Perspectives* (pp. 165–186). Westport, Conn.: Praeger, 1991.

Lederach, J. P. *Preparing for Peace: Conflict Transformation Across Cultures.* Syracuse, N.Y.: Syracuse University Press, 1995.

Lee, J., and Hwee, T. H. *An Asian Perspective on Mediation.* Singapore: Singapore Academy of Law, 2009.

Lincoln, W. F. "Presenting Initial Positions." Unpublished manuscript, National Center for Collaborative Planning and Community Services, Watertown, Mass., 1981.

Lipsky, D., Seeber, R., and Fincher, R. *Emerging Systems for Managing Workplace Conflict.* San Francisco: Jossey-Bass, 2003.

Macdonald, G. "Where Words Harm and Blows Heal." *Australian Dispute Resolution Journal,* 1990, *1*(3), 125–132.

Macleod, R. *China Inc.: How to Do Business with the Chinese.* New York: Bantam Books, 1988.

Macmillan, M. *Paris 1919.* New York: Random House, 2003.

Mallaby, S. *The World's Banker: A Story of Failed States, Financial Crises, and the Wealth and Poverty of Nations.* New York: Penguin Press, 2004.

Maalouf, A. *The Crusades Through Arab Eyes.* New York: Schocken Books, 1985.

Mansbridge, J. *Beyond Adversary Democracy.* Chicago: University of Chicago Press, 1983.

March, R. *The Honorable Customer: Marketing and Selling to the Japanese in the 1990s.* Melbourne: Longman, 1990.

Maslow, A. H. "A Theory of Human Motivation." *Psychological Review,* 1943, *50*(4), 370–396.

Maslow, A. *Motivation and Personality.* New York: HarperCollins, 1954.

Mason, S., and Wils, O., *Insider Mediators: Exploring Their Role in Informal Peace Processes.* Berlin: Berghof Foundation for Peace and Support, 2009.

Matsumoto, M. *The Unspoken Way.* New York: Kodansha International, 1988.

Mayer, B. *The Dynamics of Conflict Resolution: A Practitioner's Guide.* San Francisco: Jossey-Bass, 2000.

Mayer, B. "Facilitative Mediation." In J. Folberg, A. Milne, and P. Salem (eds.), *Divorce and Family Mediation: Models, Techniques and Applications.* New York: Guilford Press, 2004.

Mayer, B. *Staying with Conflict: A Strategic Approach to Ongoing Disputes.* San Francisco: Jossey-Bass, 2009.

Mayer, B., Moore, C., and Todd, S. "The Alaska Wolf Summit." Unpublished manuscript, CDR Associates, Boulder, Colo., n.d.

McConnell, J. *Mindful Mediation: A Handbook for Buddhist Peacemakers.* Bangkok, Thailand: Buddhist Research Institute, Mahachula University, 1995.

Mcduff, I. "Your Pace or Mine? Culture, Time and Negotiation." *Negotiation Journal,* 2006, *22*(1), 31–45.

McGoldrick, M. (ed.). *Re-visioning Family Therapy.* New York: Guilford Press, 2002.

McGoldrick, M., Giordano, J., and Garcia-Preto, N. (eds.). *Ethnicity and Family Therapy.* New York: Guilford Press, 1982.

Menocal, M. *The Ornament of the World: How Muslims, Jews and Christians Created a Culture of Tolerance in Medieval Spain.* New York: Little, Brown, 2002.

"Mexico: Let's Make a Deal." n.d. http://executive.planet.com/index.php?title= Mexico:_Let%27s_Make_a_Deal%21 .

Mizutani, O. *Japanese: The Spoken Language in Japanese Life.* Tokyo: Japan Times, 1981.

Mole, J. *When in Rome: A Business Guide to Cultures and Customs in the European Nations.* New York: AMACOM, 1990.

Moore, C. "The Caucus: Private Meetings that Promote Settlement." *Mediation Quarterly,* 1987, *16,* 87–101.

Moore, C. "Implementing Peace Accords on the Ground." *Track II,* 1993, *2*(2), 10–13.

Moore, C. "Dispute Systems Design: A Pragmatic Approach for the Development of Procedures and Structures to Manage Ethnic and Political Conflicts." *Pacifica Review,* 1994, *6*(2), 43–55.

Moore, C. *The Mediation Process: Practical Strategies for Resolving Conflict.* (3rd ed.) San Francisco: Jossey-Bass, 2003.

Moore, C. J. *In Other Words: A Language Lover's Guide to the Most Intriguing Words Around the World.* New York: Levinger Press, 2004.

Moore, C., and Brown, G. "Designing Dispute Resolution Systems and Building Local Capacities for the Settlement of Land and Property Disputes in Post-Conflict and Post-Crisis Societies." In C. Zelizer and R. Rubinstein (eds.), *Building Peace: Practical Reflections from the Field.* West Hartford, Conn.: Kumarian Press, 2009.

Moore, C., and Santosa, M. A. "Developing Appropriate Environmental Conflict Management Procedures in Indonesia." *Cultural Survival Quarterly,* Fall 1995.

Moran, R., and Stripp, W. *Successful International Business Negotiations.* Houston, Tex.: Gulf Publishing, 1991.

Morley, I., and Stephenson, G. *The Social Psychology of Bargaining.* London: Allen & Unwin, 1977.

Mulder, N. *Inside Thai Society: An Interpretation of Everyday Life.* Bangkok: Editions Duangkamol, 1992.

Mulder, N. *Inside Indonesian Society: Cultural Change in Java.* Amsterdam: Pepin Press, 1996.

Murithi, T. "African Approaches to Building Peace and Social Solidarity." Unpublished manuscript, 2006.

Murray, J. "The Cairo Stories: Some Reflections on Conflict Resolution in Egypt." *Negotiation Journal,* 1997, *13*(1), 39–60.

Myers, F. *Pintupi Country, Pintupi Self: Sentiment, Place and Politics Among Western Desert Aborigines.* Berkeley: University of California Press, 1991.

Nader, L. *Harmony Ideology: Justice and Control in a Zapotec Mountain Village.* Stanford, Calif.: Stanford University Press, 1990.

Nakane, C. *Japanese Society.* Berkeley: University of California Press, 1972.

Nasmyth, P., Ku, A., and Pun, N. (eds.). *Georgia: In the Mountains of Poetry.* New York: Routledge, 2007.

No. 126, Original, Supreme Court of the United States, *State of Kansas* v. *Nebraska and Colorado,* Final Settlement Stipulation, December 15, 2002.

Noel, B., Shoemake, A., and Hall, C. "Conflict Resolution in a Non-Western Context: Conversations with Indonesian Scholars and Practitioners." *Conflict Resolution Quarterly.* Summer 2006, *23*(4), 427–446.

Nydell, M. *Understanding Arabs: A Guide for Westerners.* Yarmouth: Me.: Intercultural Press, 1987.

Ohanyan, A. "Negotiation Culture in a Post-Soviet Context: An Interdisciplinary Perspective." *Mediation Quarterly,* 1999, *17*(1), 83–104.

Olszanska, J., Olszanski, R., and Wozniak, J. "Do Peaceful Conflict Management Methods Pose Problems in Post-Totalitarian Poland?" *Mediation Quarterly,* 1993, *10*(3), 291–302.

Orendain, A. *Skills and Values of Barangay Justice.* Mandaluyong City, Philippines: Alpha Omega Publications, 1989.

Owomoyela, O. *A ki i: Yourba Proscriptive and Prescriptive Proverbs.* New York, Lanham, 1988.

Pastor, R., and Castañeda, J. *Limits to Friendship: The United States and Mexico.* New York: Vintage Books, 1989.

Patai, R. *The Arab Mind.* New York: Scribner, 1983.

Peck, C. *The United Nations as a Dispute Settlement System: Improving Mechanisms for the Prevention and Resolution of Conflict,* Boston: Kluwer Law International, 1996.

Pipes, R. "International Negotiation: Some Operational Principles of Soviet Foreign Policy." Memorandum prepared at the request of the Committee on Government Questions, U.S. Senate Committee print, Jan. 1972.

Potter, D. *People of Plenty: Economic Abundance and the American Character.* Chicago: University of Chicago Press, 1958.

Princen, T. *Intermediaries in International Conflict.* Princeton, N.J.: Princeton University Press, 1992.

Pruitt, D. *Negotiation Behavior.* Orlando, Fla.: Academic Press, 1981.

Putnam, L., and Jones, T. "The Role of Communication in Bargaining." *Human Communication Research,* 1982, *8*, 262–280.

Putnam, R. *Making Democracy Work: Civic Traditions in Modern Italy.* Princeton, N.J.: Princeton University Press, 1993.

Pye, L. *Chinese Commercial Negotiating Style.* Cambridge, Mass.: Oelgeschlager, Gunn & Hain, 1982.

Quandt, W. "Egypt: A Strong Sense of National Identity." In H. Binnendijk (ed.), *National Negotiating Styles.* Washington, D.C.: Foreign Service Institute, 1987.

Quinney, N. "U.S. Negotiating Behavior." Washington, D.C.: U.S. Institute of Peace, Oct. 2002.

Rajan, M., and Graham, J. "Nobody's Grandfather Was a Merchant: Understanding the Soviet Commercial Negotiation Process and Style." *California Management Review,* 1991, *33*(3), 40–57.

Reader, J. *Africa: A Biography of the Continent.* New York: Vintage Books, 1999.

Regan, D. *For the Record: From Wall Street to Washington.* New York: St. Martin's Press, 1989.

Reischauer, E. *Japan: The Story of a Nation.* (4th ed.) New York: McGraw-Hill, 1989.

Riesman, D., Glazer, N., and Denney, R. *The Lonely Crowd: A Study of the Changing American Character.* New York: Doubleday, 1953.

Renwick, G. *Australians and North Americans.* Yarmouth, Me.: Intercultural Press, 1980.

Richmond, Y. *From Nyet to Da: Understanding the Russians.* Yarmouth, Me.: Intercultural Press, 1992.

Richmond, Y., and Gestrin, P. *Into Africa: Intercultural Insights.* Yarmouth, Me.: Intercultural Press, 1998.

Riding, A. *Distant Neighbors: A Portrait of the Mexicans.* New York: Random House, 1986.

Rothman, J. *From Confrontation to Cooperation: Resolving Ethnic and Regional Conflict.* Thousand Oaks, Calif.: Sage, 1992.

Rothman, J. *Resolving Identity-Based Conflicts.* In *Nations, Organizations, and Communities.* San Francisco: Jossey-Bass, 1997.

Rowney, E. *It Takes One to Tango.* New York: Brassey's, 1992.

Rubin, J., Pruitt, D., and Kim, S. H. *Social Conflict: Escalation, Stalemate, and Settlement.* New York: McGraw–Hill, 1994.

Sakwa, R. (ed.). *Chechnya: From the Past to the Future.* New York: Wimbledon, 2005.

Salacuse, J. "Ten Ways That Culture Affects Negotiating Style: Some Survey Results." *Negotiation Journal,* 1998a, *14*(3), 221–240.

Salacuse, J. "So, What Is the Deal Anyway? Contracts and Relationships as Negotiating Goals." *Negotiation Journal,* 1998b, *14*(1), 5–12.

Salacuse, J. *Making Global Deals: Negotiating in the International Marketplace.* Cambridge, MA: PON Books, 2002.

Salacuse, J. *The Global Negotiator: Making, Managing and Mending Deals Around the World in the Twenty-First Century.* New York: Palgrave Macmillan, 2003.

Salem, P. "A Critique of Western Conflict Resolution from a Non-Western Perspective." In P. Salem (ed.), *Conflict Resolution in the Arab World: Selected Essays.* Syracuse, N.Y.: Syracuse University Press, 1997.

Samovar, L., and Porter, R. *Intercultural Communication: A Reader.* Belmont, Calif.: Wadsworth, 1988.

Sampson, A. *Mandela: The Authorized Biography.* New York: HarperCollins, 1999.

Sanger, J. "Tales of the Bazaar: Interest-Based Negotiation Across Cultures." *Negotiation Journal,* 2002, *18*(3), 233–250.

Schama, S. *The Embarrassment of Riches: An Interpretation of Dutch Culture in the Golden Age.* New York: Vintage, 1997.

Schecter, J. *Russian Negotiating Behavior: Continuity and Transition.* Washington, D.C.: U.S. Institute for Peace Press, 1998.

Schein, E. *Organizational Culture and Leadership.* San Francisco: Jossey-Bass, 1985.

Schön, D., and Rein, M. *Frame Reflection: Toward the Resolution of Intractable Policy Conflicts.* New York: Basic Books, 1994.

Schneiter, F. *Getting Along with the Chinese for Fun and Profit.* Hong Kong: Asia 2000, 1992.

Seligman, S. *Dealing with the Chinese.* New York: Warner Books, 1989.

Senge, P. *The Fifth Discipline: The Art and Practice of the Learning Organization.* New York: Doubleday, 1994.

Shook, E. *Hooponopono.* Honolulu: East-West Press, 1992.

Simon, H. *Reason in Human Affairs.* Stanford, Calif.: Stanford University Press, 1983.

Slaats, H., and Portier, K. *Traditional Decision Making and the Law: Institutions and Processes in an Indonesian Context.* Jogyakarta, Indonesia: Gadjah Mada University Press, 1992.

Slaikeu, K., and Hasson, R. *Controlling the Costs of Conflict: How to Design a System for Your Organization.* San Francisco: Jossey-Bass, 1998.

Slocombe, W. "Negotiating with the Soviets: Getting Past No." In L. Sloss and M. Davis (eds.), *A Game for High Stakes: Lessons Learned from Negotiating with the Soviet Union.* Cambridge, Mass.: Ballinger, 1986.

Sloss, L., and Davis, M. (eds.). *A Game for High Stakes: Lessons Learned from Negotiating with the Soviet Union.* Cambridge, Mass.: Ballinger, 1986.

Smith, K., and Berg, D. *Paradoxes of Group Life.* San Francisco: Jossey-Bass, 1987.

Smith, R. *Negotiating with the Soviets.* Bloomington: Indiana University Press, 1989.

Smyser, W. R. *How Germans Negotiate: Logical Goals, Practical Solutions.* Washington, D.C.: U.S. Institute of Peace Press, 2003.

Snyder, S. *Negotiating on the Edge: North Korean Negotiating Behavior.* Washington, D.C.: U.S. Institute of Peace, 1999.

Solomon, R. *Chinese Political Negotiating Behavior, 1967–84.* Santa Monica, Calif.: RAND, 1995.

Solomon, R. *Chinese Negotiating Behavior: Pursuing Interests Through Old Friends.* Washington, D.C.: U.S. Institute of Peace, 1999.

Songsamphan, C. "Vendetta and Buddhist Mediator in Southern Thailand." In F. Jandt and P. Pederson, (eds.), *Constructive Conflict Management: Asia-Pacific Cases.* Thousand Oaks, Calif.: Sage, 1996.

Sowell, T. *Migrations and Cultures.* New York: Basic Books, 1996.

Spencer D., and Spencer, W. "The International Negotiation Network: A New Method for Approaching Some Very Old Problems." *Columbia International Affairs Online,* Nov. 1992.

Stevens, C. *Strategy and Collective Bargaining Negotiation.* New York: McGraw-Hill, 1963.

Stewart, E., and Bennett, M. *American Cultural Patterns: A Cross-Cultural Perspective.* Yarmouth, Me.: Intercultural Press, 1991.

Stoertz, H. "Observations on Soviet Negotiating Practice." In L. Sloss (ed.), *A Game for High Stakes: Lessons Learned from Negotiating with the Soviet Union.* Cambridge, Mass.: Ballinger, 1986.

Storie, F. *Trainees' Manual: Community Mediation Program.* Colombo: Sri Lankan Ministry of Justice, Law Reform and Integration, Canadian International Development Agency, 2003.

Sunshine, R. *Negotiating for International Development: A Practitioner's Handbook.* Dordrecht: Martins Nijhoff, 1990.

Tannen, D. *You Just Don't Understand: Men and Women in Conversation.* New York: Morrow, 1990.

Tannen, D. *The Argument Culture.* New York: Random House, 1998.

Tauroa, H., and Tauroa, P. *Te Marae: A Guide to Customs and Protocol.* Auckland, N.Z.: Heinemann Reed, 1986.

Taylor, J. *Shadows of the Rising Sun.* New York: Morrow, 1983.

Terrill, R. *The New Chinese Empire.* New York: Basic Books, 2003.

Thomas, K. W. "Conflict and Conflict Management." In M. D. Dunnette (ed.), *Handbook of Industrial and Organizational Psychology.* Skokie, Ill.: Rand McNally, 1983.

Thompson, L. *The Mind and Heart of the Negotiator.* Upper Saddle River, New Jersey: Prentice Hall, 2001.

Trade Media Ltd. *Negotiating in Asia.* Chicago: Probus Publishing, 1991.

Triandis, H. C. "The Self and Social Behavior in Differing Cultural Contexts." *Psychological Review,* 1989, *96*(3), 506–520.

Trompenars, F. *Riding the Waves of Culture: Understanding Diversity in Global Business.* London: Economist Books, 1994.

Tseten, D. "Tibetan Art of Divination." *Tibetan Bulletin,* Government of Tibet in Exile, Mar.–Apr. 1995. http://www.tibet.com/Buddhism/divination.html.

Tutu, D. *No Future Without Forgiveness.* New York: Doubleday, 1999.

Ury, W., Brett, J., and Goldberg, S. *Getting Disputes Resolved: Designing Systems to Cut the Costs of Conflicts.* San Francisco: Jossey-Bass Publishers, 1988.

Von Benda-Beckmann, K. *The Broken Stairways of Consensus: Village Justice and State Courts in Minangkabau.* Dordrecht: Foris Publications, 1984.

von Bertrab, H. *Negotiating NAFTA: A Mexican Envoy's Account.* Westport, Conn.: Center for Strategic and International Studies and Praeger, 1997.

Wall, J., and Callister, R. "Malaysian Community Mediation." *Journal of Conflict Resolution,* 1999, *43*(3), 343–365.

Wallerstein, I. *The Modern World-System: Capitalist Agriculture and the Origins of the European World-Economy in the Sixteenth Century.* Orlando, Fla.: Academic Press, 1976.

Walton, R., and McKersie, R. *A Behavioral Theory of Labor Negotiations: An Analysis of a Social Interaction System.* Ithaca, N.Y.: ILR Press Books, Cornell University Press, 1991.

Wanis-St. John A., "Cultural Pathways in Conflict Resolution." In M. Moffitt and R. Bordone (eds.), *Handbook of Dispute Resolution.* San Francisco: Jossey-Bass, 2005.

Watkins, M. "Building Momentum in Negotiations: Time Related Costs and Action-Forcing Events." *Negotiation Journal,* 1998, *14*(3), 241–256.

Wedge, B., and Muromcew, C. "Psychological Factors in Soviet Disarmament Negotiations." *Journal of Conflict Resolution,* 1965, *9*(1), 20–33.

Wehr, P., and Lederach, J. P. "Mediating Conflict in Central America." In J. Bercovitch (ed.), *Resolving International Conflicts: The Theory and Practice of Mediation* (pp. 5–6). Boulder, Colo.: Lynne Rienner Publishers, 1996.

Weiss, J. "Trajectories Toward Peace: Mediator Sequencing Strategies in Intractable Communal Conflicts." *Negotiation Journal,* 2003, *19*(2), 109–115.

Westin, A., and Feliu, A. *Resolving Employment Disputes Without Litigation.* Washington, D.C.: Bureau of National Affairs, 1988.

Whelan, J. *Soviet Diplomacy and Negotiating Behavior: Emerging New Context for U.S. Diplomacy* Washington, D.C.: U.S. Government Printing Office, 1979.

Wildau, S., Atkins, D., Moore, C., and O'Neill, E. *A Guide to Designing and Implementing Grievance Mechanisms for Development Projects.* Washington, D.C.: Compliance Advisor/Ombudsman, International Finance Corporation, 2008.

Williams, G. *Legal Negotiation and Settlement.* St. Paul, Minn.: West Publishing, 1983.

Wilson, S., and Putnam, L. L. "Interaction Goals in Negotiation." *Communication Yearbook,* 1990, *13*, 374–406.

Wilson, T. *Strangers to Ourselves: Discovering the Adaptive Unconscious.* Cambridge, Mass.: Harvard University Press, 2002.

Woodrow, P. "Time, Money and Morale: Reducing the Costs of Unresolved Conflicts Through Dispute Resolution Systems Design." *Track II,* Aug. 1998, *7*(2) 6–11.

Wyle, L. "French Value Orientations." In L. F. Luce (ed.), *The French Speaking World.* Lincolnwood, Ill.: National Textbook Company, 1991.

Yamada, H. *Different Games, Different Rules: Why Americans and Japanese Misunderstand Each Other.* New York: Oxford University Press, 1997.

Yenson, H., Hague, K., McCreanor, T., with Kelsey, J., Nairn, M., and Williama, D. (eds.). *Honoring the Treaty: An Introduction for Pakeha to the Treaty of Waitangi.* Auckland, N.Z.: Penguin, 1989.

Young, K. T. *Negotiating with the Chinese Communists: The United States Experience, 1953–67.* New York: McGraw-Hill, 1968.

Young, O. "Intermediaries: Additional Thoughts on Third Parties." *Journal of Conflict Resolution,* 1972, *16*(1), 51–65.

Zandvliet, L., and Anderson, M. *Getting It Right: Making Corporate-Community Relations Work.* Sheffield, U.K.: Greenleaf Publishing, 2009.

Zartman, I. W., and Berman, M. *The Practical Negotiator.* New Haven, Conn.: Yale University Press, 1982.

THE AUTHORS

Christopher W. Moore is a partner of CDR Associates, an international stakeholder engagement and conflict management firm based in the United States. Moore specializes in mediation and facilitation of international and domestic negotiations to resolve political, natural resource, and civil transactions and disputes. He has worked with government agencies, the private sector, and civil society in over thirty countries and has served as an intermediary in multinational negotiations in southern Africa, the Middle East, and North America. Moore also consults on peacebuilding initiatives, design of dispute resolution systems, and intercultural negotiation training. Past clients include United Nations agencies and the Organization of American States; the World Bank and the International Finance Corporation; the U.S. State Department, Agency for International Development, and Department of Interior agencies; GTZ (Germany) and the Asia Foundation; and Levi Strauss & Company, Sprint, and Pitney Bowes. Moore holds a Ph.D. in political sociology and development from Rutgers University and is the author of *The Mediation Process: Practical Strategies for Resolving Conflict* (third edition, 2003) and numerous other journal articles and monographs.

Peter J. Woodrow is codirector of the Reflecting on Peace Practice Project at CDA Collaborative Learning Projects in Cambridge, Massachusetts, an effort dedicated to improving the effectiveness of peacebuilding initiatives worldwide. He is on leave as a partner of CDR Associates in Boulder, Colorado. Woodrow is an experienced mediator, facilitator, trainer, and consultant who has worked with the private sector, international organizations, governments, and nongovernmental organizations. He has mediated and facilitated multiparty environmental, organizational, and public policy disputes and has implemented programs in consensus building, problem solving, decision making, and dispute systems design in over thirty countries in Asia, Africa, and Eastern Europe. Woodrow holds a master's degree in public administration from the John F. Kennedy School of Government, Harvard University, and a B.A. in government from Oberlin College. He is the coauthor (with Mary B. Anderson) of *Rising from the Ashes: Development Strategies in Times of Disaster* (second edition, 1998), as well as several other books and numerous articles in the field of peacebuilding and conflict resolution.

NAME INDEX

SUBJECT INDEX

The Mediation Process
Practical Strategies for Resolving Conflict, 3rd Edition

Christopher W. Moore

ISBN 978-0-7879-6446-7 • Paper
Available wherever books are sold
www.josseybass.com

"A classic in the field. Clear, practical, sensible advice invaluable to novices and professionals alike. I recommend it highly!"
—**William Ury, coauthor,** *Getting to Yes,* **and author,** *The Third Side*

"Recently updated, this continues to be the best book ever written about mediation. A sophisticated, thorough treatment of the subject, it is clearly written and contains a trove of useful examples. This new edition is a must for anyone seriously interested in the subject of dispute resolution."
—**Margaret L. Shaw, principal, ADR Associates, LLC, and former council member of the ABA's section on dispute resolution**

"The latest version of Moore's classic book *The Mediation Process* includes a much more in-depth look at the evolution and cultural understandings of mediation. This text should be on the bookshelf of every trainer, teacher, and practitioner in the field of mediation."
—**John Paul Lederach, professor of international peacebuilding, Joan B. Kroc Institute of International Peace Studies, University of Notre Dame**

Since it was first published in 1986, *The Mediation Process* has become a landmark resource for mediation practitioners, trainers, students, and professionals in corporate, legal, health care, education, and governmental arenas. This thoroughly revised and expanded third edition has been updated to include coverage of the most contemporary issues in mediation practice and to provide updated bibliographical resources.

Christopher W. Moore is a founding partner in CDR Associates, a mediation, conflict management, and training firm based in Colorado with clients worldwide. In addition to working with companies and many levels of government in the United States, Moore has conducted training programs in countries such as Indonesia, Russia, Guatemala, and South Africa.

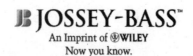

JB JOSSEY-BASS™
An Imprint of **WILEY**
Now you know.

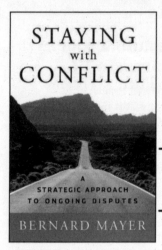

Staying with Conflict
A Strategic Approach to
Ongoing Disputes

Bernard Mayer

ISBN 978-0-7879-9729-8 • Cloth
Available wherever books are sold
www.josseybass.com

"Perhaps the biggest secret of the conflict resolution field is that many conflicts are not ready for resolution—nor need they be resolved. In this wonderfully thought-provoking and practical book, Bernie Mayer shows conflict specialists how to help parties engage constructively with their differences and stay with their conflicts in a productive way. I recommend it!"—**William Ury, coauthor**, *Getting to Yes* **and author**, *The Power of a Positive No*

"Once again, Bernie Mayer is two jumps ahead of the field. *Staying with Conflict* opens up a new way of thinking about our work and is essential reading for any practitioner who suspects the underlying conflict won't be over just because the parties have now signed something."—**Christopher Honeyman, managing partner, CONVENOR, and conflict management editor**, *The Negotiator's Fieldbook*

In this groundbreaking book, Bernard Mayer, a pioneer in the field of conflict resolution, offers a new paradigm for dealing with long-term disputes. Mayer explains that when dealing with enduring conflict, mediators and other conflict resolution specialists need to move past the idea of how quickly they can resolve the conflict. Instead, they should focus on how they can help people prepare to engage with an issue over time. Once their attention is directed away from a speedy resolution to a long-term approach, new avenues of intervention become apparent.

Staying with Conflict builds on the lessons learned and the skills honed from years of effective conflict resolution. Mayer takes the process to the next level and outlines six strategic challenges that this new long-term process will address. The book is filled with illustrative examples from a broad variety of conflicts, from the interpersonal to the international. As these stories demonstrate, this new model for working with enduring conflict offers hope for dealing with our struggles as social beings.

Bernard Mayer, mediator, facilitator, trainer, and researcher, is a professor at the Werner Institute for Negotiation and Dispute Resolution at Creighton University and a founding partner of CDR Associates, based in Boulder, Colorado. In addition, Mayer is the author of *The Dynamics of Conflict Resolution and Beyond Neutrality*.

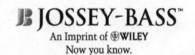

JOSSEY-BASS™
An Imprint of **WILEY**
Now you know.

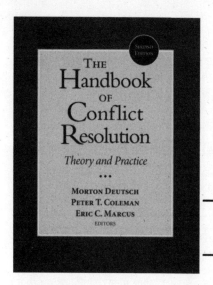

The Handbook of Conflict Resolution
Theory and Practice
Second Edition

Morton Deutsch • Peter T. Coleman
Eric C. Marcus
Editors

ISBN 978-0-7879-8058-0 • Cloth
Available wherever books are sold
www.josseybass.com

The Handbook of Conflict Resolution, Second Edition, is written for both the seasoned professional and the student who want to deepen their understanding of the processes involved in conflicts and their knowledge of how to manage them constructively. It provides the theoretical underpinnings that throw light on the fundamental social psychological processes involved in understanding and managing conflicts at all levels—interpersonal, intergroup, organizational, and international. *The Handbook* covers a broad range of topics including information on cooperation and competition, justice, trust development and repair, resolving intractable conflict, and working with culture and conflict. Comprehensive in scope, this new edition includes chapters that deal with language, emotion, gender, and personal implicit theories as they relate to conflict. The book also includes:

- An extensive review of the current state of theoretical work and research in the field
- The most current methods and models of practice for training, mediation, and large-group intervention
- Approaches for developing conflict resolution skills in children, adolescents, and adults
- Discussions relating to the understanding and management of intractable conflicts that may involve moral, religious, or human rights issues

In addition to its value as a vital resource in the field of conflict resolution, *The Handbook of Conflict Resolution, Second Edition*, also makes an important contribution toward understanding the basic social psychological processes involved in any type of social interaction. A complete resource, *The Handbook* provides professionals with many ideas and tools that will be useful in their practice. It also provides students with the knowledge and methods to help them understand conflicts and manage them more constructively.

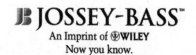
JB JOSSEY-BASS™
An Imprint of **WILEY**
Now you know.

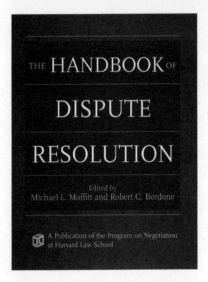

THE HANDBOOK OF DISPUTE RESOLUTION

Michael L. Moffitt • Robert C. Bordone
Editors

ISBN 978-0-7879-7538-8 • Cloth
Available wherever books are sold
www.josseybass.com

This volume is an essential, cutting edge reference for all practitioners, students, and teachers in the field of dispute resolution. Each chapter was written specifically for this collection and has never before been published. The book's contributors draw from a wide range of academic disciplines and represent many of the most prominent names in dispute resolution today, including Frank E. A. Sander, Carrie Menkel-Meadow, Bruce Patton, Lawrence Susskind, Ethan Katsh, Deborah Kolb, and Max Bazerman.

The Handbook of Dispute Resolution contains the most current thinking about dispute resolution. It synthesizes more than thirty years of research into cogent, accessible chapters that assume no previous background in the field, perfect for new students and practitioners. At the same time, the book offers path-breaking research and theory that will interest those who have been immersed in the study or practice of dispute resolution for years. *The Handbook* also offers insights on how to understand disputants. It explores how personality factors, emotions, concerns about identity, relationship dynamics, and perceptions contribute to the escalation of disputes. The volume also explains some of the lessons available from viewing disputes through the lens of gender and cultural differences.

Published as part of a special series with the Program on Negotiation at Harvard Law School, *The Handbook of Dispute Resolution* offers the most complete and authoritative synthesis of the field available.

Michael L. Moffitt is an associate professor and the associate director of the Appropriate Dispute Resolution Program at the University of Oregon School of Law.

Robert C. Bordone is the Thaddeus R. Beal Professor of Law and the director of the Harvard Negotiation and Mediation Clinical Program at Harvard Law School.

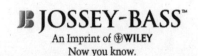

JB JOSSEY-BASS™
An Imprint of **WILEY**
Now you know.

THE PROMISE OF MEDIATION

THE TRANSFORMATIVE APPROACH TO CONFLICT

NEW AND REVISED EDITION

ROBERT A. BARUCH BUSH
JOSEPH P. FOLGER

ISBN 978-0-7879-7483-1 • Cloth
Available wherever books are sold
www.josseybass.com

"*The Promise of Mediation* has been the single most significant influence on the modern ADR movement. This brilliant work serves as a constant reminder that mediation is about more than settling cases. Any serious student of the mediation process would be enlightened by the imaginative approach taken by the authors, and this new edition adds a wealth of new detail and substance about the approach, drawn from a decade's experience applying it in many different contexts.''
—**James Alfini, president and dean, South Texas College of Law, Houston, Texas**

In this new edition, the authors draw on a decade of work in theory development, training, practice, research, and assessment to present a thoroughly revised and updated account of the transformative model of mediation and its practical application, including:

- A compelling description of how the field has moved toward increasing acceptance of the transformative model
- A new and clearer presentation of the theory and practices of transformative mediation, with many concrete examples
- A new case study that provides a vivid picture of the model in practice, with a commentary full of new information about how to use it effectively
- Clarifications of common misconceptions about the model
- A vision for the future that shows how the model can coexist with other approaches and where the ''market'' for transformative mediation is emerging

This volume is a foundational resource on transformative practice, for both readers of the first edition and new readers—including mediators, facilitators, lawyers, administrators, human resource professionals, policymakers, and conflict resolution researchers and educators. More generally, this book will strike a chord with anyone interested in humanizing our social institutions and building on a relational vision of society.

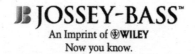